BEYOND PEEK-A-BOO AND PAT-A-CAKE

ACTIVITIES FOR BABY'S FIRST TWENTY-FOUR MONTHS

THIRD EDITION

Evelyn Moats Munger and Susan Jane Bowdon

D1607202

DEDICATION

To Dennis Munger for his good humor, support, and endurance.

To our parents, Georgia and Orin Moats and Jane Bowdon and Dr. Arthur Bowdon, for their confidence in their daughters.

Lastly to Marilyn Moats Kennedy, the sister who paved the way.

Library of Congress Cataloging-in-Publication Data

Munger, Evelyn Moats, 1946-
    Beyond peek-a-boo and pat-a-cake : activities for baby's first 24 months / Evelyn Moats Munger and Susan Jane Bowdon.
        p.   cm.
    ISBN 0-8329-0504-6 : $14.95
    1. Infants—Miscellanea.   2. Play—Miscellanea.   3. Creative activities and seat work.   I. Bowdon, Susan Jane, 1947-   .
II. Title.
HQ774.M85   1993
649'.122—dc20
                                                            93-1421
                                                            CIP

Printed in United States of America

CONTENTS

FOREWORD

As a developmental psychologist who studies infants and carries out research in infant and child behavior, I was immediately struck by the unique features of this book. *Beyond Peek-a-Boo and Pat-a-Cake* combines current information from pediatrics and psychology about child development with a number of techniques for interacting with or stimulating an infant. These techniques do not require that the parents have a Ph.D. in child development or years of experience in dealing with infants; they do serve as very practical guides to help parents become sensitive observers and to accept a complementary rather than a passive ("I really don't know what to do") role during the early months.

Beyond Peek-a-Boo and Pat-a-Cake provides a basis for strengthening parents' confidence in their own abilities by explaining infant behavior in comprehensible terms; structuring approaches for essential infant-stimulation experiences through parent-child interactions using games, songs, and activities; and, perhaps most important for the parent, by suggesting workable solutions to the inevitable frustrations that accompany the normal development of any infant. The reader will be continually impressed by the many useful ideas and practical suggestions that the authors have provided to help parents cope with the realities of life with a baby. The ideas are ones that any reasonably intelligent, sensitive, and well-read parent might develop . . . if only he or she had a decade or so of experience with infants, didn't have to worry about other pressures, and weren't faced with the need for an immediate solution.

It is important to note that not all hints on management have to do with babies. Mothers and other caregivers count too, and necessary emphasis is placed on the caregiver's needs not only for time by oneself but also for contact with other adults.

This book promises to be one of the few really valuable sources to help parents learn about, survive with, and, above all, relax with and enjoy their new baby. I cannot think of a better way for parents to begin to adjust to the demands and respond to the delights of their infant than by using the ideas so well presented here.

William Fullard, Ph.D.
Associate Professor Human Development
Temple University

ACKNOWLEDGMENTS

As this book and the knowledge it represents has grown over the years, so have the contributions of others. We want to thank all of the parents and staff of the Children's Garden Nursery Schools for their creative ideas and suggestions. In particular, we thank Janice Walton, Diana Quintana, Cheryl Fitzsimmons, Kathy Cromwell, Donna McDonald, Cathi Dobson, and Leslie Beatty.

INTRODUCTION

The abundance of research on infants in the last ten years has dispelled the once held notion of a baby's total helplessness. We now know that babies are highly responsive, eager to experience, and curious about the world around them. Studies have shown that not only can six-month-olds enjoy finger painting, but also that three-month-olds can, if they are given the opportunity, learn to control their crib mobiles through movement. *Beyond Peek-a-Boo and Pat-a-Cake* is designed to encourage parents, friends, and admirers of infants everywhere to follow their instincts and to watch, play with, talk to, stimulate, and, most of all, enjoy their babies. We hope that you will, with our help, learn just a little bit more about what your baby is truly capable of.

Beyond Peek-a-Boo and Pat-a-Cake was arranged chronologically for the sake of convenience. We wish to make it *very* clear that we are not trying to project a developmental timetable. Babies are people. Each infant has his or her own unique temperament, likes, dislikes, capabilities, and rate of growth. Because your baby may enjoy doing many of the activities out of sequence, we suggest that you skim through the entire book at the beginning of the year. What we have written is an idea book, a personalized journal, and a guide to help you learn along with your child during this first eighteen months.

We learned from experience that parents do not need another book describing babies, but that they desperately do need advice—specific suggestions about how to play, what to say, shortcuts for everyday routines, tips on handling babies in general.

For ease of readability we have used the masculine pronoun throughout the book. The masculine pronoun has been used exclusively in order to avoid cumbersome construction. It in no way implies that any activity or suggestion applies only to male infants.

Beyond Peek-A-Boo and Pat-A-Cake is divided into *eighteen* chapters, one for each of the first *eighteen* months of life. The *first year and a half* of an infant's life is a demanding time physically and emotionally—for both child and parents. Each chapter of this book is organized to lead you from fun in the "Activities, Games, and Songs" section to the everyday basics of bathing, sleeping, feeding, and dressing and changing in the "Routine Times" section. The "Helpful Hints" section provides suggestions for living more efficiently with your baby; and the "Parents, Friends, and Admirers" section suggests ways of including others in your child's life. The "And for Yourself" features focus on activities and routines a new mother or caregiver might indulge in when Baby becomes too much.

We hope that *Beyond Peek-A-Boo and Pat-A-Cake* will be useful to parents, grandparents, baby-sitters, and caregivers alike. We hope that this book will provide you with many memorable moments with your baby.

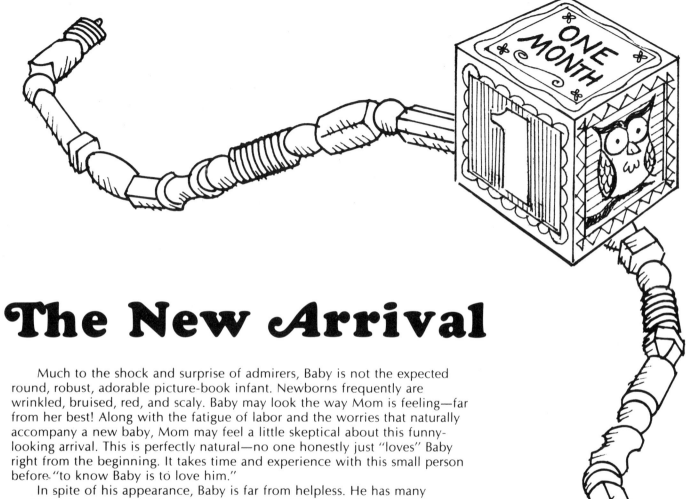

The New Arrival

Much to the shock and surprise of admirers, Baby is not the expected round, robust, adorable picture-book infant. Newborns frequently are wrinkled, bruised, red, and scaly. Baby may look the way Mom is feeling—far from her best! Along with the fatigue of labor and the worries that naturally accompany a new baby, Mom may feel a little skeptical about this funny-looking arrival. This is perfectly natural—no one honestly just "loves" Baby right from the beginning. It takes time and experience with this small person before "to know Baby is to love him."

In spite of his appearance, Baby is far from helpless. He has many sophisticated survival skills from the moment of birth. Equipped with innate abilities such as the rooting reflex, Baby can turn his head to the proper side and "root," or search, for a nipple when his cheek is stroked. Baby also has a persuasive cry he can use to summon help or secure fulfillment of his needs.

1

Although he seems sleepy much of the time, Baby is working to capacity to stabilize his vital systems. He is learning to breathe, digest food, and regulate his body temperature. Baby also has many environmental adjustments to make. No matter how comfortable one makes his surroundings, it is impossible to duplicate the womb.

At birth Baby can see well for from six to twelve inches from his body. He seems to prefer black and white patterns of any size or type to color in the items around him. Within a few weeks, as you play with Baby, you will notice that he can follow an object from side to center and back again. Now that Baby is alert for about one hour in ten, he is continually working with his eyes; he particularly enjoys focusing and will try to establish eye contact.

Baby possesses excellent hearing at birth. By the end of the first month, he will respond to voices, especially that of his primary caregiver. Although Baby loves attention, he will protect himself from overstimulation by simply not processing all the information that comes to him. When Baby is overtaxed, he will become suddenly more active or go to sleep; both mechanisms protect him from overstimulation.

The first few weeks with a new baby require that everyone involved get enough rest and a generous dose of tender loving care. This is a time of self-doubt for Baby's special people, who have been suddenly overwhelmed with an awesome responsibility. Even for those for whom parenting is not a new skill, it takes time to feel comfortable with a newborn again. As the weeks go by, you will become aware of how Baby signals for food, comfort, a change, or just peace and quiet. Familiarity will breed confidence, so take heart!

ACTIVITIES, GAMES, AND SONGS

Far from being a helpless little lump, Baby is born with many skills. The activity and game sections of this book will make the best use of these skills by suggesting fun learning experiences and enjoyable ways for Baby to practice what he knows.

Baby under Glass

Observing Baby is one of the most enjoyable and important activities for this first month. It's fascinating and exhilarating to watch this tiny being. Discover his uniqueness, his likes, dislikes, and abilities. Careful observation will alert you to the best time for play and learning. This can also be a restful time for recovering Moms and adjusting family members.

Blanket Play

It's not too early to allow your baby some freedom of movement and a change of surroundings. Encourage him to kick, stretch, and wiggle. If the room is warm, let Baby practice on a blanket on the floor.

A Ball for Baby

Hang a soft yarn pompom from Baby's crib mobile for him to watch. You may want to make more than one from different brightly colored yarns. Add some bells, too. Baby will enjoy the music.

Rattles

Put a rattle in Baby's hand, and watch to see if he can hold it for a few seconds. At this age, babies can let go of things only by chance, so you may have to remove the rattle after a short time. You can't expect too much grip this early.

Tape Magic

Place several three-inch strips of colored plastic tape on the crib sheet. Use bright colors for best results. Baby will enjoy trying to grasp and pick up the lines of color.

Beads and Bobbles

Wear a string of washable beads or a colorful pin. These will be of special interest to Baby as you hold him, and will enrich his visual environment. Baby's vision is best within twelve inches.

How Big?

A simple but enjoyable game to play is:

How big is Baby?
Soooooo big! (stretch arms)

How big is Baby?
Soooooo big! (stretch legs)

As Baby grows, so will his love for this game. Soon he will anticipate it with glee, raising his arms in delight. If you play this game regularly, Baby will gleefully respond to your questions with the proper motions by the time he is about ten months old.

Trips

A great trip to break up the day is a quick jaunt out the back door and once around the house. Do this several times a day. On a sunny day, try just sitting out in front of the house for a few minutes. You'll appreciate the change and Baby will get his introduction to the great outdoors.

Crazy Quilt

A crazy quilt can provide an exciting new environment of bright, intriguing colors for Baby. Maybe our ancestors knew more than we thought about infant delights. On the wall, under Baby when it's tummy time, or overhead at nap time, the patterns will intrigue him as he grows.

Snuggling

Slings, snugglies, and front carriers allow you to walk around your home without losing contact with Baby. These carriers hold Baby against your chest—a comforting position. There are many variations. Easy instructions for making baby slings can be found in craft or pattern books. Our variation is on page 106.

First Mobile

You can make Baby's first mobile. Keep it very simple and black and white. Research shows that newborns prefer the stark contrasts of black and white. Another study shows that babies also respond well to the human face.

Large circles, squares, triangles, and other geometric shapes readily appeal to infants. Position the mobile approximately eight to twelve inches from Baby. Make sure the mobile is safe for Baby. Always use short strings to hang the mobile so that he cannot become entangled in the strings. Change the mobile every week or so by adding shapes or switching their positions.

Best Time

Because you are taking cues from Baby, you already know when he is comfortable and relaxed. Allow him the opportunity to be himself and you'll know when he's ready to play. Be alert so you can join him in these happy moments.

The Young Cyclist

Even a young infant will enjoy a bit of cycling. Move his legs and bring his feet up to his body, one at a time or together. Do the same thing with his arms. This is an exercise either you or Baby can initiate.

Tone of Voice

How you speak to Baby matters. Very loud noises will startle him or cause him to cry. A smile and cheerful tone will make him coo or brighten. Soft tones will calm and soothe him. Hearing your voice is very important to his sense of well-being. Talk to him whenever you are together. Getting into the habit of talking to Baby early leads to better and earlier speech development.

Mmm Good

One of Baby's favorite pastimes is sucking his fingers. Sometimes he has difficulty finding his mouth. A little help will be appreciated, so give him "his hand." Sucking is very relaxing for Baby. Learning to use this skill for comfort is a first step toward self-reliance.

Set the Mood

Babies love mood music, too. Some babies, like adults, sleep best with background music. Try a variety of music—classical, jazz, blues, country and western—and notice Baby's responses.

Listen

Baby loves to listen to happy sounds. Add a wind chime to Baby's room. An inexpensive one can often be found in import shops.

What's Up?

Baby is often most alert when he is close to an upright position. Help him explore new things by holding him close enough to things that he can see using his good close-range vision. Moving about like this can be a game for Baby.

Where's Baby?

Place a cloth over Baby and say, "Where's Baby?" Raise the cloth and say, "There he is!" This favorite game becomes more and more fun as the child grows.

Mobile Mobile

Move the cradle gym or mobile you have hung at the level of the crib rails from side to side. This helps Baby notice change and practice focusing. Research suggests that by the end of the first month babies notice when objects have been so changed.

Looking Bonanza

Line the crib or bassinet with bright simple pictures for Baby to look at. He can see these pictures very well because they are close, and he will spend many happy moments studying them carefully.

Minimassage

Baby will enjoy a minimassage. Use a little lukewarm baby lotion or baby powder. If you decide to use baby powder, avoid Baby's inhalation of clouds of talc by pouring or shaking the powder into your hand before applying. Start at the neck and work down, talking or humming as you go. This promotes body awareness and feels good.

Light On

Light is an exciting stimulus to an infant. A dim lamp or nightlight will provide Baby with an opportunity to look around his bed and his room. It is never too early for Baby to practice entertaining himself before sleeping and upon waking.

Rocking

The rhythmic movement a baby feels when being rocked is very comforting. Research suggests that most babies respond best to being held upright as they are soothed using the motion achieved by an old-fashioned rocking chair. Some rocking speeds are better than others; medium to high seems best. If you do not have a rocker, consider buying one.

For other hints on handling a fussy baby, see Appendix A.

Chase the Light

A small flashlight can be the beginning of a "chase the light" game. For fun, tape colored cellophane over the light; red and yellow are Baby's favorites. Catch Baby's eye and slowly move the light from one side to another. It will take some practice, but you will soon see Baby's eyes track the colored light.

Sing That Lullaby

A very special time in these early weeks of life can involve singing some soon-to-be favorite songs as you cuddle and rock Baby.

The traditional lullaby "Rock-a-Bye Baby" goes like this:

Rock-a-bye baby, in the treetop,
When the wind blows, the cradle will rock.
When the bough breaks, the cradle will fall,
And down will come baby,
Cradle and all.

Maybe you'd prefer a show tune such as "Lullaby of Broadway," or a favorite popular song. Better yet, make up your own. See "Ode to Baby" in the Chapter 2 section on "Parents, Friends, and Admirers" for tips on writing baby poems.

Shimmer, Sparkle, and Spin

Sparkly or shiny objects often catch the eye of a newborn. Make a simple object out of crumpled aluminum foil suspended by string, ribbon, or dental floss.

ROUTINE TIMES

If you are convinced that *nothing* is routine with an infant, you are probably correct, especially during this first month. However, there are certain things that must be done every day and certain needs that must be met.

As you grow to know your child, you will become aware of his preferences and internal timetable. Throughout this book, "Routine Times" will deal with day-to-day issues such as feeding, toileting, bathing, dressing, sleeping, and so on.

BATHING

Baby's first baths are far more frightening for Baby's friends than for him. There are many ways to bathe an infant. We have included some suggestions, but certainly not all. The important thing is that you find one method with which you feel comfortable so that you can enjoy bathtimes with Baby.

Frog Position

Use just a little water, and place Baby in a frog position, your hand under his chest and his head on your arm.

Alternatives

Invest in a large bath sponge or a foam-backed mat to put Baby on in a small basin with very little water. This will be safer and more comfortable for Baby. The mat can be returned to use as a bathmat later.

Rather than kneeling and bending over the bathtub, try the sink. You'll find it's a perfect size for Baby, and a lot less precarious for both of you.

Or consider a sponge bath until you have gained confidence and the umbilical cord has come off. Better yet, have your mother or friend help the first few times, for moral support.

Warranty: Your baby is fully guaranteed not to break for one full year. With reasonable care these models last a lifetime.

Bath Bucket

Remember the small plastic bucket you used to carry your bathroom gear to the bathroom when you were in college? This is a great way to store Baby's things for bathing, assuring that you won't need something you didn't bring.

Baby's Reaction

Here's a space to record Baby's initial reactions to his earliest baths.

_____

_____

_____

_____

SLEEPING

As with every other aspect of Baby's adjustment to life, sleep needs and patterns may undergo many changes before stabilizing. Baby's pattern may be as much as eighteen to twenty hours per day or as few as twelve for the first few weeks. Each infant is unique.

Young Sleeper's Chart

	A.M.	P.M.	NIGHT
S.	_____	_____	_____
M.	_____	_____	_____
T.	_____	_____	_____
W.	_____	_____	_____
TH.	_____	_____	_____
F.	_____	_____	_____
S.	_____	_____	_____

Carriage Sleeping

Use Baby's carriage as a second baby bed. When Baby naps, you can simply wheel it to an adjoining room. This will save a recovering mother or a busy caregiver many steps.

If you live in a two-story house, keep the carriage on the first floor so that you can easily hear Baby when he cries.

Color

Babies like color and pattern in their cribs. Sheets, bumpers, blankets, and pajamas should be bright and printed. Pastels appeal only to adults.

Extra Bed for Baby

Need an extra bed or sleeping space? Try a padded bureau drawer. Betty Ford claims all her children used them for the first few months.

Noise

Babies' sleep patterns are a highly individual matter. Some settle into a predictable routine; others will keep you guessing. Many infants can sleep through all but the loudest bangs and jolts, so go ahead and converse, use various appliances, and know that members of the household need not tiptoe and whisper. It's better to begin this way. It's also fairer to anxious siblings.

FEEDING

Bubbling (Burping)

Not all babies require bubbling or burping, but some need attention before, during, and after feeding. You will quickly come to know your own infant's needs.

Bubbling usually produces a quick burp that gets rid of any air that may have collected in Baby's stomach during feeding. Try one of these three techniques, positioning a clean towel between you and Baby.

1. Lay Baby on his tummy over your lap. Supporting his head with your hand, turn Baby's head to one side and gently pat him on the back. This is a good technique to use with newborns. Remember, easy does it.
2. A sitting position works well for some babies. Using both your hands to support head, neck, shoulders, and back, Baby can be rocked or patted.
3. Try rubbing up and down along Baby's spine, especially between the shoulder blades, while he rests over your hand or shoulder.

Breast or Bottle

Regardless of which manner of feeding you choose, most babies will not only survive but thrive. Essential to the success of either method is the manner in which you carry out each feeding. Feeding is, after all, a high point of Baby's life. Beyond food, it is a social exchange of affection.

Bottle-feeding parents should be sure to cuddle and hug Baby while he drinks. Mutual satisfaction is the goal. This is one of the many ways Baby and you get to know each other.

Mothers who are nursing can get information and support from

La Leche League International
9616 Minneapolis Ave.
Franklin Park, IL 60131

First Month Feeding Chart

A.M.

_____   _____   _____

_____   _____   _____

_____   _____   _____

_____   _____   _____

P.M.

_____   _____   _____

_____   _____   _____

_____   _____   _____

_____   _____   _____

Sucking

One way an infant can reduce tension and comfort himself is to suck his fist and later his fingers. Because the mouth is really at the center of Baby's world, sucking is as important as feeding or nourishment.

Extra Satisfaction

If your child enjoys a pacifier, fine; if not, that's fine, too. No research we know of suggests that use of a pacifier is harmful for infants. Some theorists indicate pacifiers may have psychologically beneficial effects. Only Baby knows, and he's not telling.

Both Sides Now

Feed and change Baby from alternate sides. This helps him develop a sense of self.

DRESSING AND CHANGING

"Shape" Your Surface

Instead of buying a changing table, cut and cover your own. Use a piece of foam rubber two to four inches thick. Personalize this work surface by cutting the foam rubber into a creative shape. Cover it with cheery printed oilcloth, contact paper, or a vinyl tablecloth. Place on top of a low dresser or on the counter of a large bathroom vanity or cabinet.

In Vogue

Designer fashions have limited value in the early weeks of life. Any item of clothing made of special fabric or of intricate design will prove impractical.

The fact is that Baby may need a complete change of clothes with each fresh diaper. This could mean as many as eight outfits a day.

Keep newborns' togs simple, washable, durable, and free from fasteners that might be gummed or swallowed. Many babies dislike shirts or outfits that must be pulled over the head. Snaps in front are the answer. Babies like the loose look.

So that outfits need not be discarded after three or four weeks, starting size should be size 6 months.

Tips for the Changing Table

Don't wait to gather all your supplies together. Set up diaper areas in several spots and keep them stocked. A laundry room can be converted by putting a towel or mat on the dryer and keeping a basket of diapers and wipes and a trash can nearby.

Different Folds for Different Folks

For those who choose not to use disposable diapers, there are three basic techniques for folding cotton diapers. Try any or all to determine which gives you the best coverage for your infant. Remember that boys need extra thickness in the front, girls more coverage in the back.

The Square is a good folding technique to try with a newborn, especially if the baby is on his back much of the time. This style has less flexibility in adjustment than do the other two. It's the loosest style, good for a summer day.

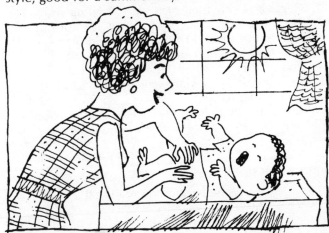

The Kite is a particularly neat-fitting diaper for a boy because there is more up front where it counts. Kite-folded diapers fit well inside plastic pants. There are also prefolded cloth diapers with fitted legs in nice colors and prints which are 100 percent cotton and washable.

The Oblong provides the most complete coverage front and rear, but tends to appear a bit bulky. This style is an excellent choice for night use.

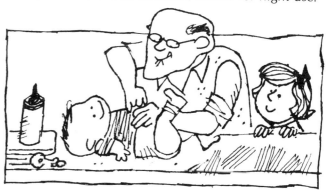

Diaper Service?

If you opt to use cloth diapers, do use a diaper service. It's a tremendous time saver; for many busy moms it's a necessity. The cost will be about the same as using disposables.

Disposable diapers, another option for cutting your work load, are more costly than cloth diapers.

HELPFUL HINTS

Learning from others' experiences can certainly make life with a new baby easier and more pleasant. The "Helpful Hints" sections of the book are designed to help you use your time and materials more efficiently. They are a compilation of tricks and shortcuts others have found valuable.

Reminder

Yes, women have been having babies since the year one. And things *have* improved considerably in this modern age. Still, having a newborn to look after is an enormous undertaking. So remember to *ask for help*. You can make this easier and more rewarding for all by developing a list of small errands and tasks to be done.

It matters that you are doing more than just coping. What makes you happy, secure, and relaxed?

Ring, Ring

If you have several extension phones, make copies of a list of numbers you use most frequently and place one next to each extension. For example,

Doctors _____

_____

Best Friends _____
(Advice)

_____

Relatives _____

_____

Baby-sitters _____

_____

Get to know businesses or services that pick up and deliver—that difference is worth your money.

Grocery store _____

Laundry/cleaners _____

Diaper service _____

Drugstore/pharmacy _____

Bookstore _____

Temporary cleaning help _____

Dinner on Tap

Food may be the farthest thing from your mind, but then again. . . ? A week's worth of dinners will allow you a social meal with family and friends. For instance, spaghetti sauce to be used for chili, chicken cacciatore, and spaghetti can be made in bulk and frozen. With a little planning, many basic meals made in quantity can be varied to provide a few days' worth of delicious meals. Write out complete menus, attach recipes or page numbers cited. Keep a file of these menus handy in your kitchen.

Energy Cycle

Mother or not, this new baby is putting you through some major changes. You are a different person. Anyone involved at any extended level with an infant, will discover that pace is everything.

Rest is a number one priority. So rest. The "found moments" when Baby is resting will make a difference when you need to gear up to cook, clean, or collect yourself enough to face the latest low-level crisis.

Matters of diet, recreation, and health are of prime importance. Taking care of your health, physical and mental, is essential to your good relationship with Baby.

Cheap, Cheap

With the excitement of a new arrival, remember to buy special equipment only as a last resort. Think about borrowing and swapping. Buy only if all else fails. Check your neighborhood newspaper, children's resale, and consignment shops for good buys on slightly used baby equipment.

Night-Light

Eliminate late evening stumbles by placing simple night-lights in dark hallways and rooms. Some nice ones recently spotted had shells and sand dollars glued in front of the bulb. Try some of the new ones with a sensor feature which turns the light on and off as needed.

Letting Go

Households will endure despite dust, fuzz, bathtub rings, and dirty windows. Your needs are of the utmost significance. Adjustment is the key word. Hassle yourself as little as possible; let go of some of those perfectionist standards. If you do not have regular cleaning help, this is where you can guiltlessly splurge this month!

A Cup of Comfort

Install a small (single-cup size) electric teapot in Baby's room. When feedings continue longer than you had anticipated, a mug of tea, bouillon, or hot chocolate can be very relaxing. Stock up and enjoy. You'll always remember these few minutes of watching your darling in blissful slumber.

Fast Eats

Fast foods are a necessity for busy working households. They don't need to be limited to greasy burgers—there are healthy choices, too. Develop a creative list of choices for when you must eat out or order in.

Peace of Mind

Since 1973, all full-sized baby cribs have been required by law to meet the safety standards of the Consumer Product Safety Commission. These standards are very stringent requirements and do ensure product safety. If you plan to use an antique crib (one made before 1973) be sure to check its features against federal safety standards.

Mattresses can be custom-made to fit cribs of unusual sizes, but they may cost much more. Things to watch for include distance between slats (no more than 23 in.); secure locking devices on crib sides, ones that an older child cannot move; nontoxic, lead-free paint; and safe metal hardware. The mattress should fit snugly into the frame; if you can fit more than two fingers between the mattress and the frame, the mattress is too small.

Health Record

An up-to-date chart of all Baby's medical information can be invaluable when faced with an emergency, a change of doctor, or a move to a new location.

	DATE	DATE
DPT (diphtheria, whooping cough, tetanus)	___	___
	___	___
	___	
Polio	___	___
Smallpox	___	___
Typhoid	___	___
Mumps, Measles, Rubella	___	___
Tuberculin Test	___	___
HIB (haemophilus b)	___	___

Frantic

Baby's first illness will be very frightening. Don't panic. First, gather the facts. Then, call the doctor.
Facts to know:

Symptoms _____

   (diarrhea, vomiting, appearance)

Baby's mood _____

Sleep pattern _____

   (last twelve hours)

Eating pattern _____

   (how much, what, when)

Temperature _____

   (how taken)

First Doctor

One of the most important relationships is the one between you and your child's doctor. This can be a long-relationship and merits investigation, time, and thought. The right physician is a lifelong friend, counselor, and resource. Recommendations from other parents and a local hospital referral service is a good way to begin your search.

Baby's Physician

Name _____

Address _____

Phone: Office _____

Home _____

Office hours _____

Hospital affiliation(s)

_____

Paint

Start out right and think *latex*. Water-based latex paints are nontoxic, easy to apply, and easy to clean up. You can touch up scratches and use a roller over dirt without repainting the whole room.

Beauty Parlor

Clip Baby's nails while he's asleep. This is a good way to accomplish a tricky task.

Organize

If you need to gather and group small items, consider using a set of colorful canisters, graduated plastic boxes, metal cans, or wicker baskets. By doing so, you can keep all those necessary but dangerously small items out of sight and reach. Babyproof now!

Odors

Help Baby to put his best foot forward. You may be immune to Baby's smells, but others are not. Besides keeping him clean, you will need a plan for handling soiled clothes and diapers. Make sure that

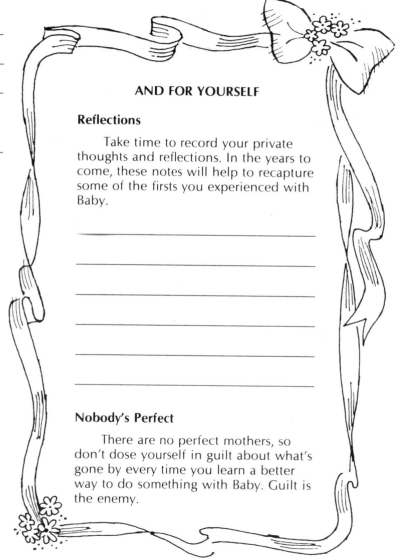

AND FOR YOURSELF

Reflections

Take time to record your private thoughts and reflections. In the years to come, these notes will help to recapture some of the firsts you experienced with Baby.

_____

_____

_____

_____

_____

_____

Nobody's Perfect

There are no perfect mothers, so don't dose yourself in guilt about what's gone by every time you learn a better way to do something with Baby. Guilt is the enemy.

diapers are placed in containers with tight-fitting lids. Empty frequently.

Air Fresheners

Use room deodorizers to keep your environment pleasant. The commercial brands that attach to the wall are especially convenient. Whatever you choose, remember to place these dispensers up and out of the way of little hands.

Crying

Yes, babies do cry, often and loudly. Although not a solution, it may help to know that crying does indicate something. Frequency of crying will begin to diminish in the next few weeks.

Most educators feel that you can't spoil an infant. In fact, research has found that prompt response to Baby's crying results in a decrease, rather than an increase, in crying.

Hang on. Your patience and tolerance will be rewarded.

First Cold

When Baby gets his first cold, make him more comfortable by doing the following.

Use a cold-mist humidifier. Also try raising one end of the crib several notches so Baby's head will be elevated slightly; you can also accomplish this by placing bricks or books under the front feet of the crib.

Give him lots of tender care and fluids and follow your doctor's advice. Do try not to become overly distressed.

The Old Rope Trick

If you have a rocking cradle or a buggy, place it near your bed and attach a string. When Baby cries, pull the string and rock Baby—this helps you get the rest you need too. (See Chapter 2, "Routine Times: Crib Springs" for a way to convert your crib into a rocking crib by changing the casters.)

Hot Flashes

Newborns are more sensitive to heat than to cold. Keep Baby warm, but don't overdo it. Many babies are kept so well dressed that they suffer from prickly heat rash or from the "drowsies." Experiences in other countries have shown that infants stay healthier in cooler rooms. So do adults.

Quick Slips

If you would rather have cotton closest to Baby's skin, consider slipping colorful pillowcases over the changing pad. These easy-to-clean cases provide Baby with new and stimulating things to look at, as well as a cool, crisp touch.

Extra Bed

If Baby is sleeping in his own room, furnish it with a cot or an extra bed for Mom or Dad. On those long, fussy nights (and there are bound to be a few), parents can catnap during Baby's restful moments.

Someone Sleeps

Many parents we know claim that the only viable method for coping with a baby's erratic sleeping needs and patterns is a rotation of duty. The one-night-off, one-night-on, or one-feeding-off, one-feeding-on procedure allows at least one parent to sleep.

Fathers of nursing babies can still help out. Dad can get up and retrieve Baby, change him, and bring him to bed for his feeding.

PARENTS, FRIENDS, AND ADMIRERS

The "Parents, Friends, and Admirers" sections of the book address the needs of Baby's best friends: parents, grandparents, siblings, admirers, and caregivers. It includes ideas for them to use, things to buy, ways to help, and plans for good times.

Let Me See

Everyone, even people you thought would never know or care, seems to have heard about *this* baby and decided to call or visit. Although flattering, it can be overwhelming. Don't be afraid to schedule these admirers and well-wishers.

You can say no without guilty feelings or lengthy explanations. Time flies and soon you and Baby will not be as sensitive.

Door Note

A note on the door, "We'll be delighted to see visitors after _____ ," is one way of letting neighbors know when to come.

Operators

Take the phone off the hook for part of the day, or use an answering machine to relay your message of "good times to call," along with a little news about the new arrival. This can be a great service to everyone.

Flag Pole Alert

To announce the new arrival, hoist a fabric flag in front of the house to alert friends that Baby has indeed arrived. This banner can then be used to indicate good times to visit or stay away.

Chain Announcement

Write a letter to your best friend with all the information on the new baby; have this friend start the chain to send from friend to friend. Each person can add his or her best wishes and whatever new information has been gathered. When the letter is finally returned to you, it will be a warm and cherished keepsake about Baby, drafted with love by dear friends.

For the Teacher

Let your class or neighborhood help you announce the new arrival. Before delivery, have students draw pictures of the new "baby and company" on postcards to be used for the announcements.

If you're not a teacher, consider enlisting the artistry of kids in your neighborhood. This is one way of discovering just how this baby is viewed by young friends.

Small Town

Place your announcement as an advertisement in the local newspaper. It's a sure way to spread the good news.

Siblings

Even if you have spent time preparing children for Baby's arrival, expect times when they are less than enthusiastic about sharing their world with an infant.

Reading stories that reflect their feelings can provide siblings with a guilt-free outlet. It will also give them opportunity to discuss and decide ways in which brothers and sisters can be involved happily with Baby.

Some books we like are:
Peter's Chair by Ezra Jack Keats
Nobody Asked Me If I Wanted a Baby Sister by
  Martha Alexander
We are Having a Baby by Vicki Holland
The Berenstain Bears' New Baby by Stan and Jan
  Berenstain
William's Doll by Charlotte Zolotow

Meet Fido

When Mom enters the house for the first time, Dad or someone else should carry Baby while Mom greets Fido. Usually this will be enough for Fido to understand that Baby is no threat. Treat Fido as a wordless sibling unless he/she is used to Baby.

Special Call

Having Mom in the hospital can be a disturbing experience for young children. Hearing her voice over the phone can make a real difference and quickly assure them that everything is just fine. Or have Mom leave a happy cassette recording, made with the child, for playing during a lonely time.

Thank You

Looking for a different way to thank the gang from work? A blow-up poster of Baby surrounded by the nice gifts he received is a great way to say thanks for everything and to introduce Baby.

Grandparents Only

Baby's first baby-sitters will probably be his grandparents. Only they can give this special gift to new parents who need a break but are too uncomfortable to leave their young infant with just anyone. Grandparents can provide new parents with renewed confidence and necessary moral support. They can be an endless source of information.

Little Red Riding Hood

Little Red Riding Hood had the right idea. A great gift for the exhausted parents of the new arrival is a "bring-in-dinner" left on the doorstep. Complete the package with plastic stemware, wine, and a candle or two. You might even add a little mood music in the form of a favorite album or tape.

Mysterious Maid

Your time can be a very helpful gift. Doing the dishes or the laundry or fixing a few meals that can be warmed up when needed can certainly be a relief to a woman too tired to do the work herself but concerned about how the rest of her family is faring.

Gifts Received

GIFT	GIVER	DATE THANKED

Hints

A short pleasant call from a thoughtful grandparent can brighten the day for a recuperating Mom. Include a little news and perhaps an invitation for dinner later this month.

The "Stork" Truth

From the first moment of birth, everyone knows who Baby looks like. No one will believe us, but the truth is Baby only really looks like himself.

Real Class

Got a classy baby? Consider a printed "At Home" card for the debut.

Baby's Name

after the seventeenth
of May 19 ___

29 East Penn Street
Philadelphia, PA

New Moms

Besides jewels, furs, and flowers, new Moms are receptive to the following gifts:
1. A best-seller to read in the tub
2. New lipsticks, nail polish
3. Flashy running shoes or new street skates to provide an incentive
4. A sexy but loose-fitting nightgown with a lovely neckline
5. A favorite music tape or CD
6. Colorful sheets to brighten her corner
7. A comfy rocking chair you found at a yard sale and covered with a new coat of cheerful paint

Photographs

There is nothing more valuable than early pictures of famous and successful people.

Start immediately to capture Baby's formative months. If Baby's parents are not shutterbugs, photos and videotapes can be a wonderful present from friends and admirers.

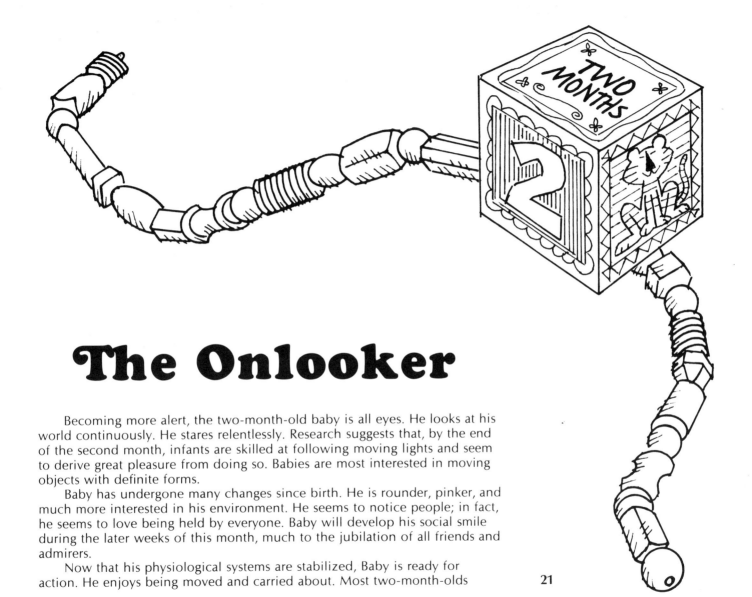

The Onlooker

Becoming more alert, the two-month-old baby is all eyes. He looks at his world continuously. He stares relentlessly. Research suggests that, by the end of the second month, infants are skilled at following moving lights and seem to derive great pleasure from doing so. Babies are most interested in moving objects with definite forms.

Baby has undergone many changes since birth. He is rounder, pinker, and much more interested in his environment. He seems to notice people; in fact, he seems to love being held by everyone. Baby will develop his social smile during the later weeks of this month, much to the jubilation of all friends and admirers.

Now that his physiological systems are stabilized, Baby is ready for action. He enjoys being moved and carried about. Most two-month-olds

21

enjoy vehicular travel. The trusty baby swing can begin to be a pleasure for Baby and grown-ups starting this month; it can be a lifesaver for the difficult-to-soothe baby.

Baby can now hold up his head and grasp things voluntarily; he may even try swiping at objects. Baby will show his delight and excitement when new objects are presented to him by cooing and making throaty noises.

Caregivers and parents will find Baby's behavior easier to predict. His feedings will be more regular, as will be his sleeping patterns.

There are more opportunities for getting to know Baby now that he stays awake for longer periods of time. When he's played with, he may even perform a little for his friends. He prefers people to toys, and will clearly discriminate among individual voices. Being touched, held, and fed are still Baby's favorite activities.

ACTIVITIES, GAMES, AND SONGS

Baby is delighted by a variety of sensations, sounds, lights, and textures. This month try some activities that will enhance his growing awareness of his body.

Sounds Like

Babies are attracted to noises. Make sure that your child's world is full of interesting sounds. Not only should toys be attractive, touchable, and mouthable, they should also provide the extra dimension of sound.

Cool Breeze

Before throwing out that paper-towel or tissue tube, consider Baby and paint it. He will enjoy the cool stream of air that you can direct toward his tummy or leg, etc. A large straw or piece of plastic tubing would also work well and help Baby to focus on different parts of his body.

A Ball for Baby

Baby would probably enjoy a cloth ball that tinkles. Such a ball is easy to make from assorted cloth scraps and jingle bells. Make sure bells are permanently embedded inside the toy.

Clothesline Art

A great eye delighter is this simple crib item made from elastic cord and several one-inch bulldog paper clips. Thread the clips onto the cord and stretch it across Baby's crib; tie it to the rails on either side. From the clips, hang anything and everything you think might interest Baby. Consider a feather, flower, ribbon, bow, or a small stuffed toy. What is especially nice about this item is the ease with which the assortment can be changed.

Dancing Face

Direct the gaze of that wide-eyed baby by making him a fantastic face! You can use a paper plate or styrofoam meat tray as a base. The best part is up to you. A simple design should include all the basics. Use a bit of colorful yarn for hair. Present to Baby. This cheerful face could be hung within Baby's view or danced before his eyes by a parent or admirer.

Are You Singing?

Keep those tunes simple, but keep singing; oldies are still goodies for Baby. Remember:

"Twinkle, Twinkle Little Star"
"You Are My Sunshine"

Finger Fancy

How about trying this one with Baby, fondling each finger as you go along? Either recite it or make up your own tune.

This is little Tommy Thumb,
    round and smooth as any plum;
This is busy Peter Pointer,
    surely he's a double-jointer;
This is mighty Toby Tall,
    he's the biggest one of all;
This is dainty Robin Ring,
    he's too fine for anything;
And this little wee one, maybe,
    surely he's the Finger Baby;
All the five we've counted now,
Busy fingers in a row,
All together they work best,
Each one helping all the rest.

Soft Sounds

Whisper, whisper, whisper. A sweet nothing is something of a surprise and a treat for Baby. Some parents report that this is a sure way to comfort a fussy baby.

Sing Along

Do join in on Baby's own songs, too. Imitate his every sound and then wait for his response. Babies like this game.

Head Lifts

Babies need time to practice raising their heads. Place Baby on his tummy and encourage him to look up at toys you dance before his eyes. Using brightly colored toys that also make a noise gives Baby that much more incentive to see what's up.

Voices

Try changing your tone. Notice the difference? Babies are soothed by a high voice. They are attracted to a voice that is low in tone.

Centerfold

Snap! . . . whether this is the first baby or not, take lots of pictures. How about one of Baby at play or with his favorite playmates?

It's hard to say enough good things about camcorders and their usefulness in recording Baby's every move. Invest in a system early. Baby's grandparents may want to assist with the cost.

Pulling Power

Since birth, Baby has had quite a grasp. Recent studies demonstrate that infants have up to two pounds of power in each hand. Up to now, Baby has been able to "hang on," but this survival skill will begin to disappear at around six weeks of age. Be sure that you support Baby when you bring him to a sitting position by pulling him up by his fists or shoulders.

Fist to Fingers

Baby's fist may be opening up a bit now to reveal fingers. Do things together with those hands. Wiggle the fingers; call attention to them. Wave your own. Touch, clap, shake, and tickle his palm.

Footing Around

A paint project for you and Baby to begin now is footprinting. Using a colorful stamp pad, a bit of water-based paint or any other substance (even chocolate pudding) as a medium, collect a sample every two or three months for the first three years of life. These prints can become a developmental graphic. Each print might contain comments on Baby's size, and perhaps a special anecdote.

Name

As you sing a tune, or play with rhymes, remember to include Baby's name whenever possible. This is just another important way to personalize your playtime together. The best songs are those you make up just for Baby.

Puppet Power

Rather than buying stuffed animals which are soon discarded, new and interesting faces can be provided for Baby through the use of puppets. A good investment, the puppets will be a source of delight throughout his child-hood. If possible get puppets that have accompanying stories.

Porcupines and Rhinos

Prickly porcupines, frogs, rhinos, fish with rubber scales, and other toys designed for puppies provide interesting textures, and are especially easy for infants to hold. These soft, sturdy toys don't object to being mouthed. They also make delightful squeaking noises at unexpected moments.

Swipe and Grab

Move a ball of crushed foil to a place where Baby can practice beginning to swipe. Add to Baby's pleasure by concealing a small bell inside the ball.

Swing Easy

You may want to try a commercially available wind-up swing. It's a favorite of babies at this stage. The swing also relaxes many babies at fussy times. For extra fun, attach a suction-cup toy to the tray of the swing so Baby has things to swipe at as he flies through the air. Please do not overuse this idea. Too much swinging can mesmerize Baby rather than calm him.

Wrist Wear

You like jewelry; why shouldn't Baby? How about bangles made of colorful cotton braid or ribbon? Baby will admire his lovely wrists and become more aware of his body.

Rapping Duck

Make those feet move. Help Baby keep the beat by dancing his feet to your favorite tape or CD.

Ceiling Sights

Baby spends most of his crib time looking at the ceiling and the walls of his crib. Why not put your efforts where they count?

African, Mexican, or other ethnic wall hangings and small rugs have marvelous colors and patterns for Baby's gaze. A Southwestern God's Eye or a baby banner of your own design can be entertaining when hung from the ceiling or wall near Baby's crib.

Joyride

Place Baby in his infant seat and then place the seat on top of your washing machine during the spin cycle. The gentle vibration and humming noise will delight Baby during this short joyride, while you're standing by.

A Little Outdoors

If the weather is too bad to take Baby outside, bring a little of the great outdoors in to Baby. Snip a branch from a tree or bush and place it near Baby, where he can carefully study it and smell its freshness. A small bird or colorful butterfly from the dime store can add extra interest.

Design Thought

Researchers emphasize that Baby's view is not the same as ours. When designing mobiles and crib toys, remember that Baby is looking up and sees the bottom of the objects placed over him.

Not Us

One researcher reports that if babies are left in cribs or playpens for long periods during their alert, learning times, their sense of curiosity can be severely crippled by the time they are fourteen or fifteen months old. Not so for our baby. With all the stimulation he's getting, his lack of curiosity will not be a concern!

ROUTINE TIMES

BATHING

By now, Baby is two feet long and probably enjoying his bath. If you use washcloths, the baby-sized ones are more convenient, but regular-sized towels are fine. To keep a young wiggler from sliding around, place a towel in the bottom of the sink or plastic tub.

A Bath Toy

Cut a clean sponge into a shape for Baby to hang onto and squeeze. Baby will enjoy watching and touching this textured item, which jumps back into shape upon being released.

Infants Only

Strip Baby and let him kick and wiggle. Total body freedom, at least for a few minutes before the bath, is an activity often reserved only for the young. Baby deserves the opportunity to learn about his environment and body in many different ways. Wearing only one's birthday suit does feel much different than a creeper, and can be exhilarating.

Stack-ups

To streamline the bathtime ritual, organize by the stack method. This arrangement begins as the laundry is sorted. On the bottom of the stack, put Baby's outer garment, then his undershirt. Next, add Baby's diaper, and top off with his towel.

Towel-Time Rhyme

Try this with Baby after each bath as you dry him. Dry the parts of his body in conjunction with the poem. He will soon look forward to his after-bath game. Our three-year-old friend Carla can recite it herself.

After a Bath

After my bath, I try, try, try
To wipe myself till I'm dry, dry, dry.
Hands to wipe, and fingers and toes,
And two wet legs and a shiny nose.
Just think how much less time I'd take
If I were a dog and could shake, shake, shake.

Warm Lotion Treatment

Place a container of baby lotion near the tub as you begin the bathing routine. Taking the chill off the lotion will add to the pleasure of Baby's after-bath rubdown.

SLEEPING

Routine

Babies do get attached to specific toys and their crib environment. Making Baby feel at home with his blanket and special things can help in establishing sleeping patterns. A song or special pat can create a napping routine that Baby will grow to associate with rest.

Cozy Corner

Baby does not need the entire space of his crib for sleeping. Some babies feel more comfortable and sleep better in a cozier space. If this is true of your child, use only part of the crib and place some of Baby's soft cuddly toys in the corners to decrease the space.

"Belly Down"

All babies have preferred sleeping positions. Be observant and learn Baby's preferred position. This can make naptime easier. Recent studies suggest that the safest position for Baby is on his side. Adding several pillows behind him will make him more comfortable in this position.

Settle Down

Give Baby a chance to settle himself for rest. Some babies routinely cry before they drift off to sleep. Of course, you'll check to see if there is a problem. Then, watch a clock to reassure yourself that this crying lasts for only a few minutes.

Nightgear for Kickers

Keep little kickers warm throughout the night by dressing them in sleeping bags, sacks, or jumpsuits. These measures will assure you that Baby is cozy and help reduce the number of trips you make to the nursery "just to check" on his coverage.

Baby Bed Bumpers

These cheery devices not only add warmth and eye appeal to a crib, they are also a great safety precaution. Bed bumpers come in prints, colors, tex-

tures, and fabrics, even in clear inflatable plastic. If you enjoy sewing, you may want to make your own out of fabric-covered foam rubber bolsters.

Crib Springs

The casters on Baby's crib can be removed and replaced with a set of specially made springs. These springs allow the crib to be rocked; they also permit Baby to bounce the crib and jostle his mobiles himself.

Research has shown that infants will try to control the movement of their mobiles and, if successful, will try to perfect their act. Having made the association that their movements caused the mobiles to sway, these infants enjoy entertaining themselves.

Crib springs can be purchased at any store carrying infant furniture (approximately $6.00 per set).

FEEDING

Atmosphere

Feeding is an important time, Baby's favorite. A pleasant atmosphere is something worth planning for, for both you and Baby.

Think about yourself in a restaurant; low lights, sparkling conversation, and mood music can make all the difference. More is happening here than just the satisfaction of hunger. Mealtimes are traditionally happy, sharing times among family and friends. Get off to a good start with Baby!

Burps . . .

Older babies can now rest their heads comfortably on someone's shoulder for bubbling. Massage Baby's back gently. Cover your shoulder with a bold-colored towel to enhance Baby's widening visual experience. By now, Baby has a preferred position for burping. It is

---

Preferred Position/Date

I'm Ready

Baby will begin to anticipate feeding time. He may make sucking noises—real smacking sounds to let you know that he is preparing himself. He will probably be able to both suck and stare, a new development for Baby.

Sucking

One way to determine if Baby is really aware of you is to observe his sucking patterns. The curious baby will stop briefly to consider something and then focus his gaze on an object of interest. The contented baby sucks because sucking is a source of genuine pleasure.

Researchers say that the happiest babies suck the most. Babies will try nipples, their fingers, their thumbs, their toys, and their bedding. By sucking, babies can reduce muscular tension and calm themselves.

Pacifiers

To the young infant, there is not a great deal of difference between a thumb and a pacifier. Both soothe and satisfy the need to suck. Although research suggests that neither is harmful, pacifiers are less likely than thumbs to cause orthodontic problems. Pacifiers are frequently discarded by Baby at about six months of age.

DRESSING AND CHANGING

Hooks and Knobs

Place a set of colorful enamel hooks and knobs on the wall near Baby's changing table or dresser. Arrange them in an interesting pattern. These are handy for you now; later, when Baby becomes a "me-do" toddler, they can be moved to a lower position and continue to be useful.

Instant Shelves

A small shelf above Baby's changing area can be indispensable. Try a wicker or stainless steel bathroom shelf. These are easy to hang and require only two holes that can be covered by a picture when you are past the changing table stage.

Head to Toe

An attractive and fun way to store some of Baby's clothes is to use tiered lettuce baskets, which can be found in gourmet shops. These are so handy in the kitchen or pantry, why not try them in Baby's room? Or use graduated wicker baskets. Hang several from cup hooks; fill each with a complete change of clothing, starting with shirts and working your way down. You can quickly dress Baby from head to toe. The baskets are easy to see and reach and require little space.

Up and Out

After you change your baby, you might do a few exercises. Raise his arms up and out. Legs, too. Baby will think this is fun. Talk to him and praise his wiggles and kicks.

HELPFUL HINTS

Concentrate on getting to know your baby rather than on having all the right answers.

Everything in Its Place

An attractive, organized way to store Baby's paraphernalia is to keep it in a shoe storage bag. Hang one by the changing table, and perhaps another near the bathtub.

Shake, Shake, Shake

If you are using cornstarch instead of baby powder, a large salt shaker might make a handy dispenser.

Magic Box

Now is the time to become a collector of all the noncommercial toys and objects (feathers to fabric, balls to bells) that you'll introduce to Baby. You'll also want materials out of which to fashion your own creations. Store your goodies in a shoe bag or covered box. With an eye to the future, keep your

box or bag in a convenient place, but out of reach of little groping hands.

Small-Item Storage

A desk organizer drawer insert can be used to separate and organize all those little things, such as pins, swabs, and so on.

Toy Tip

Baby will be the recipient of many thoughtfully chosen toys, although some may be too large, fancy, or advanced for his immediate use. These selections can be attractively displayed if a curtain ring or loop is stitched to the back. Hang these gifts in place of pictures, posters, or other wall decorations until Baby is ready to play with them. They will add appeal and dimension to Baby's room.

Cuddle Along

Let Baby come along when you do a little light housework. Just place him in his front carrier or sling. He will feel cozy and content being close to you, and you will have both hands free to work.

Plan Ahead

By now, there is a pattern to Baby's crying. Like all of us, there are times of the day when Baby is not at his best. Half the battle is discovering these times so that you can plan ahead.

BABY'S BEST

Playtime _____

Eating time _____

Loving time _____

Baby's less than best time _____

_____

Fireproof

Mix—
1 gal. of warm water
9 oz. Borax
4 oz. boric acid solution

To fireproof Baby's bedding and clothing, pour this solution into a bucket in which you can soak all items. Then let the items dry. The protection lasts for from fifteen to twenty washings. You can get the boric acid solution at a pharmacy.

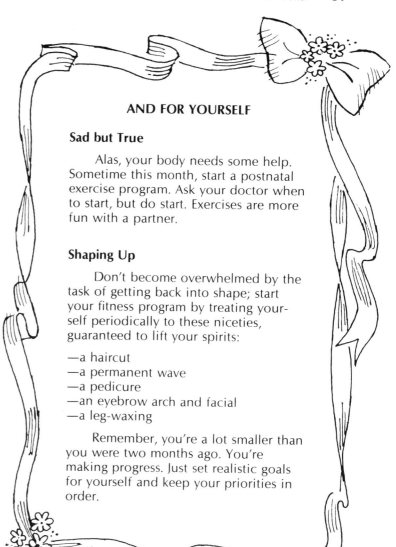

AND FOR YOURSELF

Sad but True

Alas, your body needs some help. Sometime this month, start a postnatal exercise program. Ask your doctor when to start, but do start. Exercises are more fun with a partner.

Shaping Up

Don't become overwhelmed by the task of getting back into shape; start your fitness program by treating yourself periodically to these niceties, guaranteed to lift your spirits:

—a haircut
—a permanent wave
—a pedicure
—an eyebrow arch and facial
—a leg-waxing

Remember, you're a lot smaller than you were two months ago. You're making progress. Just set realistic goals for yourself and keep your priorities in order.

The Real Thing

More visually alert, Baby prefers three-dimensional objects to photographs or drawings.

A Bike Basket

Need an easy-to-install, inexpensive (about $4.00), and attractive catchall? Try a bicycle basket. You can attach several to the end of a standard changing table; or you can mount them on the wall in a convenient place. They come in chrome, wicker, and plastic. Use as is, or spray paint with latex enamel.

Twice Washed

Sensitive skin may react to detergents or special rinses.

To minimize diaper rash or to keep Baby forever free of bumps, wash clothes once with the hottest water and mildest soap. Rinse twice in plain water without rinse additives.

When it comes to the way clothes are dried, be aware that fabric-softener cloths used in the drier are often the culprit.

For sensitive skin, good old petroleum jelly, A & D ointment, and baby oil are still good treatments for minor diaper rash.

Uniform Measure

If your name is Mommy, part of the daily uniform is a colorful apron with shoulders and large pockets. These practical garments are essential when living with a young baby, so select several. A durable model made of vinyl can be cleaned with the swish of a sponge. Try a washable sweatshirt and pants with pockets as an alternative. Pockets is the operative word.

Nasal Aspirator

A nasal aspirator is a very useful tool when your baby gets a cold. These aspirators, designed for clearing congestion from tiny noses, are available in drugstores. Ask your pharmacist to demonstrate their use and instruct you. Your pharmacist, by the way, is a very knowledgeable resource person.

Some physicians suggest the use of an ear syringe as a nasal aspirator. These syringes fit little noses very well.

Furniture for Adults

The most important pieces of furniture for the adults in the nursery are a cozy rocking chair and a footstool. A sturdy table adjoining the chair to hold items used in feeding or comforting Baby is also handy.

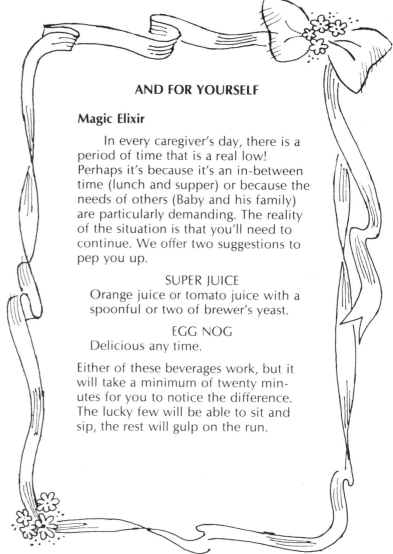

AND FOR YOURSELF

Magic Elixir

In every caregiver's day, there is a period of time that is a real low! Perhaps it's because it's an in-between time (lunch and supper) or because the needs of others (Baby and his family) are particularly demanding. The reality of the situation is that you'll need to continue. We offer two suggestions to pep you up.

SUPER JUICE
Orange juice or tomato juice with a spoonful or two of brewer's yeast.

EGG NOG
Delicious any time.

Either of these beverages work, but it will take a minimum of twenty minutes for you to notice the difference. The lucky few will be able to sit and sip, the rest will gulp on the run.

Things to Try

Many parents report that their infants have fussy periods in the early evening when little seems to help. Here are some remedies that you can try.

—Put Baby in his infant sling or front carrier and go for a short walk.

—Take Baby for a short spin in the car.
—Place Baby in his infant swing.
—Use your trusty rocking chair and sing a lullaby.

All of these suggestions include rhythmic movement, which has been found to have a comforting effect on young infants.

PARENTS, FRIENDS, AND ADMIRERS

Handling

Don't worry about Baby's endurance when it comes to being picked up, moved about, or stimulated. Babies were designed to be handled. One of the ways to truly connect with Baby is to comfort him when he is distressed. This mutual experience, very satisfying to both Baby and admirer, encourages other types of communication.

Waiting

Baby's grandparents are just as close as the telephone. Now that things are settling into a routine, why not call and share with them Baby's latest achievements. These devotees will be delighted to hear every detail of these accomplishments, and your thoughtfulness will be appreciated.

A Must

Do indulge at least once a month in a romantic dinner for two. This is a must for the new parents.

Use candles, wine, flowers, and music. Steak is always a treat; it takes only minutes to fix and is well worth the cost once a month.

Comfort Counts

For the late-night feeder or the caregiver who needs to walk with a light tread, how about a pair of fleece-lined moccasins or a bright pair of down booties? Either choice is unbeatable for cheer and warmth.

Toys

Buy something special for Baby! He has informed us that he loves red and other bright-colored things. Toys must be mouthable. They must have an interesting texture or nooks and crannies for fingers to explore. Please make sure that toys make a noise or have moving parts that won't fall off.

Two-month-olds like teething beads and teething toys. They like soft, rubbery creatures that squeak, mobiles that jump when they do, cradle gyms that have reflecting surfaces and make noises when they finally hit them. Rattles are OK, too.

Ode to Baby

Write your own poem for Baby. Try free verse, rhyme, or even a cinquain, a five-liner. Here is how you do it.

Line 1—one word, title
Line 2—two words, description
Line 3—three words, action
Line 4—four words, feeling
Line 5—one word, a title substitute

For example,
Son
First baby
Experiencing, smiling, wiggling
Such aliveness, such joy
Christopher

YOUR POEM

_____

_____

_____

_____

_____

Men

Given the chance, men can be as sensitive caregivers as women. Research shows that men are more playful and visually attractive to young infants. Learning the features of a variety of loving relationships is very important. One parent or friend does not replace the other. Rather, each adds his or her own unique contributions.

Siblings

Brothers and sisters may be among the first to tell you what they think about Baby. The truth is that Baby cannot play with them, cries a lot (and loudly), receives lots of attention from all the grown-ups, and may not be very cute. There are several things you can do to alleviate the situation.

Special times together without Baby will help relieve anxiety. Brothers and sisters need reassurance that there is enough affection and attention for them, too.

Children under two years of age are probably not going to understand what's happening if they are taken to someone else's home for baby-sitting. It would be easier for the child to remain in his or her own surroundings, even if he or she has to share them.

Three-year-olds and up often find having a baby of their own a way to cope with their mixed feelings. A baby doll with diapers, bottle, bed, and a few pieces of clothing can be used by a child while you deal with Baby's needs.

Schedule

Friends and relatives will want to see Baby, so decide when it's best for both of you. Choose one of Baby's active times so that they can see your bright, alert baby. Introduce them to some of Baby's favorite games.

Thoughtful

Going to visit a friend who just had a baby? Why not take some new fingernail polish and your nail care supplies in a lovely basket. You can trade a manicure for a cup of coffee and help Mom with Baby while her nails are drying.

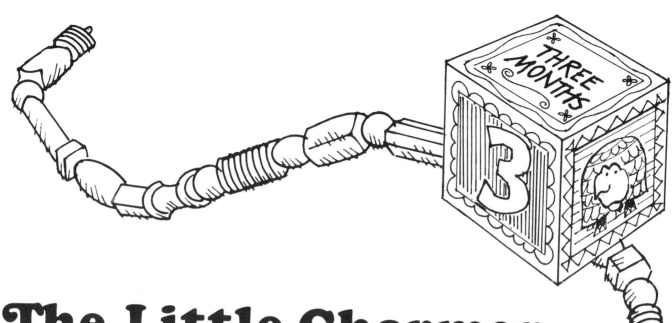

The Little Charmer

The three-month-old is a charmer—rounder, fuller, and more responsive. He is a "real baby," truly becoming a member of the family. Among his most winning ways are the beginnings of stable sleep patterns—finally, a good night's rest! Another welcome change is a decrease in crying.

Baby's verbal achievements now include talking back, cooing, and vocal play. Social skills have grown so that Baby recognizes voices and associates them with his favorite faces. He has developed an authentic social smile.

Baby is beginning to have greater control over his body. He has discovered his hands and, better still, his feet. He likes to look at his world from a variety of vantage points. Babies prefer novel, rather than familiar, visual stimuli beginning at about ten weeks of age. Spending time on their stomachs provides a change and helps them develop control of their neck and head muscles.

Though still unable to grasp objects, mobiles and other eye entertainers are an endless source of fascination. They also provide practice for grasping attempts, which resemble a boxer's roundhouse swing. Baby enjoys playing with the rattles placed in his grasp and will retain them. Baby is only able to drop these objects by chance.

Baby strains to sit up and shows his pleasure at being propped up. Whether in a special infant seat, on a lap, or positioned in the corner of the sofa, Baby thrives on being part of the passing scene.

In addition to looking, Baby enjoys listening to music and voices. He uses his voice to attract attention, the first sign of assertive behavior.

ACTIVITIES, GAMES, AND SONGS

A Ball for Baby

Baby might enjoy a small sponge ball. The ball should be tightly textured to withstand constant mouthing.

Timing

Remember that timing is all-important. Playtime will be a "ball" if Baby is well fed, awake, alert, and dry.

Toe Bows

The three-month-old is just discovering that he has toes. A bright red bow on his big toe makes playing with his toes special fun.

Baby makes a swipe for bow but can't quite grasp it

_____

Baby got hold of left bow _____

right bow _____

Oldie but Goodie

Play Peek-a-Boo, still Baby's favorite game. Playing this game is a sure way to see Baby's beautiful smile. There are as many variations to this discovery game as you have time to invent.

To Baby, who does not yet know that things he no longer sees continue to exist, the reappearance of your smiling face is a real surprise.

Easy Listening

Music is a great mood changer, pacesetter, and calming agent, so turn on the record player, tape recorder, or radio. Sing or play an instrument; determine Baby's choices.

BEETHOVEN OR BEATLES

Baby seemed to like:

Record _____

Song _____

Instrument _____

Letting Go

Watch out for bumps. Baby still hasn't quite got the hang of letting go of toys, so save those great wooden toys for later. Lightweight and soft toys are best for now. Baby can accidentally bop himself on the head with the others.

The Mobile

The experts agree that mobiles are "musts" for Baby. They provide color, motion, interest, and incentive for Baby's earliest reaching efforts. The best are mobiles of bright color or shiny features placed within ten to twelve inches of Baby, with the objects facing down to give Baby the best view.

Recent studies have suggested that, given the opportunity, babies will learn to control the movement of their mobiles by kicking and squirming, provided that the mobile is attached to the crib in a way that allows this to occur.

One father made instant mobiles with coat hangers and fishing line. He finished his creations with several balls of crumpled aluminum foil.

Tug-of-War

Sew a loop of elastic through a thread spool. Let Baby grasp the spool while you pull gently on the loop. Baby will think this is great fun. Later, these spools can be hung from the crib rail and used for a pulling game that Baby initiates himself.

Talk, Talk, Talk

Baby will now probably begin to recognize your voice by its pitch, volume, and intonation. Include him as you go about your tasks by telling precisely what you're doing—preparing his food, putting on a new striped shirt, getting ready to take a walk, or going to meet new friends. Baby is learning by listening as well as by looking. Give him the opportunity to watch you speak as he listens.

Our Own Game

Our own game together was:

_____

_____

_____

_____

_____

_____

Tracking Practice

Now that Baby's vision allows him to see across the room, he will enjoy games of visual tracking. A flashlight beam on the ceiling or wall is a fun way to lighten a dark room and give Baby's eyes a chance to chase the light.

Cuddle Toys

Baby's earliest companions in the crib, day seat, or on the floor will be a range of furry, soft objects. Check all toys to make certain that decorations cannot be removed by an exploring mouth. The best choices are washable, durable, and make a low sound.

Already there is a favorite toy.

It is a _____

Given by _____

Rattles

This classic toy takes on new meaning as Baby's skills and interests change. Remember that variety is the spice of life. This month a shiny rattle that tinkles has the greatest appeal for Baby.

Tickle Me

Tickle me, tickle me,
Tickle me, whee . . .
Oh, that tickle feels
Good to me.

(Under the chin, on tummy.)

Exercise

Passive exercises were used last month as a way to develop body awareness. They are also a fine way to relax a tense infant. Cycle those legs, rub those arms, pat the tummy, and shake the fingers. If you hum or sing a lullaby, this will aid the relaxation process.

A Name Song

Baby will begin to recognize his own name if you sing it each time you approach him or at special times. Sing to a melody of your choice:

Tell me what your name is.
My name is Grandma (Uncle, Daddy).
I'll tell you what your name is.
Your name is (Lisa).
I'm very glad to see you.

One-Man Band

Colored plastic bangle bracelets make great toys for Baby. Why, with a few bracelets to clang and some bells sewn onto elastic for his ankles, Baby is a one-man band. He will enjoy the music as he kicks and squirms.

Tummy Time

Although Baby may initially resist time on his stomach, this position will give him new sights to see and will also provide practice at raising his head and strengthening his neck. Start slowly—five to ten minutes a day after meals. If you lie down beside him and converse, there will be a real reason for him to raise up and look around.

Rainbow Colors

Buy a package of colored acetate sheets at a school supply store. Cut them into 4 in. x 6 in. panes and sew bias binding around them on your sewing machine.

Tie them onto the crib, between the bars. The light from the window will cast a lovely parade of colors across Baby and his crib.

Yodda-Lay-Dee-Hoo

Listen for those early chortles and gurgles. They are a demand for response. Talk back and Baby will talk, talk, talk. . . . This early imitation game will delight Baby. Someone is finally speaking his language.

Echoes

Baby's responses to my mimicking him were:

_____

_____

_____

_____

_____

Date _____

Kicking Toy

For a change of pace, make a kick toy by hanging a foil pie plate from Baby's mobile. Position it just in reach of his feet or attach the pan to the footboard of the crib. Add bells or a rattle to make successful kicks delightful.

Before you attach the kick toy to the crib, think through how you will attach it. Make sure that Baby cannot catch a foot in the kick toy and become distressed.

Clear-View Envelope

You can make your own clear-view envelope for Baby. Take a piece of heavy, clear vinyl and make a bag or pocket with a finished size of 7 in. x 10 in. Turn back the top edges of the bag 1 in. to form a casing. Now stitch along the edge. Thread two pieces of 36-in. colored ribbon through the casing so that you have two tying ends on each side. Sew or glue velcro tabs or strips along the inside of the opening so the bag can be securely closed.

Stretch the bag across the crib about 12 to 15 inches above Baby's head and tie securely to the crib railings. You can then place all kinds of good things inside for Baby's viewing—a flower, bells, tinsel, pretty fabrics, lollipops, plastic Christmas tree bulbs. Only your imagination will limit you.

If you can't sew you can convert a clear plastic pencil case (the kind intended to fit in a three-ring binder). The zip tip will allow items to be changed, extending Baby's interest.

Sit Box

By the middle to the end of the third month, you will want a secure way of letting Baby practice sitting for a *short* period of time. Use a small cardboard box, about 9 in. x 12 in. x 9 in. Place Baby in a sitting position in the box. The sides of the box should fit snugly under Baby's arms. Baby's feet should be touching the front of the box. This gives him plenty of support and he can practice sitting without fear of falling. Attach some bells or a toy to the box for Baby to explore.

Move Baby and his box as you go about your daily routines. He will enjoy the companionship and the view, and boredom will not become an issue. This should be only one of many position changes for Baby.

I Wanna See

A curious baby will enjoy observing you doing things for and to him. Mirrors and shiny surfaces hold a special fascination anyway. They never lose their ability to attract Baby's eyes. Mirrors that are mounted so that Baby can see himself are desirable now and later.

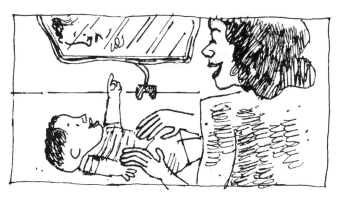

A mirror over the changing table can be reassuring. As Baby gets older, the mirror will be a visual pacifier. Reflective surfaces that will work well as mirror substitutes include sheet aluminum and shiny contact paper. With these, there is no danger of broken glass.

Portrait Gallery

Babies love faces, especially eyes. Favorite faces are those of family and friends, so why not put a gallery of several pictures inside Baby's crib. A clear sheet of contact paper will protect the pictures from exploring hands and tongues later on.

ROUTINE TIMES

Enjoy these daily activities with your very cheerful baby.

BATHING

Three Tips

By now, most babies are accepting the bathing routine. Remember—
1. to add oil to bathwater to keep Baby's skin soft
2. to select an unscented soap to ensure thorough cleansing and protect sensitive skin
3. to always gently pat Baby dry—brisk rubdowns are reserved for adults

Share a Shower

Share water fun with your infant by showering together. A gentle mist or spattering is a welcome surprise, and refreshing, too.

Mothers who have tried this report that their babies were eager, early participants in aquatic programs. Some facilities have courses for infants as young as six months. Call your local YMCA or park district for additional information.

Netted

Use a netlike sack (one that held oranges or potatoes) to hold bath gear—toys, scrubbies, etc. Hang sack over the faucet and allow to dry after bathing.

SLEEPING

Noise

A surprise to many is how little the sleeping patterns of infants are affected by noise. Members of the household need not tiptoe or worry about waking Baby with normal conversation, use of appliances, or television.

Tired babies sleep and wide-awake ones don't. It's important not to force Baby to sleep much longer than he needs by controlling the environment. He has much to learn and needs to be up and doing when he's alert.

Zzzz

Both morning and afternoon naps are more predictable. Baby may sleep two hours in the morning and one and a half in the afternoon.

Baby's schedule is:

_____ A.M. _____ P.M.

_____

_____

_____

_____

_____

(Comments)

Two Are Better

To cover Baby at bedtime, use two or more lightweight blankets rather than just one heavy coverlet. With the multiple blanket approach, there is less bulk, the temperature is easier to regulate, and you have a greater chance of keeping Baby covered. This approach also allows you to wash a blanket at any time and still have a covering for Baby.

Warming Touch

A hot-water bottle takes the edge off cool sheets, enabling Baby to relax and rest. We recently spotted some bottles cleverly concealed as barnyard animals. More like a toy, these bottles were welcomed by a baby we know. These thoroughly washable "pals" can be used to hold ice in case of a bad bump.

FEEDING

A Spoon for Cereal

Most experts recommend that you avoid the shortcut of mixing cereal with milk and putting it into a bottle. If you plan to start solids with Baby, why confuse him? Solids are eaten with a spoon; bottles are for liquids only.

Yum, Yum

By three months, some babies are ready for "real food." They will let you know by showing that they are no longer satisfied with milk. Check with your doctor before adding any new food or beverage to Baby's diet. This decision is strictly between you and your doctor.

Start slowly; a tiny sugar spoon (or demitasse spoon) worth of food each day should be enough. One new food item per week is an easy way to begin.

Don't panic if Baby seems to stop eating altogether. Much is happening—he's learning to swallow, to close his mouth, and to assimilate many new tastes and textures.

Water

Don't forget about plain water. Some babies cry not because they are hungry but because they are thirsty.

Although some nursing mothers advise against ever offering Baby a bottle, more say that getting Baby accustomed to an occasional bottle gives them more freedom in the long run. Don't forget that pumped breast milk can be left in a bottle with a caregiver.

Having a drink of water with Baby is a healthy habit for Mom, too, especially if she is nursing.

Bottle Ready?

By now you can usually anticipate the time of the next feeding. Be prepared, have the gear together and the bottle ready on demand. It is frustrating for a child to have his signal cries for food misunderstood, delayed, or denied. Baby will associate your coming for him at feeding time with the appearance of his bottle.

Blending Ahead

Although Baby may not be ready for solids yet, leftovers can be mashed in a blender or food processor and frozen in ice cube trays. The cubes, each the right size for a meal, will be ready to use in the weeks ahead.

DRESSING AND CHANGING

Favorite Article of Clothing

One of the best ways to dress Baby for fashion and comfort is to join the T-shirt craze. Whether you make your own or purchase souvenir shirts, T-shirts are a welcome change from fussier garments. Brightly colored, inexpensive, usually all cotton, these shirts are fine day or night. Longer shirts can be converted to baby sacques by hemming the bottom and adding a drawstring.

Save outgrown shirts for super toy decorations to make in the months ahead.

Three-Month Poll

Parts of routines Baby has learned to like (or at least accept):

Bathing _____

_____

Sleeping _____

_____

Feeding _____

_____

Dressing and Changing _____

_____

_____

Parts of routines Baby *still* protests (or actively dislikes):

Bathing _____

_____

Sleeping _____

_____

Feeding _____

_____

Dressing and Changing _____

_____

_____

Cold Hands, Warm Heart

Babies frequently have hands and feet that are cold to the touch. Don't consider this a true test of body temperature; the place to check is the tummy. If your home is within a normal temperature range (68° F or above) and Baby has his "work" clothes on (a T-shirt, coveralls or creepers, and diaper), he is probably adequately dressed. If you are concerned about his feet, slip on extra footwear.

HELPFUL HINTS

Reminder

The happy three-month-old baby deserves and delights in more social contact. Let him see and be seen.

Beware of Glare

Babies like soft light from interesting sources. A Mexican tin lantern can provide Baby with a fascinating pattern of light on walls and ceiling.

For a special treat, add a little atmosphere with candlelight while you are with Baby. Baby will be entranced by the flame. Think safety.

Pins and Tape

Keep diaper pins sharp by poking them into a bar of soap when you are not using them.

If you are using disposable diapers, masking tape or plastic tape can be used to replace diaper tape that has been accidentally coated with powder or baby cream.

Perfume or After-Shave

Ah, the sweet, fruity or spicy fragrance of your choice need not wait for a special occasion. The aroma will lift both your spirits and will tantalize Baby's nose. You can spray the air with scent, or sprinkle a bit on the top of a lightbulb to fill the room with interesting smells. You'll find Baby appreciative.

Guilt Fighter

Babies may look frail and helpless, but by the age of three months they do have some toughness. Forgetting to change a diaper occasionally or not doing something right on schedule is not a crisis. Baby will forget and forgive; so, no needless guilts!

Sweet Soakers

Carry a sponge or cloth that has been soaked in a solution of baking soda and water to clean up Baby's bibs and feeding mishaps. Odors will be absorbed quickly.

A Good Night's Sleep

Parents, rejoice! Many infants sleep a continuous ten hours a night by the end of this month. Sleep is guaranteed to make your life easier, so get your rest . . . and thank you, Baby.

Hang Ten

A wall-type hat rack placed close to Baby's changing table will save many steps. Hang washcloths, not-too-soiled undershirts, bibs, etc., on the rack.

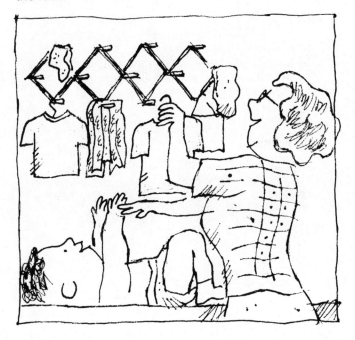

High Polish

To polish the first silver spoon for a tasting baby, try toothpaste. It is absolutely safe, quick, and inexpensive. This works well on rattles and cups, too.

Seat Safety

Now that Baby is becoming more active, never leave him unattended in an infant seat placed on a table or counter. These little seats are tippy, and a sudden jerky movement by Baby could cause an accident.

Sizewise

Planning to make a custom garment for Baby? The only statistics you need for three-month-olds are:

Weight _____

Length _____

These measurements will usually provide a designer with enough information to create a garment that Baby will be able to wear for many weeks. Think comfort and loose-fitting styling. A simple style means quick and easy sewing, and easy laundering, too.

The Entertainer

Baby can keep himself happily occupied for many minutes if there are interesting things to look at in his crib. Give Baby an opportunity for discovery and experimentation, especially in the morning or at the end of a nap. Provide Baby with time and some dangling objects to swipe at or kick. Don't worry, Baby will call you when he needs you.

Fasteners

The fewer snaps, buttons, and zippers on a garment, the easier and speedier dressing will be. An all-fabric fastener, velcro is tufted nylon material that adheres when pressed to itself. Check it out—strips tabs, patches, all are great for quick changes.

Bulletin Board

To keep track of supplies, or to record feedings, hang a bulletin board. An invaluable organizer, the bulletin board with pushpins, pen on an attached ribbon, and paper, is a sanity saver.

Diaper Storage

Disposable diapers are cheaper in larger quantities. If you can buy in quantity, an easy way to store a large number is to stack them vertically in a garment bag. The bag can hang, out of sight, in a closet. Besides neatness, you have the advantage of being able to check your supply at a glance.

Place to Go

Remember the library when you need information or inspiration. Whether you need specific answers regarding your child or yourself, it's a quiet and helpful place to spend time.

Fewer Tears

Now is the time when Baby can really accompany you on some small excursions. Most

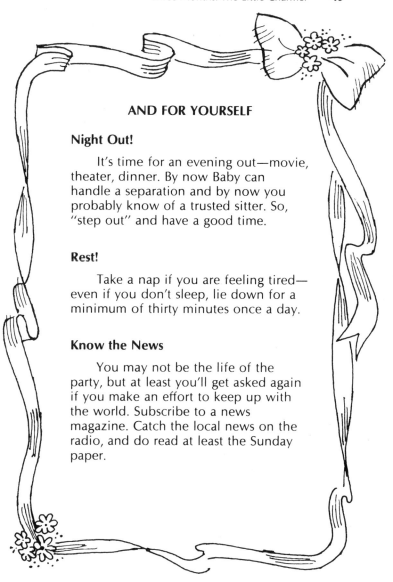

AND FOR YOURSELF

Night Out!

It's time for an evening out—movie, theater, dinner. By now Baby can handle a separation and by now you probably know of a trusted sitter. So, "step out" and have a good time.

Rest!

Take a nap if you are feeling tired—even if you don't sleep, lie down for a minimum of thirty minutes once a day.

Know the News

You may not be the life of the party, but at least you'll get asked again if you make an effort to keep up with the world. Subscribe to a news magazine. Catch the local news on the radio, and do read at least the Sunday paper.

caregivers agree that there is a marked decrease in crying at about three months. If you've only risked a trip to the mailbox until now, it's time to start trying the supermarket, a department store, or even lunch with a friend. Baby can enjoy the view or cuisine from his carriage or infant seat. A change of scene is essential for both you and that smiling, social baby of yours.

Un-stuck

To remove a Band-Aid or adhesive tape from Baby's skin, saturate a cotton ball in baby oil and rub over the tape. No pain, no strain.

On-the-Go Baby

For the baby who goes to an early learning program, get a cute rubber stamp and a pad of indelible ink. Soon all his belongings will sport a jumping frog, duck, etc., and will be quickly recognized by all. This is far easier than sewing on labels or writing on masking tape.

of a standard crib. Add elastic in a casing to the corners to keep the new sheet secured and smooth.

A "Must"

To keep you and Baby happy, part of the daily routine should include some time out of the house. Except in the most extreme type of weather, even a short jaunt will do you both good. A change of scene means new things for Baby to see. Other people and stimulating sights can lift your spirits. This planned activity period will minimize the sense of isolation that often occurs when caring for a young child.

Fresh Air

And while you and Baby are out, don't fail to allow Mother Nature an opportunity to contribute to Baby's room. Push back the shutters, open wide the windows, and let the fresh air in to circulate and sweeten. This is by far the fastest and surest way to deodorize a stale room.

PARENTS, FRIENDS, AND ADMIRERS

For "My" Baby

A sibling or other young child will often want to "do" for Baby. Here are a few projects to keep him or her busy.
1. A Cloth Book—pages need be nothing fancier than a few colored fabric swatches. Older children might pink the edges of the pages for a fancy touch. Two holes along one edge laced with a ribbon will hold the book together. Completely

washable and visually appealing to Baby, the book can be a crib toy and a gift of love.
2. Young Decorator's Sheets—stretch a portion of a white or solid-colored sheet over an embroidery hoop to hold it steady, then let the child draw, design, or doodle with indelible markers or special fabric crayons. Baby will follow the colors first with his eyes, and later on with his fingers. It's a one-of-a-kind item.

Men

Grandpas, uncles, big brothers, and fathers deserve the thrill of time alone with Baby. Make certain that they know where supplies are located. Post phone numbers and a list of things Baby likes to do. Setting the stage helps ensure success with Baby.

Working Mothers

Here are a few quick thoughts for the mother returning to work.

It is quality time, not quantity time, that counts with Baby.

Baby will always have only one Mommy with whom he shares a very special relationship. Working will never change this. The more you grow as a person, the better mother you will be.

Chitchat

A new face provides a lift for you and Baby. A neighbor child or sibling can entertain and respond to Baby as no adult ever could—just watch! Most older children want very much to really participate in Baby's world, if only anxious parents would let them. Children teach and recognize cues from each other in fresh, spontaneous ways. So disappear and let the "small talk" begin.

Special Folks and Grandparents

Including these not-so-secret admirers in Baby's world is often a challenge. Although proudly possessive, these friends have much to share. Keep them informed by postcard or a quick call if distance separates you; send photos as soon as possible. They are eager to help, so make your suggestions regarding needs, schedules, and routines specific. Showing them in this way that you are on top of the situation will put everyone at ease. These measures will ensure that their efforts will be justly rewarded. Fortunate parents can rely on these people for the best in child care.

BABY VISITED

People	Date

THEY CAME TO SEE BABY

People	Date

Moccasins

If an admirer is traveling to a part of the Old West, a great gift for Baby is a pair of moccasins.

More than a mere novelty, these coverings are an excellent choice for a child who is preparing to crawl. Many are fleece-lined for extra warmth. Soft and flexible, you can make your own from widely available kits.

Remember

What Baby accomplished and how you coped this month will grow difficult to recall all too soon. So take the time now to do some quick jotting.

TIME OUT TO REFLECT ON THE HAPPY MOMENTS
OF THE MONTH

_____

_____

_____

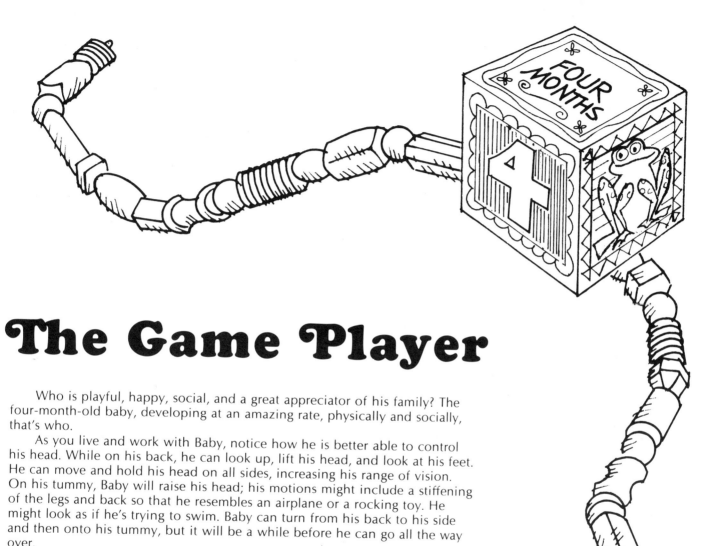

The Game Player

Who is playful, happy, social, and a great appreciator of his family? The four-month-old baby, developing at an amazing rate, physically and socially, that's who.

As you live and work with Baby, notice how he is better able to control his head. While on his back, he can look up, lift his head, and look at his feet. He can move and hold his head on all sides, increasing his range of vision. On his tummy, Baby will raise his head; his motions might include a stiffening of the legs and back so that he resembles an airplane or a rocking toy. He might look as if he's trying to swim. Baby can turn from his back to his side and then onto his tummy, but it will be a while before he can go all the way over.

His arms and hands are a continuing source of pleasure, delight, and information. Hands are more and more like toys, especially now that Baby can

53

bring them together. Little fingers, sensitive to touch, will explore all surfaces, objects, and clothing before bringing whatever possible to Baby's mouth, the taste-tester and first source of information. Arms that are growing strong are being used for pushing up while on his belly and for snaring objects within reach.

Routine times provide opportunities to socialize. Baby wants to talk and to respond to your comments. Just listen for the spontaneous chortles, gurgles, and coos. Bathtime is bliss. Feeding times are the best times of all, but prepare for the mess. This could be a time for fun with father and siblings.

Baby loves to be played with and handled, from casual hugs to gentle roughhousing. Siblings will enjoy this not-so-fragile Baby and can both help out and interact with him easily. Baby's responses will be squeals, smiles, and demands for more. He is a performer, too. Allow him access to a mirror and watch. Baby is a willing participant in any game.

Baby may also grow to prefer a particular toy—one favored above all others. This object may play a special role at rest time, or might help soothe him when he is fussy.

ACTIVITIES, GAMES, AND SONGS

Baby enjoys doing some of his first activities even more now than he did the first time. Do go back and provide lots of opportunities to repeat old favorites.

OUR CHOICES	YOUR CHOICES
1. How Big? (Chapter 1)	_____ _____
2. Wrist Wear (Chapter 2)	_____ _____
3. Tracking Practice (Chapter 3)	_____ _____

Games

Everything you present to Baby is a game. How playful he has suddenly become! If you don't initiate a smile, watch to see if he does. We bet you'll be surprised.

Hot Air

A bunch of brightly colored balloons can be an exciting new toy for Baby. Attach the balloons to his infant seat so they will sway as he moves his body. Keep an eye out for the new foil balloons, too. Their reflection quality is mirror perfect.

Hide-and-Seek

A fun game for an older sibling to play with Baby is hide-and-seek. While Baby is on someone's lap, have a friend call his name and let him turn to find the friend. Baby will enjoy the fun and repetition of this simple game. This is a great activity anytime, especially during routines.

Rolls

Remember the neck-roll pillows your Granny had? These are easy to make and great fun for a young baby getting ready to move. You can place the roll, for short periods of time, under his chest, tummy, or knees, giving his body a new position in space.

A Ball for Baby

Baby will enjoy playing with a multitextured cloth ball or with a molded ball with lots of indentations for exploring fingers.

Changes

As you redecorate, become a collector. A theme approach is just one way to gather posters, prints, and clippings. Try flowers, barnyard animals, food, faces, seasons, wildlife, etc. All your finds can be used for books, puzzles, or games. Remember to cover everything with clear contact paper.

Faces

Use fabric crayons or markers to design the features of an animal or sew a felt face on the top part of Baby's socks. Attach yarn for hair, add buttons, bows, and other finery for a special touch. A fine pair might be a dog and cat, Mom and Dad, or twins. Baby will enjoy watching his feet move and trying to grasp these funny faces.

Body Work

Baby is now really working to know himself—feeling himself, exploring himself and his world. Allow him an opportunity to play alone—perhaps when he awakens in the morning. Such times are learning times; he'll let you know when he wants or needs assistance.

Hands Plus

Because Baby is using his hands more and more, encourage his efforts by giving him a gold star or two. This sparkly reward, stuck onto his wrist, will provide interest for hands and eyes. Place them on other parts of the body, too, perhaps his knee or big toe. Try alternating the stars, red on the top of his wrist, gold for the inside arm. Lately we've spotted piglets, hearts, puppies, and teddy bear gift seals that would also please Baby. If one of these scraps of paper is taste-tested, it will not be a catastrophe.

Dance Partner

A ready partner, should the time be suitable (record, radio, or tape), is Baby. Lift him and waltz, swoop, sway, dip, or jitterbug. Hold each other close and move out onto the dance floor often.

I Can

Baby can, through trial and error, learn to manipulate his own crib gym if he's given the opportunity. Try placing Baby in his infant seat near his gym so that the knobs or things to grasp or hit are suspended just above his lap. He will be delighted with his success. This is the time to include noisemakers, such as a set of metal measuring spoons or jangling plastic bracelets.

Sound Bonanza

Babies learn to listen through practice. "Sound Bonanza" can be a fun game. Put together in a box four or five of Baby's favorite sounds.

OUR LIST	YOUR LIST
Bells	_____
Crinkly paper	_____
Spoons	_____
Squeaker	_____

Play the game by providing Baby with an opportunity to hear each different sound. Start by introducing one or two and slowly include the other sounds until you've presented the entire "Bonanza" to him. Over time you'll notice how Baby learns to anticipate and enjoy this game.

Remember that each room in your house has its own sounds. Baby will grow to associate these sounds and respond to them with recognition and delight.

A Touch of Color

Baby loves his fingers. Examining them is a favorite game. You can add a new dimension with a touch of colored polish on a tiny fingernail.

Rolling Room

Baby can roll now. Make sure to allow room for this activity and give him some incentive. Seeing an item of interest out of the corner of his eye might encourage a roll. For now, these movements may be more like flops, but they are an important stage in his motor development.

Never leave Baby alone on a sofa or bed, no matter how large. Now that he can roll, falls are all too possible.

Mirror Fun

Mirrors are a must for Baby. Use your imagination and place them in places that are accessible to Baby. Nonbreakable mirrors in a variety of shapes and sizes can be purchased at most toy or educational supply stores. Mirrors never lose their intrigue, and can help Baby learn a lot.

Oh Yes, Toes!

Tickle those toes. Remember:

This little Piggy went to market.
This little Piggy stayed home.
This little Piggy had roast beef.
This little Piggy had none.
And this little Piggy cried, "Wee, wee, wee,"
  all the way home.

Fish

Baby loves to watch goldfish. Bright orange and always on the move, they're a real Baby fascinator. A few stalks of fishbowl fern will add additional color and help keep these friends alive.

Be sure to position the bowl close enough to Baby's crib for "live entertainment." But the bowl must be far enough away so that someday soon Baby won't surprise you with a fish in his hand and water all over his crib.

Horsie, Horsie

To the tune of "Here We Go 'Round the Mulberry Bush," sing the following verse as you gently bounce Baby on your knee.

This is the way the lady rides,
  the lady rides, the lady rides.
This is the way the lady rides,
  when she goes into town.
This is the way the gentleman rides . . .
  when he goes into town.
This is the way the farmer rides . . .
This is the way the hunter rides . . .
This is the way the Indian rides . . .

Watch Baby's behavior; see how he shows that he wants you to continue the game. Men seem to be especially good at this game.

Children's Records

Children's records that include action songs can be a good investment. Buy a sturdy child's record player, one an elementary schoolchild can learn to operate. Baby will enjoy listening to the records now. He will try to do the actions with you as a toddler, and sing along as a preschooler. Children like to hear the same several songs many times and are just getting the hang of things about the time adults are ready to scream, so do plan to listen a lot to the ones you choose. Remember that a lot of learning takes place through the medium of music.

Lower, Please

Baby is no longer happy simply watching toys sway before his eyes. He may even wail in frustration. He wants to touch and inspect now. Lower the crib gyms and sturdy, safe mobiles so that they are within easy reach of Baby. He will enjoy practicing this new game of eye-hand coordination. He will diligently work, adjusting his aim until he is finally able to touch and hold these tantalizing toys.

Other Babies

An exciting experience for Baby will be meeting and watching his first other baby. It will be fun for you, too. You will be amazed at the two babies' instant awareness of and interest in each other. Lay the two infants side by side on a blanket where they can truly investigate each other. It would be fascinating to know just what they are thinking.

ROUTINE TIMES

BATHING

Splashes

Happy splashes will be part of bathtime for both of you by now. Remember to wear an apron (oilcloth or vinyl) if you don't want to be dampened. A nice addition to the bath might be a drop or two of food coloring. Don't use too much, or you'll have a strawberry or blueberry baby.

Body Wise

Naming parts of Baby's body is a good thing to remember at bathtime. Start at the head and work down, giving an order to this body awareness routine. Telling him what is being done as you proceed is very reassuring. "I am now washing your arm, your hand . . . give me your other foot . . ." In time, Baby will learn to respond by presenting the appropriate part for a scrub.

Water Play

Baby is not too young for water play. He will enjoy paddling hands and feet in warm water. For the reluctant bather, this mini-experience might be a help in learning to cope with a larger tub.

Bath Toy

A fluffy nylon net flower makes a tickly bath toy. You can often buy these at local bazaars or craft outlets.

Best Bath

Baby likes his bath best after his meals, when he is full, relaxed, and happy. Often this will be the time when he needs one. Experience will quickly teach you when not to bathe Baby; for example, when he is overtired or hungry.

Rub-a-Dub-Dub

An open-weave plastic laundry basket is a safe way to secure Baby in a tub, if you don't have a tub ring, which is commercially available. Run an inch or two of water in the tub, and watch him enjoy his new environment. This is also a great way to have fun outside with water; use a small inflatable pool.

SLEEPING

Sleep Time?

Baby is growing quite comfortable in his bedtime routine. Make sure that stability continues by sticking to the same bedtime with as few exceptions as possible. Put him down in the way he prefers, with or without favorite toys. Make him cozy, sing, say goodnight, and leave calmly.

Baby on the Go

It is important that parents be aware of Baby's napping routine, even if Baby spends most naptimes away from home. By providing some continuity, weekends can be more enjoyable. Having a bedfellow who comes and goes with Baby can be helpful. So is knowing whether Baby naps in a quiet room or if his crib remains in a lighted room where other children are playing. Good communication among Baby's favorite people benefits all.

FEEDING

By now Baby probably no longer requires a late night feeding. During the day, he is steadily eating every three to four hours. Since Baby is beginning to try "people food," you might consider:

—bananas in thin slices
—a toast finger
—a graham cracker
—a popped pea or two (a pea that has been poked by a fork)
—a tablespoonful of applesauce

Baby's Treat Sheet

ITEM PRESENTED   DATE   REACTION

_____

_____

_____

_____

_____

Food Facts

Keep food simple; no combinations, please. By presenting a single serving, food intolerance can be immediately detected. When Baby wants to be fed again, he will let you know.

A handy way to keep a variety of food for Baby is to use a plastic popsicle kit. A few tablespoonfuls of fruit or vegetable easily fit into each well. Cap to preserve flavor and taste.

Remember that your homemade concoctions should not be kept longer than three days. If you have any doubts, throw it out.

Bib

Playing with food is nearly as interesting as eating to Baby. So make a couple of quick bibs; use washcloths or kitchen towels, 13 in. x 10½ in. These will help keep Baby clean and covered. Cut a half circle for the neck, bind edges with bias tape, and stitch long lengths for ties.

DRESSING AND CHANGING

Jingle-Bell Jack

A nifty shirt is one that has several things going for it. Baby and Mom like it to be easy to get into, washable, and an unexpectedly brilliant color. You could make a surprise shirt by sewing on a bell or a noisemaker. Attach the item securely or conceal it artistically so that it is worn, not swallowed. Baby and Mom will love it.

Bells and noisemakers are also great additions to shoes or booties.

Clothes Horse

Looking at those adorable clothes that no longer fit is discouraging, so may we suggest:
1. Cutting the sleeves out of shirts for that "muscle beach" or layered look
2. Stuffing old socks and booties for a soft sculpture or mobile
3. Saving the best and favorite items for Baby's larger stuffed friends and dolls to wear

4. Swapping with a friend whose children are older *and* younger than Baby

The Strap

Your little wiggler, in a fit of temper, could launch himself right off a changing table. For security, both yours and his, remember the strap. A midriff belt will do the trick.

Flat Out

If you are caught off guard by the telephone, doorbell, or some emergency, and you need free hands or arms, remember that the floor is the best place for an infant halfway between being diapered and dressed.

Diaper Rash

Some suggestions:
1. For an easy and often successful treatment, lay a large plastic tablecloth on the floor and cover with a sheet or mattress pad that can be laundered easily. Allow a diaperless baby to play there with his toys for at least thirty minutes, giving the affected area time to thoroughly dry in the warm room air. If routinely done several times a day for three to five days, this treatment can promote healing. This can also be used as a preventive measure.
2. Rubber pants are often the culprit. Use them only when really needed because they limit the circulation of air around Baby's bottom.
3. Cornstarch works as well as talcum powder in a pinch.

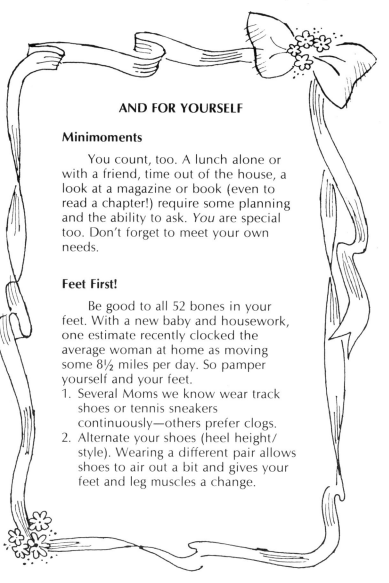

AND FOR YOURSELF

Minimoments

You count, too. A lunch alone or with a friend, time out of the house, a look at a magazine or book (even to read a chapter!) require some planning and the ability to ask. *You* are special too. Don't forget to meet your own needs.

Feet First!

Be good to all 52 bones in your feet. With a new baby and housework, one estimate recently clocked the average woman at home as moving some 8½ miles per day. So pamper yourself and your feet.
1. Several Moms we know wear track shoes or tennis sneakers continuously—others prefer clogs.
2. Alternate your shoes (heel height/ style). Wearing a different pair allows shoes to air out a bit and gives your feet and leg muscles a change.

HELPFUL HINTS

Reminder

We will bet that if you are bored, Baby is too. Think for two; plan ahead. The smallest changes make the hour, morning, or day a special one.

Rested

Have you noticed that things are getting easier? Everyone, including Baby, is getting more rest. Certain routines are becoming established. Baby is more predictable and you can plan the best times to play with him.

Sit Box

Keep your sit box (see Chapter 3, "Activities, Games, and Songs") for a safe alternative to Baby's infant seat. Great to have handy when you travel or must make a quick trip to the second floor. Try covering it with washable, printed contact paper.

Beach Blanket Bingo

Since Baby will be spending more time on the floor, change his surroundings by putting him down on a large, colorful beach blanket or bath sheet. The texture will amuse him and so will the design. This is especially handy when visiting friends.

Last Diaper

Tired of reaching into a box or drawer of diapers only to find that someone has used the last one? Buy a wicker wine rack and stack diapers (cloth or disposable) in the handy sections. This attractive and orderly way of storing diapers lets you see how many are left. After Baby's diaper days are over, you can move this storage item to the pantry and use it for its intended purpose.

Sniff-less

Two deodorizers for the refrigerator, now full of odd baby food concoctions, are:
1. A box of baking soda
2. A chunk of charcoal
   Both items will absorb odors and keep foods tasting the way they were meant to taste.

Medical Note

By now Baby should be halfway through his immunization program. Completion of this program ensures a healthy baby. Check to make sure things are on schedule; keep a record at home.

Heloise?

My Helpful Hint for Heloise this month would

be: _____

_____

_____

Your Observer

Baby wants to see you doing things. The most common household task is still new to him. Companionship is part of what Baby is after. He also loves an opportunity to chatter with you. So move him with you in his sit box, sling, high chair, or swing, or make a place for him on the floor. Make sure he is positioned so that he has a good view of the action and that you are not far away.

The Packed Baby

One way to make the quick trip a more frequent happening is to have an extra bag of gear ready to go. Just like an overnight bag that can be grabbed for a dash to the airport, prepare so that you and Baby can leave with a minimum of fuss.

Include

—diapers (disposable/cloth)
—powders or cream (sample size)
—a complete change of clothes
—a sweater
—a blanket
—wipes

Repack your bag after each trip and you'll be ready for next time.

Stroller Tips

Storage tips for your umbrella stroller—the greatest invention since disposable diapers—include

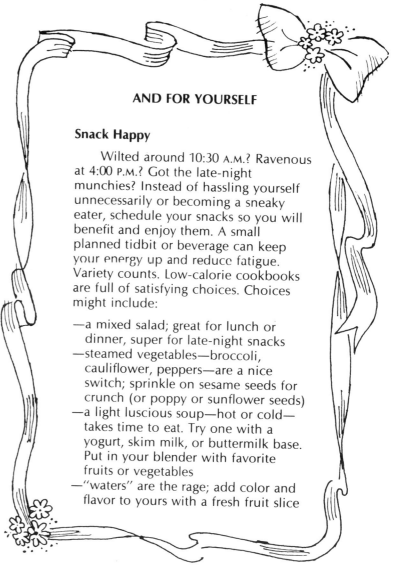

AND FOR YOURSELF

Snack Happy

Wilted around 10:30 A.M.? Ravenous at 4:00 P.M.? Got the late-night munchies? Instead of hassling yourself unnecessarily or becoming a sneaky eater, schedule your snacks so you will benefit and enjoy them. A small planned tidbit or beverage can keep your energy up and reduce fatigue. Variety counts. Low-calorie cookbooks are full of satisfying choices. Choices might include:

—a mixed salad; great for lunch or dinner, super for late-night snacks
—steamed vegetables—broccoli, cauliflower, peppers—are a nice switch; sprinkle on sesame seeds for crunch (or poppy or sunflower seeds)
—a light luscious soup—hot or cold—takes time to eat. Try one with a yogurt, skim milk, or buttermilk base. Put in your blender with favorite fruits or vegetables
—"waters" are the rage; add color and flavor to yours with a fresh fruit slice

—hanging it on an old-fashioned clothes hook
—setting it in an old wicker umbrella holder or tall
  wicker basket
—storing it in a bottom bureau drawer

Lickety-Split

A baby front-carrier can be turned into an
emergency high chair for Baby by placing him in the
sling and tying it to a chair. This will give Baby's
back needed support. It also provides an element of
safety in that he is securely tied to the chair. It can
be handy when you are at a friend's home and want
to have your arms free to sip your coffee. It also
allows your social baby to stay close to your side.

"Two in One" Bag

It's worth the effort and time to develop a "two-
in-one" bag to take Baby and his belongings to day
care or the baby-sitter. Ideally the bag should allow
for the large section of the bag to remain during the
week. The small bag should be detachable so that
soiled clothes can be taken home daily. It can also
be used to transport daily food and needed extras.

Pop-Tops

A "fashion" poncho can provide quick coverage for a busy Baby. These easy pop-tops can be made for rain, sun, or cool temperatures at the beach or in the backyard.

1. The Raintop can be made of lightweight vinyl or a similar fabric. No hemming required; just bind neck edge with ribbon or seam binding.
2. The Suntop, a cool, absorbent cover to keep the ultraviolet rays away from sensitive skin, can be made from an extra hand towel, standard size. A fringe front and back adds a festive look.
3. For cooler days—an extra blanket from Baby's collection will make a fine washable cover.

PARENTS, FRIENDS, AND ADMIRERS

Special Toy

A simple rag doll or a monkey made of socks is a good choice for Baby this month. Soft enough to gnaw on without teeth, durable, and cuddly, these toys are easily made at home. Patterns and kits are readily available. Or, make up your own little creatures from your scrap bag.

Brothers and Sisters

Baby is becoming more responsive and no one is more delighted than his siblings. Baby can do more and is less apt to cry when bumped, startled, or loved by his family. Rivalries will at last be under control.

Sound Machine

The most patient interpreters of your little noise machine are probably grandparents. These admirers, long on experience, will be best able to imitate and initiate Baby's sounds. Watch them, and pick up some valuable techniques.

Young Art

Baby will enjoy the colorful art of brothers, sisters, or young neighborhood friends. He especially likes faces that can be dangled for his amusement or used to brighten his room.

Frame especially nice artwork from Baby's siblings and hang in his room. This is a good way to flatter the brother or sister who may need a pat on the back just about now.

Sprouting

Baby is growing fast.

Current length _____

Current weight _____

Favorite Toys _____

_____

_____

An Early Start

Now that Baby is four months old it's time for friends and admirers to think about his future. A piggy bank may be corny and old-fashioned, but it's a nice way to start thinking ahead for this special baby.

Notes for Special Host/Hostess

Here are some suggestions that should make Baby's stay with a special admirer especially fun. Prepare now and have these items close at hand.

—This book, so you will know Baby's favorite games
—Some well-chosen toys
—A cozy, safe place to sleep
—A familiar toy and blanket from home

Instant Bed

The floor is a perfect place for a visiting baby. Place a plastic mat from a playpen or an air mattress on the floor, cover with an old quilt or blanket, and partition off a cozy space with pillows. This will provide a safe place for this little wriggler to sleep in comfort.

Napping Hints

Techniques you might use when napping your visiting baby are:

—Lay Baby down, dim the lights, turn on the radio very softly, and creep out. Wait about five minutes to see if he falls asleep.
—Rock and walk Baby until he starts to fall asleep, then lay him down.
—Pat or rub Baby's back as he lies on his tummy in bed until he quiets and slips off to sleep.

Voices

Baby will respond to a new voice. Notice how alert he becomes when a visitor or stranger appears. It is one of many ways Baby learns about people in his world. Give him exposure to new voices.

Fathers

Dads and other involved men play a continuing role in Baby's development. These important people communicate with Baby their special way of handling, care, and concern. Their body language is picked up in ways that many babies respond to positively and with delight. Men are great caregivers and can change, bathe, and feed successfully.

Personality Chart

Baby has a very definite personality and temperament. Take time to jot down a few notes about Baby's emerging style.

_____

_____

_____

_____

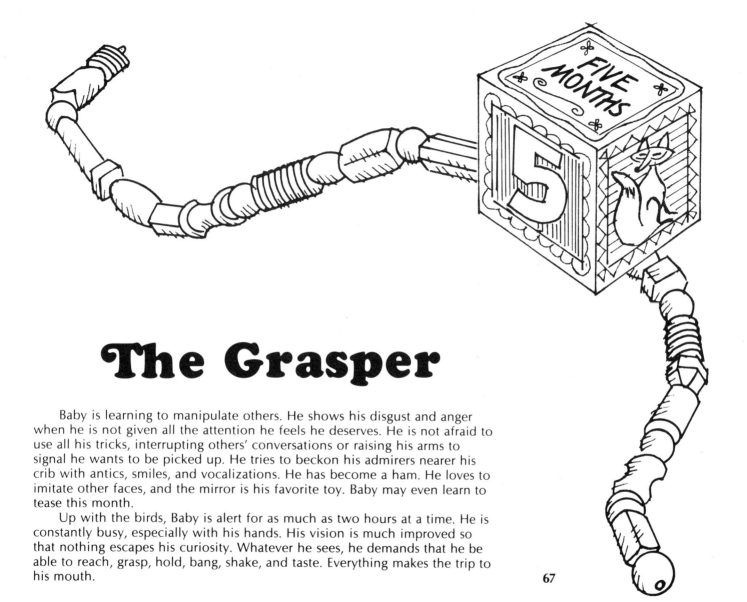

The Grasper

Baby is learning to manipulate others. He shows his disgust and anger when he is not given all the attention he feels he deserves. He is not afraid to use all his tricks, interrupting others' conversations or raising his arms to signal he wants to be picked up. He tries to beckon his admirers nearer his crib with antics, smiles, and vocalizations. He has become a ham. He loves to imitate other faces, and the mirror is his favorite toy. Baby may even learn to tease this month.

Up with the birds, Baby is alert for as much as two hours at a time. He is constantly busy, especially with his hands. His vision is much improved so that nothing escapes his curiosity. Whatever he sees, he demands that he be able to reach, grasp, hold, bang, shake, and taste. Everything makes the trip to his mouth.

67

He now looks after fallen objects and recognizes familiar objects. He is developing a memory and remembers some of his own actions. With his good vision, he can now recognize members of his family and may bounce and wiggle with delight when he spots them approaching. By the same token, he is likely to be more wary of strangers.

Baby is beginning to understand language. He knows his name and babbles to gain attention. He enjoys experimenting with sounds and inflection patterns, trying to imitate what he hears. He vocalizes to himself, his toys, and his admirers. He watches mouths very carefully, sharpening his skills.

Motor skills may be developing rapidly. On his tummy, he lifts his head chest-high off the bed as he bounces and wiggles. He is beginning to locomote by rocking, rolling, twisting, or pushing against flat surfaces. He can sit supported for thirty minutes. He likes to stand when supported and will sway, stomping his feet. Remember, however, that babies are individuals; not all will develop this rapidly.

Baby is leaving the quiet months of looking and is about to become very mobile, someone from whom nothing is safe. This is the time for parents and others who have infants in their homes to begin babyproofing.

ACTIVITIES, GAMES, AND SONGS

Swinging Eggs

An inexpensive crib gym for Baby can be made from metallic egg-shaped panty hose containers. Simply add rice, beans, or bells, a string, and seal the eggs tightly. These can then be dangled from a piece of elastic stretched across the crib. Babies love shiny objects, and will enjoy hearing them jingle and trying to catch them as they sway.

Bubbles

Babies love bubbles and will sit spellbound watching you blow them. Make your own mix using ½ cup dishwashing liquid, a tablespoon of glycerine, and a small amount of water. A straw or the frames from an old pair of sunglasses will make the perfect blower or wand. If time is money, buy a jar of bubbles at the dimestore. They are still inexpensive and a very good buy.

Surprise

Hide a squeak toy under Baby's sheet or blanket. Show Baby how to squeak it with his hand. Soon, with a little practice, he'll learn to squeak it himself. For an additional surprise, hide a squeak toy in the pocket of Baby's coat or in the jacket of a friend.

Puzzles

It's not too soon for knob puzzles (puzzles with little knobs on each piece for easy lifting and holding). Babies enjoy looking at them, chewing on them, and distinguishing their colors and shapes. Add knobs of your own to wooden puzzles. It's difficult to lose pieces with these quick-to-attach handles.

Music

Music is a language of its own, one that Baby can enjoy and understand. A nice way to start a nap might be with a little soft classical music. Playtime can include lively music to sway to. Watch Baby's reactions.

Musical Instruments

Baby will enjoy making music with bells. In Chapter 3 he had an anklet with bells. This month he will be able to grasp some bells joined together. Another fine choice would be a pair of maracas for him to shake.

Handles

Toys with handles will be special fun this month. A stuffed chick with wings to hang onto or a friend with a tail would be great; so would an octopus, monkey, rhino, or elephant. Pick durable and washable toys.

A Left Hook

Waiting in a high chair can be more bearable for Baby if you place a few toys with vacuum-cup bases on his tray. These inexpensive items are fun to hit and they will stand still for a swinging baby. One child we know liked a little bear, circle of balls, and several small animals. Most of these toys will jingle or make a noise when poked or squeezed.

Slick and Shiny

Stuffed oilcloth shapes with bells and rattles inside are welcome new toys. Since Baby is involved with carrying around, holding, and mouthing objects, these washable playthings are practical, too. The fabric itself can determine the final shape. A cheery vinyl pattern with luscious oranges, grapes, and cherries inspired a fruit basket of goodies stuffed with foam rubber. The fruits were also perfect for bathtime toys.

Fire trucks, apples, and hearts drawn freehand, cut from red oilcloth, and stuffed with polyester batting give Baby a slick and shiny surface that will tickle his tongue. A quick sponging or immersion in soapy water and the toys will look great again.

A Ball for Baby

Try stringing three or four table tennis balls on a fishing line. Baby will enjoy grasping and shaking them. In the months to come, they will be fun for the crawling Baby to roll and chase.

Knots

Play teaches Baby about himself and his world. An intriguing toy for Baby this month is a one-inch-thick cotton cord with knots tied at intervals. This simple string toy—approximately six inches long—satisfies Baby's desire to touch and explore.

Making Faces

Baby loves to imitate your funny faces. He will also try to imitate your voice inflections, so use lots of them. See how Baby watches your mouth and then experiments.

Imitator's Notebook

Describe below some of Baby's best imitations of friends and family members.

_____

_____

_____

_____

Pat-a-Cake

A hand-clapping game for you and Baby is:

Pat-a-cake, pat-a-cake,
Baker's man;
Bake me a cake
As fast as you can.
Roll it and pat it
and mark it with B,
And put it in the oven
For Baby and me.

Custom T-shirt

A T-shirt for Baby, one that will be fun for you both, is one that includes a detachable toy. How about a sunny breakfast shirt with snap-on eggs (fried, of course) and bacon strips. Or a fluffy mama cat with a kitten attached with velcro strips.

Produce Exploration

An unlikely but fascinating source of items for exploration is as near as the fruit basket or vegetable bin. Baby will examine, in the greatest detail, texture, shape, and aroma when a basket of these goodies is placed in front of him. Excellent choices include a stalk of leafy celery, a shiny purple eggplant, a fuzzy peach, a slick onion, and a pungent orange. If Baby actually manages to pick anything up, his toothless attempts to gnaw can do little actual harm to these pieces of produce.

Changing Terrain

Lifting one end of Baby's bed can create a new dimension in his environment. He will enjoy this new hill and slide on which to climb and roll. For safety's sake, do this only when you can be present to supervise.

Sing

Sing "Pop Goes the Weasel"—bring Baby's hands together to make the popping sound or clap your hands. Within a few months, Baby will be clapping hands on his own.

All around the cobbler's bench
The monkey chased the weasel.
The monkey thought 'twas all in fun
Pop . . . goes the weasel.

Just Out of Reach

Baby will be working hard this month to make his body move. His rocking, wiggling, arching, and rolling may eventually lead him to crawl. Encourage him to move forward by positioning toys and attractive objects just beyond his grasp. To help a noncrawling baby give the technique a try, sit with the toys yourself an arm's length away to persuade him to move his body.

Inner Tube

A favorite toy is a black rubber inner tube. It is great fun to sit in, pat, and poke. It adds the security of a bit of extra support for the beginning sitter and provides a challenging embankment to scale for the very active baby.

Inner tubes are still easy to come by; check your local tire store or service station. During the summer months, inner tubes of brightly colored lightweight plastic are often sold as beach toys.

Just Like Me

Now that Baby enjoys imitating motions, you can help him develop these gestures into a game. Pick actions that Baby can do spontaneously. Sing as you do them together. For example:

Pat, pat, pat the table,
Pat, pat, pat the table,
Just like me.

As you play, Baby will get the idea and follow along. This is also a good learning experience. Baby hears the words as you do the actions. Other actions might include pull your toe, touch your head, pat your tummy, etc.

ROUTINE TIMES

BATHING

Shampoo Tips

Dealing with Baby's fuzz or first hair can be accomplished if shampoo or bath soap is applied first to a washcloth and then to the head. Baby shampoo is gentle and seems not to bother infants' eyes.

Best Water Toy

Your sitting baby is beginning to play gleefully at bathtime. And you are relaxed and enjoying this ritual more, too.

A few simple bath toys can add to the experience. Besides a cup and sponge, several table tennis balls will add new interest. These lively balls will float and bob for Baby. With a permanent laundry marker, draw happy faces on the balls or decorate them with a stripe or two.

For a jellyfish, just draw a face on one of the balls with an indelible laundry marker and cover with an 8 in. x 8 in. square of nylon netting. Secure with a rubber band. These bobbing jellyfish make nice soft scrubbers for dirty knees, and they are great bath toys.

Jingle, Jingle

Add a jingle to bathtime. Make washcloths easy to locate by sewing a bell onto the corner of a terry cloth washrag.

SLEEPING

Five More Minutes

Now that Baby is rising at dawn, you may be able to grab a few more minutes of sleep by making sure his crib is an interesting place. Put a full array of toys, including his special friend, in Baby's crib at bedtime. Most babies are willing to play happily alone if they don't realize that you are awake. Stay in bed until you hear his loudest protests.

Crib Time

Baby is quickly approaching the size and age when the only truly safe sleeping place is his full-size crib. Time to put away the cradle or bassinet and to limit the use of the pram to strolling.

FEEDING

Eating and Feeding

Baby is all action where food is concerned. Messy times are to be expected. Baby's way of tasting includes lip licking, fist smearing, face painting with food, and inserting utensils and fingers into dishes for just one more taste. It's apron time for you. A cheery apron of wipe-off vinyl or very washable cotton can help you enjoy these antics. An old shower curtain, drop cloth, plastic tablecloth, or plastic sheet will minimize cleanup.

Bottle Sensation

A cover for his slippery bottle is a pleasure for Baby. A colorful sock makes gripping his own bottle easier and provides a tactile experience. A terry cloth handle cover, one designed for a tennis racket, makes a quick cover and helps identify his bottle at day care.

Slip a cover you've made from flannel or stretchy knit material over the bottle and Baby will have something that will help him keep the bottle within his grasp.

The Teether

Got a drooling or grumpy baby? Is he playing with or banging his head? It may not be an earache, but rather the emergence of a new tooth. A teething goody would probably help. See Chapter 7 for "Teething Tips" and "Grandma's Teething Biscuits."

Before Dinner

Keep a busy, hungry baby occupied while you prepare his meal by handing him his own special sponge. Just for the sheer joy of patting, poking, punching, and gumming there are few toys that compare to a dampened sponge. Pick the brightest, most durable one you can find.

Disaster-Day Cooking

On a day that ends as if a national emergency had struck, or on one when cooking for anyone is a low priority, keep an emergency kit containing Baby's favorite foods, ones that need no cooking, in the pantry or refrigerator to see him through mealtime.

Some things to have on hand:

—applesauce
—baby cereal
—yogurt
—a few jars of commercial baby food

Routine Times

The Cup—it's time to master something new! Babies seem to prefer a sturdy cup: a plastic, two-handled, weighted model is a fine beginning. Expect little nourishment to actually reach Baby. These first attempts at drinking will be truly experimental. Remember to use the nonspill drinking lid that comes with the cup while Baby experiments with upside down.

Beauty Parlor Trick

Slipping several tissues, a soft paper napkin, or some toilet tissue around Baby's neck before you put on his bib can make cleanup easier. Learning to eat solids is a messy task. It seems much of his meal becomes liquid feed and rolls down his chin and neck. Using this borrowed idea will keep Baby comfortable and his clothes dry.

DRESSING AND CHANGING

Dressing

Babies are often irritated by fabrics, wool and plastic in particular. They often react to the ties on bibs. Clip the strings and add

—preshrunk grosgrain ribbon
—cloth strips
—bias tape
—two clothespins and a length of string

Diapering Safety

Do, do, do use your safety strap on the changing table. You no longer have a little stay-put baby. Don't, don't ever turn your back on this wiggler, even with his safety strap fastened.

Homemade Baby Wipes

Baby wipes recipe

2 cups water
2 Tbs. mild baby bath liquid soap
2 tsp. baby oil
1 roll strong paper towels
1 baby wipe plastic holder (stand-up type for rolls works best)

This recipe calls for you to reuse an empty plastic baby wipes holder. CHUBS works best.

Cut the paper towel roll in half to make two rolls. Remove the cardboard center.

Mix 1 cup of water, the baby bath soap, and the baby oil in the container. Place one of the paper towel halves in the container standing upright.

Add the last cup of water to the container. You now have your own homemade baby wipes.

Save the other half of the paper towel roll for the next batch of wipes.

Note: The wipes will pull out from the CENTER of the roll—just as other stand-up roll wipes do. Begin pulling from the center hole to get the wipes started. The first few may be difficult. Persist.

Size Chart

Shirt size _____   Weight _____

Suit size _____   Length _____

Jot these measurements down and refer to them when you shop for Baby.

Favorites

Baby's favorite sleepmates:

_____

_____

Favorite foods:

_____

Favorite toys:

_____

_____

Favorite games:

_____

Favorite song/music:

_____

_____

Best way to make baby smile:

_____

_____

Baby's current achievements:

_____

_____

HELPFUL HINTS

Reminder

When planning for play, think safety first. Then, make sure there are a lot of opportunities for practice in babyproofed surroundings.

Relaxing

If Baby wants to sit alone but still needs a little support, consider letting him use a pillow with a back and arms like those used for reading in bed. This will provide three-way safety for an easily toppled infant.

Baby Fun

A fun game for Baby, one that is often no fun for busy friends, is "Watch the Toy Fall." Use short elastic bands to attach several toys to his high chair; this can be a backsaver. Baby is not yet able to retrieve his own toys, but this will make the job easier for you.

Remodeling

It's time for a change of environment for Baby. Take down the remaining eye-only tantalizers and bring out the made to touch, taste, wave, and bang ones. Baby is at a stage where he is frustrated by eye-only things. He's into touching in a big way!

Busy boxes and mouthable, soft rubber toys will catch Baby's attention. A selection of wooden spoons of different shapes and sizes makes an inexpensive toy that he will enjoy. Plan Baby's

environment to include safe crib toys he can play with while the family gets a few extra winks.

Odor Control

A good way to control changing-table odor is to tie heavily soiled disposable diapers in plastic bags before putting them in your trash can. Taking out the trash regularly and using long-lasting solid deodorizers also help.

Vanity

Mirrors are still pleasing. A quick way to handle a crying baby is to take him to a mirror. He is so pleased with himself that a sneaky peek will convince him to quiet down and show his better self.

Group Care

Feeding more than one baby at a time? You can heat several bottles at once in an electric bottle sterilizer. These appliances, which hold from six to eight bottles at one time, can be left running throughout the day. They need only a little water added periodically. This is how day-care centers do it.

Milk Stains

To remove milk stains, soak in cold water for about fifteen minutes. Hot water will set milk stains.

Babyproof Now

Start changing your habits now, before it's absolutely necessary. Evaluate everything you do. For example, start now to turn all pot handles in when cooking on the stove. Return all caps and lids to bottles immediately, and give them an extra turn. Sweep often to remove all dangers from Baby's favorite play surface, the floor.

Outlet Covers

For electrical cords you cannot remove from their sockets, there are socket protectors that fit over the sockets and plugs; this makes them safe for Baby. These protectors are also handy for items you do not wish to unplug, such as lamps, stereo, and TV. You'll be glad you have done this when Baby surprises you by reaching for the socket.

Coverage

When visitors come to call, do not hesitate to offer them a diaper, towel, or lap pad along with Baby. This measure is essential if Baby is to be invited back to the visitor's lap.

Softeners

Most mothers are very careful about the soaps they choose for laundering their infants' clothing, but they may not pay equal attention to their choice of fabric softeners. Many softeners that are fine for the family's clothes can irritate Baby's delicate skin. If your child has a problem rash, consider these softeners as possible culprits.

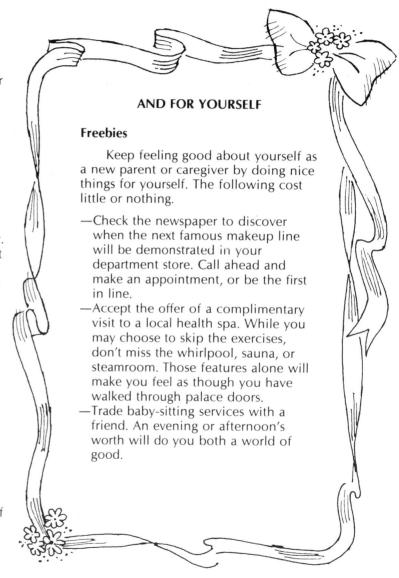

AND FOR YOURSELF

Freebies

Keep feeling good about yourself as a new parent or caregiver by doing nice things for yourself. The following cost little or nothing.

—Check the newspaper to discover when the next famous makeup line will be demonstrated in your department store. Call ahead and make an appointment, or be the first in line.

—Accept the offer of a complimentary visit to a local health spa. While you may choose to skip the exercises, don't miss the whirlpool, sauna, or steamroom. Those features alone will make you feel as though you have walked through palace doors.

—Trade baby-sitting services with a friend. An evening or afternoon's worth will do you both a world of good.

A Man's Magic Meal

Plan ahead for the day when nothing short of an all-out rescue will save you. Most men have at least one meal they find easy to prepare. Ask the man in your life to share his specialty meal with you. Then, *always* have the ingredients on hand. This is your contribution to the magic-making.

When you need help—yell. Who knows? This special person may have been secretly hoping for an opportunity to dazzle you with his skills.

MAGIC MENU   ITEMS TO HAVE ON HAND

_____   _____

_____   _____

_____   _____

Window Safety

If you live in an old house with wide window sills, prepare now for the safety of your crawling, climbing baby. Adjustable gates can be used across these windows to protect Baby from the hazards of glass and screening. This is particularly important for second-story windows.

Boy or Girl?

If mistaken identity regarding your baby really bugs you, try this solution. Neatly embroider across the seat of your child's pants the simple words, "I'm a girl" or "I'm a boy."

PARENTS, FRIENDS, AND ADMIRERS

Beware of the Beast

An admirer's friendliest, most loyal pet may not take kindly to an invitation by Baby. Babies often emit strange sounds and make quick movements that pets may misunderstand, causing them to become aggressive. Beware and be extra careful.

Meals on Wheels

When you are cooking and taking something special to Baby's house, don't forget him. He will enjoy your goodies, too. How about chicken noodle soup? Baby loves noodles plain, or with a touch of butter. Or how about some of the stew vegetables—

mashed, of course. Or some applesauce made from the leftover apples you used for the apple pie.

Family Pictures

When you're exchanging pictures of the family, don't overlook Baby. He will enjoy pictures of his admirers as much as they like snapshots of him. Big ones are especially good.

Something from the Oven

Would you like to make goodies for your favorite baby? How about some freshly baked graham squares. Try our highly acclaimed recipe. Babies who have sampled them find them irresistible.

3½ cups graham flour (unbleached, unsifted)
½ tsp. baking powder
1 tsp. salt
1 tsp. cinnamon
¼ lb. butter
¼ cup brown sugar
¼ cup honey
1 tsp. vanilla
¾ cup water

1. Mix flour, baking powder, salt, and cinnamon.
2. Cream butter, sugar, and honey until light and fluffy. Then, add vanilla.
3. Alternating water and flour, add to butter mixture. Beat well after each addition.
4. Cover dough and allow to stand at room temperature for 30 minutes.
5. Divide dough in half. Place dough on a lightly greased cookie sheet; pat into a ½-in. thick rectangle. With floured rolling pin, roll dough almost to the edge of sheet. Using a pastry wheel or knife cut lines in the dough.
6. Bake at 325° F for 30 minutes or until brown.

Yield: 40 3-in. squares.

Poem

Here is another way to send a personal greeting. This verse, which might well become a keepsake, is easy to write. The style, called Haiku, refers to an unrhymed Japanese poem of three lines. Haiku often contains a seasonal motif.

Here is how you do it:

First line   5 syllables
Second line 7 syllables
Third line   5 syllables

Oh, darling baby
A joy to all of us now
Bloom in the sunshine.

YOURS:

_____

_____

_____

Jewelry

Ever wonder why grandmothers are such a hit with babies? It may be because they are such a visual treat, especially when it comes to accessories. Those touches of costume jewelry—brooches, buttons, and buckles—have great eye appeal. Baby is captivated by a sparkling pair of earrings or a tinkling bracelet.

Needlework

It's not too late for an admirer to embroider something special for Baby. An heirloom of this type is always appreciated. Handwork is a lifetime treasure, not only for Baby, but for Baby's babies, too.

Bread Basket

A basketful of bread sticks, objects, and animal shapes can be shaped from any frozen bread dough. These are quick and easy with lots of room for creativity. This easy project will please both Baby and his health-conscious mother. The basket provides a great snack for any outing.

Artist's Plate and Cup

Now that Baby is eating more and more "people food," a friend, especially a young one, might enjoy creating a mug or plate just for him. Your artist can draw, decorate, or design on a special surface using the crayons or markers that come as part of a kit. Some kits come prepared with a cup and saucer ready for design. Others provide paper and marking pens/pencils; upon completing the design, the artist sends the design to the company where it is reproduced onto the cup and saucer.

Invite this friend to create a mug for herself or himself so that she or he can share a snack or light meal with Baby. Check local craft stores for details.

Prints and Postcards

Make something special to send to friends who would appreciate early evidences of Baby's art. One of a kind, yours and Baby's alone, are the prints that come from thumbs. No two thumbprints have ever been found to be exactly alike.

Make your own ink pad; use a small hunk of sponge or an absorbent, folded piece of fabric that has been saturated with food coloring.

Press Baby's thumb down on the printing surface and then onto paper. Give the print a minute or so to dry.

The fun comes by adding lines, squiggles, and dots to your blob. Books on thumbprint drawings of all kinds are available—faces, animals, insects, and action designs.

Memo

Why is it that you inevitably spot things that would be "perfect" for Baby in a few months only when you are not looking or buying? As you discover them, make a note of these "finds" so that they are on file when you *are* ready to buy.

ITEM	STORE/LOCATION	COST

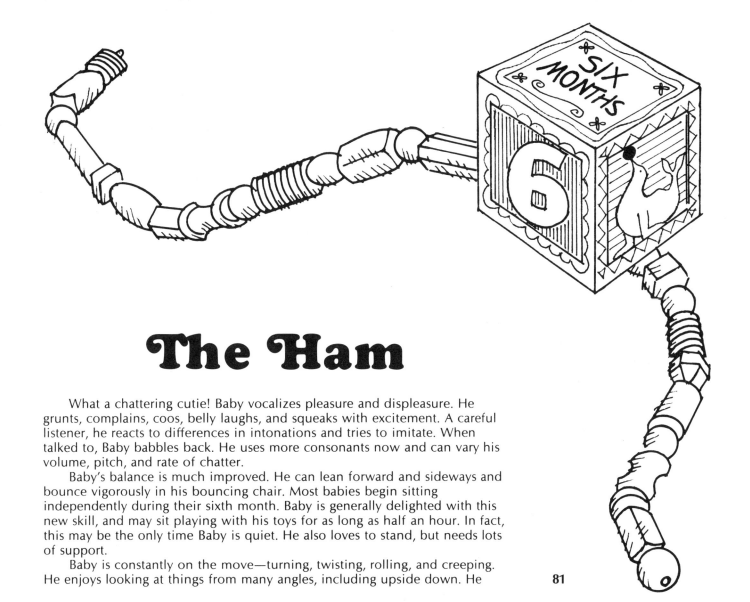

The Ham

What a chattering cutie! Baby vocalizes pleasure and displeasure. He grunts, complains, coos, belly laughs, and squeaks with excitement. A careful listener, he reacts to differences in intonations and tries to imitate. When talked to, Baby babbles back. He uses more consonants now and can vary his volume, pitch, and rate of chatter.

Baby's balance is much improved. He can lean forward and sideways and bounce vigorously in his bouncing chair. Most babies begin sitting independently during their sixth month. Baby is generally delighted with this new skill, and may sit playing with his toys for as long as half an hour. In fact, this may be the only time Baby is quiet. He also loves to stand, but needs lots of support.

Baby is constantly on the move—turning, twisting, rolling, and creeping. He enjoys looking at things from many angles, including upside down. He

81

loves playing peek-a-boo, especially if you create a version that involves movement.

Baby is most content when he is holding something and can transfer his treasure from hand to hand. His grasp has become quite sure; he can hold his own bottle. He can also reach to grasp with one hand now.

Mirrors top the list of baby entertainers. Baby now differentiates himself from the mirror image. He also loves music: listening and dancing to records, singing with others, and making music with toy instruments begin to be favorite activities. Baby has also noticed people writing. He can be entertained and fascinated just by watching you write.

Baby's favorite toys are the people close to him. He loves other babies but may be wary of adult strangers. He can now use his voice to get attention and will yell for help when frightened.

Routines are becoming more reliable. By now, Baby is well established on some solid foods. He enjoys trying to feed himself with finger foods and is starting to manipulate his cup. Best of all, this busy, sociable baby sleeps through the night.

ACTIVITIES, GAMES, AND SONGS

Edible Games

A few cheese squares, bits of crisp toast or banana, dry cereal shapes, or other tempting morsels can be placed in a clear plastic bottle or in a little gift box. Baby will enjoy playing with these containers, and in trying to open them he will be practicing his fine-motor skills. He will be delighted, too, to find this game has such a delicious ending.

Easy-Grasp Blocks

Babies love handles and flaps that make toys easier to grasp. Blocks with easy grasp handles are simple to make. Start with a square of foam rubber. Cover each face of the block with a fabric circle. Simply glue the overlapping fabric around the blocks. This overlap fabric will allow for a rounded flap on each block edge.

Right-Side Up

Baby will enjoy showing everyone that he knows things have a right-side up. A great game to play is to place things at different angles and let Baby right them: shoes, cups, teddy bear—and don't leave out Baby and yourself as things to be righted!

Baby cannot always put himself in the position he would like and this can be frustrating. Now that he knows when things are right-side up, he will enjoy seeing the world from many different angles.

Who, Me?

Now that Baby responds to his name, be sure to call him often. He's delighted with this new skill, too.

Where's the Baby?

"Where's the Baby?" and other such search-and-find games are baby-pleasers. Get down on the floor, crawl around, and search for Baby. Call out, "Where is Baby? Where's the baby?" Ask others if they've seen Baby. Look under and around and near Baby. Finally, find him. "Here's Baby!" The more animated you are, the more fun! Soon Baby will learn to scramble away in delight as the game begins. He will laugh loudly and anticipate being found.

A Ball for Baby

Give Baby a tennis ball. This round, fuzzy little ball will be a favorite thing to carry. It is fun to drop several in boxes or cans. "Dead" tennis balls are perfectly acceptable to Baby. On the court or off, these balls are a hit.

Knee Game

A must is a ride on somebody's knee. Try this classic while singing or reciting:

Ride a cock horse
To Banbury Cross
To see a fine lady
Upon a white horse.
With rings on her fingers
And bells on her toes,
She shall have music
Wherever she goes.

Don't Pick Him Up Yet!

Because of his interest in finding out about things, Baby can play happily by himself for twenty to thirty minutes. Enjoy this phase while it lasts! When Baby gets restless, a change in position or a new toy will do.

Gotcha!

A perfect toy to chase is an aluminum-foil pie plate. This inexpensive and recycled item from your kitchen is fun to push, grasp, bang, throw, and chew. Baby will relentlessly stalk this toy as he improves his creeping. Add a face made of plastic-tape strips or turn it into a UFOB (unidentified flying object for Baby)—a disk from outer space.

Baby's Own

When you put safety latches on low kitchen cabinets and cupboards to keep your inquisitive infant out of harm's way, save some kitchen space just for him. (Remember, even with safety latches, tops for all potentially harmful items should be baby-proofed.) Let him know what is his by tying a bell or noisemaker to his special cabinet door. With this incentive, Baby will find added delight in opening and closing his own cabinet. Be sure to put some of Baby's favorite toys, or kitchen utensils you have chosen just for him, inside.

The Barnstorming Baby

For the infant who enjoys a different slant or perspective on his world, try a few gentle aerial feats. Rotate him upside down and roll him through space like a stunt plane. Listen for his squeals of delight. A few zooming sounds add to the fun—after all, you are the pilot, at least for now.

Another Old Favorite

Two Little Dicky-Birds

Two little dicky-birds
  (use index fingers to represent the birds)
Sitting on a wall,
One named Peter, the other named Paul
  (lift one finger for each bird).
Fly away, Peter; fly away, Paul
  (put each finger behind your back).
Come back, Peter; come back, Paul
  (bring each finger back).

Your Own Kind of Music

By now, you've done a lot of singing. You've developed some rather good numbers and Baby has crooned along. So now, before you forget the words, record your own music below.

_____

_____

_____

_____

_____

Better yet, tape record a few of your favorites for your and Baby's enjoyment.

Cans

Add the shimmer of silver to Baby's toy collection by saving a series of cans. Once opened, emptied, washed, and dried, check the interiors for rough edges. Try three tuna cans in the 3-, 7-, and 13-oz. sizes. The cans in which tomato paste, puree, and sauce come are good, too.

You can cover the cans with colorful fabric, contact paper, or pictures under clear contact paper.

Or, make a graduated stacking-puzzle by attaching drawings to or painting three graduated cans. Use the smallest size for the head, the middle- and large-sized ones for the body. One parent made a snowman, another created a robot.

Talking Time

When you need a peaceful moment, place Baby in front of a mirror. He will chatter to his image endlessly, just as he talks to you.

Place the mirror low enough for Baby to pat his image, and make sure the mirror cannot tip over. Some parents put mirrors on baseboards, where Baby will see himself as he crawls. We like the commercial non-glass mirrors available in most toy stores.

Infant Obstacle Course

Gather together several towels, throw pillows, and stuffed toys. Lay them on the floor in variously sized piles. Now top with a blanket or a large sheet. Baby will enjoy this new, interesting terrain with things to creep around, over, and push off from—a challenging obstacle course for Baby.

Baby Mystery

If you have a non-glass double boiler, let Baby try to put it together. It's an intriguing mystery. It's a perfect early stacking toy for Baby. An old stove-top percolator can also present a challenge for Baby.

Tummy Tickler

A little tummy tickler is always a favorite baby game. These silly little rhymes are only a mechanism for helping infants learn the fun of anticipating something to come. Use this rhyme or invent your own.

Jelly in the bowl (shake Baby's tummy)
Jelly in the bowl (shake Baby's tummy)
Wiggle, waggle (sway him by his shoulders)
Wiggle, waggle (sway him by his shoulders)
Jelly in the bowl (tickle delighted Baby).

Photo Finish

Capture your busy and mature six-month-old at play. What a change six months can make!

Box Table

You can make a sturdy baby-sized work table from a cardboard box. Select a box that allows you to slip Baby in his infant seat under one side, forming a desk or tabletop. The box should be lying on its side with the top flap against the floor. The weight of the infant seat will hold the table steady. Now, to the

surface that will serve as the top of Baby's table, add a little edge or rim. This will keep Baby's work materials from sliding off.

ROUTINE TIMES

BATHING

Bath Toys

Keep an eye out for new bath toys. Seasonal gift catalogs are usually fine sources. Keep bathtime fun.

Boats

Inexpensive plastic boats may turn out to be no bargain. Many of these toys do not really float; they sink and allow water to be trapped inside, which can breed mildew.

Wooden boats, although more expensive, are more seaworthy and durable. They will last throughout Baby's preschool and primary years. Remember not to leave them sitting in water.

Making a few of these boats is a great project for a handy admirer.

Sponge boats have many nice features. They are easily made by simply cutting the boat parts from colorful sponges and then assembling the pieces with glue designed to withstand water. There need be no waste as the scraps can serve as decorations. These toys, which can be squeezed out after use, make bathing more fun if used as scrubbers.

No Slips

A bath mitt is handy for scrubbing a slippery baby. You can make your own by copying a kitchen hot mitt; use terry cloth or two washcloths.

Niagara Falls

While fun is to be encouraged during bathtime, splashing may not be as enjoyable for you as it is for Baby. Try wearing a thin, lightweight raincoat for complete coverage on days you'd rather stay dry.

Bath Bag

You can make a handy carryall in a few minutes from a face towel and plastic coat hanger. Flip the short side of the towel in so that a small triangle is formed on either side of the hanger hook. Stitch securely close to the hook.

To form the "bag," fold the towel in half bringing the lower edge up and over the horizontal hanger bar. Stitch close to the hanger and you have a great holder for bath toys.

FEEDING

Bottles and Cups

Baby is beginning to manipulate his own bottle. Sometimes he is even able to manage a cup. Encourage either or both of these skills. Although Baby still relies on the bottle for nourishment, practice with the cup is an important advance that should be supported. Let him practice drinking in the tub, where spills don't matter.

What Baby's Eating/When

A.M.   ITEMS

_____   _____

_____   _____

_____   _____

P.M.   ITEMS

_____   _____

_____   _____

_____   _____

Meals with Music

Baby loves music, now as never before. He will stop to listen to almost any type of music, reason enough for you to set the mood at mealtimes. Try presenting the classics if he's only heard the "Top 40," or country and western if he's listened only to jazz. It should contribute to more tolerable mealtimes.

Not Eating for You?

Without warning, Baby may suddenly decide to eat better for anyone but you. So *do* let fathers, friends, and siblings help. Sit back, relax, and enjoy.

Feeding Tips

Many parents and friends think that the only place to feed Baby is the high chair—not so. Just as you enjoy a change—spreading out a blanket for a picnic or sitting on low cushions for an Oriental meal—so does Baby. If you're finding it hard to contain an active Baby in his high chair, consider his jumping seat. The seat gives him an outlet for his energy and may allow you to get more of his meal into Baby.

Dual Feeding

Make mealtime a participatory experience for both you and Baby. Giving him something to do while you are feeding him may make this task somewhat easier. Food items he can handle on his own include banana disks and dried cereal pieces.

Now that baby is using his high chair and is constantly in motion, consider adding a foam cushion for him to sit on. A simple piece of foam rubber without a cover will keep him firmly in place. Even with his new cushion, always use the safety strap on the chair. At times he will protest but safety shouldn't be compromised.

Convenience Food

If you like yogurt, you may discover that your infant does, too. A real convenience food, yogurt is easy to make or to purchase in economically sized containers. Finely chopped fruits or vegetables (fresh or cooked) add appeal and nutrition.

Yogurt can be breakfast, lunch, dinner, or a snack. Portable, too, yogurt can travel to day care or Grandma's house.

SLEEPING

Bad Habit

Many parents have found, much to their dismay, that what started as a good idea became something they wish they had never begun. We are referring to the practice of taking Baby back into your bed. Baby may, after the second or third time, actively look forward to this chance to be with you. He may awaken in the middle of the night and demand to join you. Don't give in. Check to see that he is safe, turn off the light, and leave. Being too responsive can encourage bedtime games. A change in Baby's routine can quickly become a habit.

Wee Baby Moon

This is a delightful song or poem to share with your child:

There's a wee baby moon
Just a-lyin' on his back
With his little tiny toes in the air.
And he's all by himself
In the deep blue sky
But the funny little moon doesn't care.

With Baby, any tune will do. He will enjoy and appreciate your efforts. It doesn't matter if your voice is flat or sharp—just be natural and try.

DRESSING AND CHANGING

Transitional Game

If Baby is engrossed in play or motor activity, you may find that he resists your efforts to diaper or change him. To make him more cooperative, try playing a game such as "Gotcha."

Fist Problems

One way to keep an impatient baby's hands busy while you proceed with the dressing process is to simply give him something to hold in each hand. This same idea can make dressing Baby in his bulky snowsuit easier, too. When you give Baby things to hold, make sure they are small so that you won't have a problem with sleeves. How about pieces of fabric, or celery leaves on which he can munch.

Finding and pulling a tightly clenched fist through a sleeve is far easier than trying to force the sleeve over an open hand. It also eliminates the possibility of bending tiny fingers the wrong way.

Work Clothes

Because Baby is entering a more active phase, why not replace his kimonos and creepers with sturdy overalls or coveralls. He'll enjoy this graduation to long pants and so will you. These new work clothes will afford Baby the protection and freedom he now requires. Believe it or not, they do make blue jeans, farmer's overalls, and workman's coveralls in Baby's size.

HELPFUL HINTS

Reminder

Baby will let you know when he wants company. He's very social now. Just watching you work is as absorbing and interesting as a new toy.

Recycling

Recycle some of Baby's earlier toys. Every time he reaches a new level of development, he regards familiar items with new insight. A block once used for carrying is now something to bang or drop. When Baby seems to tire of a toy, put it away for later. When you bring it out again, Baby will treat it as a new discovery.

A Planter with a Plus

Add a touch of green to Baby's room by hanging a green plant in a toy planter. Consider a fire truck with ivy or a doll buggy filled with fern. This is one way to use and admire Baby's special gifts until he is old enough to enjoy them.

Shining Brightly

If Baby received a traditional silver cup, mug, spoon, or rattle, now is the right time to catch his eye with the sheen of polished metal.

Place the item in a large aluminum container. Add 1 tablespoon of baking soda to each quart of water. Leave the silver piece immersed for 15 minutes. Rinse in hot water and dry. (Note: this method is not recommended for antiqued silverware.)

Larger Is Better

Everything that Baby finds goes directly to his mouth—everything and anything! Do check his toys to make sure there are no small parts that may be removed by this determined workman. Larger toys are best now—things to bang, shake, and throw.

Hide a Stain

If one of Baby's garments has a nonremovable stain, hide it with a colorful appliqué from the fabric store. The stitched-on appliqué will be a delightful eye-catcher, sure to please Baby and his admirers. Fabric paint added in a design will work equally well.

Jumping

A jumping seat or walker may be of real value this month. In these, Baby will be safe and yet not too confined at those times you just can't watch him so closely. Make sure the chair is well balanced. In later months, you may want to weight the chair for added stability.

Emergency Rations

Most babies travel in the back seat of the car where they are safer than they would be next to the driver. Sometimes the back seat is not acceptable to Baby and, on longer errands, he may begin to wail. If talking, singing, and the radio fail to do the trick, stop and pull out your trusty tin of crackers, which you keep in the glove compartment for just this purpose. It may help you both get home safe and sane.

Less Mess

Petroleum jelly in a plastic squeeze bottle makes it easy for you to handle this gooey substance less and ensure that you get a more precise amount on just the right spot.

Phone Calls

If Baby's not hungry, a sprinkle or two of baby powder or cornstarch on his high-chair tray will keep him happy and busy while you make a phone call. A dab of baby lotion can also be an interesting distraction.

Traveling

When Baby is travelling, travel light. Wear a fanny pack and carry only the sample size of each thing you need. Travel can and should be fun for all—including Mom.

The First Tooth

Some babies get their first teeth, usually the lower central incisors, as early as four months. Boys seem to cut teeth somewhat earlier than girls.

_____

Baby's name

_____

Date

_____

First tooth (location)

AND FOR YOURSELF

Celebrate

Congratulations. It's time for a celebration. You have made it through the first half year of life with Baby. Think of the changes, your abilities to cope, and the many things you've noticed about yourself and your child.

How about a trip to your local ice cream parlor to celebrate with Baby? He will enjoy people-watching while you indulge.

And then, how about an evening out without Baby? Parents need and deserve some time without Baby.

Women Together

Join a women's group or professional organization whether you're working or not. No one is duller than the woman who only talks about her kids and the weather. You must meet your needs, too. Spending an evening with your peers will keep you sane. Be wary, however. Don't buy into the old animosity between stay-at-home mothers and working mothers.

Teething

Research does not substantiate the claim that teething causes diarrhea. Like the common cold, diarrhea is passed on by germs. If Baby develops persistent diarrhea, consult your doctor. Nor does research substantiate the claim that teething causes a significant temperature of 101° F or so.

Pretzel Teethers

None of the fine Philadelphia-born-and-bred babies we know would be caught without their Pennsylvania Dutch pretzels. These pencil-thick, hard snacks are preferred over crackers and other teething biscuits. Our young friends gnaw, nibble, and bang these pretzels, which fortunately rarely crumble into a mushy mess. Saltless pretzels are best; just brush the salt off before giving to Baby.

A Spoon for the Teether

Dusting a wooden spoon, one of Baby's favorite toys, with a little powdered sugar might bring a smile to a teething sufferer.

Drooling

Babies drool when teething; some drool more than others. Here are some suggestions for coping with a drooler. The obvious ones are:

—small bibs
—"total body" aprons

_____

(Yours)

Less obvious ones include:

—a cowboy's bandana
—a handkerchief strategically tucked inside the front of Baby's shirt
—a little spray-on fabric guard secretly and subtly applied to the front of Baby's best duds

Drooling will not end until Baby's teeth arrive.

Freezer Tip

Teething is no fun. Remember your last toothache? Anything that will cheer Baby up or make him more comfortable is well worth your time and effort. Experiment to see what seems to help. One suggestion is a hard rubber toy, one that can be made more effective as a teething device by being placed in the freezer for an hour before use. Special toys made for freezing can also be bought.

New Life

Tired of the pale pink, yellow, orange, and brown stains on Baby's little, almost white, T-shirts? A quick remedy and one that will bring Baby into the fashion spotlight is to dye them in fabulous fall shades. Easier to use than the dyes you remember, today's dyes are safe, inexpensive, and simple to use. For the craft-fair look, remember tie-dying. Bunch fabric and wrap with rubber bands or tie at intervals with string. For vibrant color, used prepared liquid dye at double strength.

Quick Dispenser

Sometimes it is easy to overlook the obvious. A mother recently shared an idea that seemed so simple we were amazed we had never thought of it. She had installed a toilet-paper dispenser near the changing table. What could be a better choice for cleaning Baby's tender bottom than soft toilet tissue? A paper-towel dispenser would also be a good idea. Not only is this a very convenient and sanitary system, but it is far less costly than commercially packaged baby wipes.

PARENTS, FRIENDS, AND ADMIRERS

Color

The latest polls reveal that red is still Baby's favorite color. Think bright when you select clothes for your child or someone else's. How about a pair of glorious red socks for tiny feet? Or maybe a pair of warm mittens or a cozy hat?

Old Pros

Since you have been a successful parent/friend/caregiver for six months, why not share some of your insights and triumphs with folks who have just begun. One way might be a chain letter describing helpful hints and time-savers. Here is how to begin.

Write out your tip and a list of three friends and their addresses with your name at the top of the list. Send these to six other friends instructing them to send their helpful hint to the top name on the enclosed list of names. They should then remove the name of the person to whom they send the tip and place their own name on the bottom of the list.

Centers and Sitters

Parents who take Baby to a day-care center or baby-sitter should not view this as only a paid, professional service. You pay for the care of your child, but all the love he receives there comes free. Thoughtful parents quickly recognize this and realize that any addition they make to this environment benefits Baby.

Since most of Baby's waking hours are spent at the center, why keep all of Baby's toys at home? Sending in toys you're willing to share with all the babies and which you do not expect returned is only logical. Suggestions of things to send include mobiles, crib gyms, learning toys, safety mirrors, and a batch of graham crackers. Even a little chocolate pudding for a finger-painting experience or a jar of hand cream for Baby's caring friends says you understand and appreciate the loving kindness these people are giving your baby and your family. Do return it in kind.

Toys

Find yourself with a baby who is bored without his favorite toys? Or, perhaps a baby who is unexpectedly visiting needs a little something with which to play. Present Baby with a piece of colored tissue paper, aluminum foil, or cellophane and watch the fun. Make sure he doesn't eat these items!

Joyride

Baby is very attracted to social play with his admirers. Make a sliding board out of your legs and help Baby get up and down. Here's a little rhyme to accompany Baby.

Slide, Baby, slide
Now it's time to ride
Up here on my knees
Anytime you please.
Come now let's have fun
We have just begun.

Get Down, Too

Because of their willingness to get down on the floor and romp with Baby, men seem to be favorite playmates. Baby enjoys gentle rough-and-tumble.

T-shirt Togetherness

The matched look for your favorite family could be matching T-shirts with or without logos. These could be real pieces of nostalgia, particularly if captured in an admirable historic photo.

Thoughtfulness

One sister-in-law told us that her in-laws kept her in contact with the world while she was recuperating and adjusting to life with her baby. About every other week, her mother-in-law would send a letter and a little envelope of clippings from current magazines, newspapers, and books. This interesting assortment was greatly appreciated by the new mother, who was too busy to read a whole book or magazine, much less hunt down a tasty new recipe.

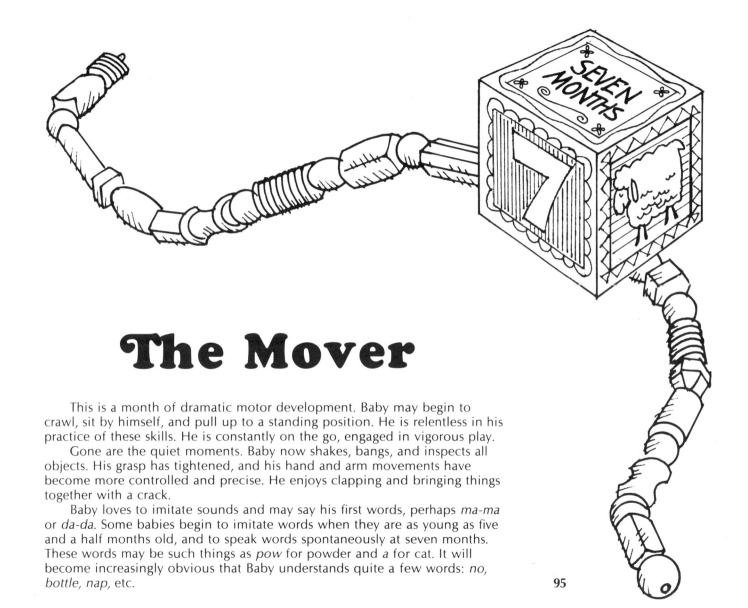

The Mover

This is a month of dramatic motor development. Baby may begin to crawl, sit by himself, and pull up to a standing position. He is relentless in his practice of these skills. He is constantly on the go, engaged in vigorous play.

Gone are the quiet moments. Baby now shakes, bangs, and inspects all objects. His grasp has tightened, and his hand and arm movements have become more controlled and precise. He enjoys clapping and bringing things together with a crack.

Baby loves to imitate sounds and may say his first words, perhaps *ma-ma* or *da-da*. Some babies begin to imitate words when they are as young as five and a half months old, and to speak words spontaneously at seven months. These words may be such things as *pow* for powder and *a* for cat. It will become increasingly obvious that Baby understands quite a few words: *no, bottle, nap,* etc.

95

By this month, Baby has learned to discriminate between different familiar faces. Categories of recognition are also developing. Baby can often tell the difference between men and women, or boys and girls, but not yet between two women or two men unless, of course, they are close friends or family.

The seventh month may also bring another heralded event—Baby's first tooth. The lower incisors generally come in first. At this stage, infrequent fussiness might be due to teething.

Baby is now beginning to make associations and to anticipate his routines. When his bib is put on, he knows that food will come. He demands some independence during mealtimes and may refuse to relinquish his spoon and cup. Finger foods are a welcome compromise for both Baby and adult.

Baby will display some new emotions at this age. Your social seven-month-old infant will want to be a part of the grown-up world. He can tease and is beginning to have a sense of humor. He remembers bits of games and invites friends to play with him. But, confronted by strangers, your outgoing, vocal infant may show "stranger anxiety," a very normal reaction.

ACTIVITIES, GAMES, AND SONGS

Seeing Me

Mirrors continue to be among Baby's favorite toys. He is recognizing himself. Make sure there is an accessible mirror for an admiring Baby. If Baby is sitting up, place a mirror where he can see himself eat and bathe. This will fascinate him.

Baby Talk

Playing back a recording of Baby's chatter can be lots of fun for everyone. Years from now your child will love hearing it himself.

Eyes, Nose, and Mouth Game

One of Baby's best games is to point to his eyes, nose, and mouth (with your help). Played in front of a mirror this game is especially fun. Soon Baby will learn to recognize the words and associate them with the correct features.

A Ball for Baby

Try a small colorful beach ball. Baby will enjoy holding it, having it rolled to him, or crawling after it.

Mouth Harp

Mickey was able to play on a harmonica at seven months. He enjoyed using both draw and blow notes up and down the scale. His parents said they merely demonstrated how to play and were delighted when Mickey imitated them. Don't underestimate Baby's interests. Mickey still delights his day-care center with his daily playing.

First House

A large cardboard box can be converted into a great A-frame playhouse. Simply remove two opposing sides of the box and the top. Leave the bottom attached. Securely tape the remaining sides together so that you now have a triangular structure. Cut large holes out of the sides for windows. You can paint the house with latex enamel. Baby will enjoy crawling through, peeking out of, and sitting in his house.

Bubbles

Take out your jar of bubbles again. It can provide lots of fun for Baby when you need a different activity and have a few moments to spare. Bubbles never seem to lose their appeal.

Bare-footing

Assemble a variety of textures in a path; use a rug sample, grass mat, bath mat, pillow, etc. With your help, Baby will enjoy toddling and crawling across these various surfaces.

Peek-a-Boo

Baby is now ready to play this game in many ways. For variety, you can place your hands over his eyes, hide from Baby, put something in front of Baby's face (diaper, magazine), or stand behind the door and peek out. These easy variations will delight Baby.

High-Chair Fishing

Objects and toys on elastic strips are one way to save your back, since everything Baby touches ends up on the floor! The elastic lets Baby play a fishing game—throw away the toy, then reel it in.

Kitchen Collection

Cooking equipment makes an intriguing collection of toys. Pots, pans, and lids are popular, as are wooden bowls and spoons, measuring cups, whisks, plastic cups and saucers, plastic bottles, and ice cube trays.

Place Baby on the kitchen floor, a safe distance from your working area, surrounded by these toys. You'll find that you are able to get your work done and that Baby will be working right along with you.

Wrappings

A box of fancy cards, bits of wrapping paper, pretty fabric, wallpaper scraps, and ribbon can captivate Baby's interest in detail.

Finger Painting

Place Baby in his high chair. Put about one tablespoonful of chocolate pudding on his tray and stand back! Baby will enjoy tasting, patting, smearing, and creating an artistic design on his tray. You can save his earliest efforts by quickly blotting up the design with a piece of paper.

Roll Toy

A metallic, egg-shaped container for panty hose can make a great roll toy. Put some bells, sand, beans, or rice inside and seal carefully with a strong glue. Tape securely shut for good measure. Baby will enjoy chasing this shiny bauble.

Puzzle

Even a seven-month-old can benefit from puzzle play. Simply screw small wooden cabinet knobs

(½ in.) purchased at your hardware store into several blocks. Arrange these blocks so they fit snugly into a cardboard box. Baby will enjoy taking them out of the box and putting them back in.

Easy Blocks

You can make a set of durable and wipeable blocks from a variety of milk cartons. Using two milk cartons, fit the bottom ends together and cut off the tops. Cover with colorful contact paper; Baby especially likes prints. If you add some beans or bells, Baby will enjoy rattling and banging these blocks together.

Kitchen Drum

A saucepan and two fat carrots make a great drum set. This is a good game to promote when you must be in the kitchen. Invite a sibling to join Baby.

Step Blocks

Baby is now interested in climbing stairs, much to the horror of all concerned. After all, there are motor skills to be learned from the challenge of negotiating stairs. If you do not have a set of preschool stairs on which Baby can safely practice, make a set out of cardboard boxes stacked and secured in formation. Fill several boxes (approximately 6 in. x 12 in. x 18 in.) with newspapers to weight them. Seal the boxes and cover with colorful contact paper. Baby can now safely practice.

Dumping

Baby loves to dump things. A wide-mouthed, plastic, five-gallon jar filled with a variety of things to dump and pull out—clothespins, cups, blocks—soon becomes a favorite toy. When Baby is finished, the loose items can be neatly stored in the jar.

Puppy Toys

Soft rubber toys designed for puppies are excellent for babies, too. They squeak easily. Their softness makes them easy to hold. Many puppy toys have unusual textures and vibrant colors.

Does this idea sound familiar? We did suggest buying these cute critters earlier. Remember, Baby will enjoy using them in different ways now. He will bang them, throw them, and stuff them into other toys or clothing.

Walking with You

Hold both Baby's hands and he will enjoy strutting as you let him practice walking. Baby never tires of this game.

Pat-a-Cake

Now that Baby can clap his hands, "Pat-a-Cake" is a favorite.

Pat-a-cake, pat-a-cake,
Baker's man;
Bake me a cake
As fast as you can.
Pat it and prick it
And mark it with B,
And put it in the oven
For Baby and me.

Do the motions with Baby as you chant the verse.

View from the Floor

Baby likes to look at pictures, too. Drawings or photographs, especially those of other babies, puppies, and cats, will enrich his visual environment.

Hang the pictures at Baby's eye level. Clear contact paper protects special favorites. Completely seal the pictures for best results.

Oldies but Goodies

Finger stories have stood the test of time. All babies love them. Do you remember this one?

Knock at the door (forehead),
Peep in (peep through circled thumbs and
    forefingers),
Turn the latch (twist nose),
Walk in (put a finger into Baby's mouth).

Eency Weency Spider

An eency weency spider
Climbed up the water spout
    (one hand climbs up arm to shoulder).
Down came the rain
    (raise hands high in air and drop them down
    quickly)
And washed the spider out
    (hand slides down arm).
Out came the sun
    (arms form circle over head)
And dried up all the rain.
The eency, weency spider
    (hand goes back up arm to shoulder)
Climbed up the spout again.

At first, you will be doing the motions on Baby. He will be delighted and anticipate the movements. As he grows to know them, he will vocalize and eventually try to gesture.

Books

Don't forget to look at picture books with Baby. A good time for this activity is before nap- and bedtime. Looking at books in this way can set the tone for early learning. A desire to read starts with a love of books.

Sorting

A cupcake or muffin tin can be great for sorting pretzel nuggets or wooden blocks. Sometimes a finicky eater will be intrigued by morsels placed in these tins to retrieve and nibble. Try a few cheese squares, banana disks, or small teething biscuits.

Talking

Baby loves to chuckle and coo. He really thinks he can talk. It's not too early to let him try his conversational skills with you. Talk to him and he will answer. Often he will try to initiate the conversation, so be sure to answer.

Poker

It's time to bring out the wooden sorter boxes with holes through which to put blocks. Baby is learning to poke his little fingers into small places and loves it. Although Baby may not yet be able to put the blocks into the right holes, he will enjoy poking his fingers through the holes.

ROUTINE TIMES

Cause and Effect

Baby hears the water running and knows it's time for a bath. He perks up at the sound of familiar footsteps, he grows still at the mention of a nap, and calls when he needs assistance. All these examples reflect Baby's growing ability to recognize and anticipate the workings of his surroundings. Baby is taking a more active part in getting what he needs.

BATHING

Squeeze Bottles

Additions to the tub that will appeal to Baby are squeeze bottles. Thoroughly clean clear plastic detergent or colored food bottles such as those containing margarine, mustard, or syrup. Then, let Baby play with them in the tub.

Bathtime is the perfect time to experiment with dipping, squeezing, and squirting. Best of all, these free toys float.

Fingernails

As you've surely noticed, Baby's tiny fingernails, although almost transparent, can scratch delicate skin. Put a little powder or cornstarch under each nail and you will be able to see what you are cutting. As suggested earlier, this task is best done while Baby is sleeping.

Bathtime

No longer content to just sit in his bath, Baby needs the closest and most constant type of supervision. Protect him from a quick pull-up or an attempt to get out of the tub.

SLEEPING

Crib Comfort

A very crafty mom we know developed crib interest for her child in a most unusual way. She selected two sheets, one solid and one print. She then followed the design on the printed sheet and machine-quilted large forms. The result was a reversible sheet or comforter to amuse a restless seven-month-old who enjoyed tracing the puffy forms with his fingers while drifting off to sleep.

Bedcheck

Rachel's mom reminded us to check again when a seven-month-old is cranky at bedtime. Even though you've just changed him, Baby could be wet again. Urine, which becomes more acidic around this time, stings or burns, keeping Baby from settling down to sleep.

Shorter Naps

Baby's morning nap may be shorter now. Some babies will, over the next few months, be giving up their morning nap entirely. However, the need for sleep varies among children. Fill in the chart. This

information can make naptime an easier process for you both regardless of the number of rest periods required by Baby.

Baby rests well when _____

_____

_____

What helps (toys, blankets, music, reading a story)?

_____

_____

_____

Baby prefers his body in _____

_____ position.

FEEDING

The Cup

Now is the time to start using a cup. A two-handled, weighted model is a good choice because there is more for Baby to hold. While his initial attempts may be disastrous, practice is important. If Baby is teething, a cup may be preferred because it places less pressure on tender gums. At the beginning, do use the special spill-proof lid; it will make this new experience easier.

First successful use of Baby's cup
(date and comments).

_____

_____

_____

Mealtimes

Feeding can be hectic now that Baby is fond of
spoons. One useful trick may be to have two spoons.
You hold yours while Baby holds his. Through a
process of frequent spoon exchanges you'll find that
you can get through the meal with minimal stress.

Endurance is the only real answer. It won't be
long before Baby can feed himself. Don't discourage
his efforts at self-help. Relax and try to appreciate
Baby's antics for what they are—steps toward
independence.

Bottle Straws

Bottle straws are very handy small plastic straws
that fit into the standard bottle nipples. They can be
easily used by a sitting baby and eliminate the need
for the bottle to be inverted at a special angle. Many
parents swear by them.

Finger Foods

This month marks the beginning of the great
escape for Baby's feeders. Baby will work hard and
enjoy the challenge of feeding himself. Beginning

goodies include toast, cheese bits, cooked potatoes,
green beans, carrots, zucchini, and asparagus, cut
into small pieces.

Food Preferences

LIKES   DISLIKES

_____   _____

_____   _____

_____   _____

_____   _____

_____   _____

More Firsts

First food eaten successfully with fingers:

_____

_____

_____

_____

Traffic Patterns

With your social baby wanting to share his
mealtime with you, keep in mind the traffic pattern
in your kitchen or dining area. Plan ahead when

positioning Baby's chair. He will drop (or throw) occasional bits of food that will be tracked about the home unless you give him his special spot. A layer of newspaper, an oilcloth, or an old tablecloth under his chair can make cleanup easier. Baby may perform less when he doesn't have an audience of laughing family members.

Meat Matters

Baby is growing rapidly and needs his protein. Remember his meat. If necessary, mix it with his favorite vegetables or other preferred foods, but make sure he gets some meat daily. Cheese and fish are also good protein sources.

Babies don't have the same concerns as we do about what foods go together. Applesauce and spinach may be a special favorite.

DRESSING AND CHANGING

Getting a wiggly baby into clean clothes is often a tussle. Show him how he can participate in this ritual by grasping and pulling down his shirt or picking up his shoes or socks. You can chant this little rhyme while helping him:

Hurry Up

It's time for a change
And so much more.
When I'm dressed

I'll head for the floor.
So pull on my shirt
And cover my knees.
I'm ready to play,
So quick, if you please,
Slip on my socks
And forget the shoes,
Hurry up now
I've no time to lose.

Better Fit

There are diapers designed for extra absorption. Consider using the overnight ones or pull-ups. Also check the size you're buying to make sure they're not too large.

Double Diaper

Yes, you can double diaper with disposable diapers. A mother who takes her baby home on the subway explained this little trick.

Put two diapers together, soft sides touching each other. Now cut away the plastic in the seat area of the top diaper. Add a diaper liner if Baby can't tolerate the remaining plastic against his skin. This arrangement allows the second diaper to draw most of the moisture during those long trips.

HELPFUL HINTS

Reminder

Take care . . . experts tell us that your tension can be transmitted to an infant. None of us enjoy all aspects of child care. That's why it's important that you take breaks and be good to yourself. Community hospitals often have childcare newsletters. If you aren't on the list, ask to be included.

Call Out

Vocal contact is comforting for Baby. If you leave the room, call often to Baby and let him know what you're doing and that you will return. Out of sight need not mean left alone.

Fancy Framing

Every baby receives special articles of clothing. Many are lovingly made or chosen, some are heirlooms, others are exotic or of foreign design. Once outgrown, or before their debut, show them off! Place these treasures inside a clear plastic box-type frame and hang on the wall for decoration in Baby's room.

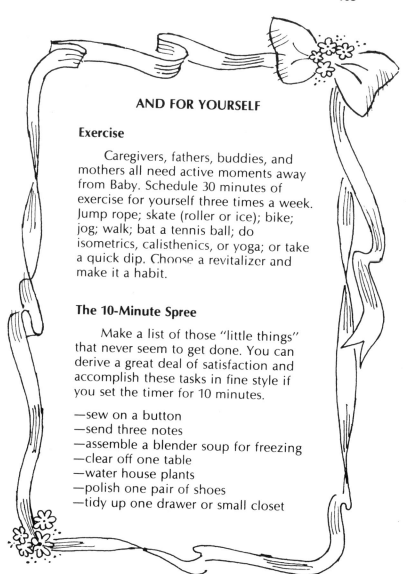

AND FOR YOURSELF

Exercise

Caregivers, fathers, buddies, and mothers all need active moments away from Baby. Schedule 30 minutes of exercise for yourself three times a week. Jump rope; skate (roller or ice); bike; jog; walk; bat a tennis ball; do isometrics, calisthenics, or yoga; or take a quick dip. Choose a revitalizer and make it a habit.

The 10-Minute Spree

Make a list of those "little things" that never seem to get done. You can derive a great deal of satisfaction and accomplish these tasks in fine style if you set the timer for 10 minutes.

—sew on a button
—send three notes
—assemble a blender soup for freezing
—clear off one table
—water house plants
—polish one pair of shoes
—tidy up one drawer or small closet

Pull-up

Baby may now begin to pull himself to a standing position. This is a signal for caregivers to rethink furniture arrangements. Furniture should be put away if Baby is strong enough to pull the pieces over on himself.

Taping Cords

Protect your exploring child and your furniture. Secure lamp cords with transparent tape close to furniture base.

Fussin' and Fallin'

Tumbles and bumps are part of exploring, learning, and playing. To minimize the tears, provide quick comfort. Sometimes Baby's reaction depends on yours. If you simply smile, Baby may shrug off his "injury" and start to laugh. If not, a pat, a hug, a kind word, and Baby will be back in action again.

Crafty Kid

Make a note of the first time your baby intentionally teased you.

_____

_____

Who else has noticed? When did it happen?

_____

_____

_____

Hip Sling

Bokki's mom showed us a quick, colorful way to move around when a stroller is too cumbersome and hands are full. She used a piece of African fabric, draped it across her body, and tied it on her shoulder, making a sling in which her child could sit. Bokki could now sit comfortably, with one leg on each side of his mother's hip; he could ride safely, enjoying the nearness of his mom.

Stranger Anxiety

Babies need time to get acquainted with new people. You play an important part in this process. Don't be alarmed if your once happy baby becomes shy when approached by strangers. This normal reaction is quite common at seven months.

You can help Baby by sitting him on your lap while talking, giving Baby an opportunity to look the new person over before introducing him or her.

Pillow Play

Remember those cute T-shirts and other items that Baby outgrew (see Chapter 3)? Get them out, stitch all openings but one together, stuff with polyester filling, and close up the last opening for durable, colorful pillows. These toy-togs will serve as buffers in the playpen or crib; they are ideal for a baby who likes to toss or throw things.

Margin of Error

Everything takes longer now. Allowing enough time is essential if you are to keep your sense of humor.

On those days when being on time is crucial, tack an additional 30 minutes onto your preparation time and see what a difference it makes.

Egg Poacher

Use this handy kitchen appliance to keep the meal of the leisurely-eating seven-month-old warmed to the proper level. Salton and Oster both make easy-clean models.

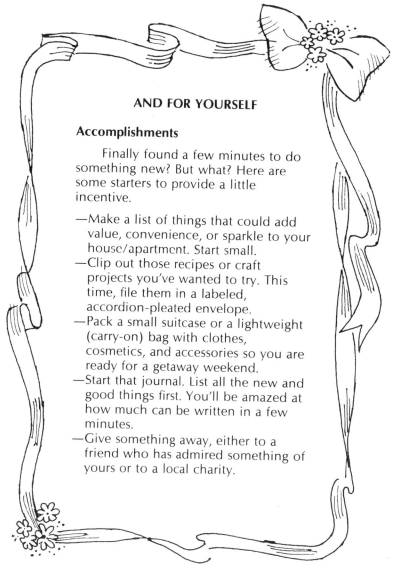

AND FOR YOURSELF

Accomplishments

Finally found a few minutes to do something new? But what? Here are some starters to provide a little incentive.

—Make a list of things that could add value, convenience, or sparkle to your house/apartment. Start small.
—Clip out those recipes or craft projects you've wanted to try. This time, file them in a labeled, accordion-pleated envelope.
—Pack a small suitcase or a lightweight (carry-on) bag with clothes, cosmetics, and accessories so you are ready for a getaway weekend.
—Start that journal. List all the new and good things first. You'll be amazed at how much can be written in a few minutes.
—Give something away, either to a friend who has admired something of yours or to a local charity.

Food-Carton Baby-Food Caddy

A handy way to store all those baby-food jars and keep them from getting lost in the refrigerator is the baby-food caddy. This organizer also limits the number of trips to the refrigerator when preparing meals. Look for small six-pack cartons (the type that hold single servings of mixers or wine). Cover the carton with bright contact paper or paint with latex enamel paint and you have your caddy. Later on these carriers can be used by Baby himself as a carry-all for toys as he moves from room to room.

Cleaner Toys

Stuffed toys look cleaner and brighter after an application of cornstarch. Rub the cornstarch into the soiled toy and set aside briefly. Remove the powder with a stiff brush.

Think Safety!

Very little will escape your baby's exploring hands. Careful babyproofing is a must at this stage. Strings and electric cords become irresistible; beware of everything in Baby's reach. It's not too early to start using safety plugs in all electric sockets.

Teething Tips

Here are some soothing suggestions for a baby with tender gums: a breadstick, a bagel necklace, a frozen carrot, a wooden clothespin (old-fashioned style), or a puppy's hard rubber ring.

Happy Hands

Prepare now for the inevitable accidents that will occur as Baby becomes more mobile. Nothing soothes a cranky teether or a baby bumped on the mouth like the Happy Hand. Fill a surgical glove with water, tie a knot at the end, and freeze. Children who may not want you to hold an ice cube over a sore will be more than willing to suck a finger or thumb of the Happy Hand. The thumb and fingers are the right size for a baby's mouth so the ice goes where it will do the most good.

PARENTS, FRIENDS, AND ADMIRERS

Baby Gallery

Did you save pictures from months 1, 3, and 5, or, better still, from each month? If so, select your favorites and blow them up for all to see. Baby will soon begin to recognize himself. Include a portrait of VIPs, too. Special caregivers deserve space in Baby's room.

Invitations

Grandparents can provide the young family with affordable ways to get away from home. A weekend invitation to visit grandparents who live out of town or an invitation to come for Sunday dinner are to be looked forward to; such events eliminate a great deal of hassle and stress. They also provide a large, very reassuring dose of admiration, appreciation, and loving support for the still less than self-confident new family.

Thrifty Tip

Check local papers or bulletin boards for best buys in toys and infant equipment. Kiddie gyms, jumper chairs, and pushtoys are worth looking and waiting for. Yard sales can be especially rewarding.

Quick Change

How long has it been since you changed Baby's surroundings? At seven months Baby is active, but also easily bored. Keep things lively, for both your sakes! Move the crib, bring in a plant or bouquet of flowers and place just out of Baby's reach. Tack up a big bright poster or two. Babies respond to primary colors. Don't forget the ceiling.

Quality Trip

A piggy-back ride on a taller person's shoulders is a good trip that *never* grows old. The view from the top is exciting.

I Love Daddy

According to some researchers, Baby prefers playing with Daddy at seven months. Apparently games with fathers tend to be more physical and, in this mobile month, Baby responds enthusiastically to such play.

For the Admirer, the Knee Ride

Here is a little game to play with Baby once you have become acquainted. Cross your knees and sit Baby on one side. Hold on to both his hands, bounce him to the rhyme, and on "Whoops" swing him by uncrossing your knees.

Leg over leg
A dog went to Dover.
He came to a wall—
Whoops—he jumped over.

Face Book

A special friend (sibling or child) might make a "Face Book" for Baby. Any face, animal or human, is suitable. To ensure durability, glue choices onto cardboard and then cover with clear contact paper; remember this book will be tasted, poked, and handled at lot.

Baby Loves Babies

Better than Mommy, another child, or special friend, is another baby. Just watch how infants intently observe and imitate each other's actions. They learn from each other. Now may be a good time to consider joining (or forming) a playgroup.

Playgroup

Join with three or four other parents to form a playgroup. Children within four months of each other will enjoy being together regularly for an hour or so two times a week. Because they are, after all, just babies, keep plans flexible and simple. Snacks or preparations should be completed before the group gathers. Limit the play area, closing off all other parts of the house. These occasions provide adults an opportunity to exchange stories, information, and tips on child care. Even at this tender age, the friendships formed often last for years.

To Grandma

Maybe it's not your luscious chocolate chip recipe, but it will receive rave reviews from all your favorite babies.

Grandma's Teething Biscuits

1 egg yolk, beaten
3 tbsp. corn syrup
1 tps. vanilla
1 cup flour
1 tbsp. quick-cooking oats
1 tbsp. powdered milk

1. Blend egg yolk, corn syrup, and vanilla; then add dry ingredients. Dough will be stiff.
2. Roll out dough thinly and cut into finger length "T" or barbell shapes.
3. Bake at 350° on an ungreased cookie sheet for 15 minutes.
4. Cool and store in an airtight container.

Makes about 2 dozen, depending on the shape used.

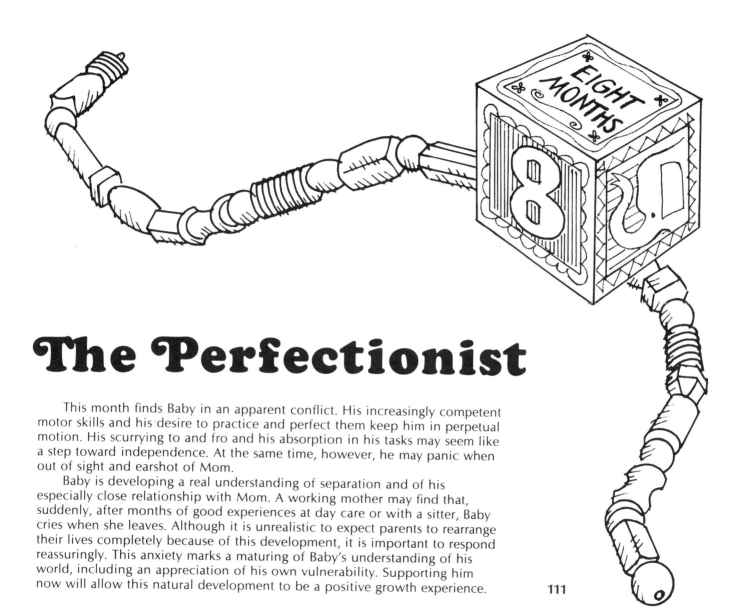

The Perfectionist

This month finds Baby in an apparent conflict. His increasingly competent motor skills and his desire to practice and perfect them keep him in perpetual motion. His scurrying to and fro and his absorption in his tasks may seem like a step toward independence. At the same time, however, he may panic when out of sight and earshot of Mom.

Baby is developing a real understanding of separation and of his especially close relationship with Mom. A working mother may find that, suddenly, after months of good experiences at day care or with a sitter, Baby cries when she leaves. Although it is unrealistic to expect parents to rearrange their lives completely because of this development, it is important to respond reassuringly. This anxiety marks a maturing of Baby's understanding of his world, including an appreciation of his own vulnerability. Supporting him now will allow this natural development to be a positive growth experience.

111

Baby will probably practice pulling up and standing this month. Unfortunately, he can't always get back down once he's on his feet. His attempts may include many falls, so protect him by padding areas where he is allowed to practice.

His drive to be mobile may actually wake Baby up at night. You may find him practicing pulling up in his crib. This will be particularly frustrating until he can get down and stops crying for help. You can try to teach Baby how to let himself down, but he will probably learn how all by himself. Once you are sure he can do it, be firm about these nighttime workouts. If you do not encourage him to stay awake, they will gradually cease.

Baby is now developing a true pincer grasp. Being able to handle objects with the thumb and forefinger is one characteristic that distinguishes humans from other animals. Baby will use this new skill in order to learn about his environment. Objects that are unsafe or that you want to protect must be put away for now.

Baby has been listening to you speak since birth. Words that have a special significance for him may crystallize in meaning for him this month so that he will understand them every time they are spoken. He may also develop "words" that have true meaning behind them, even if they don't seem to resemble words you know. Some babies do speak their first real words this month.

ACTIVITIES, GAMES, AND SONGS

Chase Game

One of Baby's greatest pleasures will be you imitating his style. So, down on all fours; Baby will take the lead and look to see if you are following. He'll squeal with delight as you chase and follow him about the room. "Here I come, I'm going to catch you!" Don't fail to hug and hold him close after he's been caught.

In and Through

Curious babies love challenging crawling experiences. Make a quick tunnel out of cardboard boxes. Another sure winner is to open a few suitcases and place them in different spots in one room. Put a few enticing items in each suitcase. Baby will crawl from one to another, sitting for a while in each.

Simon Says

Now that Baby uses gestures, he will enjoy games of imitation. He can do as you do but will like you doing as he does best. Simply observe until you see a gesture to repeat (table-patting, hand-waving, etc.). Now repeat this gesture exactly. It won't take long for Baby to catch on. His sudden beaming smile will convey his delight.

Pat the Pillow

A quick game for Baby can be fashioned from an old pillow. Sew four or five velcro tabs onto the pillow. Sew the other side of the tabs onto cloth shapes cut from a variety of colorful textured scraps. Baby will enjoy pulling off these scraps and patting them onto the pillow again. In time, he will be able to play this game alone.

Hide-and-Seek

"Hide-and-Seek" around an overstuffed chair or around the door can be great fun, especially if you're on your knees and crawling along with Baby. When you play this game, include others—teddy bears, dolls, and siblings.

A Ball for Baby

Baby will enjoy chasing a 4-in. rubber ball as he crawls around the floor.

Plates of Food

Do you have extra paper plates from a picnic? Cut out a few colorful pictures of food from magazines and glue them to the center of each plate. Now cover the pictures with a square of clear contact paper. Baby will enjoy sorting, stacking, touching, and mouthing these new toys.

It's Following Me!

For your crawler who likes to take something along on his excursions, toys with short strings that jangle as he crawls are special fun. These pull toys are easy to make from an assortment of whatever is handy.

Hole-in-One

Baby likes boards with holes in them. A pegboard with giant pegs (2-in. diameter) can be fun. This is a simple toy to make. Three or four colorful pegs are plenty. Paint with colorful, safe, latex enamel.

"Moo"

Remember the cylindrical noisemaker you had as a child, the one that said "moo" or "meow" when you turned it over? These are still available. Seal one of these in a plastic food storage container so it is safe for Baby to taste. Now that Baby is learning *upside down* and *right-side up,* a picture of a cow glued inside the lid will make playing even more fun and a real learning experience.

Books

Homemade books are special fun and they help Baby learn. They can be picture books of Baby's things—bottles, shoes, cats, dogs, etc. A "people book" with photographs of all the family and friends is also fun. Durable books can be made by covering the pages with clear contact paper or slipping pictures into the plastic photograph holders that come in all sizes.

"Touch and Feel Books" of many textures can include a variety of interesting items such as well-attached bows, buttons, and zippers. These books will provide practice for Baby in the years to come.

"Pat Books" that include noisemakers between the pages so that they squeal when patted are great fun. Inexpensive noisemakers can be purchased at novelty or carnival supply stores. Be sure to attach and conceal them well.

Container Fun

Don't throw away those old boxes, cans, and plastic bottles. The top-of-the-line containers are the great plastic cosmetic cases that are a part of special gift promotions. Clean these containers carefully and let Baby play with them. Different sizes are fun. Big ones are to stick your arm into and retrieve toys. Small ones, which require a finger to coax out the contents, are another favorite. A few interlocking ones and some with lids too big to swallow will provide a challenge for little fingers.

His Own Language

Baby names and calls his friends now:

Mom _____

Dad _____

Siblings _____

Pets _____

His friend _____

Write these names phonetically so that you and others will recognize them. Baby will be delighted that you are finally beginning to decode his language.

Guess Who's Coming to Dinner?

Baby will enjoy being taken to the window to anticipate the homecoming of special people. This is a great learning experience. Be sure that Baby knows the name of the person arriving.

The Crate

A plastic storage crate on wheels is a good investment. Attach a rope and you have a wagon to push, tug, or slide as you clean and straighten. With luck Baby will enjoy putting his toys into the crate almost as much as trying to get in and out of it.

Chorus Time

The timeless song "A-Hunting" can be fun to sing.

A-hunting we will go.
A-hunting we will go.
We'll catch a fox
  (reach for Baby)
And put him in a box
  (bear-hug Baby)
And then we'll let him go
  (sit him down a few inches away).

Make up your own songs, too.

Do You Like My Hat?

Baby will enjoy a hat to plop on his head, especially when he's in front of the mirror. Hang several on a low knob near the mirror, and watch Baby ham it up.

Tickle Times

Tickle games are great fun. Use your hands or Baby's to mime the actions suggested by the words.

Play this tickle game on your squirming baby. He will squeal in anticipatory glee as he becomes familiar with the actions.

Slowly, slowly, very slowly
Creeps the garden snail.
Slowly, slowly, very slowly
Up the wooden rail.
Quickly, quickly, very quickly
Runs the little mouse.
Quickly, quickly, very quickly
Round about the house.

Toes

Baby enjoys playing with his toes. You can make this more fun by playing "Terrific Toes." Baby is beginning to develop a memory, which makes this even more enjoyable.

Terrific Toes

I knows those toes.
I love those toes.
They are a part of me that grows.

Cute and round they touch the ground;
In the air they kick around;
What a sight, and not a sound.

Footprints

If you have been recording Baby's growth periodically, it's time for another footprint.

For contrast, use Baby's white shoe polish on a dark piece of paper. It's amazing to see how much growth has occurred in a few months. Toddlerhood is just around the corner.

A framed series of these prints makes a lovely gift for grandparents or other admirers.

Soapy Magic

Amaze yourself and Baby too by blowing bubbles. A perfect time to practice is bathtime. You need only a bar of soap and your fingers. Curl your index finger and wrap your thumb around it. Rub across a bar of soap. Slowly and gradually release your index finger to form a circle. Blow gently to form a bubble. It is a matter of coordination, determination, and a bit of luck.

"The Sandy Shore"

Now that Baby sits well and loves to crawl, he is ready for some sand play. A sandbox can be a great experience. Pack his favorite measuring cups and bowls, and be off to the park.

You will need to show him the ropes, but soon Baby will master this new environment and look forward to trips to the sand area.

Cut the bottoms off handled plastic milk or juice containers at an angle; these make handy, handled sand scoops. An old big-toothed comb is another fun sand toy.

You can also bring this game to Baby at home. Sprinkle a cup or two of cornmeal in the bottom of a dishpan. Set Baby and the pan on a newspaper-covered floor. Indoor sand play!

Blocks

Cover a half dozen or more 5-in. foam-rubber cubes with cheery fabric for one of Baby's first sets of blocks. This group of toys will be used in many ways. Blocks will be thrown, kicked, gummed, banged, stacked, and carried about.

More High-Chair Art

Instead of chocolate pudding, you can use mashed potato flakes. Sprinkle on Baby's tray. Add a touch of tomato juice (1 tbsp.) and a little warm water. This is tasty fingerpaint for Baby. A good time to use this activity is while you're cooking or busy at the sink.

Touch Board

Baby's busy hands will return again and again to a quick-to-fix, easy-to-change board with a variety of surfaces. Cover a 16 in. x 18 in. piece of corkboard, cardboard, or wood with colored oilcloth or contact paper. Add swatches of material of different textures: sandpaper (scratchy), thick yarn (stringy), etc. Use your imagination. Make sure each item is securely attached.

ROUTINE TIMES

BATHING

Baby's Bath

I'm taking this bath
So I can be
Clean and sweet
And more like me.

A little soap
A little rub
And I will be
Out of this tub.

Then quickly dry
I'll tell you why
I like to smell
. . . just swell.

Tub Time for Two

Baby may enjoy taking his bath with a brother or sister. Trying to get two kids clean at one time means keeping alert . . . and can they splash! Bathwater need only be 3 to 4 inches deep.

Ear Care

Experts tell us that you should not use cotton swabs or anything smaller than your little finger to clean Baby's ears. This is because in trying to remove the wax you might actually force more down into the ear than you remove. The wax can gradually build up and become hard, so that it will have to be removed by a doctor. Washing tiny ears with a little soap and water and a washcloth is all that is necessary and recommended.

Soaps

Let Baby help you at bathtime. Give him some part in this routine. Soap on a rope is one way not to lose the bar, or try a soap that floats.

Toweling It

Do you know Baby's favorite color? Select a terry towel that he will like and indulge his first attempts at drying himself. If given a good example, Baby will, as usual, pick up this technique. This "pat, pat" imitation will delight Baby.

SLEEPING

Bedtime Boss

With so much to see, do, touch, and taste, Baby may not wish to sleep, rest, or even slow down. Bedtimes may become difficult, trying times. Baby's determination to continue even at the end of a busy day is a force to be reckoned with. As the caring adult, it's up to you to set the standards. Decide on a bedtime procedure and, when the lights go out, stick to the plan. Baby needs his rest despite loud, angry, wailing protests to the contrary. Waiting for Baby to signal his desire for sleep could keep you up indefinitely.

Baby's Bedtime Routine

For the world to know, this *is* Baby's routine.

_____

_____

_____

_____

_____

FEEDING

Feeding Himself

Baby has a growing fascination for his spoon. But first, how to use it . . . ah, the problems. Give Baby an opportunity to practice by presenting him with a short-handled wooden spoon. Let him dip the spoon into something stiff or sticky that will adhere to the spoon. Babies have experienced success with mashed potatoes and peanut butter.

Fiddling, Fingers, and Eating

Is Baby finding bananas nice but boring? Now that he has become accomplished with finger foods, a pinch of *pizzazz* would be appreciated. Try these munchies:

—a little lettuce
—a piece of pear (peeled, please)
—watermelon fingers (without seeds)
—slivers of raw apple
—a waffle finger

Another Feeder

A sibling is often preferred to any other caregiver at mealtime. Somehow it's more fun, or perhaps it's the change of face. A brother or sister who has the time and patience to feed a messy eight-month-old deserves encouragement, watching, and an apron. The social nature of the mealtime banter is usually high kitchen comedy, with Baby initiating much of the conversation.

What I'm Eating

Just so you will have it in writing, complete the following list of what Baby is and is not eating. Caregivers and friends will appreciate it.

	LOVES	HATES
Juices	_____	_____
Cereals (types)	_____	_____
Fruits (strained)	_____	_____
Vegetables	_____	_____
Meats and other proteins	_____	_____
Snacks and finger foods	_____	_____

Very favorite food:

_____

Poorest choice—likely to be refused:

_____

Mixing Your Own

Meats and vegetables are the best buys when it comes to commercially available baby food. Fruit juices and mixed dinners may have a high percentage of fillers and water. Fruit drinks and baby desserts have the lowest food values and are loaded with sugar.

If you like the combination idea, why not mix your own? Choose the meat and vegetable items Baby likes, or ones that you want to introduce.

Open Sez Me

The young mimic loves to imitate faces, especially at mealtime. However, such silliness sometimes keeps him from his food. Don't forget to try these old standbys when facing a baby with a clamped jaw.

Here comes the bee into the hive—buzz buzz buzz
  (aim the spoon toward the mouth)

The airplane is looking for the airport—lay
  out the runway(tongue)—here comes the
  airplane in for a landing.
Here comes the plane into the hangar
  (fly the food into Baby's mouth).

DRESSING AND CHANGING

Cowbell

An eight-month-old who is getting into everything and who is trying to extend his reach so that he may touch untouchables can be hard to keep track of. Attach noisemakers, bells, or clickers to knees, shirts, coveralls, and shoes so that the exploring child will disclose his location with a jingle or two.

Keep Talking

Allow Baby to participate in the dressing process to make this routine more bearable. Remember to chat with the child, "Here is a super red shirt from Aunt Jane with a strawberry on the front . . . over your head it goes. Give me your arm so we can slide it into the sleeve." This is the time to focus on body parts.

Changing Safely

Never take your hand off that baby when it's time for a change. Baby can perform amazing feats of strength while waiting for clean clothes or a dry diaper. Maintain an iron grip and safety will become an automatic part of this routine.

Position

Now that Baby can sit, you may find dressing easiest when he is in a sitting position, rather than trying to dress a squirming Baby determined to practice rolling over. Those with an active baby should consider any strategy that works. Dressing a baby with "things to do" can be a very frustrating experience. Standing may be another position to try.

Suggestions for a Quick Change

These can be invaluable for a sitter or caregiver.

What works _____

_____

_____

What doesn't work _____

_____

_____

Winners (for unexpected reasons) _____

_____

_____

_____

Baby Hats

Babies do not like things that tie under their chins. Hats that do not require ties, such as a knit helmet type, are the best choices. Hooded garments are another alternative.

First Choice

Jogging togs are available for infants. These clothes, made in bright, light, stretchy, and durable fabrics, have features that make them favorites with parents. Elasticized ankles keep walkers from tripping over dangling hems, and elasticized wrists keep arms and hands free for action. Most outfits are two-piece and can be layered for warmth. The hooded, zippered jacket is one that babies like.

HELPFUL HINTS

Reminder

Talk to Baby in complete sentences. He is very interested in patterns of speech and will be experimenting with intonation and rhythm patterns.

Incentives

Now that Baby is pulling up to almost any piece of furniture or object that will support his weight, add incentive to his efforts. Give Baby reasons to pull up. Think about rooms he is probably exploring. Plant surprises and treats for the inquisitive child. Position a toy just beyond his grasp on the seat of a chair. Let a portion of a blanket hang over the edge of the couch. Place his Busy Box on the outside edge of his crib so he can pull up to play with the toy.

Too Much Togetherness

Mom and Baby need not (and should not) be together all the time. Both of you deserve occasional rest and time away from each other. These early "time-outs" help Baby begin to handle separations. The first experiences pave the way for handling social situations, sitters, and nursery-school years with greater ease. Understand that no one will ever do everything just as you do. Baby will always have only one mother. However, others can provide him with loving care while you are away.

Baby Food Safety

Remember to check the safety center on the lids of the baby-food jars you buy. The small circle must be concave to ensure that the jar has remained properly vacuum-sealed.

Toughening Togs

Clothes will be expected to withstand extra wear now and in the months to come. Buttons will stay on longer if sewn with durable thread (heavy-duty #8); try using a shank. A small strip of twill tape sewn to the garment before the button is attached will add considerable strength and keep the button from pulling a hole. Buttonholes can be reinforced with heavy-duty thread as well.

Pick, Pick, Pick It Up

Make it a game, but now is the time for Baby to learn to pick up his things. Baby is involved with taking everything out and, with your encouragement, he will soon find putting things back equally fun.

Baby can begin to learn where to find clothes, toys, and other items to play with or wear if they are placed at his level. Graduated wicker baskets are a help.

His Own

A low drawer is a wonderful learning experience for Baby. A challenge to open, to jiggle, to pull and balance, a drawer is something to sit in, put things in, and take things out of. Add a surprise from time to time and keep the explorer happy.

Carpet Safety

It's important to keep your area rugs from sliding and slipping now that Baby is so mobile. Nonslip mats that go under the rug are available for just this purpose. There is also a special double-faced tape that works well with smaller rugs.

Snow Weather

Even though it takes time to bundle up Baby in his snowsuit, do get yourself dressed first. Dressing Baby as quickly as possible will keep him from getting overheated and fussy from the delay. Snowsuits with zippers from neck to toe are the most convenient.

Heating Reminder

Don't warm baby food in glass jars unless you're sure you'll use the entire jar. Instead put a serving in a small dish and warm in the microwave for 10-15 seconds.

Compartments

Baby is a little clutter-creator. Think about a cleanup strategy with a future. Cube-like compartments that can be made or bought commercially can hold and display toys and books now. The units are convenient because they can be stacked or rearranged. In a few years, the cubes can hold puzzles, games, clothes, and gear for the older child.

For a Window Watcher

Next to becoming a master crawler, Baby's favorite activity is looking. Researchers have projected that up to 20 percent of Baby's time is spent viewing objects close at hand. And now Baby is interested in those farther away, too. Baby especially loves to look out of windows—just for the sheer joy of seeing what's out there. Keep windows clean and bright. When cold weather comes, rub salt water or alcohol on the outside of the windows and polish with newspaper.

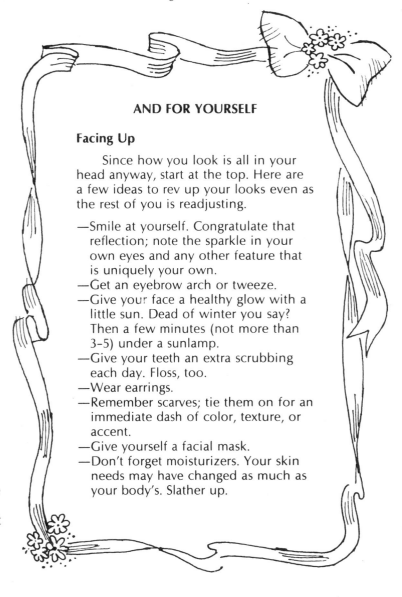

AND FOR YOURSELF

Facing Up

Since how you look is all in your head anyway, start at the top. Here are a few ideas to rev up your looks even as the rest of you is readjusting.

—Smile at yourself. Congratulate that reflection; note the sparkle in your own eyes and any other feature that is uniquely your own.
—Get an eyebrow arch or tweeze.
—Give your face a healthy glow with a little sun. Dead of winter you say? Then a few minutes (not more than 3-5) under a sunlamp.
—Give your teeth an extra scrubbing each day. Floss, too.
—Wear earrings.
—Remember scarves; tie them on for an immediate dash of color, texture, or accent.
—Give yourself a facial mask.
—Don't forget moisturizers. Your skin needs may have changed as much as your body's. Slather up.

Falling, Falling

Baby is into everything. He is testing his body to the upper- and outermost limits. As a result, there may be a temptation to protect him by confining him to a playpen. While this eases your mind, Baby's growth and development can be hampered if he is left alone too long. One solution is to stock up on ice and aspirin. The ice is for the inevitable bumps and bruises; the aspirin for your predictable headache. Be prepared to console and cuddle.

Spotless

Some people *do* think of everything! One mom uses furniture casters on the four corners of the playpen when she takes it outdoors. This neat housekeeper reports that bringing mud, dirt, and grime inside is no longer a problem because of this simple measure.

The Beach Baby

Why exclude Baby from a trip to the shore? He will have a happy time and so will you by following these suggestions offered by beachcombing parents:

—Take several jugs of water for drinking, rinsing off, and keeping cool
—Take or rent an umbrella; Baby is especially sensitive to sun
—Turn a playpen upside down for a safe, protected play or sleep space
—Circular, portable, expandable gates are a nifty way to give Baby play space while keeping him from dashing into the ocean

Rocker

There is no place like a rocking chair for comforting and cuddling. Keep the chair in operation and the floor beneath it in good repair by protecting rocker arcs with adhesive tape or felt dots (the kind used on the bottom of lamps).

Telephone Tip

The phone rings or a call must be made. Try spaghetti, wet or dry, to keep Baby busy and happy while you converse.

Dry: Two or three strands of spaghetti or noodles will respond to the grasp of a young child by breaking, snapping, and popping. Baby will be intrigued by trying to pick up the little pieces.

Wet: A cooked noodle or two of any width will wiggle about on Baby's feeding tray. A noodle can slip, slide, swirl, and be chased by little fingers. It tastes good, too.

Super Swing

One creative father we know quickly made a supersafe swing out of an infant car seat. He hung the well-designed, padded, and belted seat from the limb of an apple tree. His baby enjoyed the swing all summer long.

No Mud

We were walking after a rain one day and noticed a baby carriage with wheel covers coming towards us. Always on the alert for helpful hints, we stopped and asked about them. The woman told us that they were just plastic bowl covers (they look like little shower hats) she puts on the carriage when it's wet and muddy outside. She can slip the covers off when she gets home without having to worry about tracking mud into the house.

Hat Trick

A quick way to shape and dry Baby's hats and caps is to place them on an inflated balloon. They'll soon be restored to their original size.

Instant Boots

For added protection in inclement weather, reach for two plastic bags or several sheets of clear food wrap to cover Baby's shoes. Secure these instant boots with rubber bands or shoelaces. In an emergency, these boots will also work for adults.

Ten-Minute Blitz

Setting a kitchen timer for ten minutes when cleaning a part of your home out of baby's sight has become an absolute necessity. This blitz technique allows you to concentrate all your energies for short periods of time. We have found that this method also soothes the conscience. You will discover that a lot can be accomplished in these short periods.

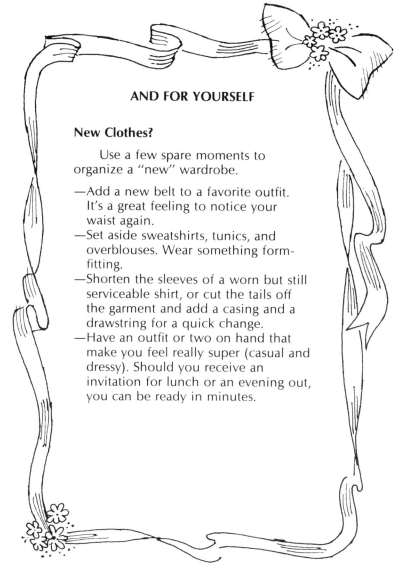

AND FOR YOURSELF

New Clothes?

Use a few spare moments to organize a "new" wardrobe.

—Add a new belt to a favorite outfit. It's a great feeling to notice your waist again.
—Set aside sweatshirts, tunics, and overblouses. Wear something form-fitting.
—Shorten the sleeves of a worn but still serviceable shirt, or cut the tails off the garment and add a casing and a drawstring for a quick change.
—Have an outfit or two on hand that make you feel really super (casual and dressy). Should you receive an invitation for lunch or an evening out, you can be ready in minutes.

PARENTS, FRIENDS, AND ADMIRERS

The Human Chair

We recently spotted a very delighted baby having a splendid ride in an instant apparatus created by a "special male friend." The baby's chair was made by clasping the friend's hands together and arranging the rider so that his back was supported against his friend's chest. The infant's feet looped over the top of the friend's arms. Security and closeness were created by drawing the friend's arms in toward his own chest.

Toys Are for Babies

Yesterday's toys may be totally forgotten for now. The cruising eight-month-old may forgo all objects save those that share his crib. If he chooses any favorite items, they are most likely ones that are of use to you—pots, pans, utensils. Share your wealth with Baby . . . or buy a second just for him. Those measuring spoons, cups, utensils, bowls, and small pots will be used for sand toys, for playing house, and for other dramatic adventures in the months to come.

Chipless Dip

When planning a get-together for friends, consider Baby, too. Before you add spices or other exotic items to your dip, take out a portion for Baby. A touch of food coloring will catch his eye. Baby may try to use his treat like the big folks or he may prefer his finger. Mothers tell us that using dip is a fine way to introduce vegetables.

Saving Memories

Take the time to jot down several of Baby's latest antics. These prized memories will be appreciated later. So record them now.

_____

_____

_____

_____

_____

_____

_____

Guests

Visitors may be surprised by Baby's response to their presence. At this age, Baby will need additional assistance and attention in order to respond easily to company. This social shyness is typical of nearly all infants of this age. Kind words, hugging, and information about the guests will make a difference. Let Baby make the first move. He will let you know when he is ready to be held or handled by others.

Away

Prepare Baby in advance for times away from home. Verbal reassurance helps. So does taking familiar toys and one special surprise. Move slowly.

Spend time talking to Baby and prepare him for new experiences. This will be rewarding.

Mountain-Climber

Baby will enjoy the adventure of climbing a human mountain. Have one of Baby's bigger admirers spread out on the floor and let Baby enjoy the closeness and challenge of crawling over this special friend. This is a good motor-development game for Baby.

Tapes

Remember the archive. Tape a sample of the talking baby who may be putting syllables together: *dada, mama,* etc. These recordings will be savored now and become a source of amusement later.

Snapshots

How about a family photo while you're capturing special moments?

Funny Face

A cookie that looks good and tastes even better could have a face like Baby's. This fun-to-frost-and-create treat might be made by an older sibling or young friend. Decorate a plain, nonsweet cookie with a touch of icing and draw a face.

Soft Sculpture or Pillow Plus

While primarily interested in climbing and cruising about, Baby will still opt for a comfy place in which to curl up. Make a tomato, a cushiony doughnut, a naugahyde cucumber, or a fluffy cloud to roll over. Consider including handles or crawl-through spaces in these material sculptures. Baby will climb over, lean against, and explore this form, which will be the site of many games for years to come.

For the less creative, attach three or four pillows of odd or standard sizes to make a "magic mass." This challenging terrain will help the child practice motor skills as it becomes a favorite lounging spot in the future.

A friend who made a pillow plus for her baby found that it was still being used by her teenager.

Gifts

An Activity Box is a great present for Baby. The best boxes have things to push, pull, poke, and turn. All parts of this box should make noises. Best of all, nothing comes off, so no cleanup. Baby will continue to enjoy this toy until he is two or so.

A homemade busy box with a variety of things to try, touch, turn, and test is indeed a special gift. Items to include in your design:

—a caster with a wheel to spin
—a lock with a permanently attached key to twist back and forth
—a bell to ring
—a handle to turn
—a bicycle horn (bulb type) to poke or squeeze

—a latch to lift
—a chain to rattle
—a bolt to throw

Consider any hardware-store item that moves, emits sound, pushes or pulls, slides, or rolls.

Beads

One of our favorite grandmothers from the Midwest regularly makes "bread beads" for her favorite baby. First, she reserves some bread dough and molds it into interesting shapes. After poking a large hole in each bead, she allows the beads to rise, and then bakes them. For a finishing touch, she likes to glaze them with a little egg white and water.

She strings four or five of these shiny shapes on a thick cotton cord or yarn. This easy-to-make gift is fun to wear and is a fine teething toy.

For a slightly older sibling, the baker made a lovely tinted heart to wear and nibble. Both items were designed and intended for immediate consumption.

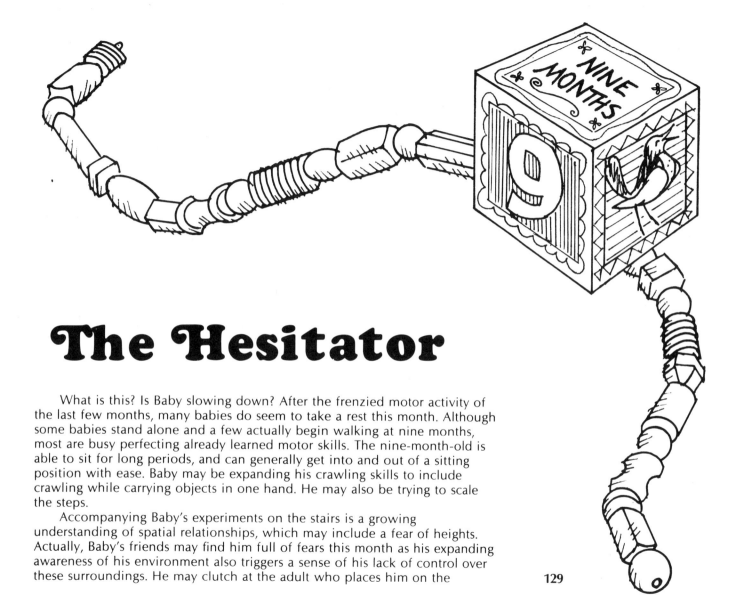

The Hesitator

What is this? Is Baby slowing down? After the frenzied motor activity of the last few months, many babies do seem to take a rest this month. Although some babies stand alone and a few actually begin walking at nine months, most are busy perfecting already learned motor skills. The nine-month-old is able to sit for long periods, and can generally get into and out of a sitting position with ease. Baby may be expanding his crawling skills to include crawling while carrying objects in one hand. He may also be trying to scale the steps.

Accompanying Baby's experiments on the stairs is a growing understanding of spatial relationships, which may include a fear of heights. Actually, Baby's friends may find him full of fears this month as his expanding awareness of his environment also triggers a sense of his lack of control over these surroundings. He may clutch at the adult who places him on the

129

changing table or in the tub. He may react with tears to loud noises. These events are all part of Baby's growth; with a little time and sympathy his fears will subside.

Baby is making cognitive leaps this month. His growing understanding of spatial relationships and his greater dexterity give him the ability to build towers out of two or three objects. His memory is developing rapidly; he searches for objects that have been removed from his sight and recalls recent events and routines. For example, if his daily bath follows dinner, Baby will let you know that he expects this.

You may hear Baby imitating noises as well as words this month. He is learning to cough, click, make airplane sounds, etc., deliberately. He will also be practicing his words, sometimes in long sequences such as *da-da-da-da-da-da-da*. Some babies can respond to verbal commands during the ninth month and will comply with great satisfaction to a simple request such as "Pick up your bottle, Josh."

ACTIVITIES, GAMES, AND SONGS

Ring Toys

Give Baby a spindle toy with which to play. With your help and encouragement, Baby will learn to put the rings on the spindle. Once he has learned this, he will practice again and again with great satisfaction.

Spindle toys are easy to make. Use your imagination. A hand with a big thumb to ring, a stuffed teapot, or a pumpkin with a big stem would all appeal to Baby. Use doughnut shapes cut from wood and pad them thoroughly with stuffing. Now make a fabric cover for your creation.

Clapping Song

Baby especially enjoys hand clapping. Play this little clapping song as the words suggest (to the tune of "Little Brown Jug"):

Clap your hands, one, two, three,
Play a little game with me.
Now your hands have flown away.
Come back hands so we can play.

Help Baby clap his hands and then hide them behind his back. As Baby learns the song, he can do more and more by himself. He will also like being the one to initiate this game.

Balloons

Baby will enjoy kicking, pulling, and chasing a fast-moving balloon on a string.

Strutting

During this month and until Baby is walking independently, his favorite game will be walking and stomping his feet while you hold his hands. Baby needs this motor practice, so play often.

String-along

Baby is learning to use tools. String toys are a fascination as he learns that pulling the string will fetch the toy. These fun-to-make toys are great gifts. You can assemble impromptu toys from an assortment of other toys and gadgets or make them from scratch. The important thing is to include moving parts that will make noises when moved— measuring spoons, wooden spools, blocks, plastic bangle bracelets, keys, etc.

Collage

Pasting a collage of colorful scraps of paper, fabric, and trim can be fun for Baby. Tape a piece of colored paper to his high-chair tray that will contrast with the scraps.

Dribble a trail of white nontoxic glue around the paper. Next show Baby how to push the scraps onto the dribbles of glue. Now stand back and let the artist create.

These artistic creations can be mounted in a clear plastic block frame and given to an admiring grandparent or friend, or they can brighten Baby's own room.

The Cat Says "Meow"

Baby is alert to all sorts of environmental noises and tries to imitate them. Animal sounds and pictures hold special interest.

Naming the animals and imitating the sounds they make will provide beneficial early experiences with beginning books. Encourage Baby to actively participate by pointing and imitating.

Such songs as "Old MacDonald Had a Farm" have not lost their popularity with young children. Many of the songs sung to a child at an early age will give special pleasure when he learns to sing them himself. This can be a fun family game, especially for young brothers and sisters.

At Last

Baby can at long last retrieve toys that are tied to his high chair or walker. This is a sign of beginning problem solving, and Baby enjoys practicing this new accomplishment.

76 Trombones

Musical instruments provide exciting experiences for Baby. Bells, tambourines, and sand blocks can be purchased or easily made. In order to make sand blocks, cover several wooden blocks with sandpaper and use a small drawer knob for a handle. A tambourine can be made by lacing two aluminum pie pans together with a string of jingle bells so that the bells are around the edges. Baby will enjoy playing along with a song like John Philip Sousa's "Stars and Stripes Forever."

All in a Row

Wooden clothespins are great baby toys. Just dumping them from their bag is a lark. And there are many other great games that can be played with clothespins.

Line them up on the edge of a loaf pan and let Baby take them off and drop them into the pan.

A plastic container can be combined with the pins for a great game of "Dropping In and Shaking Out." Hard work for Baby, but what satisfaction.

Catchall

By now there are lots of odd pieces of games that no longer exist among Baby's toys. These odds and ends can be stored in a dump can, solely intended, as the name implies, for dumping. Baby will enjoy emptying and filling this container of goodies. A large plastic food container makes a great "dumper," but any container will do. Add a few new treasures such as fabric squares, junk mail, and a ring box with a little cereal inside to reward Baby's thoroughness.

Snap, Pop

If you have more money than time, giant plastic pop beads are an inexpensive learning toy for Baby. They make great necklaces, bracelets, and crowns.

Plumber's Special

An eight-to-ten-inch section of clear plastic hose (3-in. diameter) or pipe with edges that have been smoothed can be a versatile baby toy. Show Baby how to drop small objects through the pipe so he can watch them fall. Try whispering through the pipe or blowing gently.

Buy extras for the bath and beach.

Sock Bottle

Cut a medium-sized plastic bottle about 6 inches from the bottom. Now, using the bottom half, pull an old sock up over the bottle's bottom. What you have is a safe, intriguing toy for Baby, a mystery bottle. Fill the bottle with several of Baby's small toys—blocks, rattles, or jingle bells on an elastic wristband. Show Baby how to put his hand into the bottle and pull out a treasure.

Not Too Young

Baby is not too young to enjoy coloring with felt tip markers (nontoxic and nonpermanent color) or crayons. If possible, use slick finish paper; it will make the most of his marking efforts. He will need your help at first to get the idea of marking, but will be excited to see the results of these efforts.

Painting

Your baby will enjoy painting with stubby half-inch pastry brushes. A little chocolate pudding, colored whipped topping, or tomato sauce will make a great paint. A roll of masking tape can be used to attach a small pot-pie paint pan to Baby's high-chair tray.

Watching the World

Babies enjoy looking out of the window. If you have glass patio doors, Baby can safely look out while he is in his walker or jump seat. Placing Baby securely in his high chair in front of a window will also allow him to visually explore his neighborhood between outings.

Talk Time

Baby is just beginning to discover a new toy, the telephone. By playing the telephone game, Baby gets the idea of conversation.

Toy telephones are inexpensive and can provide hours of fun. Help Baby by playing "Hello" together.

Once Baby becomes interested in phones, remember to keep the real phone out of reach. It may end up off the hook if you don't.

Rag Bag

A basket of cloth scraps of various textures and colors will surely be scattered all over the room, but Baby will have great fun with them. Add several features and little bits of yarn, too.

Take Time

Take the time now to record some of your favorite anecdotes about Baby. There are only a few months left before Baby will enter his toddler years.

_____

_____

_____

_____

_____

Just the Right Size

Baby is becoming a climber and trying to get into or on everything. He will enjoy being able to climb into a low child's chair. One of the safest types is a molded plastic cube chair. These versatile cubes come in sets of three. Depending on which surface is up, the cube is a very low chair, a slightly higher chair, or a table. The three together make a colorful table and chairs that Baby can use now and throughout his preschool years. They are sold at educational supply stores.

Stairs

Baby is ready and interested in practicing going upstairs. Stairs are a developmental challenge for Baby. The safest way to provide this experience is with his own set of two or three low steps that he can safely negotiate.

Anyone handy with tools can build a set, or you can make them from cardboard boxes that have been weighted by filling with newspapers. The steps can be covered with colorful contact paper or vinyl wallpaper. They will provide Baby with safe climbing practice.

Here's a Ball

Here's a finger play for Baby. Just use your fingers to make balls of graduated size as you say the simple words and count. The first ball is formed with thumb and index finger, the second ball with two hands, and the third ball by both arms. Help Baby make the movements, too.

Here's a ball,
and here's a ball,
and here's a great big ball!
Let's count them,
One, two, three.

Roll the Ball

Simple but fun, roll a ball to Baby. He will enjoy sitting straddle-legged across from you as you roll the ball back and forth. Brothers and sisters can enjoy this game, too. Knowing that Baby likes playing ball may be quite reassuring to them. Maybe Baby's not so bad after all.

ROUTINE TIMES

BATHING

Reminder

While dressing or bathing Baby, sing some of the tunes or play the games (see "Activities, Games, and Songs") that develop an interest in body parts. Baby will play a real role in these games now and may try to say the words or indicate that he knows what you mean if you give him the opportunity.

Bathtime Safety

Never, never leave Baby alone in the bathtub. While he may look peaceful and content, bathtime is the time to give him your complete attention. Even in only several inches of water, there is real danger.

A rubber bath mat is a good safety precaution. It is reassuring to Baby since its texture is less slippery than the tub's.

Hanging On

Some babies experience temporary fear of the tub at nine months. A time or two in the tub with you might help. An old pair of cotton work gloves will improve your grip.

More Practice

The tub is a fine place to practice handling a cup. Drinking bathwater is not a serious offense, and mess is of little or no concern. Drinking from a cup is still a game. Provide the essential link by bringing Baby's favorite cup to the tub.

SLEEPING

Bedtime Buddy

A small unbreakable mirror attached to Baby's crib where he can see himself can give you a few extra minutes of shut-eye. If a mirror is already part of the crib, move it to a new location and watch Baby amuse himself anew.

Baby's Nap

An important part of successfully bedding Baby down for his nap is establishing a routine and sticking to it. The routine need not be unpleasant, but it must be consistent. Here is a little poem to say as you lay Baby down, cover him, and then snuggle and pat his back a few moments until he falls asleep. This helps Baby know what to expect.

Here's our Baby ready for his nap,
Lay him down in his mother's lap;
Cover him up so he won't peep,
Rock him till he's fast asleep.

FEEDING

Enough Is Enough

Feeding reminder—babies will truly eat only what they need to eat and no more. Unless you, the caregiver, force him to continue, Baby will stop. Yes, you can overfeed Baby! So be alert to his signals. An additional snack or a minimeal is a nutritionally sound and efficient alternative to three big meals.

A Tea Party

Baby will probably develop his cup-drinking skills this month. Fun and learning occur when your little imitator has a tea party with an older sibling. Baby will watch the child use a cup and will copy the action, especially if the beverage is delicious.

Me First

Feeding Baby first can save all members of the family from a lot of frustration. That Baby has very little patience is an understatement. By starting his meal with a few things he can eat independently, the rest of the family may get started before he requires more attention.

Reminder

Do remember to use some of the suggestions from earlier months about ways to secure Baby's dish to his tray when he is practicing his emerging spoon skills, lest you have a disaster.

Spoons

Now that Baby is beginning to use a spoon, there are many special ones from which to select. Most mothers seem to prefer small metal spoons or baby-sized spoons. Spoons with special coatings that are easy on tender gums are nice, too.

Plastic spoons will not work as Baby has more crunch to his bite than you think and may break them.

Bowls

A large plastic soup bowl with sloping sides is the best serving dish for Baby. Its sides allow food to be cornered and forced onto the spoon.

Brown Bag Delight

When fixing Baby's lunches to be eaten away from home, keep portions small, tasty, colorful, and easy to eat. Baby can feed himself better these days.

Many of the best ideas will be inspired by those good hors d'oeuvres sampled at Mom's and Dad's last get-together. Many of these goodies can be made up ahead of time and frozen. Thus lunch can be assembled quickly and will be thawed at room temperature when it's time to eat.

Suggestions for easy lunches include:

Fruit
Applesauce
Fruit cup (your own or canned)
Seedless tangerines
Mandarin orange slices
Banana disks

Vegetables (blanch lightly so still firm, but not impossibly hard)
Carrots and zucchini sticks spread with peanut butter
Broccoli/cauliflower flowerets with a dip
Cherry tomatoes stuffed with cream cheese

Bread and Crackers
Cheese crackers
Toast in fancy shapes (buttered, please)

Bagel in bite-sized pieces
Pita bread cut into wedges
Graham crackers
Animal crackers
Wheat crackers (make your own and add wheat
  germ, cheese, and parsley)
Croutons; for dessert add honey or cinnamon

Miscellaneous
Yogurt with fruit
Cottage cheese with mixed vegetables
Dab of egg salad
Bits of cooked chicken or shrimp
Fingers or chunks of cheese
Spinach balls made with stuffing mix
Peas
Cold rice salad
Peanut butter balls
Cheese puffs
Tapioca pudding
Grated carrot and fruit salad
Thick cereal; oatmeal or farina with fruit and yogurt
Melted cheese sandwiches, open-faced

DRESSING AND CHANGING

Diapering

Some babies may begin to fight you if you try to diaper them lying down. So try the procedure with Baby standing up, holding onto your shoulders. If possible, allow Baby to hand you the diaper and tell him what you are doing and why.

Mother's Little Helper

If Baby is not already helping you, why not encourage him to remove certain items of clothing, but only when you are ready. He can certainly manage shoes, once untied, and probably socks.

Shoes and Socks

Baby can now take off his shoes and often his socks. Sometimes it's important to keep them on. Save the exasperation and double knot! You can also buy bells and infant shoe "barrels" that will serve this purpose.

Shoe Business

Now that Baby is cruising or beginning to take a few steps, try some of these suggestions about his shoes:

—Remember to have Baby try on both shoes with socks that are the correct size. Recheck the fit after four to six weeks; feet grow fast.
—To keep shoes shiny after polishing, paint several thin layers of shellac over the tips. This treatment will protect shoes from nicks and scratches.

Socks Up!

If your baby is walking, he is probably wearing shoes and, of course, socks. To keep those socks from sliding down his ankle and disappearing altogether, place a strip of adhesive tape inside the shoe above the heel.

HELPFUL HINTS

Reminder

If Baby seems uninterested in his toys and other activities, be patient. He is concentrating all his energy on developing his new mobility skills. He may be crawling, cruising, pulling up, or walking, but, regardless of his style, Baby is working hard.

Table Tips

Baby has discovered that he can get many things by pulling. Baby can get himself up and he can bring things down to have a look. With this in mind, rethink the tables and ledges in your home. Beware the fringe or attractive tablecloth edge; be aware of tassels on the end of a runner. For now, it may be best to reposition coverings or to remove them altogether.

Gates

With Baby's cruising, pulling up, and exploring, now is the time to evaluate living and playing sites in the environment in order to determine to which areas you wish to limit him. Are there any areas you want to close off? Someone handy with tools can make a simple gate out of plywood. Such gates are desirable because Baby cannot see further than the top of the barrier. Lattice-type gates are to be avoided, as we have known many a bright, ingenious baby who has learned to climb over by gaining a toehold and vaulting over. A sturdy gate with baby-proofed latches can maximize your child's safety and security and minimize your anxiety.

Diet Planning

As you plan Baby's diet, keep in mind that fruits and fruit juices tend to soften stools. Prunes, apricots, and peaches help to prevent constipation when homogenized milk is introduced. Cheese, milk, highly processed breads, and cereals tend to firm stools. Vegetables and whole grains add needed roughage and bulk. Adequate fluids, including water, are important items in any child's diet.

Out Spot!

Oops! Baby's diaper has leaked on the rug! This common accident needs to be dealt with as quickly as possible. The high alkaline concentration can change the color of the carpet. Be prepared with a premixed solution and a clean sponge.

First, using lukewarm water, sponge the area several times. Blot up as much moisture as possible with a second clean sponge or cloth.

Next, apply a mixture of 1 tsp. white vinegar and 2 tsp. lukewarm water. With a medicine dropper, saturate the spot using a circular motion. Allow the solution to remain on the stain for 15 minutes. Blot up excess solution. Sponge area several times with lukewarm water. The last sponging should follow the direction of the pile. Allow to dry completely.

Emergency Closing

To discourage curious fingers, seal a lower cupboard in a new room or at a friend's home quickly with a short piece of strapping tape.

Bent Out of Shape

Are rubber and plastic toys looking a bit worn and misshapen? Improve their form by dipping them in very hot water for a few minutes. Then restore them to their original proportions.

While at this task, see the suggestions for cleaning plastics.

Keep Plastic Fantastic

Many of Baby's utensils will be made of plastic. Durable as these items can be, they tend to need periodic sprucing up. To keep bottles, bowls, and containers looking fresh, use liquid cleansers that have the kind of mildness yet effectiveness to do a good job on the smoothest surfaces.

Textured plastic responds well to a light sprinkling of cleanser or a hand soap containing pumice particles. Scrub well with a knitted plastic mesh sponge to avoid additional scratches.

Brown Bagging It

For the baby who eats away from home—at a sitter's, day care, or with friends—pack his lunch in one of these unusual ways:

—a backpack/duffel bag
—an artist box (many are plastic)
—a tour pack (check bike shops)
—the classic fisherman's bag with leather fasteners (check sporting goods stores)
—a wicker hamper, perhaps a rectangular or Chinese "wedding" basket (circular shape); line these with vinyl for added durability

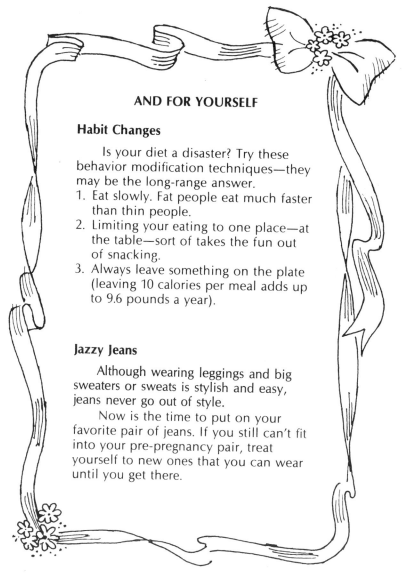

AND FOR YOURSELF

Habit Changes

Is your diet a disaster? Try these behavior modification techniques—they may be the long-range answer.
1. Eat slowly. Fat people eat much faster than thin people.
2. Limiting your eating to one place—at the table—sort of takes the fun out of snacking.
3. Always leave something on the plate (leaving 10 calories per meal adds up to 9.6 pounds a year).

Jazzy Jeans

Although wearing leggings and big sweaters or sweats is stylish and easy, jeans never go out of style.

Now is the time to put on your favorite pair of jeans. If you still can't fit into your pre-pregnancy pair, treat yourself to new ones that you can wear until you get there.

Remember that most of these containers will hold bottles, jars, and plastic bags. They need to be flexible and sturdy at the same time.

Make certain that these "lunch boxes" can be hung or left flat. In warmer weather, an insulated container is probably a good idea. And remember a label with Baby's name and phone number.

That's Mine

Nothing is more frustrating than discovering that Baby and his possessions have become separated while he has been away. Increase the chances of keeping what's rightfully his. It's not too soon to order special name tags for a baby who is away from home. These printed cloth tags can be ordered from stationery stores. Perhaps a stencil with his initials can be applied to his paraphernalia. For the patient parent, an embroidered trademark is nice; a bunny, sun, or strawberry are easily identifiable.

Code System for the Lunch Box Set

Whenever more than two babies get together, the equipment begins to look amazingly alike. To keep confusion to a minimum, may we suggest the following ideas for marking bottles, jars, lunch boxes, and containers that will be washed daily and subjected to the hardest sort of use.

—A ring of several strips of colored plastic tape. Choose a color scheme; tricolors are pleasing.
—An indelible laundry marker
—Nail polish (avoid frosted hues); the brush can do whatever you like
—A kit for marking sporting equipment works well on baby gear

—A stencil with small letters (from the hobby shop)
—A family insignia (think of what some famous designers have done with initials)
—Use puffy paint or glitter paint

Soft Parts

Toss a stiffened pair of plastic pants into the dryer with a batch of towels to soften them. Or, add a little baby oil to the final rinse to keep the plastic from cracking and stiffening.

Leave-taking

Baby has become a careful observer with a memory. Based on clues he has picked up, he can predict when you might leave the house. So, do not attempt to sneak out. It is far better to deal with a few tears and explain your departure than to alarm him by having him suddenly discover that you have already gone.

Keep Calling

Baby is a getaway artist. His movements have grown refined. He can turn on a dime and scurry away. Keep in touch by constant calling. Make this a routine game and insist on a response. Immediately track down a player who stops returning a call.

Spotless Socks

To get the socks of a busy baby clean, try:

—Soaking socks in a solution of washing soda and warm water for 30 minutes before washing
—Boiling white cotton socks briefly in water with a tablespoonful of cream of tartar before washing
—Adding a bit of borax to the wash

PARENTS, FRIENDS, AND ADMIRERS

Jack-in-the-Box

Baby will be captivated by a jack-in-the-box. He will soon learn to anticipate the appearance of Jack. Turning the handle of a musical box will add to his fun.

Remember:

Jack-in-the-box,
You sit so still.
Won't you come out?
Sure I will.

This is also a favorite action song for young children. Hold Baby with his feet on the floor in a partial squat as you recite the poem. Ask Baby to come out and then help him spring from his position. Later he can play this exciting game alone.

Boats

A brother or sister might enjoy making a boat for himself or herself and one for Baby, too. These easy-to-assemble toys start with a milk carton, or a small, 4-oz. juice carton or whipping-cream container. To assemble:

1. Wash carton and dry thoroughly.
2. Close top, staple or tape shut.
3. Add smokestacks, sails, and portholes. Use pieces of paper straw for the smokestacks and masts.
4. Decorate with colored plastic tape.
5. Sail in or out of the tub.
   These boats could become the first portion of a flotilla—all child-designed and created.

Block Covers

One of the greatest dimestore discoveries we've made lately is paper block covers in an inexpensive cutout book. These paper covers—trucks, cars, buildings, etc.—are designed to be used over a variety of empty paper milk cartons. They make a delightful set of blocks.

The nonartistic admirer who wants to make a special gift should keep these in mind. Clear contact paper will make these beauties last.

Baby's Phone List

By now you've discovered that Baby prefers the company of other babies, perhaps to the exclusion of all other people, toys, or routines. So, make a list of Baby's favorites and invite a friend over soon.

NAME	PHONE NUMBER
_____	_____
_____	_____
_____	_____

A Day Outside

An opportunity for a splendid day begins with a lightweight stroller. Take a blanket, pack a light snack for a picnic, and off to the great outdoors.

Your strutting baby will revel in the textures, sights, and sounds of the outdoor world. No matter what the weather, you and Baby will have an exciting, easy day.

Visiting Safely

If Baby will be coming to stay for a week or more, remain his faithful admirer by preparing your home and yourself in the following ways:

—Put all breakables out of reach
—Remove all lightweight furniture
—Cover electrical outlets with tape as a temporary measure
—Beware of all sockets and cords; move as necessary or reposition
—Limit the number of rooms Baby will frequent
—Select a variety of small items from your kitchen and put them in a basket or box ready for use when Baby gets bored
—Have a card table ready to use as an instant gate (to block off a stairway, etc.); place a heavy chair behind the table
—Make a note of the phone number of a trusted baby-sitter so that you and Baby's parents can arrange a night out

These measures will be greatly appreciated by Baby and will allow you to show your hospitality and concern in practical ways.

Baby Photography

Babies and children are the most photographed of all subjects. Successful child photography involves nothing more than capturing on film the spirit of childhood. Infant pictures often have this quality because babies are not as aware of the camera as older children; they're not as easily distracted.

Don't try to direct the action, rather capture the child involved in the activity of his choice. Picture series showing complete stories can be especially effective. Since most babies repeat enjoyable activities, the opportunities to snap the action are ample.

Lower the level of your camera so that it is even with the child's eyes, giving you Baby's perspective of the world.

Needlework

A piece of needlepoint that captures faithfully one of Baby's artworks can be a gift of love. This can easily be done by reproducing the artwork on the needlepoint canvas with acrylic paint after tracing the outline onto it with carbon paper. Maybe not the professional way, but it works. This can also be done with embroidery.

These masterpieces could also be reproduced onto your favorite child's clothing.

Picture Books

Colorful picture books such as *The Three Little Kittens* or *Animals and Their Babies* are good beginning storybooks for Baby. These books, made of sturdy, wipeable cardboard, are welcome gifts that a friend can send across the miles to surprise Baby and his family.

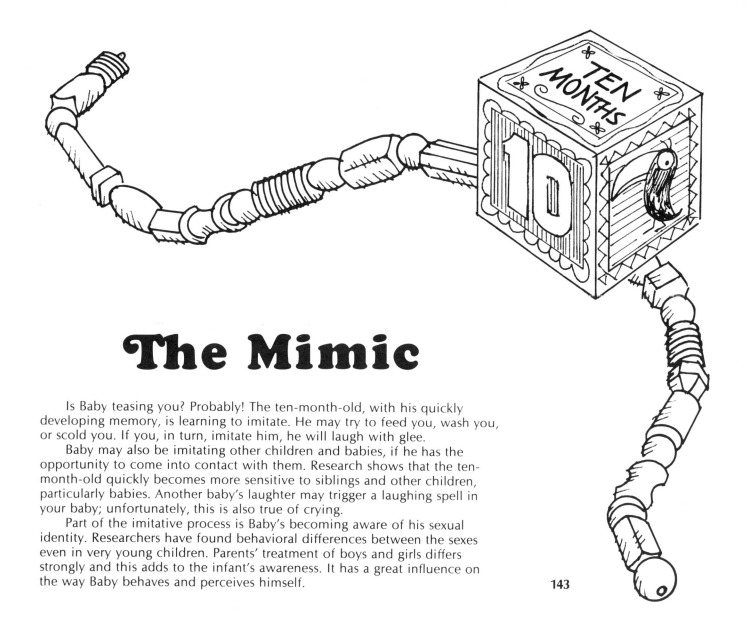

The Mimic

Is Baby teasing you? Probably! The ten-month-old, with his quickly developing memory, is learning to imitate. He may try to feed you, wash you, or scold you. If you, in turn, imitate him, he will laugh with glee.

Baby may also be imitating other children and babies, if he has the opportunity to come into contact with them. Research shows that the ten-month-old quickly becomes more sensitive to siblings and other children, particularly babies. Another baby's laughter may trigger a laughing spell in your baby; unfortunately, this is also true of crying.

Part of the imitative process is Baby's becoming aware of his sexual identity. Researchers have found behavioral differences between the sexes even in very young children. Parents' treatment of boys and girls differs strongly and this adds to the infant's awareness. It has a great influence on the way Baby behaves and perceives himself.

Baby's fine-motor skills are developing noticeably this month. Although you may not always notice it, Baby is distinguishing between what he does with his left and right hands. The hand he uses for sucking is often his passive hand; he leaves the other free for exploring and manipulating. And explore he does, particularly with his index finger. He is interested in probing and poking everything, and is particularly delighted when he can insert his finger into something. Now it becomes especially important to cover plugs and sockets, and to remove from harm's way any utensils, etc., that might cause an injury.

Baby is adding gestures to his words. He may wave "bye-bye," shake his head "no," or smack his lips to "eat." Sometimes these words and gestures are practiced to the extent that they lose their practical meaning and become a nonsense game for Baby.

Although Baby's ninth month motor lull will probably continue, he may begin "cruising." This is when Baby walks along the furniture, steadying himself with a hand-over-hand procedure. Some babies develop this preliminary to walking, others don't.

ACTIVITIES, GAMES, AND SONGS

A Ball for Baby

This month baby will enjoy playing with a clear plastic ball with moving objects inside. Baby will be interested in this object-within-an-object concept.

Music Magic

Now that Baby has the idea that strings are to pull, he will enjoy an assortment of musical toys that "talk" when their strings are pulled. He will enjoy most pull toys that make a noise.

Fit Togethers

Look around the house for the interlocking things that might make safe stacking toys for Baby. He is very interested in putting things inside each other. Measuring cups are the most obvious, but certainly not the only, household items that can be used this way. Anything that is safe and comes in graduated sizes will delight Baby.

Baby Toss

Baby is learning to throw. A variety of colorful beanbags can make throwing great fun. Since Baby is aware of differences in texture, fill the bags with several different materials—split peas, lima beans, macaroni, navy beans, etc. This will give Baby things to compare and problems to solve. You might slip in a bell or two as a surprise.

Make sure that the beans are securely inside and will stay there. A double lining is a good precaution.

Bags can be made up in a variety of shapes, from a simple square to a frog.

Having something into which to throw the bags makes this game more fun. Depending on the time you want to spend, let Baby toss the bags into a wastebasket or onto a homemade beanbag toss face.

Let Me Get to It!

Remember the storage ideas from earlier chapters? As you start to rearrange Baby's things so he can take a more active role, consider recycling the ideas for toy storage. Arrange his toys so that he has access to them.

A "Sit In"

The rubber tub that came with your changing table or that you used for Baby's first baths can become a favorite toy. Baby will enjoy climbing in and out of it, or filling it with toys and then dumping them out. A plastic milk crate is also great fun, as is a cardboard box.

Roll the Ball

Rolling balls back and forth is a favorite game at this age. This is a great way for older brothers and sisters to play with Baby. It is also a good group game for several babies.

Hiding Game

Now that Baby knows that objects have permanence, that they exist even when they are not in view, hiding games have taken on new meaning. Baby will search with new determination for the hidden toy. Baby rarely tires of hide-and-seek. There are endless variations—hide the toy, you hide, Baby hides, etc. All are fun.

Building

Baby is beginning to learn about tower building. It's time to bring out blocks of heavy cardboard or wood instead of the cloth ones. The latter can still be used for throwing and squeezing.

At first, Baby will need to watch you and others to get the idea of building, but, as we all know, he is a great mimic. Soon building will come into its own.

Let's Try It Again

It's time to review some of the songs and finger games you've been playing. Baby can now take an active part. Remember "Just Like Me," from Chapter 5? Now Baby can initiate the game and you follow. Or how about "Pat-a-Cake," (Chapter 7). Here is a new one. It involves a little more activity but is sure to become a favorite.

CUP OF TEA

Here's a cup
  (form cup with one hand),
And here's a cup
  (form cup with other hand),
And here's a pot of tea
  (form teapot with both hands).
Pour a cup
  (pouring motion),
And pour a cup
  (pouring motion),
And have a drink with me
  (pretend to drink).

Squat and Jump

Baby's interest in his new upright position and in a sense of movement makes this game special fun. Hold Baby under the arms while he is standing on a table or chair. Show him how to relax and bend his knees as you say "squat." Then, when you say "jump," help him jump. This can be played until your arms say "no more." You can add excitement and anticipation by adding a buildup such as "are you ready" or "get ready."

Baby Reads, Too

Hear the long series of syllables that Baby says as he looks at picture books? He's reading to you. Do read and discuss pictures with Baby often and allow him to join in. Baby understands much more than he can say. A love for and interest in books is an important step toward becoming a good reader.

Snap Caps

Gather an assortment of plastic bottles, small boxes, and their corresponding lids and tabs. With a piece of elastic and two plastic curtain rings, put the containers and lids together so that the rings are on the top side of the lid and bottom of the jar or box. String the elastic between the rings, through the inside of the container. Allow enough elastic so that when Baby pulls the ring the lid will snap to the container.

Direction Game

With Baby's receptive or understanding vocabulary he can now follow a few simple directions. This is very pleasing to everyone and can be great fun. You can begin to develop this new skill in simple games. For example, empty a basket or box of familiar toys onto the floor close to Baby. Now, while you hold the basket, ask Baby to bring you each item to refill the basket. Accept any object Baby brings. He is learning the concept of *bring me,* not that of identifying all the objects correctly. Just say, "Yes, you brought me a block," etc.

Poke Carton

Baby likes to explore holes and crevices with his probing forefinger. Use an egg carton to develop an easy game for Baby. To the inside lid of the carton, directly in line with each egg cup, glue some texture or object that would intrigue an exploring finger— fur, feathers, sandpaper, double-faced plastic tape. Securely tape the carton closed. With a sharp knife, cut a hole in the bottom of each egg cup through which Baby can stick his finger. Now allow Baby to discover this new game.

Outside

Playing outside is a delight for Baby. He will enjoy crawling and cruising about, but do keep an eye on him as he will try to eat grass, leaves, dirt, dead bugs, and anything else he may find. Although a little will not hurt him, it's a good idea to police the play area before Baby arrives.

Instant Toys

Band-Aid boxes are always fun toys—just the way they are with their easy to fasten tops and cozy storage space. Infants love to bang them, open them, shut them, and fill and empty them.

Recycling

Some of the earlier toys you have put away can now be recycled and used by Baby in a different way. He will enjoy having new toys every now and then, rather than too many all at once. Rattles can now be great drumsticks and teething beads something to dress up in.

Take-Aparts

Baby loves to take things apart, but, like most of us, he can't put together many of the things he took apart with ease. Take-apart games that are great fun include sorter boxes, puzzles, undressing dolls, and preschool toolbenches. Many of the safe but more sophisticated toys may be introduced now for their take-apart properties. Later they can be used for their other functions.

Painting

Now that Baby finger paints and uses a pastry brush, you might try several new ideas. Use adhesive tape to tape together three or four cotton swabs to use as a brush. Or, Baby might find an old toothbrush appealing.

Reassurance

Mothers of infants who paint with food report that their babies do not seem to play with their food more than do children who do not paint with food. Babies are smarter than that; they know the difference between mealtime and playtime. There does seem to be an earlier interest in self-feeding, however, on the part of babies who paint with food.

New Challenge

If Baby enjoyed playing with clothespins on a loaf pan last month, now is the time to add additional challenge to this game. Mix in a few spring-type pins for him to play with.

Winter Alternative

Flour or cornmeal play can be a winter alternative to water play. Place Baby in a wading pool on a discarded shower curtain or old sheet. Now give Baby a dishpan with about a cup or two of cornmeal or flour in the bottom. Add a few simple objects such as several cups, a funnel, plastic comb, etc. When Baby is finished, brush him off and shake the curtain or sheet outside. The birds will love you.

Paper Magic

Babies love paper. Keep a box of scraps for Baby. Include waxed, tissue, wrapping, cardboard, cellophane, brown, and flocked paper. On a day when nothing seems to interest Baby, this box might hit the spot.

Greeting Cards

Go ahead and save all those cards you receive and hate to throw away. Baby will appreciate them almost as much as you did. He likes cards for all occasions and will get lots of practice turning pages as he inspects them, especially if you seem interested, too.

Cards are also a great source for homemade storybook pictures. Cut out the rabbit, add a cotton tail, and you have the first page of a pat-and-touch book.

Doll Bath

Baby will enjoy giving his dolls a dunking in a dishpan. A few inches of water will be enough. Add a washcloth or sponge and maybe some bubbles. If you watch, you'll get a good imitation of Baby's interpretation of his own bath routine.

Game Chart

What games does Baby initiate?

_____

What games does Baby like best?

_____

What games does he play with siblings and friends?

_____

What games does he play with men?

_____

What games does he play alone?

_____

ROUTINE TIMES

BATHING

Steamy

If Baby's baths are steaming up the bathroom or kitchen, fill the tub or sink with a couple of inches of cold water before adding the hot water. This will keep windows and mirrors clean and clear.

The Duck

The classic bath toy and frequent companion of babies and young children is the rubber duck. Today ducks come in many colors, sizes, and materials. The very best duck floats and is not too tippy.

Here is a perky poem to share with Baby while he plays with his duck in the bath.

My-oh-my-oh-my what luck,
Here he comes, my rubber duck.
While I get my daily scrub,
Float him with me in the tub.
Stroke his back
And he will quack.
Rub a dub-dub.
Rub a dub-dub.

Faucet Fascination

Now that Baby is bathing in the tub, take this additional safety measure. Wrap the shiny faucet, a source of fascination, with a washcloth once the water has been drawn. Baby will be protected from touching a hot fixture and, should he wiggle, he will avoid a bump.

Tender Touch

Don't forget those little niceties. A squirt of baby powder or a splattering of lotion is an experience guaranteed to get a positive response. Sometimes we tend to skip these things as Baby grows older, but now is the time when Baby really appreciates them.

SLEEPING

PJs

Be very careful about sleepwear you choose for Baby. Sleeping bags and long nightgowns will get caught under his feet and may cause a baby who has begun to pull up to stumble and hit his head against the rail of the crib. Creepers or loose-fitting garments will allow greater freedom.

Night Owl

Baby may suddenly have become a night owl. The level of energy expended during the day may rouse him long after he has been put to bed. Parents who have just gotten used to a child's sleeping through the night may not appreciate this new routine. While there is little you can do to reverse this trend, do not promote this break in his schedule. Do not, for example, feed your wide-eyed baby. With small amounts of attention and a pat of affection, Baby will probably go back to sleep.

FEEDING

Don't Eat Too Fast!

By now Baby is undoubtedly fully involved with his own feeding. This messy process is not to be rushed. Baby may take anywhere from twenty to forty-five minutes to sample, fiddle with, and finally consume his meal.

Give Baby an opportunity to begin the meal by feeding himself. Later you may decide when it's time to help him finish.

Baby Utensils

Use plates and bowls with edges so that Baby has a surface against which to push his spoon. To keep plates or dishes from sliding away, attach small suction cups to their bottoms. For a change, present a meal in a TV tray, small baking pan, or colored paper plates or bowls.

A Drinking Problem?

Encourage neat drinking habits by pouring only a small amount of liquid into Baby's cup. Refill often.

Try a straw if Baby seems to be having trouble. Watch closely. He may not catch on.

We know of one mother who guided her baby's drinking by allowing her to use a sugar bowl. The baby held one handle, Mom the other.

Cleanup Tips

Baby usually finds feeding an absorbing and entertaining experience. It's all fine except for cleanup. Here are two ideas that should involve him and make the later part of the process relatively painless.

1. Oil him up! A thin, glistening layer of petroleum jelly or baby oil applied to cheeks and chin will protect skin and make cleanup quick.
2. Hand Baby a washcloth and let him spruce himself up. You may decide to finish the job, but Baby will appreciate a head start on the task.

Bibs

To cover, catch, and absorb is the aim of the bib. So, for a change of pace, tie on an old bandana or a lobster bib (share yours after the feast).

In an emergency, use safety pins and several layers of paper towel with a bottom layer of aluminum foil. Mold a drop catcher from a sheet of foil cut longer than the toweling.

Eating Song

To the tune of "Baby Bumble Bee":

I'm eating all the green peas I can see.
They're round and small and green as they can be.
So I'm eating all the green peas I can see.
Yummy, yummy, in my tummy,
Good for me!

DRESSING AND CHANGING

Ask for Help

Baby can begin to speed the routine of dressing if you give him adequate information. Remember that it is easier to pull down than push up. Start a

T-shirt over his head and ask that he pull it down and push his arms through the holes. These directional terms are ones he will soon begin to appreciate.

Fancy Patch

The knees and bottoms of Baby's pants will soon start to show wear and tear. Patches on his corduroy coveralls can be a source of pleasure with a little imagination. Use prints, textures, or metallic-appearing mylar fabric for these reinforcements.

Stepping Out

You can buy inexpensive non-slip toe and heel pads to put on the bottom of dress shoes. Put strips of adhesive tape on the bottom of Baby's socks to make them non-slip if Baby is cruising around in his socks.

Shoe Biz

If Baby is crawling, he may require only socks or stockings. Soft slippers plus socks will keep toes warm if it's cold. Should Baby be a beginning cruiser, he may be pleased with soft booties or sneakers.

The Terrific Star Chart

Your little achiever deserves the recognition that comes with recording, so get a pen or pencil and jot:

Baby's latest accomplishment:

_____

Dressing/undressing skills:

_____

Dining habits:

_____

Social skills/parlor tricks:

_____

HELPFUL HINTS

Develop Antennae

Don't be surprised to find Baby climbing upstairs, taking things apart on top of a table, etc. Silence is no longer golden (unless Baby is asleep); nowadays it's a state worth checking.

Baby, Books, and You

Baby deserves to have his own "working library." Develop one that will satisfy his fondness for variety and color by saving old magazines, catalogs, and worn-out children's books. Read a magazine together: an old one for Baby and a current one for you. After all, Baby wants to do as you do. Perhaps he prefers your lap over his own chair or the floor.

Reading out loud, no matter what the material, will please Baby; in fact, he will probably join in. This experience with books is the best sort of imitation and is educational as well.

An excellent way to limit Baby and save yourself from repeatedly reshelving your own collection of books is to pack them very tightly on the shelves. Those tricky fingers can be foiled.

Reminder

Baby is going through many impressive developmental changes. He is far from the predictable infant of a few months ago. Baby is capable of all manner of unexpected feats because of his mobility, agility, probing forefinger, and iron grasp.

The Talker

The best way to help Baby develop his language skills is for you to listen attentively. Response is important, too. Answering Baby in an appropriate adult manner will enhance his speech and language patterns.

Careful listening in the next few weeks may yield the "magic moment"—hearing Baby's first words. Even if this first word is not a real word, you will know it's what you've been waiting for because it will be used on an occasion when it clearly has specific meaning.

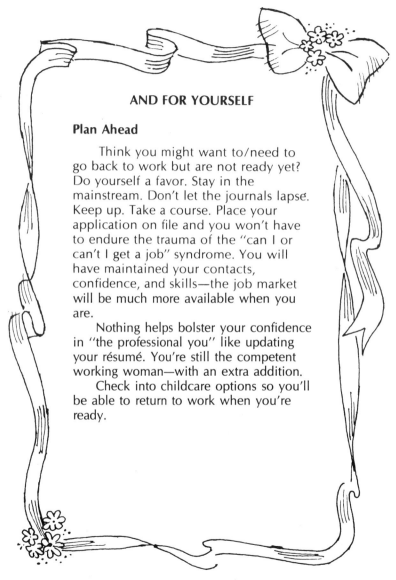

AND FOR YOURSELF

Plan Ahead

Think you might want to/need to go back to work but are not ready yet? Do yourself a favor. Stay in the mainstream. Don't let the journals lapse. Keep up. Take a course. Place your application on file and you won't have to endure the trauma of the "can I or can't I get a job" syndrome. You will have maintained your contacts, confidence, and skills—the job market will be much more available when you are.

Nothing helps bolster your confidence in "the professional you" like updating your résumé. You're still the competent working woman—with an extra addition.

Check into childcare options so you'll be able to return to work when you're ready.

Planter Priorities

Ah, plants—beautiful to behold, living things to nurture, accents to your decor, but a hazard to Baby. The moving, cruising ten-month-old may well be attracted to those robust plants. Some growing things are particularly poisonous. Others will give the taster a stomachache. Check with a reputable florist or greenhouse if you have questions.

Here is a partial list of plants you should keep out of Baby's way.

Azalea
Buttercup
Calla lily
Daffodil
Daphne
Diffenbachia
Elephant ear
Holly
Iris
Poinsettia
Oleander
Rhubarb
Wisteria

Don't let Baby drink water in which cuttings have been soaking, suck plants or stalks, or nibble leaves—these are toxic substances.

Unusual Appetite

Pica is a medical term given to a condition that occurs with some infants. These babies need special observation and protection because they crave inedible substances such as crayons, chalk, plaster, dirt, cigarettes, and paint chips.

A true case of pica is uncommon, but talk to your doctor if you feel that your child is unusually fond of eating nonfood substances.

Handiest Helper

The tool never to be without, especially now, is a large safety pin. Somehow having one or more available makes a busy parent or caregiver feel more secure. They are great for quick bibs, jacket closing, and other emergencies.

Patches

Keep patches on permanently by pinking the edges of iron-on tapes or patches. These are fun for Baby if cut in amusing shapes—free-form, geometric, animals, flowers, or favorite toys.

Netting

If you are an apartment dweller with a balcony or if you have a patio or deck that is aboveground, protect your baby by installing some sort of barrier. It takes a mobile infant little more than a split second to journey from the inside to the outside.

The fencing used around these outdoor places often has openings large enough for Baby to fit through. Check a hardware store for mesh nettings, chicken wire, or plastic screens that could be real lifesavers.

Strategy

Like most people, babies have trouble with impulse control. Moods rise and fall, tempers flare. Punishment is not very effective at this stage; in fact, it is a drain on adult energy. The best measure is prevention; plan ahead to avoid scenes.

Fingerprints!

Touching is a way of learning about the environment. Baby is not only touching everything, but he is also leaving his marks. Try some of these tricks to remove unwanted fingerprints.

—Chunks of stale bread can be rubbed over the marks
—A little dab of toothpaste on a damp cloth is a good way to remove fingerprints from the TV screen; rinse well
—A weak solution of baking soda and water makes a good spot remover

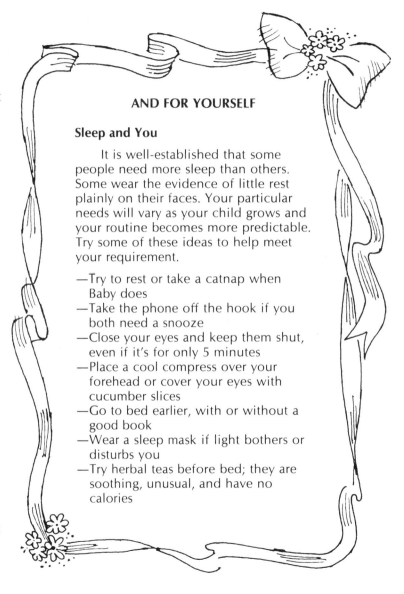

AND FOR YOURSELF

Sleep and You

It is well-established that some people need more sleep than others. Some wear the evidence of little rest plainly on their faces. Your particular needs will vary as your child grows and your routine becomes more predictable. Try some of these ideas to help meet your requirement.

—Try to rest or take a catnap when Baby does
—Take the phone off the hook if you both need a snooze
—Close your eyes and keep them shut, even if it's for only 5 minutes
—Place a cool compress over your forehead or cover your eyes with cucumber slices
—Go to bed earlier, with or without a good book
—Wear a sleep mask if light bothers or disturbs you
—Try herbal teas before bed; they are soothing, unusual, and have no calories

Orange Juice

To remove orange juice stains, presoak in cold water with enzyme-based detergents. This will lift the stains from the front of Baby's T-shirts.

Fido's Dish

The young activist has undoubtedly discovered your pet's dish. We know of one baby who surprised his parents by engaging in water play in liquid he found in the bowl. Splashing about and slapping the floor was a source of considerable pleasure and some mess. A great game idea, but a better idea is to plan ahead by selecting a container and setting the scene with an oilcloth.

And What About Fido?

Your pets are probably not as understanding as you are about having their mealtimes interrupted. To avoid mess and possible injury to Baby, plan to serve the pets in an inaccessible area.

By now your kitty litter should be out of Baby's reach.

PARENTS, FRIENDS, AND ADMIRERS

An Assist for Brothers and Sisters

Siblings may find dealing with a busy baby a trial. Older brothers and sisters may find that their possessions are suddenly no longer safe from a curious and cruising infant. Detouring Baby by taking items away seems to create a game situation. Baby thinks it's all a lark and is back for more, much to the frustration of his siblings. Your help in providing insight and strategies can promote understanding and harmony.

An Elephant for Lunch

As a special lunch treat or a snack, delight Baby and his siblings with a menagerie of animals. Use your imagination or an animal-shaped cookie cutter to shape the bread. If you use two slices of bread, the animals will stand by themselves. Spread toast with cream cheese or peanut butter. Fill sandwiches with any of Baby's favorites.

Dog and Cat Alert

Fido and Kitty will require more attention and affection from you in the coming weeks. Now that Baby can squeeze, poke, and pull with greater efficiency, your pets may find themselves in greater peril. Baby may decide that he can really chase this prey. Keep alert to safeguard both Baby and pet. It's not a good idea to leave these two alone.

We assume that the pet's shot record is up to date and complete just in case a nip occurs.

Grandpa's Light Show

This simple game involves light, shadows, and hands. In a darkened room, project a beam of light from a projector or a flashlight against a wall. Then make shadow animals with hands and props. This event recently staged by a grandpa thrilled Baby and siblings alike.

Grandma's Game

One granny delighted her grandchildren with this old finger play:

Here are Granny's spectacles
  (fingers form glasses placed up by eyes).
Here is my cap
  (bring fingertips together and place over head).
This is the way I fold my hands
  (fold hands)
And put them in my lap
  (place hands in lap).

Better Than a Kiss

With the many bumps, tumbles, and crashes Baby is taking these days, a collection of decorated Band-Aids makes a thoughtful gift. Make your own by keeping a package of self-adhesive dots next to your supply of Band-Aids. Add stars, stripes, or drawings with permanent magic markers. This surprise for Baby could be the beginning of a family tradition and a must for a toddler. Take a few with you when you travel by car or carriage. You could decorate each Band-Aid as needed while Baby watches.

Busy Baker

All of us are concerned about the amount of sugar children eat. For those who would love to bake for Baby, may we offer this compromise? Try your famous cupcake or cookie recipe in a two-bite size pan often used for making candies or dainty teacakes. These delicious miniatures can get past even the most finicky mom.

A Quickie

A nimble-fingered admirer can knit or crochet a mitten string for Baby in a matter of minutes. All but impossible to find, these cords are indispensible for keeping mittens and other small items together.

Approach Is Everything

For friends and admirers who have few opportunities to visit Baby, here are some time-tested techniques for approaching Baby.

—Eyes first! Catch Baby's eye and smile.
—Win a smile! Get him to smile at you. Make a few funny faces.
—Speak! Say something to him. Use Baby's name. Say, "Hi, Chris, how are you, what are you doing?"
—Encourage him to come to you. If Baby seems reluctant, slowly move toward him but *do not* touch him. Continue to talk and smile.
—Get down. Squat or kneel to get on Baby's level.
—Spend time. Speak for a few minutes while on Baby's level. Encourage him to move toward you.

—Share! If you have a surprise (book, toy, etc.), now is the time to present it to Baby. Don't give it away—yet. Don't pick up Baby. Take his hand and see if he will sit down with you and investigate the present you've brought.
—Remember that slow starts often lead to the warmest sorts of relationships. The best things develop over time.

Baby's Feelings Will Be Known

At ten months, Baby shows us his opinions! They are:

EMOTION	EXPRESSED
Delight	_____
Anger	_____
Frustration	_____
Self-satisfaction	_____

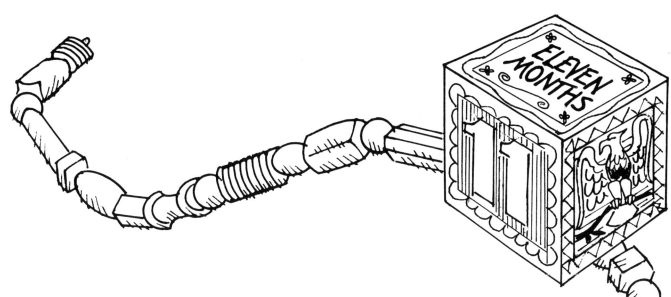

The Little Mechanic

At eleven months, Baby is probably standing alone. He will be very tentative about this at first, letting go of his support for only a moment. He will probably not be upset by his falls if you don't make too much of them. As he becomes more self-confident, Baby may become obsessed with standing and insist on spending most of his time practicing. This is the time to be careful when he is in his high chair or stroller; if you turn your back, he may tumble out.

Baby is developing very nimble, dextrous little fingers. He can probably use his cup fairly well if he holds it in both hands. He can also feed himself, and probably insists upon doing so. In other routines he may not be as helpful. For instance, he probably likes to help you by taking off his socks and untying his shoes. You will notice Baby's new abilities with spindle toys. He may enjoy taking the objects on and off the spindle incessantly, giving those hands practice.

159

Last month's imitation play is more marked now. Baby will follow you from room to room, assisting you in your chores. Encourage him to pick up or dust with you—he'll enjoy it and you'll get more done.

Baby's growing conceptual understanding of his environment can be observed in the way he relates to objects around him. Objects suddenly have definite, different properties. You may catch him swaying his toy airplane in the air, or racing his car along the rug.

Beginning with this month, Baby seems able to really differentiate between good and naughty behavior. He is starting to understand what pleases you and will consciously try to obey you and seek your approval. This may also be the month in which he begins real "testing" behavior; he is interested in knowing the limits you will impose.

ACTIVITIES, GAMES, AND SONGS

Dress-up

Baby is learning to do more for himself. He will enjoy a few dress-up items with which to practice. A diaper bag or purse, hats, and a few shoes, scarves, skirts, or shirts can be added to his play wardrobe. Of course, he may not wear the clothes appropriately, but he will admire himself in the mirror and entertain the entire family with his choice of adornment. Clothes that would fit an older child are the best size choice for this little performer.

Loving

Bring out the rejected stuffed animals. Now that one of Baby's latest tricks is to give affection, hugs, and kisses, he will enjoy showering his affection and tenderness on a multitude of play friends. It's rewarding to see Baby's awareness and imitation of the loving he's learned through your gentle care.

Chair Walker

You may find Baby is only interested in walking and that other activities frustrate him. Because he is a new or developing walker, his balance may not be up to his desire to go. Help Baby by giving him a fast-moving walker to push and hold as he scurries about. Any small wooden chair will do the trick. It can be tipped over so that the back is at an angle to the floor. This chair can then be pushed around the open play area by Baby as he relentlessly practices his walking skills. Felt adhesive dots will protect the chair and floor.

See What I Have

Baby comprehends many phrases such as "Show me what you have" and "Give it to Mommy." Baby is very proud of this new understanding and enjoys practicing these skills in a game. You can make up simple games. Give him simple directions and let him bring things to you.

Funny-Face Game

As you've noticed, Baby delights in mimicking other people's gestures. He can be caught scolding his bear just as you scold him.

You can turn this skill into a hilarious game by playing "Make My Silly Face." A mirror will help Baby get the nose wrinkle, wink, or frown just right. You may find him in front of the mirror some days later playing this funny-face game by himself or with a toy.

Puppet Friends

Remember the hand puppet you used in earlier months? Baby is now ready to try hand puppets on his own hands. You'll need to help him at first, but he will soon enjoy these new friends, especially in front of a mirror. This is also an entertaining game brothers and sisters can play with Baby.

A Ball for Baby

Let Baby play with a football this month. He will enjoy chasing this unpredictable rolling ball with its funny shape and texture.

Me Too

Baby will enjoy a game of flashlight play just like his older friends. A lightweight, disposable flashlight in a dimly lit room can be an excellent baby entertainer. Make sure that there are no removable parts to the flashlight; Baby's a good mechanic, given the opportunity.

Red Nose

Baby is beginning to be aware of the difference between himself and his mirror image. Play "Red Nose" with him to help develop this skill. Place a little blusher on a tissue and rub it on Baby's nose. Then let him see himself in the mirror. Does he notice his nose?

Flannelboard Fun

A flannelboard is a versatile, inexpensive toy. To make one, get a sturdy cardboard box. Cut two sides at an angle, retaining the top and removing the front panel. You will end up with a slanted desk top. Tape the sides so your desk is sturdy. Cover the slanted surface with felt. Because the surface slants, pieces won't fall off.

Simply cut out shapes of colored felt for Baby to arrange on the board. Pictures from magazines or old books can also be included if they are mounted on cardboard and felt is glued to the back of the cardboard. Baby will enjoy patting the picture and shapes onto the board and then peeling them off. Commercially produced items are available at school-supply stores; these include favorite storybook characters and learning sets.

Talk about and identify the objects on the board. Tell stories using the pieces. As you and Baby play with the flannelboard, his language skills will grow.

Teatime

Baby will enjoy a make-believe tea party with you and his stuffed friends. He will especially enjoy feeding them with his cup and spoon or sharing some cereal pieces or cheese squares.

Hinges, Latches, and Hooks

Baby will be intrigued with hinged boxes and cabinet doors. Latches and hooks can also be a source of problem solving. If you are handy with tools, make a busy board for Baby that includes these items. Or, have a friend make one.

Wooden or cardboard boxes, such as cigar boxes, will attract Baby's attention, especially if the box holds some of Baby's small toys.

A utility storage box like the ones used to store nails is also an excellent baby occupier. Its small drawers and many compartments are intriguing to explore. Later this box can be used for more complicated sorting and number games, or for storing childhood treasures.

Color Fun

A simple toy for a problem-solving baby is a clear plastic bottle, particularly one filled with colored water and securely sealed. Add a few pebbles for good measure. Baby will like shaking, turning, and studying this fascinating object. For better buoyancy add one part corn syrup to two parts water.

Turn Toy

Baby loves to point to familiar pictures as you name them together. As a variation of the picture identification game, use a lazy Susan instead of a picture book. Simply cover the tray with paper and paste the pictures of familiar objects around the tray. Baby will enjoy helping you turn the lazy Susan and watching the pictures go around.

Self-Image

Baby's awareness of people is growing. He is noticing subtle details such as eyebrows, eyelashes, and freckles. If he has a baby doll with similar features, it will make comparisons easier. You may notice Baby at play closing the doll's eyelids and then his own eyelids.

Baby's Toys

This little action song will have special meaning for Baby now that he understands some of the words. The more you sing the song, the more fun it becomes.

Here's a ball for baby,
Big and soft and round
  (touch fingertips, forming ball).
Here's baby's hammer,
See how he can pound
  (pound one fist on other).
Here's baby's music,
Clapping, clapping so
  (clap hands).
Here are baby's soldiers,
Standing in a row
  (hold ten fingers erect).
Here is baby's trumpet,
Toot, too-too-too-too
  (pretend to blow trumpet).
Here's the way that baby
Plays at peek-a-boo
  (do peek-a-boo).
Here's a big umbrella,
To keep the baby dry
  (make an umbrella with hands).
Here is baby's cradle,
Rock-a-baby bye
  (pretend to rock a baby in your arms).

Winter Style

One mother decided not to store her child's inflatable beach toys. Instead, she weighted the inflated animals by partially filling them with water. They made lively playmates for her baby to push and poke; he would squeal with glee when they responded to his touch.

Home Movies

If you want an attentive audience for your home movies or slides, try Baby. You'll find he is delighted by the colorful images. He may even recognize his friends or himself. This can be a great game for all. So, don't save these treasures for a once or twice a year showing. Enjoy them often. They will help raise your spirits and remind you that these are the greatest times of your life.

Stories to Read

Baby loves being read to, especially stories that include animals and colorful illustrations. Consider these:

"The Three Little Kittens"
"The Three Bears"
"The Three Little Pigs"

At this stage, Baby is not able to follow a story plot; rather he is enjoying pointing and naming the pictures with you and, most of all, being close to you. Picture books that include clear colorful pictures of familiar objects are also a good choice.

Interlocking Blocks

Bristle blocks are an inexpensive, very versatile toy. These soft, safe interlocking blocks allow

children to stick them together and form all sorts of wonderfully imaginative creations. They are also a good size to drop into all sorts of containers. Babies enjoy carrying these nubby pieces with them.

Hand Puppets

Baby will enjoy hand puppets made on the human hand. There are a variety; all are fun. Here are two easy ones.

1. Make a fist and place eyes on each side of the third knuckle of your index finger. With red paint or lipstick, color the inside of the index finger and thumb so that you have a mouth when you make a fist. If you move your fingers while in a fist, your puppet will look as if it were talking. Be as elaborate as you like; add a wig or a hat. Make a body and hold it in your fist to complete this little puppet person.

2. A second quickie involves making a hat for your thumb out of paper. Now draw a face on the area of the palm below the hat. As you move the thumb, Baby will enjoy watching the dancing, happy face.

ROUTINE TIMES

BATHING

Squeaky Clean

Here are some tips on shampooing Baby's hair.

—Remember to use baby shampoo; it is truly so mild that it doesn't sting when splashed into the eyes.
—Coat Baby's eyebrows and eyelids with a layer of petroleum jelly. This will cause soapy water to drip sideways instead of up and down. Having Baby watch in a mirror while you apply the petroleum jelly will help keep him calm.
—Slip a shower cap out of which the crown has been snipped onto Baby's head. This will reveal the back of Baby's head while protecting the front.

Soapy Sock

Baby will enjoy holding soap if it's in a nonslip sock (one of his). This is one way to let him hold soap and protect him from sampling it. Knot the top of the sock securely.

An Extra Tub

Should you find yourself visiting or traveling or just without a bathtub, try a small inflatable swimming pool. Simply position the pool in the shower stall and bathe baby as usual. Siblings will probably enjoy this novelty, too.

SLEEPING

Bedtime

Your live wire may find winding down an extremely frustrating part of his day. He will not give reliable signals as to when he is ready to rest. Stick with his scheduled bedtime and try this little poem as you make Baby comfortable.

Come little baby (or use Baby's name)
Calls the mother hen.
It's time to take your nap again.
And under her feathers
The little chick creeps.
And she clucks a song
Till he falls asleep.

Stars

Bring a little nighttime magic indoors. Cut several handfuls of stars out of luminous tape, or paint the constellations with a product guaranteed to glow in the dark. Arrange the twinkles on ceiling or walls of Baby's room. Don't forget the moon. Baby will be delighted when the lights go out.

A Few Golden Minutes . . .

If Baby is an early bird, try some of these measures to gain a few minutes of extra rest. Ignoring the jubilant shouts or initial cries of Baby is pointless. Instead make Baby comfortable.

—Change his diaper
—Offer him a drink
—Remove special sleep togs (sleeping bag, sacque, long nightie)
—Let in the light
—Move the crib toward a window; a birdfeeder or treats for feathered friends on a sill will make things more lively
—Supply a favorite toy or two
—Best of all, encourage an older brother or sister to come, stay, and play quietly. Baby can remain in his crib, which keeps both at a safe distance from each other

FEEDING

Worth the Wait

To manage mealtime preparation with a baby requiring distraction, occupy him with treats that will save his appetite.

—Discarded baseball cards
—Magazines, the glossier the better
—Old ribbons from gifts
—A bag with something grand to pull out, perhaps a long chain of knotted fabric strips or scarves

A Straw?

Just for fun, let Baby try a straw. Fruit juices or other healthy beverages are easy to follow in a nearly clear straw. Drink along with Baby to see if he can manage this trick.

Oh, Peanut Butter!

Parents concerned that their children are not getting enough protein should not overlook peanut butter. This very nutritious and comparatively inexpensive food is a real dietary standby. Many commercial brands are made with reduced salt and sugar. Or, make your own.

Combinations Baby will enjoy include:

—Peanut butter and lettuce leaf rollups
—Peanut butter balls with raisin centers rolled in carrot shavings
—Peanut butter with applesauce on toast strips (lady finger style)
—Pineapple tidbits frosted with peanut butter
—A peanut butter boat—long strips of banana filled with peanut butter

An Eating Buddy

If Baby is balking at mealtime, surprise him and invite a friend to join both of you. A doll wearing a bib or a puppet made of washable fabric holding a spoon may make the critical difference.

Carrots, Peas, and Spinach

Don't assume that Baby will not eat a food because he has refused it once. Babies are just beginning to develop preferences for tastes and textures. The best approach is to give him many opportunities to sample and experience foods he initially rejects.

When an item is pushed away, make a mental note to try it again several days later. Combining the new food with favorites is a good way to begin. Baby may relish combinations that are totally unappealing to everyone else. Remember that what Baby eats first has an effect on the taste of the next food. This awareness can work to the advantage of the feeder.

Calculated persistence and a willingness to be flexible seem to be the surest ways to get Baby to eat a well-balanced meal.

DRESSING AND CHANGING

A Dressing Helper

Plan ahead and set up a retrieving game rich in learning possibilities. Place Baby's pants and shirt in a low drawer or in a place he can reach so that he can bring them to you as dressing time approaches. This is an ideal time to help him with vocabulary and language skills.

Birthday Suit

Don't be surprised if you find a fast-fingered Baby who has taken off all his clothes, perhaps even his diaper. Resist an impulse to be angry, for this is actually an accomplishment. Dressing Baby in a one-piece jumpsuit or overalls will help keep this event from becoming a regular occurrence.

Tied!

Baby is definitely able to remove his shoes and socks. To prevent his doing so, try the good old double knot; it still works. Commercial gadgets are

fine, too; the bells and barrels that hold laces are helpful because they identify Baby's whereabouts while keeping shoes on and tied. To get a tighter pull when tying a shoe, put the shoelace into the last eyelet from the outside in.

Changing

Some parents find that keeping a special toy or two—one for each hand—near the changing table takes the "wiggle out of the warrior."

Calamity

Baby is helping with his own dressing, mealtime is a mess, bedtime is all but impossible. Do record this month's routine calamities. Think for a minute and jot down the incident or two during which you might have cried except that they were *so* funny.

_____

_____

_____

_____

_____

_____

_____

HELPFUL HINTS

Reminder

You really can't teach Baby how to walk. Baby will walk when he is ready. All that is necessary is that you provide him with a safe, interesting environment in which he can practice his emerging skills. Lots of tender loving care and encouragement will make a difference.

Exchange, Exchange

This is a fine age to sort through Baby's clothing and gear. Baby clothes are rarely worn, much less worn out, because of Baby's rapid growth. Save a few for Baby to see years from now and give the rest to a consignment store. These stores also sell used toys and baby equipment.

Spend money on good experiences and equipment for Baby rather than on clothes and gently encourage Baby's friends and admirers to do the same.

Fruit Soup

A change of pace for you and Baby is this recipe, delicious hot or cold.
1. In two cups fruit juice soak ½ to 1 cup dried, chopped fruit. (We like apple juice, apples, prunes, grapes, pears, oranges, apricots, and pineapple.) Allow to stand for 2 or more hours. Add honey to taste (1 Tbsp. to start).
2. Bring juice, fruit, and honey to a boil.
3. Mix 2 tsp. cornstarch with 1 tsp. water. Stir into mixture. Blend until mixture thickens.
4. Add 1 tsp. cinnamon.

5. To thicken and make more pudding-like, add more cornstarch. Float a bit of yogurt on top and dust with cinnamon.

An Extra Bed

Need an additional place to bed down a visiting infant, a sick baby, or a bored baby who needs a change of scene? Investigate these choices:

—a blow-up splash pool
—a playpen
—a rented port-a-crib

Another Drier

For families with the time, inclination, and preference for home cooking and food preservation, a fruit drier is a must. Baby and his family can enjoy fruit year round with this inexpensive piece of equipment, which can be found in organic food or hardware stores. When a favorite fruit—apple, peach, pear, apricot, or plum—is in season, an extra box or bag can be preserved without additives. The dried fruit will provide an excellent snack for dessert. It can be easily packed in a lunch bag or taken on trips.

Stroller Safety

Baby has become amazingly strong. More than one child we have known has reared up and pulled a stroller or buggy over on himself. Never, never leave Baby unattended in his carrier. Do not assume that he is safe while you are running an errand. Many strollers are unstable and have protruding parts or sharp edges. Check the weight limit on these portable wonders.

Neat Eatin' Ice Cream

How Baby adores the coldness and flavor of ice cream! If you can't persuade him to eat outdoors, cut a hole in a paper plate or small aluminum meat pan and poke the bottom of the cone through the hole. This is a fine time, too, for a quick mop-up with a premoistened cloth.

Circular Tip

Consider purchasing two plastic lazy Susans. With the growing supply of baby food in open jars, cans, and dishes, these disks will help keep your refrigerator organized. On the kitchen shelf, you can take a quick inventory with a slow spin of the Susan.

Just for Baby

A quick way to make a small table and chair for Baby is to cut down the legs of a piano bench, card table, or end table. Should you locate a small coffee table, no cutting will be necessary, as the table is already the right height. For small chairs, footstools or step-type stools are good alternatives. Preschool-size chairs are available commercially. Baby will enjoy his own furniture and will surprise everyone at how long he will sit in his own place.

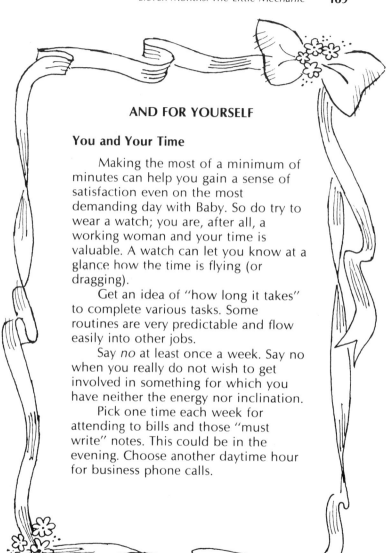

AND FOR YOURSELF

You and Your Time

Making the most of a minimum of minutes can help you gain a sense of satisfaction even on the most demanding day with Baby. So do try to wear a watch; you are, after all, a working woman and your time is valuable. A watch can let you know at a glance how the time is flying (or dragging).

Get an idea of "how long it takes" to complete various tasks. Some routines are very predictable and flow easily into other jobs.

Say *no* at least once a week. Say no when you really do not wish to get involved in something for which you have neither the energy nor inclination.

Pick one time each week for attending to bills and those "must write" notes. This could be in the evening. Choose another daytime hour for business phone calls.

Footloose

Baby receives much information about his world through his feet. These sensations can have an important effect on his learning to balance. Sometimes, it can be beneficial to delay the use of hard-soled shoes for a month or two as Baby experiments with pulling up, standing, or walking. Socks alone can be extremely slippery and dangerous; bare feet or slipper socks with nonslip soles are better choices.

Safety Hook

Bring a bit of peace to the household and install simple latch hooks, out of Baby's reach, of course. Brothers and sisters will especially appreciate this babyproofing technique because their possessions and territories will be protected. From the parent's or caregiver's point of view, this precaution minimizes worry when Baby is off exploring. This is an easy way to set limits.

Jars

Don't be overwhelmed or annoyed by the baby-food jars that may now be cluttering up your kitchen. Save them for a variety of uses throughout the home.

—In the workshop, nail lids onto a board or beneath a wooden shelf. The jars will clearly reveal nuts, bolts, washers, screws, and assorted nails.
—In the sewing room, the jars are ideal for snaps, hooks and eyes, buttons, bobbins, pins, thimbles, and needles.
—For gardeners, the jars are suitable for rooting cuttings or mixing small amounts of feeding solutions.
—For food preservers, the jars are a convenient way to create assortments of jams, jellies, or preserves for gifts.
—Freeze herbs and spices or potpourris in these small containers.
—Young artists will find the jars perfect for paint or water.

An Important Message

Should you plan to be away for the evening or several days, a cassette tape can maintain a link between you and Baby. Caregivers or baby-sitters will find these messages very helpful. Sing a favorite song or two and say good-night as you always do. This will make bedtime easier.

Still Sweet

Good old baking soda still sweetens. Try a solution of water and soda for plastic tablecloths, table mats, bibs, and other baby equipment that needs to be freshened up.

Irons

Hot irons always present a potential safety hazard. Place your hot iron on a back stove burner and make sure the cord is not in Baby's reach when you are cooling your iron.

PARENTS, FRIENDS, AND ADMIRERS

Brother and Sister

To help build a positive relationship between Baby and his siblings, help them discover games they can enjoy playing together. Suggestions include:

—Water play with measuring cups, spoons, funnels, and sponges
—Finger painting with colored dessert whip, pudding, or mashed potato flakes
—Playing "Roll the Ball"

You can also help older children accept Baby and his antics by letting them talk to you about their feelings. A good way to start such a discussion is to read a story about other children and their baby brothers and sisters. We suggest:

Couldn't We Have a Turtle Instead?
   by Judith Vigna
It's Not Fair by Robyn Supraner
I Don't Like Timmy by Joan Hanson
Tommy's Big Problem by Lillie D. Chaffin

Photo Flair

A great gift for Baby's first birthday next month is a personalized baby book from an admirer with photographic flair. A book of pictures of Baby's world would include Baby, his family, his pet, and his special friends. Don't forget his possessions: favorite toys, his cup, his crib, and maybe even his house. Such a book will be a favorite toy and a priceless keepsake, so make this chronicle of Baby durable—a real gift of love.

Baby Hand-Print Cookies

Make up your favorite sugar cookies or use ours, and use the imprint of Baby's hand as a cookie cutter pattern. Simply trace around Baby's hand on cardboard and cut out the pattern. (Baby will let you do only one or two directly from his hand.)

Sugar Cookies

⅔ cup shortening
¾ cup sugar
½ tsp. grated orange peel
½ tsp. vanilla
1 egg
4 tsp. milk
2 cups all-purpose flour
1½ tsp. baking powder
¼ tsp. salt

1. Cream together first four ingredients.
2. Add egg and beat until light and fluffy.
3. Stir in milk. Add remaining ingredients.
4. Divide dough in half. Chill one hour.
5. On a lightly floured surface, roll dough to ⅛-in. thickness. Cut out hands with a knife. Bake on greased cookie sheet at 375° F for about 6 to 8 minutes. Cool slightly and remove from sheet to cool. Makes about 2 dozen cookies.
6. Decorate with frosting, nails, or rings, as desired.

Baby and his family will enjoy these good-tasting cookies. This pattern can be used with bread dough, too. You might want to save a bread dough sample to shellac and make into a kitchen plaque for an admirer.

Birthday Present

Start now if you are planning to make or build a gift for Baby's very first birthday. Remember to make clothing somewhat larger than his current size—he's still growing fast.

Special Day

Brothers and sisters deserve a day with you and without Baby. Do plan a very special time together when you can be all theirs. How about a trip to the ice cream parlor, the zoo, or a fast-food restaurant after the park? It will make them much more willing to have Baby come along most of the time if they know they can look forward to these regular, special times.

Bronzing Baby's Shoes

Want to preserve Baby's first shoes without spending a lot of money? Fill them with plaster of Paris and spray with gold, silver, or bronze paint. You'll be delighted with their professional look.

Help the Baby-Sitter

Even the best baby-sitter will do a better job if he or she has more knowledge about his or her charges. You might want to show to your sitter the following list, or copy and post it for him or her. Do add your own ideas. Update often as Baby grows.

Best snack _____

Where _____ How Many _____

Favorite music _____

Location _____

How Baby likes to be comforted _____

_____

Bedtime ritual _____

_____

Favorite toy _____

Books to read and talk about _____

_____

_____

Location _____

Baby-sitters need ideas about how best to help Baby enjoy himself while you are away. Besides giving information on Baby's routines, tell them about Baby's favorite games and songs. Keep a few of these on index cards to share with the baby-sitter; this can make the evening more fun for everyone. Encourage baby-sitters to think of some of the favorite songs they remember from their early years and to jot them down. You and Baby will enjoy learning some new ones, too. Baby will soon begin to associate the baby-sitter's arrival with song-and-game times, making your departure much easier.

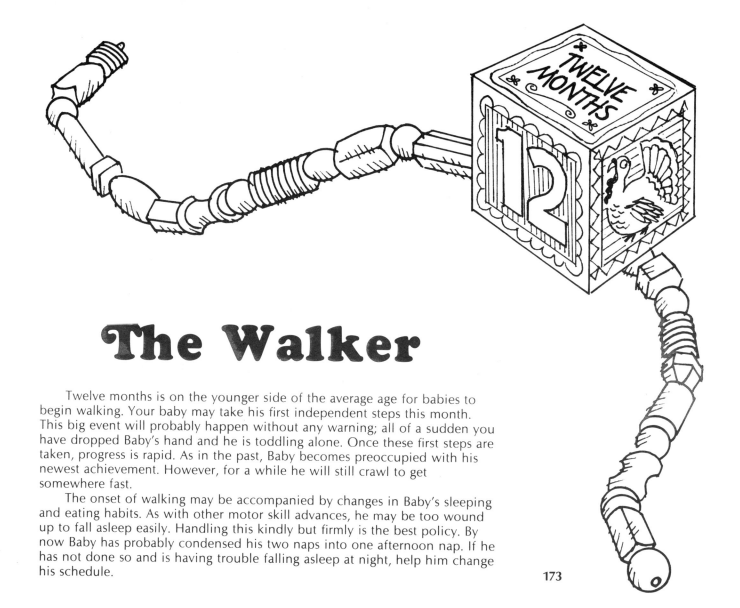

The Walker

Twelve months is on the younger side of the average age for babies to begin walking. Your baby may take his first independent steps this month. This big event will probably happen without any warning; all of a sudden you have dropped Baby's hand and he is toddling alone. Once these first steps are taken, progress is rapid. As in the past, Baby becomes preoccupied with his newest achievement. However, for a while he will still crawl to get somewhere fast.

The onset of walking may be accompanied by changes in Baby's sleeping and eating habits. As with other motor skill advances, he may be too wound up to fall asleep easily. Handling this kindly but firmly is the best policy. By now Baby has probably condensed his two naps into one afternoon nap. If he has not done so and is having trouble falling asleep at night, help him change his schedule.

Baby's newest sounds and words relate to his expanding understanding of object classification. He may identify animals or vehicles by making the sounds they make. Don't let Baby fool you; he understands many of the things you are saying to him.

The awareness of his own behavior, which began about a month ago, is increasing as toddlerhood approaches. He is testing limits constantly. He may even begin having real tantrums. The best way to handle this is to define rules that allow Baby freedom to grow but do not impinge on other members of your household. These rules must be consistently enforced. Heading off trouble before it starts is the best way to begin Baby's second year.

ACTIVITIES, GAMES, AND SONGS

A Ball for Baby

Baby will love an airy lightweight plastic ball, the kind with all the holes. These balls are great for little pitchers to practice throwing; they are also easy to hold and retrieve.

Race Car Driver

Baby will enjoy wheeled toys he can push and watch roll. Make a cardboard hill and track from a discarded paper box. Show Baby how to start his cars down the hill. He will enjoy retrieving his cars and repeating this game. Baby's enjoyment and excitement will be enhanced by your encouragement and help.

Hairdresser

Baby will like playing with his own comb and brush in front of the mirror. He will also make a game of brushing and combing his doll's and stuffed animal's hair. You can turn this into a learning time by talking to him and encouraging his efforts.

Wiggles

This little poem will be a favorite for years. Baby will soon learn to go through the motions himself with your help. Just do as the words suggest. A home movie of this would be a treasure, capturing Baby's fleeting days of babyhood. Next month he becomes a toddler.

I wiggle my fingers.
I wiggle my toes.
I wiggle my shoulders.
I wiggle my nose.
Now the wiggles are out of me.
See how still I can be.

Roller Fun

Your old plastic hair rollers make great toys. These graduated cylinders can be strung as beads or used to fill a busy baby's many containers. If you happen to have a deluxe set with its own holder for easy storage, it is truly a find. Baby will spend hours arranging the rollers on the holder pegs.

The rollers are easy to wash and almost indestructable. Remember, you slept on them for years.

Matching

Matching simple objects and pictures is lots of fun and a learning game, too. Cut out pictures of several objects that look like Baby's toys. Mount them on cardboard and cover with clear contact paper for durability.

Lay three or four of the pictures on the floor in front of you and Baby. Name the pictures and point to them as you and Baby identify them. Now hand Baby the object that matches the picture. Show him how to place the shoe on the picture of the shoe. Now, with the same object, let Baby do it by himself.

Lavish Baby with praise for his efforts. Good starting objects include shoe, cup, baby doll, and a favorite stuffed animal. The important thing is that the items be very familiar to Baby, things he knows and likes to talk about.

Something Different

A new twist for an old toy is to hang Baby's giant inflatable beach ball from the ceiling so that Baby can walk under it and push it out of the way. He will enjoy this new responsive toy that bounces back when pushed aside. Soon he will be scurrying under it with glee.

First Rider

Baby's first riding toy is a landmark purchase, exciting for all. Choose one without pedals, as the skill of pedaling does not come for some time. Baby will literally wear the wheels off this toy in the months ahead.

See this month's "Helpful Hints" for several suggestions on how to apply a furniture-saving bumper to the front of this favorite toy. You'll want to designate an open, safe area where riding is allowed, one where Baby can ride with abandonment without damaging himself or the house.

Street Strut

Baby wants to walk! You may find that the best way to keep the enjoyment in your outings is to let Baby help you push his stroller on your walks. This will give him extra stability, balance, and confidence. Your very independent baby may even be a willing rider on the return trip.

Conversion

Remember the cardboard sit box described in Chapter 3? This box can easily be converted into a new toy—or use any cardboard box of about 9 in. x 12 in. x 9 in. Attach a body or shoulder strap and cut out the bottom of the box. This gives Baby something to wear. Add a head and tail and Baby can be a unicorn, cow, or lion. Add paper-plate wheels and paper-cup headlights and you have a car. This is special fun when Baby can watch himself in a mirror.

Carpet Puzzles

Carefully cut several shapes from a square piece of carpet about 12 in. x 14 in. in size. From several other scraps of carpet, contrasting in texture and color to the first, cut the same shapes. These shapes will be the pieces in the "form board" you cut first. The form board can be glued to a piece of plywood. Baby will enjoy this colorful puzzle with its fuzzy shapes. Although he cannot yet master this puzzle by himself, he can enjoy using its parts in many ways of his own devising. As a toddler, he will learn to master the puzzle.

Color Wise

Providing Baby with early opportunities to experiment with colors is a very beneficial learning process and fun for Baby. Paint three coffee cans, boxes, or baskets the three primary colors—red, blue, and yellow. Now gather objects such as wooden blocks, rubber balls, etc., of each color to be placed in the correctly colored container. Only a few objects are necessary for each container. Play the game of sorting together. With practice and experience, Baby will learn to play this game alone. He will be extremely proud of this skill once mastered.

Rocking

Many babies gain endless pleasure from a small child's rocker, especially if someone else in the family also uses a rocker. These rockers are relatively inexpensive and can often be found at neighborhood garage sales. Rocking provides Baby with an outlet; he can keep moving while he stays nearby.

Card Deck

Busy babies enjoy rustling through things. A picture card deck can provide this opportunity. Simply cut into quarters the fronts and backs of several old manila folders. Place a bold picture of one of Baby's things on each card. Now cover with clear contact paper.

If possible, make pairs of pictures. Baby will enjoy trying to match these pictures; he has a 50 percent chance of guessing the right answer.

There are many fun games you can play together with his cards.

—Turning them all over
—Turning them all right-side up
—Saying them and giving them to each other one by one
—Dividing them in half and each laying one down

These very simple games promote complex learning later.

Presto Puppets

You don't have to be creative to make a sock puppet. They are so easy you will wonder why you never thought of them yourself. Just put a sock on your hand; the heel should be on top of your wrist. Stuff the toe back towards your palm, between your fingers and thumb. This makes the mouth. Now take the sock off and sew the corners where you pinned to hold the mouth in place. Add button eyes and nose, hair, ears, etc. Easy, quick, and fun, this is a great family project for a rainy afternoon.

No Cleanup

Baby loves to paint. For those days when you just don't have the time to get everything together, Baby will be just as happy to paint with a little colored water on the sidewalk, the fence, trees, etc. Exterior painting can be just as much fun and there is almost no cleanup. The only supplies you need are brush, bucket, water, and Baby. Several sizes of brushes add to the excitement.

Baby's Play

As this year draws to a close, reflect on Baby's play. Jot down the year-end favorites.

Song/finger play _____

Game _____

Story _____

Trip _____

Bowling

Soda pop cans make great bowling pins for Baby. Add a few pebbles for weight and then tape them shut. To add a shape, stuff the toe of an old sock and pull it down over a can and secure at the bottom. Now use a ribbon or rubber band to form the proper small bowling pin shape at the top of the sock. Add funny faces if you like. Baby will enjoy scattering these pins with his rubber ball and then setting them up again.

Books

Although Baby is still not quite ready to follow a story and your reading is really picture naming, it's not too early for nursery rhymes. These melodious tales with their funny words are fun to listen to even if their meaning is unclear. Some of the best are the sing-song type such as "Three Little Kittens."

Invest in a good book of Mother Goose rhymes. Your local children's librarian will have many suggestions of ones to buy. She or he can also suggest storybooks for admirers who want to start Baby's library. Take Baby on his first trip to the library. Start his second year off in a learning way.

Blanket Fun

Baby will love a ride on a blanket being pulled along the tile or wood floor. He will be excited by this new way of traveling. Because he is close to the ground, it is safe if done with slow stops and starts. One mom found this great fun for laundry times. As she stripped the beds, she gave Baby a ride from room to room.

Cleanup

Yes, someone in your house will enjoy cleaning with you. Give Baby a sponge or dustcloth and let him clean as you do, perhaps a low table or other accessible surface.

One mother made a glove duster for her baby. She sewed yarn pom-poms onto the palm side of a child's mitten. All her child had to do was wipe over the dusty surface. He thoroughly enjoyed the mitt with its funny features and spent many happy moments cleaning.

Sorting Boxes

Sorting boxes with a variety of different-shaped holes can now be used by Baby if you give him the right object to push through the hole.

For variety, cut different shapes and sizes out of foam rubber and cover them with colorful fabric. Baby can stuff them in any hole with great success. Save the wooden or plastic shapes that come with the box for later.

ROUTINE TIMES

BATHING

Slip Stoppers

It seems that slips and mishaps occur most frequently when putting Baby into or taking him out of his bath. Now that he may try to get out himself, consider arranging nonslip bath strips in a pattern on the inside of the tub and along the top ledge. This measure will minimize the hazard of entry and exit.

Shampoo

Many babies hate to have their hair washed because the water runs into their eyes. To stop this, fold a washcloth lengthwise and lay it on Baby's forehead. Ask him to follow some simple directions while you rinse his head. It's a game. Have Baby look up and tell you what he sees, look down, and so on. Letting Baby participate in bathtime makes it easier and more pleasant for everyone.

Peek-a-Boo Face Wash

Stop fighting with Baby at face-washing time; play a game of peek-a-boo instead. Lay the washcloth on Baby's face, rub it around, and lift it off with a peek-a-boo. Try it, it really works.

Octopus

A bath toy that pleases Baby this month is an octopus made of a whiffle or styrofoam ball, cotton cord, and a rubber band. Drape the cords over the ball and attach with the band. For added fun, draw on a face with an indelible marker or sew on buttons for eyes.

Old Bathtime Goodie

Rub-a-dub-dub
Three men in a tub,
And who do you think they be?
The butcher, the baker, the candlestick maker.
Turn 'em out, knaves all three.

SLEEPING

Zzzzzzz

On Baby's party day, try to stick to his routine as closely as possible. Make sure that Baby has napped before the festivities begin. If you are especially lucky, he will nap for an extra few minutes, which will allow the star of the party to be in fine shape. Remember: parties are not a production, they're fun.

Sleepy Time Rhyme

Wee Willie Winkie runs through the town,
Upstairs and downstairs in his nightgown,
Rapping at the window, crying through the lock,
"Are the children all in bed, for it's eight o'clock."

Two or More

Most babies take pleasure in having familiar toys or cuddly objects with them when they are put down for a nap or to bed for the night. These items become increasingly significant to a child who associates them with comfort. He knows them completely through his sense of touch and his sense of smell. Avoid a distressing situation by identifying these objects and buying or setting aside duplicates now. These favorites will inevitably grow worn, soiled, and disreputable looking. Make no mistake, however; Baby will most likely search for these objects and may not sleep without them. If you replace his cherished object with a duplicate, he will know instantly that this is not his old cherished object. He may, however, be willing to accept a look-alike substitute should the original become lost.

FEEDING

Tasty Bag

As you prepare a meal for a cranky baby who is unwilling to wait, or if you find that there will be an unavoidable delay, placate him with a "tasty bag"! Place several tidbits in a brown paper bag for Baby to find, feel, and sample.

Joining In

Baby may have indicated that more than anything he would like to eat with the rest of the family. One way to let him be part of the scene is by providing him with a matching place mat cut to fit his tray.

If Baby refuses to eat alone, remove his tray and allow him to use the table surface while strapped into his chair. Baby wants to be part of this typically social time.

Dining Tip

For special occasions, or eating-out situations, remember that, of all the people in the party, Baby is the youngest and the least able to wait. It is wise to carry a few snacks with you so that Baby will manage the waiting period with less displeasure.

Fancy Food

Add a little zest and touch of elegance to mealtime. Force mashed potatoes or carrots through a pastry tube and swirl into a small peak on Baby's plate. He'll enjoy the fancy fare.

A Change in Position

Losing patience with a finicky eater? A little change can make a great deal of difference. Let Baby sit next to a sibling or special admirer. You may both enjoy the experience and eat more of the meal.

DRESSING AND CHANGING

Shoes/Sneakers?

There is a lot of controversy about when Baby should have his first shoes. There are questions and opinions about the type and quality of the shoes; soft or hardsoled; high, low, or knit tops. The few points that experts seem to agree upon are:
1. Importance of a good fit—take him with you.
2. Shoes should never be so big that Baby may trip.
3. Sole should have a tread or some nonslip finish.
4. Shoes should be flexible.
5. Interior of shoes should be checked to ensure that there are no rough seams that could cause blisters or other discomfort.

Baby's First Shoes

Date purchased _____

Size _____

Style _____

Color _____

Store where purchased _____

Baby's reaction _____

_____

Socks Up

Tired of hassling with Baby's socks—no matter how you try, the pairs never match. Try this little trick. On the heel of each pair of socks you buy, place a symbol with a laundry marker. It takes the snarl out of matching Baby's socks. When Baby is older, he can learn to do this matching trick himself.

Reach In

We have noticed that many babies intensely dislike getting into their jackets or coats. One reason could be that small fingers are frequently bent while arms are thrust into a garment's sleeves. This jamming can be avoided if you reach into the sleeve to meet a small hand halfway.

Roll 'em Up

When it comes to fashion, Baby would thoroughly appreciate it if those who dress him would always remember to roll up his pants legs until they just graze his ankle. "Short" is a safe and comfortable length for a walking baby. Because of his ample, round belly, the most comfortable waist size will usually be accompanied by pants with legs that are *much* too long, so roll 'em up, please.

A Penny Spent . . .

Do you find it difficult to settle on a disposable diaper that fits an increasingly active and growing child? Fit is critical; it is a significant consideration when attempting to avoid accidental damage to furniture and rugs. A bit of time and a few pennies more may well help minimize aggravation. All disposables are not the same; all disposables do not have the same absorbency and fit. A more expensive diaper or pull-up may save you money in the long run. Do some serious product comparisons.

HELPFUL HINTS

Reminder

Baby's first steps are far more important to adults than to the child himself. Each baby is very different and has his own unique set of priorities. So do not be overly concerned if Baby is so pleased with his agility in crawling that he shows little more than a passing interest in walking. He will, soon!

For Safety's Sake

Even with special latches and rearranged shelves, Baby and siblings may still get too close to dangerous cleaning agents. Set up your own code system to keep everyone just a little bit safer.

Hang a small bell around the top of all toxic bottles, cleaners, and medicines. To remind yourself which bottles contain poisons, put bright orange mystic tape or permanent magic marker stripes around those that hold poisons.

Tape down the tops or completely seal lids of special cleaners after each use.

NEVER rely completely on the child-proof lid.

Helpfuls from You

What has helped the most this year? Take a minute or two, which may be all you can spare, to jot down some things too good to forget.

Supportive services, agencies, and groups:

Agency	Service	Address	Phone

Best books or magazines (some clarified issues, others raised questions):

_____

_____

_____

Keep as references:

_____

_____

Greatest time (energy) savers:

_____

_____

Splinters Out

Should your adventurer reveal a wooden splinter or two in his finger, use this fairly painless way to remove it. Soak the finger in vegetable oil and then numb it with an ice cube. Now you can remove the splinter.

Or Gum

A sibling may share his or her gum or Baby may happen upon it himself. In either case, gum is easily removed from hair with cold cream or peanut butter. Next it's into the tub for a bath and shampoo. Ice will help remove gum from clothing. Rub over the area and scrape off the hardened portion. Or soften gum with an egg white, scrape, then launder as usual.

Trash

Just as pets are tempted by aromas and must check them out, so is Baby. He will certainly investigate the trash bins, garbage pails, and wastepaper baskets. He may well try to pull the container over, just to see if there is anything good inside. He will enjoy dumping the low cans for the sheer pleasure of watching items roll or fall out. He may also try to sit in any of these cans. Prepare for these possibilities by:

—Placing a large brick or other weighty object between the garbage can and the liner, so the container will be less easily upset
—Separating out disposable items that may be harmful to Baby. Place them in a container that always remains within a latched cabinet
—Giving Baby his own trash in his own sack or basket

Advice Column

A friend is planning and preparing for a new baby. Now that you are an "experienced hand" what specific information or advice would you share?

Games and activities _____

_____

_____

Routines _____

_____

_____

Self-care _____

_____

_____

Dealing with others _____

_____

_____

Toys

Now may be the time to give Baby's toys a scrub down. Squeak toys will survive the wash if the outlet is completely taped.

Many rubber toys will tolerate the gentle agitation of a washing machine, especially if placed in a net bag.

Not What It Seems

It's not like they said it would be. What myths could you dispel regarding a year's worth of life with a baby?

_____

_____

_____

Quick Cleanup

A hint (from Chapter 10, "Routine Times") that will minimize fuss on the Big Day (Baby's first birthday) is to "oil him up." Lipstick, frosting, and other sweet treats can be easily removed from Baby's face if this procedure is followed before you sit down to celebrate.

Grape Juice

Only chlorine bleach will remove grape juice from Baby's clothing.

Camera

This is a party month so plan ahead. Get your camera ready to record the events. Check to see that the batteries are working, that a supply of film, flashbulbs, and other necessary lighting fixtures are within easy reach. Don't miss a single exciting pose.

Stains and Spots

If stains and spots are a problem (and spray-on pretreating solutions and washing aids are too expensive to use) consider using some of your spray-on all-purpose household cleaners. These are much cheaper and many mothers report they work even better.

Cushion the Crash

Now that Baby is using his riding toys and pushing his trucks and cars about, try this measure. Cut foam rubber bumpers to fit Baby's vehicles. These bumpers can be covered with durable fabric and attached directly to the toys with special glue. Not only will these additions add pizzazz to Baby's toys, they will also prevent nicks and scuffs to the furniture, walls, and woodwork. The bumpers can be purely utilitarian or as artistic and imaginative as you wish.

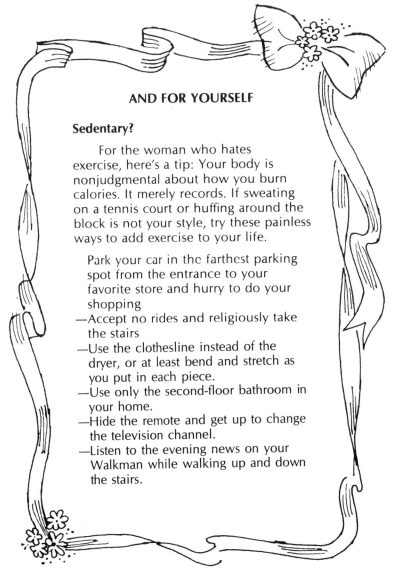

AND FOR YOURSELF

Sedentary?

For the woman who hates exercise, here's a tip: Your body is nonjudgmental about how you burn calories. It merely records. If sweating on a tennis court or huffing around the block is not your style, try these painless ways to add exercise to your life.

Park your car in the farthest parking spot from the entrance to your favorite store and hurry to do your shopping
—Accept no rides and religiously take the stairs
—Use the clothesline instead of the dryer, or at least bend and stretch as you put in each piece.
—Use only the second-floor bathroom in your home.
—Hide the remote and get up to change the television channel.
—Listen to the evening news on your Walkman while walking up and down the stairs.

Sitter

Some parents have found that hiring a baby-sitter for Baby's first birthday is a lifesaver. If Baby should demand more than he usually does, due to the arrival of guests or excitement, there will be a familiar set of hands to take extra special care of his needs. Once his presents have been opened and his time in the limelight has ended, the sitter can entertain him in his room, leaving his parents free to entertain adult guests without worry. This added flexibility will allow you to celebrate, too—after all, what an accomplishment!

Storage

If Baby's room is becoming overrun with bulky stuffed toys and animals, reclaim the floor by thinking "up." Hang a lightweight wooden ladder horizontally about 2 feet from the ceiling. This aerial shelf will keep favorite toys clean and within view, and will add interest to Baby's quarters.

Or, hang a short ladder vertically for an instant set of shelves.

Corner Interest

With a continually growing toy collection and with bulky items scattering themselves about the house, we like this "cleanup corner" strategy! One friend utilized a corner space by stringing fabric from one cup hook to another. Toys were instantly concealed behind the curtain. As her child grew, she fashioned the front of a house out of oilcloth, complete with windows, doors, and roof. By day the "house" was a versatile, dramatic play center; at cleanup time it became a warehouse behind which favorites rested close by but out of sight. She bumper-proofed the walls and moldings so that toys could even be ridden into the corner.

PARENTS, FRIENDS, AND ADMIRERS

Grandmothers Only

Only Grandma would remember such a special gift on Baby's first birthday, the "Birthday Bib." Do waterproof this family treasure to preserve it for the babies to come.

Party Goers

Even if you are a habitual early bird, do try to give the birthday family an extra ten minutes before you arrive for the party, and don't plan to stay too late. This thoughtful gesture will be most appreciated by your friends.

A Special Friend

Help siblings feel that they are a part of the excitement on Baby's party day by allowing them to invite a special friend over to play. This will assure that they will enjoy themselves, too.

Across the Miles

A nice way to share the fun and excitement of Baby's first birthday party with grandparents who can't attend is to videotape the event. Even if you don't own a camcorder, borrow or rent one. Remember to make a copy of the tape to keep.

Good Gift

Baby will like a small preschool slide. He will quickly learn to enjoy this new sensation with your help and insist on many turns. Preschool slides are very common and can often be found at local garage sales at bargain prices.

Photo Uses

Now is the time for photos. Do take a good one of Baby and his cake. Have an 8 x 10 print made for a puzzle. Cut a piece of Masonite, the size of the picture, into puzzle pieces. Now, with a mat knife, cut the picture into the same-shaped pieces. Glue the picture to the pieces of wood. Shellac each piece. You will have a personalized puzzle that will provide hours of fun.

A Friend's Gift

Give close friends a special treat for Baby's birthday. Call ahead so that a baby-sitter can be arranged for and ask your friends if you can treat them to dinner and a quiet drink following the party. Help them unwind and relax. There's something so nice about walking away and worrying about cleanup tomorrow.

Gift Ideas

Here are some gift suggestions for the year-old baby.

—A T-shirt with a big number one
—An outdoor swing with supports
—A small xylophone with attached stick for Baby to bang on
—Colorful pull toys that make noise
—Small riding toys without pedals
—A large, colorful ball

Speaking of Gifts . . .

To help reduce sibling anxiety, a special friend might bring brother or sister a small gift, too. Baby won't know the difference, but the older child surely will!

My Gift

Siblings will want to make or buy a very special gift for Baby, too. Help them do so. It is important that they have confidence in their gift. Here are some suggestions.

—A family picture book that includes favorite photos and pictures they've selected, drawn or cut out, and mounted.
—An enterprising young artist (eight years or older) may want to attempt a real painting of Baby. Poster paint can be used on an inexpensive canvas or have them use water colors on paper.
—A batch of homemade peanut butter play dough with several plastic cookie cutters. The dough will last for several weeks if kept in the refrigerator.

EDIBLE PLAY DOUGH

1 jar of peanut butter (18 oz.)
6 tbsp. honey (or to taste)
Add nonfat dry milk and knead to the right consistency.

Family Gift

Want to give a gift for the whole family? How about matching family sweatshirts or T-shirts? The Three Bears—Momma, Papa, and Baby—is one possible theme.

Thank You

If you hate to write thank-you notes, consider using one of the photos taken at Baby's party for a photo thank-you card just like the ones used at Christmas. Baby's admirers will be pleased.

An Alternative

In lieu of a large party for Baby's birthday, you may want to start a tradition of taking a special trip as part of the birthday celebration. Choose a trip to the zoo or another special place that will be a treat every year for years to come.

Reflections

You've made it through the first year. Baby isn't the only one who's grown and changed; you have, too. Take this time to reflect on your first year with Baby—a pause before toddlerhood.

Baby's Gift to Someone Else

Would you believe that babies enjoy gluing? Tape a piece of paper on Baby's high-chair tray. Sprinkle a little glue (white) on the page. Give Baby some colorful scraps of paper or fabric. Show him what to do and let the artist work. When the artist seems satisfied, retrieve the creation and mail to proud grandparents, relatives, or friends. This might make a nice card for Mom and Dad, if done at a caregiver's.

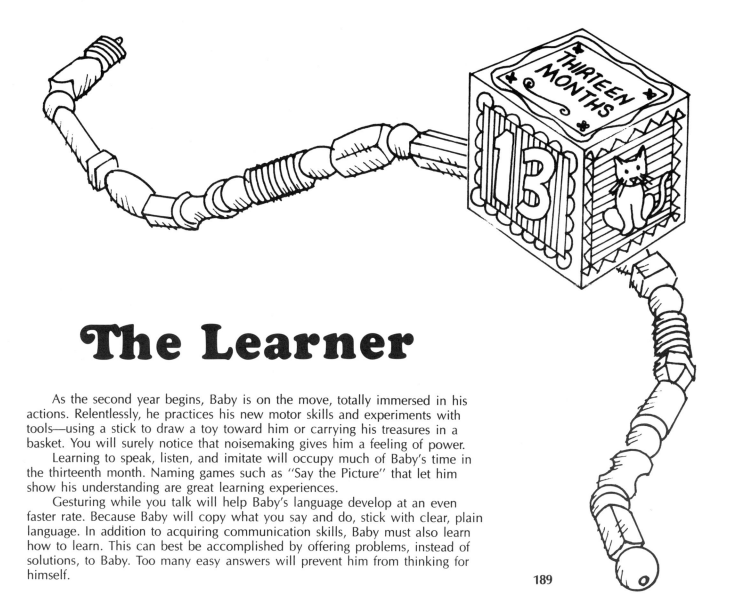

The Learner

As the second year begins, Baby is on the move, totally immersed in his actions. Relentlessly, he practices his new motor skills and experiments with tools—using a stick to draw a toy toward him or carrying his treasures in a basket. You will surely notice that noisemaking gives him a feeling of power.

Learning to speak, listen, and imitate will occupy much of Baby's time in the thirteenth month. Naming games such as "Say the Picture" that let him show his understanding are great learning experiences.

Gesturing while you talk will help Baby's language develop at an even faster rate. Because Baby will copy what you say and do, stick with clear, plain language. In addition to acquiring communication skills, Baby must also learn how to learn. This can best be accomplished by offering problems, instead of solutions, to Baby. Too many easy answers will prevent him from thinking for himself.

Play is learning for your Baby. Simple games like "Peek-a-boo" teach him how to get along in the world. You are better than any toy on the market. The time you and/or a caregiver spend playing with Baby can be the most enjoyable and rewarding period of his infant stage.

Although he is likely to react with amazement and fear when meeting strangers, Baby still needs and wants social contact. Stay close, though, because his social skills are minimal. He can become uncomfortable with someone he's gotten along with before if he's left alone with that person too quickly.

Beware! Attempts to restrain Baby may reveal his newfound temper. Baby needs a lot of parental contact at this time. As he strives for independence, his seemingly irrational fears can be controlled best by gentle exposure to and explanation about his world. No sound is as affirming for Baby as his parent's voice.

ACTIVITIES, GAMES, AND SONGS

Fill Up/Empty Out

A small trash can with a lid, either the swinging or lift type, is a novel container for a fill-up/empty-out activity. Any object too big to swallow will be good for this game. Include some pictures on cardboard.

Watch the Birdie

Baby will love to watch birds in the backyard or near the kitchen window. A bird feeder with a squirrel shield will attract a variety of birds. However, once you start feeding them they will come to depend on the food. Don't stop! A bird bath hung near Baby's bedroom window can also provide hours of delight. Use a metal dish hung from a rafter with nylon cord or fishing line.

Personal Scrapbook

Start a scrapbook for Baby that features him and his friends. Don't forget the family pets. Include pictures of Baby's favorite foods. The best scrapbook has a plastic shield over each page so pictures can be moved easily.

To Market, To Market

A miniature shopping cart will become one of your child's most beloved toys. This is such a versatile toy that Baby will play with it daily and constantly invent his own uses for it. You can purchase one very inexpensively at a discount store.

Personal Magnetism

The refrigerator door should be Baby's showcase. Not only will he enjoy magnetic letters, but other magnetic toys as well. Make your own by sewing a hardware store magnet securely into a small toy. The sewing must be very secure because Baby wants to put everything into his mouth. Baby's friends and admirers will want to contribute to the gallery. Don't forget a small picture of Baby.

Tub Fun

The baby bathtub has a new use. Filled with oatmeal flakes or cornmeal, it can be used as an indoor sandbox. Filled with water, it's great for Baby's water play. Just a few cups of water or flakes plus measuring cups, funnels, basters, and sifters provide hours of indoor or outdoor play.

Bean Bags

Bean bags provide an easy toss game that can be made instantly with a wicker basket and six or eight of Baby's old socks. Fill the socks with small objects larger than 1-in. square (to keep Baby from choking should he get at them). Knot the socks firmly. Give Baby a spot to stand on and show him how to throw the bags into a basket.

Roller Art

For the aspiring artist, you may want to try "Roller Art." Save your roll-on deodorant bottles. They can become a great alternative to markers and brushes. Just snap off the plastic ring that holds the ball, fill the bottle with paint, and replace the ball and ring. It's a novel and less messy way to paint. Use red, yellow, and blue tempera paint.

Traveling Puppet Show

Take puppets along in the car to amuse Baby while traveling. You could hide something in the puppet's mouth for variety and surprise.

Feel-ly Can

Put some small toys or kitchen utensils in a coffee can. Pull a large sock over the entire can. Your curious child will delight in putting his hand through the sock into the can to feel what's inside and try to bring out the surprises.

Listening Skills

Do invest in a child's tape recorder. Buy children's songs or stories on cassette or transfer favorite music from records to blank tape. If you start early, your child will develop listening skills and soon enjoy listening to stories with headphones. This is great for the times when Baby needs to wait or sit quietly.

Sing and Clap

For an action song—always a great favorite—try "Clap Your Hands." This simple song is sung to the tune of "Row, Row, Row Your Boat":

Clap, clap, clap your hands,
  shake them in the breeze.
Put them up and put them down
  and put them on your knees.

With a Moo-Moo Here . . .

Teach Baby animal sounds using "Old MacDonald's Farm" variations or a picture book. Learning what each animal says is just the beginning. Children will also learn how to communicate and concentrate.

Surprise Munchies

Save boxes with lids and plastic jars with plastic screw-on tops. Collect assorted sizes of these objects and wash them thoroughly. Hide a few edible morsels in them and they will become an intriguing source of fun and learning for Baby.

Hours of Activity

Filling and dumping is a favorite activity for Baby. Be inventive. Clear plastic detergent bottles (well-rinsed) and an assortment of small toys (blocks, clothespins, etc.) can provide lessons for a toddler.

Together

Matching games are challenging for Baby and a great learning experience. He can do this successfully with just a little practice. Put together sets of objects matched by colors: blocks and plastic cups, cars and box garages, or crayons and papers. Look around the house and you'll find items for a color-matching set. Keep it in a box or zip-lock bag.

Magic Tunnel

Roll tiny matchbox cars through a paper-towel roll. The disappearance and reappearance is the "magic." This is a good game to teach Baby how to solve problems. He'll want to find out what happens to the car when it goes out of sight.

Crawling Upstairs

Let Baby practice climbing stairs on a "crawl-over" box. Cover a sturdy, wide, low box with bright adhesive paper. Baby can crawl up, across, and down the other side.

Tickling

Baby's sense of humor is growing. Play this tickle game with your small squirmer. You will delight in hearing his anticipatory glee as he becomes more familiar with the motion of your fingers.

Slowly, very slowly, creeps the garden snail,
Slowly, very slowly, up the wooden rail.
Quickly, very quickly, runs the little mouse,
Quickly, very quickly, round and round the house.

Baby's New Tricks

Now that Baby is beginning to use tools, jot down five of the new tricks he learned this month that you've enjoyed watching develop.

1. _____

2. _____

3. _____

4. _____

5. _____

ROUTINE TIMES

BATHING

No More Tangles

A product that prevents Baby's hair from tangling will be very helpful. Spray it on Baby's wet or dry hair to prevent the tears and struggles that can come with combing his tangled hair.

Bath Play

Pastry brushes, sponges cut into interesting shapes, squeeze bottles, colanders, and measuring cups make good bath toys.

Puppet Persuaders

If Baby dislikes having his arms or legs held when they're scrubbed, try using a washcloth puppet. The puppet also makes it easier to grasp a slippery, wiggly body.

Spot Rinsing

We know of no toddlers who enjoy a shampoo. A squeeze bottle is an efficient way to wash and rinse Baby's hair. Fill the bottle with warm water and do the job as quickly as you can.

Sleeping

Don't ignore Baby when he wakes up crying. Find out what the problem is and try to comfort him. Babies of this age don't cry to annoy you, but because they have real fears or problems that they would like you to alleviate.

Nap Music

At this time, Baby may be beginning to consolidate two daily naps into one. If his schedule needs reinforcing, try to establish an event to mark the beginning of naptime. Use something Baby can look forward to. Try a colorful music box with a moving part that is played only when Baby is snuggled in and ready to nap.

Stories

Alert! If the bedtime routine is becoming too inconsistent, now is the time to tighten up. Toddlers who have well-established bedtime routines seem to have far less difficulty accepting an agreed-upon bedtime when they get older. Make sure that reading bedtime stores is a part of the ritual. It's enjoyable for everyone and the love of stores is fundamental to reading success later on.

FEEDING

New Spot

Baby loves to eat in a new location occasionally. Picnics, even in the back yard or on the landing of an apartment building, can be an adventure.

For Baby's outings, a holder for his juice box will help prevent those squeezed-out leaks. Consider straw cups that allow you to use your own juice and still have the convenience of sip boxes. Flip-top thermos containers are also a good choice.

Slurp

Let Baby drink from a short straw sometimes to provide variety while drinking. Keep the straw short, so the cup won't tip easily.

Portable Meal

Fill an ice cream cone with snacks other than ice cream. Try foods such as cubed cheese, peeled apple slices, or cereal. This is a good way to minimize mealtime mess when traveling. Keep a box of cones in the car.

Boxes and Bags

The new juice boxes and bags can help to wean Baby from his bottle. Start by filling his bottle only with water. Later, let him drink juice with a straw from the box or bag. This is a pleasant diversion for Baby and a convenience for you because the containers can be carried easily in the stroller or car.

Style

If Baby refuses to wear a bib at mealtime, try replacing it with a brightly colored scarf. You can give a little on small matters and save your firm insistence for the important ones.

Mealtime is Family Time

You may want to pull the high chair up to the table and give Baby some of the food the rest of the family is eating in order to make him feel he's part of this family ritual.

DRESSING AND CHANGING

Talk, More Talk

When dressing Baby, do a running commentary to keep his attention. Say, "Look, I'm putting on your shirt with buttons in the front," etc. It helps Baby learn and keeps him diverted.

Dressed-up Dolls

Save Baby's outgrown or permanently stained play clothes to use for dressing up dolls or stuffed toys.

He'll have a great time and the practice will help him learn to dress himself.

Sing a Song

It may be corny, but it works. To help your often less-than-cooperative toddler dress, try a rendition of "This is the way we put on our pants, put on our pants, put on our pants. This is the way we put on our pants so early in the morning." You get the idea.

HELPFUL HINTS

Reminder

Be sure to get him immunized against measles and German measles this month if you have not already done so.

Buckle Up!

It's the law! Everyone must wear seat belts. If you move Baby's car seat from one car to another double-check to make sure the seat has been buckled in. This is just as important as buckling Baby into the seat.

Traveling Toy Tote

A shoe bag, hung on the headrest of a car seat, is a good place for Baby's toys while you're traveling.

He can have his possessions at his fingertips, and you'll have less clutter throughout the car.

Cup Spot

To avoid spills, draw or tape a circle on the table or high chair tray to show Baby where to put his cup. If there's a designated spot, he won't topple his cup so often. Using a cup with a lid and drinking spout makes good sense, too.

Toddler Proofing

There are two things you should do as Baby becomes more active around the house.

— Arrange the furniture in a specific room in a way

that allows Baby to cruise easily between the pieces. The gaps should be no wider than Baby's stretched arm length.
— Remember to remove objects that are easy for him to knock over while he toddles through the house. A lightweight table or precariously balanced stack of books can be a real threat to Baby's safety.

Upstairs, Downstairs

Teach Baby to maneuver the stairs and help him practice when you can. There are several good approaches to teaching this skill. He can go backwards with tummy against the stairs while holding

on to the step above, or he can sit on one step while his feet are on another and go down on his bottom and hands. Practice can prevent a lot of accidents.

Interaction

To teach Baby to communicate, read short stories with short sentences that allow him to participate. Punctuate the story with questions that require some sort of response. Ask Baby to point to an object, find something, or ask him where something is. Repeat these phrases and watch his interest grow.

Learning to Listen

To build good listening habits, keep the TV or radio low while talking to your child. This way, background noises won't obscure Baby's comprehension of speech sounds.

Kitchen Cabinet Art

Use the lower doors of kitchen cabinets as an alternative site for Baby's art. He'll constantly be delighted and surprised as he moves from cabinet to cabinet, inspecting his handiwork.

Soothing Sounds

Sounds can comfort a teething Baby. Using a tape recorder, collect chuckles, water sounds, birds' songs, and your voice singing a lullaby. Play this for Baby when he needs a little soothing.

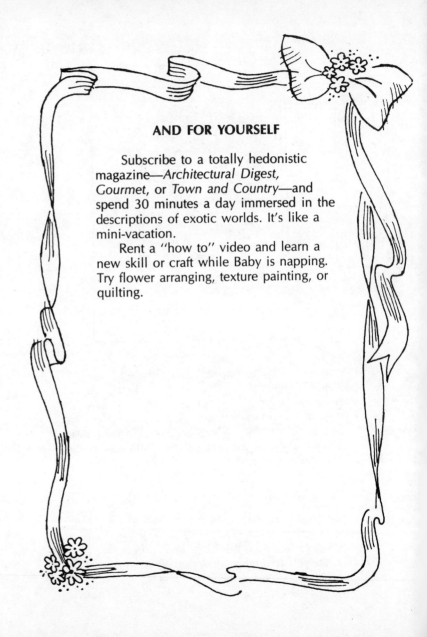

AND FOR YOURSELF

Subscribe to a totally hedonistic magazine—*Architectural Digest, Gourmet,* or *Town and Country*—and spend 30 minutes a day immersed in the descriptions of exotic worlds. It's like a mini-vacation.

Rent a "how to" video and learn a new skill or craft while Baby is napping. Try flower arranging, texture painting, or quilting.

PARENTS, FRIENDS, AND ADMIRERS

Rock Art

Save some of those rocks Baby picks up at the beach or in the park. Your child can enjoy an activity that has made some people's fortunes—painting rocks. You can preserve the best ones with shellac. Add a date and Baby has a memorable paperweight for Dad on Father's Day or for grandma on her birthday.

Hope Chest

A clever grandmother we know has saved a few early crayon drawings by each of her grandchildren by ironing them on pieces of cloth. Later she framed some and transferred the rest to sweatshirts for Baby and his admirers to wear and enjoy.

Light Show

Dad can create a colorful nightlight for the nursery by hanging a short string of Christmas lights. Baby will love their soft glow.

T's

Dad's worn T-shirts are good for more than rags. Let Baby put a crayon design on them and wear them. Won't he feel big in Dad's shirt! Iron over the design and it will be permanent.

Walk 'n Talk

Baby-sitters and friends can charm Baby by taking him for a walk through the house. Baby will see familiar objects differently through their eyes. They can ask him to say the names of things as they point to them.

Skills Book

A handy grandma could make a fabric book with something that works on each page—a heavy-duty zipper, several large buttons and button holes, large snaps, and pieces of Velcro. Baby will love the practice in grandma's book.

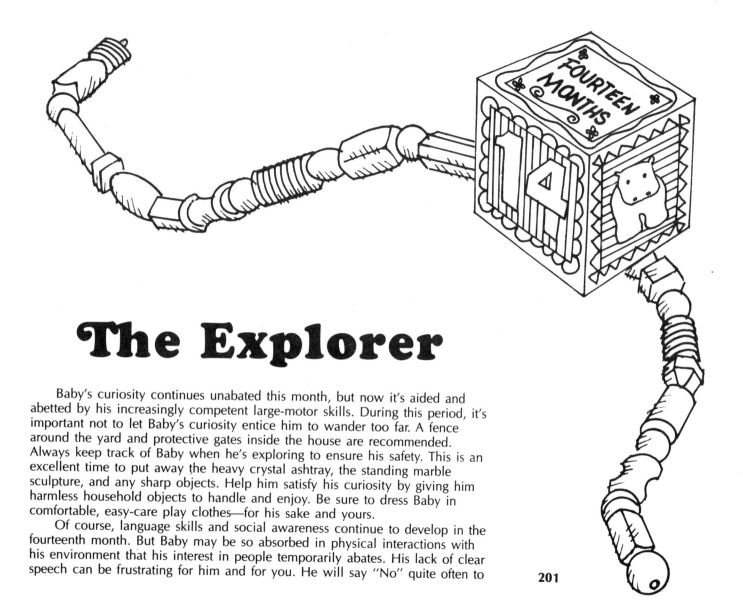

The Explorer

Baby's curiosity continues unabated this month, but now it's aided and abetted by his increasingly competent large-motor skills. During this period, it's important not to let Baby's curiosity entice him to wander too far. A fence around the yard and protective gates inside the house are recommended. Always keep track of Baby when he's exploring to ensure his safety. This is an excellent time to put away the heavy crystal ashtray, the standing marble sculpture, and any sharp objects. Help him satisfy his curiosity by giving him harmless household objects to handle and enjoy. Be sure to dress Baby in comfortable, easy-care play clothes—for his sake and yours.

Of course, language skills and social awareness continue to develop in the fourteenth month. But Baby may be so absorbed in physical interactions with his environment that his interest in people temporarily abates. His lack of clear speech can be frustrating for him and for you. He will say "No" quite often to

201

express many things. True rebelliousness will come in about twelve years; now he's just building his ego a little. Remember, Baby understands far more than he can express. Your attitude and tone of voice mean a great deal. Help him by being patient and looking him in the eye when you talk to him and when you listen. The more confident Baby feels about his ability to communicate, the more adept he will become in future social situations.

Don't be surprised if Baby's newly acquired physical abilities seem to be accompanied by regression in other areas. In particular, his interest in quiet, small-motor activities may appear to diminish. The concentration and energy required for him to master one activity detracts from the time spent on others. Continue to motivate rather than demand, and Baby will continue to learn.

Baby will acquire independence and self-confidence if you let him try to accomplish routine tasks such as eating. It will take him a little longer but he will learn more. It's difficult to spoil Baby. Give him a lot of attention, affection, comfort, assurance, and praise. These can only help a baby, not spoil him.

ACTIVITIES, GAMES, AND SONGS

Brush Box

Almost anything bristly is a worthy subject for study. Baby will enjoy a "Brush Box." Put a scrub brush, toothbrush, paintbrush, hair brush, vegetable brush, etc. in the box and let him enjoy the different sensations they give his hands. Store smaller brushes in a plastic toothbrush holder. Baby practices eye/hand coordination as he makes a game out of putting them away.

Versatile Tubes

Save your paper-towel and toilet-paper tubes. Baby can put them to many uses. For example, a tube can become a horn, a device for whispering in someone's ear, a telescope, an object that is rolled and chased, something to roll objects through, a magic wand (attach streamers), rhythm sticks (two together), or a painting device to print O's.

A Place of His Own

Toddlers love a private space. Hang a canopy in a corner (or over a loft) to create a private, special area. Maybe he would enjoy some stars on the underside. If you have a spare closet you can create a private space. Cut the door into Dutch doors and create a child's kitchen or a small quiet cozy reading corner with large cushions to sit on. This space can be changed as your child's need for privacy changes.

Stringing and Lacing

Use stiff, bendable, rubber-covered wire, such as automobile wire (you can get some at a hardware store), for stringing and lacing toys. Secure one end of the wire inside a box and tape it closed. Put the box on the floor with the wire extended upward and give your child something to string on the wire. Some objects that work well are toilet-paper tubes, mason-jar covers, lids, or aluminum pie tins with holes punched in them.

New Sounds

Sound containers can be made easily by putting beans, salt, rice, etc. into separate 35-millimeter film containers. Baby won't be able to remove the lids if you use your quick-dry super adhesive to seal them.

Learning About Sizes

Cut rings of 2 to 4 in. wide from containers of assorted diameters (juice can, toilet-paper roll, oatmeal container, salt box). Cover the edges with cloth or masking tape. As Baby arranges and rearranges them on the floor or on a string, he'll learn the concept of small, medium, and large objects.

Adventure Trip

Create an obstacle course for Baby. Get a few large cardboard boxes and cut out various doors in them. Line up the boxes and let Baby crawl through and amuse himself. Some scarves or other clothes can be hung over the doors or spread on the floor of the course.

Pop in the Ball

Games made with cans are also fun. Get two coffee cans or other cans with plastic lids. Cut out the bottom of one of the cans and cut a small hole in one lid and a large hole in another. Experiment with different-sized balls so Baby can see how they roll in, out, and through the cans.

Picture Stories

Cut out colorful, interesting magazine pictures and mount them on pieces of cardboard. Talk about them and make up stories with Baby. Store the cards in a large manila envelope.

See the Colors

Baby would love to turn the pages of a wallpaper book and look at all the colorful patterns.

Cheap Tricks

You can buy some round, plastic pot scrubbers very cheaply. These make great objects for your child to toss and roll. Variety stores are full of inexpensive household items Baby will love to play with.

Treasure Carryalls

For Baby's treasure collection, provide containers with handles that he can carry around the house or use for gathering things outdoors. Baby loves to carry a bag that reminds him of Mom's handbag. Consider a canvas carpenter's apron that ties around his waist and provides several pockets.

Laundry Room Choo-choo

Make an exciting train for Baby with old detergent bottles, container lids, elastic cord, dowels, nuts, and colored tape. Push two dowel rods through each bottle, attach plastic lids for wheels, and secure them with glued-on nuts. Add windows to the cars with tape and use assorted lids for smokestacks. Tie the cars together with elastic cord, and you have a train that Baby will love.

Play in the Laundry

The laundry room can be a great place for Baby to play. He'll love to empty and fill baskets, try on clothes, and discuss and identify different items of clothing and where they are worn. He can even do some sorting—putting all the socks in the dryer, for example. Be sure all laundry products are stored out of his reach.

Poem

Finger plays are a great introduction to language for toddlers. They are fun and absorbing while they encourage responses and visualizations. Here's one not to miss.

Frog is Coming

Frog is coming with a hop, hop, hop.
He's hopping on my tummy and he will not stop.
He's hopping on my knee and on my chest, too.
"Hop away frog, I've had enough of you!"

Of course, the poem can be easily altered to include other parts of the body.

Finger Family

Draw family faces on your nails or finger tips with a marker. Put on a show featuring Mom, Dad, and Baby.

Visit a craft fair and look for a puppet mitten. It is a glove which has characters from a story such as "Goldilocks" or "Red Riding Hood" attached to the fingers. The characters are removable. As you tell the story each character appears to play his or her part. Later Baby will tell the story and enjoy this prop himself. In Chapter 19 you can find our version of this easy craft project.

ROUTINE TIMES

BATHING

Tubby Fun

If you're in need of new bath toys, try using a sponge or cork as a buoy in the water. Another idea is to cut a large bleach bottle in half vertically. Be sure to include both handle and spout in one half. Poke holes in the bottom of it and let Baby use it as a scoop, sieve, or storage for small water toys.

Tub Safety

Baby can sit up in the tub and may even want to stand. Don't leave him alone in the tub even for a minute. Slipping is a real danger. Make yourself comfortable by sitting on a small stool while Baby plays in the water. Baby girls should avoid any kind of bubble bath product. Doctors say they cause vaginal infections.

FEEDING

Juice

For an inexpensive substitute for juice boxes, use small plastic Evian water bottles. They have a rippled texture which makes them easy and interesting for Baby to hold. A biker's water bottle is equally useful. Plastic straws and screw-on cap sets which allow you to change any bottle into a sip bottle are also available.

Ode to "Crispy O's"

If there is anything a 14-month-old never wants to be without, it's "Crispy O's." Not only are they sugarfree and nutritious, they're easy to pick up and chew, and they taste good. They also can be pasted, colored, strung, and put in a rattle box. What is more versatile?

Recycling Bonanza

Recycle "Le Menu" and other plastic frozen dinner trays. They're microwaveable and keep food sectioned in small portions. Baby may not want his foods mixed and object heartily when they are.

SLEEPING

Away from Home

When you take Baby to visit grandparents or on a vacation, you need to prepare him for sleeping in a strange bed. As much as possible, stick to the same bedtime routine you have at home. Take along favorite sleep clothes, toys, and blanket. Read beloved bedtime stories. A half hour or so before bedtime, talk about going to bed. Say, "In a few minutes, it will be bedtime and we're going to go to sleep at grandma's."

Making Your Bed

If there's no crib, Baby won't be comfortable in a large bed unless it's modified. Roll two blankets separately and put the rolls under a fitted sheet on each side of the space where Baby will sleep. These bumpers will keep him confined and make the space feel smaller.

Rentacrib

Most cities today have furniture rental companies where you can rent a crib and other baby equipment for a reasonable fee. This is especially helpful when you travel by plane or in a small auto.

DRESSING

Switch, Don't Fight

When dressing Baby is a struggle, especially when he resists putting his arms in a jacket or putting on galoshes, resort to distraction! Give him a small push-button flashlight to play with. He will probably enjoy this so much that he will begin to look forward to getting dressed and another opportunity to play with the light.

Boot Tips

Putting on winter boots will be much less of a struggle if you spray the insides with furniture polish and wipe lightly. If this doesn't do it, try putting a plastic bag on each foot before pulling on the boots. The bags also add warmth.

Preppy Tot

Leather shoestrings stay tied longer when you sprinkle a little water on the knot. If Baby's shoe won't stay tied, .turn them into slip-ons: Make a loop, then curl the shoelaces tightly around it, slipping the end through the loop and pulling tight.

HELPFUL HINTS

Reminder

Because Baby is eating more adult food, read labels carefully. Be sure you know which foods contain artificial sweeteners, preservatives, and other manufactured ingredients and take control of what your child eats.

Trade Tots Clothes

Do you have baby clothes that are too small but still usable? Organize an exchange with several other mothers where outgrown clothing can be traded. Everyone benefits. Or use one of the growing number of children's resale shops.

Love Game

Use tennis sweatbands as kneepads to protect the child who easily falls during play. They can also be added to hold up sleeves during art or when eating. Sweatbands will keep socks up and a head sweatband for your head makes a great slip-on emergency belt if Baby's pants are slipping.

Crayon Preservation

If you put masking tape around each new crayon, it won't break as easily and will discourage Baby from chewing on it.

No-Slip

Several strategically placed bathtub appliqués on the highchair seat will help Baby sit more securely.

Bumps and Bruises

Grab a sack of frozen vegetables when you need a quick ice pack. Soak a small piece of a clean sponge in fruit juice and keep it in the freezer. This can be sweet comfort for a bruised lip. A physical therapist suggested this one: Put half water and half alcohol in a zip-lock bag and freeze it. The mixture stays slushy so it conforms to a bruised knee or elbow.

Little People

You can make little people with pipe cleaners or from old-fashioned wooden clothespins. Saw off the ends and paint in bright colors.

Easy Cleanup

Keep a large, attractive basket near the door in each room. If everyone is trained to put strewn toys and other items in them, straightening up the house will be much easier. This idea is especially good if you live in a multi-storied home. Place good-looking baskets by the stairs: one at the top and one at the bottom. Switch baskets each trip you make up or down.

Easy Lunches

If early morning is hectic at your house, try making and freezing sandwiches for the whole week at one time. The sandwich or, if you prefer, finger food will be thawed by lunchtime and you won't have to worry about spoilage. Add fruit or cookies to the lunchbox each morning.

Bath Organizer

A bathtub organizer shelf which fits across the tub is a handy item for storing bath toys. Get one with drainage holes. The shelf will move out of the way when adults bathe or shower.

Shopping Safety

If your supermarket doesn't have seatbelts on its shopping carts, make your own from a webbing belt with a locking buckle. It will make your shopping trips safer and more pleasant. You might suggest to the store manager that the store provide seatbelts.

Travel Tip

Be ready for spur-of-the-moment invitations. Keep a bag packed with diapers, a change of clothes, juice in a bag, cereal, a fruit bar, a wet wipe, a few toys, and a plastic bag. Then you won't need half an hour to get ready. Keep one in the trunk of the car at all times so you can be spontaneous.

Keep a small basket with some of Baby's toys in the trunk as well. Since he will only see these on outings, he'll begin to look forward to traveling.

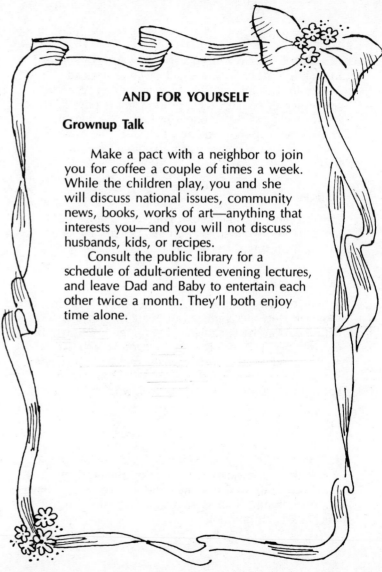

AND FOR YOURSELF

Grownup Talk

Make a pact with a neighbor to join you for coffee a couple of times a week. While the children play, you and she will discuss national issues, community news, books, works of art—anything that interests you—and you will not discuss husbands, kids, or recipes.

Consult the public library for a schedule of adult-oriented evening lectures, and leave Dad and Baby to entertain each other twice a month. They'll both enjoy time alone.

PARENTS, FRIENDS, AND ADMIRERS

Family Album

Fill a photo album with family and friends Baby doesn't see often so that he can "get to know them" by looking at their pictures. You could hang a wall album above Baby's bed so he can see grandma and grandpa whenever he likes. This will make him less shy and clingy at the next family gathering.

Baby Gourmet

Here are some food ideas that should appeal to grandmothers and babysitters. Baby can "help" make them.

1. Pudding Sandwich—Spread pudding between two graham crackers. Freeze until pudding is firm.
2. Ants on a Log—Stuff celery with peanut butter and dot with a row of raisins.
3. Banana Pop—Cut banana in half and insert popsicle stick. Spread with peanut butter and roll in granola or crushed cereal.
4. Cookie Pops—two vanilla wafers joined by frosting with a popsicle stick handle. Then dip the pop in chocolate half way up the wafer. Harden on a cookie sheet.

Friendship Gift

Need a special gift for special friends? Give your personal gift certificate for an overnight or weekend of baby-sitting with their child.

Thank You Notes

The best thank you note for a gift—short of sending Baby himself—is a picture of him using or wearing the gift. Everyone loves to see for themselves that the gift is used and appreciated.

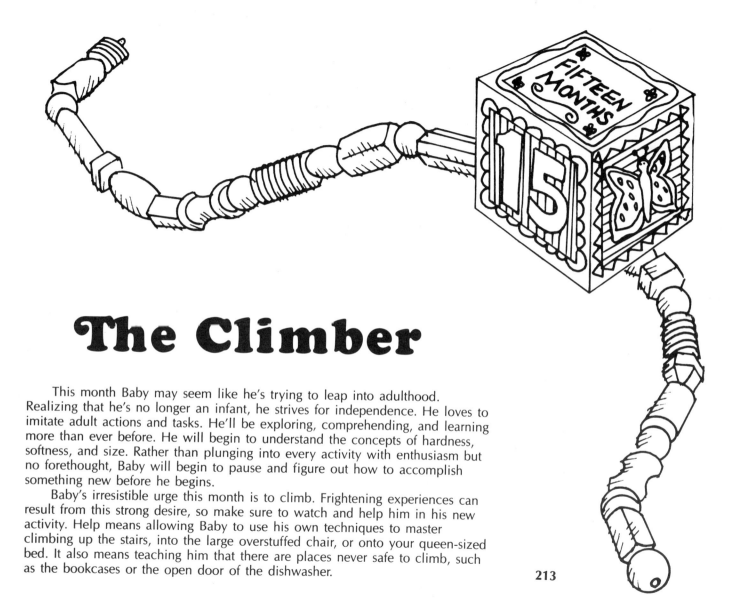

The Climber

This month Baby may seem like he's trying to leap into adulthood. Realizing that he's no longer an infant, he strives for independence. He loves to imitate adult actions and tasks. He'll be exploring, comprehending, and learning more than ever before. He will begin to understand the concepts of hardness, softness, and size. Rather than plunging into every activity with enthusiasm but no forethought, Baby will begin to pause and figure out how to accomplish something new before he begins.

Baby's irresistible urge this month is to climb. Frightening experiences can result from this strong desire, so make sure to watch and help him in his new activity. Help means allowing Baby to use his own techniques to master climbing up the stairs, into the large overstuffed chair, or onto your queen-sized bed. It also means teaching him that there are places never safe to climb, such as the bookcases or the open door of the dishwasher.

213

While the senses of sound and smell are fully established at birth, others take time to develop. All Baby's senses come into play now as tools for exploring his world. Baby's sense of touch helps him understand the nature of things around him. A variety of textures, which adults take for granted, delight and fascinate him. Continue to introduce new tastes, but not those that require a cultivated palate. The anchovies and olives will have to wait!

Another development is Baby's sense of humor. He will try to entertain you with dances and other antics that allow him to be the center of attention. You'll observe that Baby is learning that different kinds of behavior will influence those around him. Set limits on his experiments with people so that he doesn't get the idea that he can have total control over others.

Baby may try to rebel against his parents by not eating. Letting him get hungry is a good defense against this power play. He may refuse to eat, even skip a couple of meals. It won't do any harm. Eventually he'll feel very hungry and stop rebelling for the moment.

Don't force food on Baby; that's how real eating problems can develop. The eating patterns he acquires early in life will stay with him forever. The fewer fat cells he develops as a child, the fewer he will have to feed as an adult. Good eating habits established now will keep Baby healthy in the future.

ACTIVITIES, GAMES, AND SONGS

Dancin'

Baby is always ready to "dance to the music." Add to the fun by giving him some scarves or feathers, a towel cape, spoons to clank, or pie plate cymbals.

Touch and Talk

Cut different shapes from textured materials such as sponge, foam, cardboard, carpet, and sandpaper. Let Baby look at, feel, talk about, and match them.

Together

Matching games are challenging for Baby and great learning experiences. He will learn to do them successfully with just a little practice. Put together sets of objects matched by colors: blocks and plastic cups, cars and box garages, or crayons and papers. Look around the house and you'll find items for color-matching sets. Keep them together in a box or zip-lock bag.

Dust 'Em

Feather dusters are wonderful, safe, help-Mom toys. Baby can dust the chair rungs and the top of the coffee table to his heart's content and you won't have to worry about breakage.

Make Your Own

Remember the flannelboard made from a cardboard box in Chapter 11? The same technique can be used to make an easy easel just Baby's size. Do as before but instead of adding felt, use a piece of an old plastic tablecloth to cover the slant surface. Cut two holes at the top, one at each end of the easel, for clothespins to hold Baby's paper. Or use large clips. Baby can sit or stand to paint depending on where his easel is placed. Watercolors will work fine but a thick, stubby brush will improve his art. Limit the water and make sure his water dish is stable.

Treats Box

Baby loves surprises. Use a shoebox to create some. Cut a hole in this lid big enough for his hand to go through. Put small, but too-big-to-swallow toys in the box plus small packages of cereal or cookies and let him pick one by feel. He'll be thrilled.

Picture Perfect

Mount a picture on a piece of cardboard and tape a piece of paper over it. (Put the tape down the left-hand side of the paper only.) Cut the paper horizontally into strips. Your child turns over one strip at a time to reveal (and guess) the picture underneath.

Hit the Road

Give Baby some new terrain to cover with his small cars. Put about ⅓ cup of salt on a cookie sheet. He can make roads for his cars. To begin again, just give the sheet a shake.

Balancing Act

Baby is quite proud of his motor skills. You can help him practice his skills by developing a ''toddler style'' balance beam. Use masking tape to put two parallel lines on the rug about 6 in. apart. Let him try to walk between the lines. When he has mastered this, make it a little harder by having him carry a plate of toys as he walks or by changing the width and design of the lines to maze-like patterns.

Ten Little Firemen

This is a song with new sounds and lots of action.

Ten little firemen
Sleeping in a row
(Extend both hands, fingers curled, to represent
   sleeping men)
Ding-dong goes the bell,
(Pull bell cord with one hand)

And down the pole they go
(Close both fists, put one on top of the other, slide
   them down the pole)
Off on the engine, oh, oh, oh
(Steer engine with hands)
Using the big hose, so, so, so
(Make nozzle with fist)
When the fire's all out, home sooo slow
(Steer engine with hands)
Back to bed, all in a row.
(Extend both hands, fingers curled)

Mr. Alligator

This is another fun, interactive poem for you and Baby to enjoy. Here it is:

Five little monkeys
Swinging in a tree
Teasing Mr. Alligator.
Can't catch me.
Along comes Mr. Alligator
As hungry as can be.

(Swallow up thumb.)
Four little monkeys
Swinging in a tree...
(and so on until all the fingers are swallowed)
Burp—so excuse me.

Finger Printing

Fingerprint pictures can be fun for little fingers. Using colored stamp pads, you can make green leaves on a tree, red apples on the branches, and black bugs lurking below in the green "grass."

Pick a Card

Old business cards, blank on one side, can become a deck of cards for Baby. Draw or glue pictures on them and let him sort and match them.

Colorful Clips

Colorful plastic bulldog paper clips (at least 2½ in. long) can be used several ways. They can be connected, making a necklace or a leash for a toy dog, or, of course, used to clip papers together.

What Did He Say?

Now that Baby is saying a few words and maybe even attempting some two-word sentences, jot down some of his favorites.

1. _____

2. _____

3. _____

ROUTINE TIMES

BATHING

Bath Toy Basket

Another approach to organizing bath toys is an inexpensive plastic bicycle basket. The handles will fit over the bathtub soap dish so toys can drain. These baskets also fit on the end of cribs or strollers and just about anywhere else you need extra storage.

Singing in the Tub

You've always thought you sounded wonderful when you sing in the shower; now use that talent to amuse Baby in his bath. Expose him to some golden oldies—"Singin' in the Rain," "You Are My Sunshine," "Zippity Do Da," and "Oh, Promise Me."

Alllll Gone!

Should Baby decide he's not ready to get out of the tub on a day when you're rushing to make an appointment, start letting the water out. When it's all gone, even a stubborn child will want to get out.

FEEDING

Eating Independently

By now, Baby should be encouraged to feed himself. Let him eat his own way while you recommend (but not force to the point of disharmony) the use of a spoon. Any order or combination of foods Baby prefers should be acceptable. He doesn't care if the peas have ketchup on them and neither should you. Above all, try to make mealtime enjoyable.

Most babies are slow eaters—a desirable habit you should encourage. Don't rush Baby. Rather, let him help the rest of the family slow down, too.

Baby can eat almost anything adults eat. He doesn't need bland food. (Young Italians relish garlicky pesto sauce and little Mexicans thrive on salsa.) You should avoid food that he cannot completely chew, such as whole kernel corn, popcorn, and whole peanuts.

When Baby starts playing with his food or dropping it on the floor, he's telling you he is no longer hungry. You'll eliminate a lot of the messiness if you give him only very small portions. Let him have second helpings if he'll eat them.

Catching the Drips

When you give Baby an ice cream cone, make a collar of a small aluminum pie pan and slip it around the cone. It'll catch the drips.

SLEEPING

Bedtime Fussiness

Research suggests that at least 50 percent of all children between the ages of 1 and 2 make a fuss about being put to bed. There are no solutions to the problem that will work all the time or with every child. Our suggestion is a middle-of-the-road approach.

Establish a well-defined bedtime routine but, don't hesitate to comfort Baby if he's really distressed. Don't stay long, just quickly comfort him and say a final goodnight.

Helping Bobby to Bed

Focusing on someone else's bedtime may help. Try talking about getting Bobby Bear ready for bed. "Hurry and put on your 'jams so you can help Bobby get into his. You know he won't get ready until you do." "You need to go to bed and help Bobby get to sleep so he won't be crabby in the morning."

New Bed

If you are thinking about getting a new bed for Baby sometime in the not-so-distant future, be sure to consider what will be best for your family. One single bed may not be the most practical. A trundle bed provides extra sleeping room for overnight guests. If Baby's room will double as a guest room occasionally, a full-sized bed may be the most practical. There is no rule against a small person enjoying the luxury of a large bed. A bunkbed is a possibility, too. It won't be long before Baby will be having friends sleep over or maybe sharing his room with a brother.

DRESSING AND CHANGING

Portable Pocket

Pockets in toddlers' clothes are usually too small to really hold anything. Make a useful pocket for Baby of sturdy cloth or felt. Add buttonholes and sew buttons on the bibs of a couple pairs of overalls. He can use it to collect treasures, store tissues, and to play "in-and-out."

Dressing for Success

Now that Baby is more involved in the dressing process, you will have to become more flexible. Accept any dressing position, standing or sitting. Be tolerant of the clothing combinations he may insist on; a dressed child is better than one who puts on matching socks but forgets to put on anything else. Keep it simple—no ties, belts, bows, or small buttons.

Dresser Drawers

Since Baby wants to do things by himself, you have many opportunities to introduce new ideas to him. Mark his drawers with simple pictures of their contents. Soon he will learn that he only needs to pick one article from each drawer. This method will also help him put his clothes away.

HELPFUL HINTS

Tisket A Tasket

You can never have too many baskets. They are great organizers and Baby loves them. Baby is especially partial to those he can climb into or carry about.

No More Pacifiers

It's time to break the pacifier habit. Try cutting off a piece of it each week until it's gone. Changing the shape will make it less satisfying, so a single snip may be all that is needed.

Goodbye to Stains

You're probably looking for a good stain remover. Try these to combat four tough stains:

1. Urine—Soak one half-hour in a quart of warm water with one-half teaspoon liquid dishwashing detergent and one tablespoon of ammonia.
2. Baby food—Soak a few hours in one cup of bleach, one cup of dishwashing detergent, and two gallons of water.
3. Formula—Paste the spotted area with unseasoned meat tenderizer and let it sit for a few hours before washing.
4. Spit-up odor—Baking soda paste.

Remember that the quicker you attack these stains, the more likely you are to win. Consider mixing a jar of each stain remover and having them available in the laundry room, ready for action.

Plastic Clothes

To make a plastic poncho or a painting smock, cut holes in an old plastic tablecloth or rubber sheet to accommodate Baby's head and arms. Put it over his head and belt it. The poncho is not beautiful, but it is effective for rain protection and art and water play.

Toy Trading

If you're already smothered with stuffed toys, weed out the ones that are in good condition but no longer interest Baby and trade with another mom. This way both children get some new friends without additional cost to you.

Hang Them

A soft cloth shoe bag that holds ten pairs of shoes is only about 5½ in. wide and fits on the clothes pole. In Baby's room, it's a great way to maximize closet space without major alterations. Several can be hung together for garments and toys. The lower pockets will be easy for Baby to use, and the upper ones will expand your storage space for special items or toys that require your supervision.

Shelf Life

A bathroom shelf with towel hooks at child's height can be a great organizer near the back door. Youngsters can place boots, mittens, outside toys, etc. on it as they come and go. A mom we know has a white wire one that gets lots of use. When she has company, she lifts it off and hangs two pictures.

Keepsake

Do take the time now to launder those few special items of Baby clothes and place them in an airtight bag. The christening dress will be beautiful for Baby's baby too.

Friendly Comfort

When Baby has a cut that needs a bandage, apply one to the same part of his favorite stuffed animal or doll. Baby and his friend will console each other.

The Whisper Method

When Baby is in full voice with a temper tantrum, whisper in his ear. He'll have to stop yelling in order to hear what you are saying.

Hold the Rope

A short piece of rope will be handy when you're walking with a toddler and your arms are full. He'll hold onto the rope (or the strap of your handbag) as if it were your hand. Preschool teachers working with several toddlers at once use a rope with knots at intervals so each child has a knot to hold. Kids love to do it.

Zip Up

Attach a key ring with a little bauble on the end to the zipper on Baby's jacket. He can grasp it and it will help him learn to zip up.

Athletic Equipment

Baby will love an indoor slide/stair/gym combination. These are reasonably priced, often available at discount houses, and are hot items at garage sales. The gym will provide exercise, entertainment, and motor skill development. When Baby outgrows it, you can sell it at your garage sale.

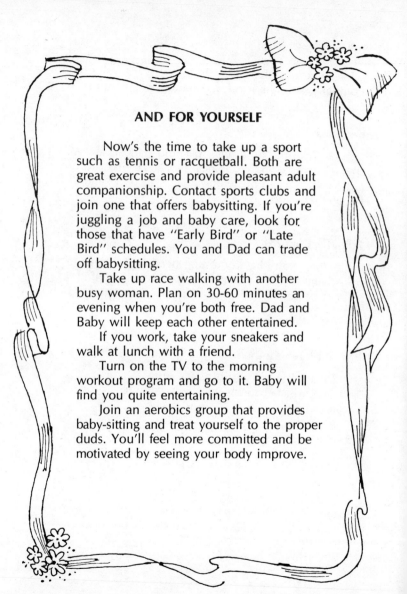

AND FOR YOURSELF

Now's the time to take up a sport such as tennis or racquetball. Both are great exercise and provide pleasant adult companionship. Contact sports clubs and join one that offers babysitting. If you're juggling a job and baby care, look for those that have "Early Bird" or "Late Bird" schedules. You and Dad can trade off babysitting.

Take up race walking with another busy woman. Plan on 30-60 minutes an evening when you're both free. Dad and Baby will keep each other entertained.

If you work, take your sneakers and walk at lunch with a friend.

Turn on the TV to the morning workout program and go to it. Baby will find you quite entertaining.

Join an aerobics group that provides baby-sitting and treat yourself to the proper duds. You'll feel more committed and be motivated by seeing your body improve.

PARENTS, FRIENDS, AND ADMIRERS

Socializing

When you have a friend over who also has a toddler, plan an activity so the adults can have a chance to talk. If you will all be in the kitchen, get some water play ready for the kids in the kitchen sink. Start with a little water, an assortment of plastic cups, spoons, etc. That will amuse them for about fifteen minutes. For an extra ten, add soap bubbles and ice cubes.

Picture Tree

Before you have a family gathering, hang a family "tree" that will help Baby learn the names and faces of the relatives he will soon see. He will become familiar with them and be much more comfortable and willing to interact when they arrive. To make the tree, prepare the snapshots by covering them with clear contact paper and putting a small hole in the top of each. Tie a string to them and hang them on the branches of a potted tree or plant in your home.

Practically Perfect Pinwheel

When a special aunt we know visits her sister, she always brings a special project to make with her favorite niece. One that was well received was a pinwheel made with just a square of flexible cardboard (or plastic), a carpet tack, and a wooden dowel about 1¼ in. × 12 in. Cut two diagonals in the cardboard that approach the center. Tape down the right corner of each triangle to the center. Put the tack through the middle and into the end of the stick.

Storage Bags

When grandma wants to buy Baby a building set that has a large number of pieces, suggest that she make a drawstring bag from colorful cotton to hold all the parts of the toy or game.

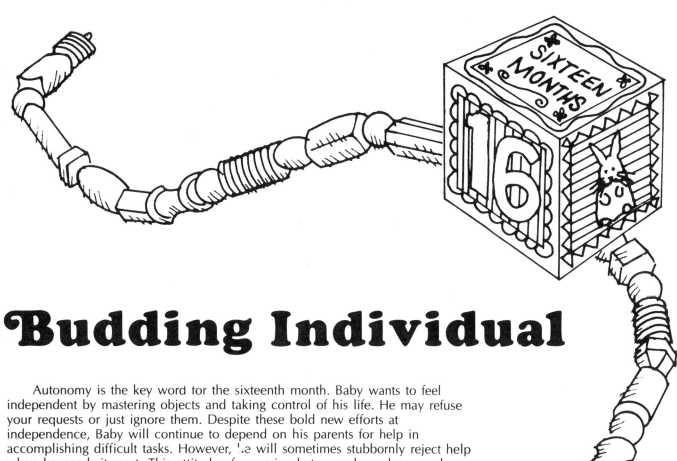

Budding Individual

Autonomy is the key word for the sixteenth month. Baby wants to feel independent by mastering objects and taking control of his life. He may refuse your requests or just ignore them. Despite these bold new efforts at independence, Baby will continue to depend on his parents for help in accomplishing difficult tasks. However, he will sometimes stubbornly reject help when he needs it most. This attitude of wavering between dependence and independence will continue through adolescence, but the objectionable aspects of this phase will pass. When your patience wanes, remember that Baby simply wants to see how he can affect his environment.

You will soon begin to see Baby's new method of trying to get what he wants—the ever-popular temper tantrum. Many parents have trouble dealing with tantrums, but actually the remedy is quite simple: Do not give in. By giving in, you encourage more, longer-lasting tantrums. Do not yell back;

225

calmly appear to ignore his cries of discontent. If Baby is very stubborn and decides to hold his breath, gently slap his face, causing him to breathe involuntarily. The tantrum is one of many ways he uses to try to control you. He tries out these ploys on his parents because he trusts them; he knows they will not retaliate.

Another popular toddler attempt at control is out-and-out defiance. If you try to force him to be totally obedient and submissive, you may hinder his social development. On the other hand, you have to let him know with discipline and disapproval that he can't indulge in biting, scratching, hitting, and other antisocial behavior. Too much permissiveness or neglect hinders social development, too. Baby will be very unpopular with other children and adults if he's allowed to do anything he wants in the interest of "letting him express himself." Be firm but patient and realize that his objectionable behavior is part of his attempts to grow up. He is expanding his horizons and testing his world. His little plots against society are manageable if approached calmly and patiently.

Baby's social exposure should help teach him right from wrong and how to get along with others. Children learn basic social skills through rewarding experiences, imitation, participation, and communication. Baby's encounters with family members, friends, and peers will help him learn them. Your reactions to the things he does will teach him the essentials of acceptable behavior. Baby will also learn a great deal about socialization if he has opportunities to mix with people outside the family. A play group or classes at an early learning center are an asset. Often, mothers feel rejected if Baby objects to coming home from a friend's house or nursery school. Be aware that throughout his growing-up years, a child will want to spend more time with his peers than with his parents or family members.

Developing self-esteem and ego go along with seeking autonomy. Babies are not born with any knowledge of self. The sixteenth month seems to be when a sense of self begins to form. Saying his own name gives Baby a sense of himself as a separate individual. Baby is now fascinated with his own image, both in the mirror and in photographs. Ego comes into play when Baby does everything possible to be the center of attention. Other important aspects of ego-building are the ability to take the initiative, learning to love oneself, and trying to influence one's environment. Although Baby's attempts to develop these traits may be distressing, they signify positive growth.

GAMES, ACTIVITIES, AND SONGS

Box Painting

Tape a piece of paper to the bottom of a shoe box. Let Baby dip a rubber ball or a jumbo-sized marble in paint and toss it into the box. Shut the lid and the shake the box; you have made a box-painting masterpiece.

Name the Picture

Using Baby's coat rack, play a game of "hang the shape" (or picture). Mount pictures or shapes on cardboard and punch a hole at the top that will fit over the hooks of the coat rack. While Baby hangs them, you name them. Soon he will do it all himself, much to his delight.

Blotto Pictures

Fold a piece of paper in half and drop a small dab of paint inside. Close the paper and smooth it out. When you open the paper, a "blotto picture" will appear. Let Baby do several pictures, then staple them together to form a book. An older child can finish the book by labeling the pictures.

Something Different

As an alternative to paintbrushes, try filling liquid shoe-polish bottles and daubers with different watercolors.

Adventure Walk

Turn your walk with Baby into an adventure. Take along a paper bag, sand pail, or basket and instruct Baby about what things to find—a red leaf, a green stick, a stone, a yellow flower. Help him on his quest and praise his findings when you return home.

Follow the Bunny

On a rainy day, your child can be amused by following bunny or bear tracks around the house. Cut a cardboard stencil of a bunny or bear footprint. Use cornstarch and a flour sifter to make the tracks and give your house that "enchanted forest" look.

Wiggle

This little poem will be a favorite for years. With your help, Baby will soon learn to go through the motions himself. Just do as the words suggest. A home video of this would be a treasure, capturing Baby's last moments of babyhood. Next month he becomes a toddler.

I wiggle my fingers, I wiggle my toes.
I wiggle my shoulders, I wiggle my nose.
Now the wiggles are all out of me.
Look and see how still I can be.

Scooter

Platforms with casters which are used to move large plants make greater scooter toys. They're low to the ground and Baby can move himself on them.

Rattle, Rattle

Metal bandage boxes make wonderful rattle toys. Fill them with raw carrot rounds or sticks (too big for Baby to swallow) and let him shake and rattle to his heart's content.

Greeting Cards

Christmas and birthday cards should be saved, too. Baby can look at the pictures and open and close them. Cards with pop-ups are especially intriguing.

Smart Talk

Now that Baby has opinions and can express some of them, it's important that you say what you mean. Asking questions when you're really giving information is a bad habit. Effective teachers know they can get children to participate within guidelines by following these rules.

1. Keep it simple.

2. Limit choices to those you will accept. For example, "Do you want to eat your apple or your raisins first? Do you want to take the monkey to bed?"

3. Separate Baby from his behavior, especially when it comes to unpleasant or negative situations. Baby is never bad. He may be acting grouchy or angry but he's still wonderful.

Little Red Wagon

Here's another short song that Baby will enjoy. It's sung to the tune of "Where is Sister Susie?"

Bumping up and down in my little
    red wagon, (three times)
Won't you be my darling.
The axle broke and the wheel
    rolled off, (three times)
Won't you be my darling.
(Child's name) is going to fix it
. . . with his/her hammer;
. . . with his/her pliers;
. . . with his/her screwdriver, etc.
Won't you be my darling.

More Artistic Ideas

Baby might like some more artistic ideas. Tie-dye a paper towel by folding it several times and dipping one corner into a bowl of thinned tempera paint (or food coloring mixed with water). Unfold the paper to see a design.

Easy-to-Make

Baby would like a trundle toy to roll around him. You can easily make one by cutting a large circle from a piece of cardboard and inserting a long stick in the middle.

Ribbon Bows

Save the bows from wrapped gifts in a bag or basket. Bring them out for Baby to play with when he needs something new to amuse him.

ROUTINE TIMES

BATHING

Vary the Bath

Where is it written that Baby must take his bath at the same time everyday? If Baby begins to resist his bath at night, bathe him before his nap or mid-morning.

Well Suited

Let him wear his swimsuit in the tub if that will distract him from fussing about taking a bath.

Dirty Dolls

When Baby's dolls are in need of a cleanup, let him scrub them clean as he sits in the tub.

FEEDING

Cleaning His Plate

Believe that your child will never starve if he is offered adequate food. If you accept this idea, you'll not worry over each meal. Consider what a child eats in a week, not a day, and you'll see the complete picture. Just like adults, children have days when they're less hungry. Resist the temptation to coax or force Baby to eat when he's not hungry. Insisting he clean his plate at each meal or making a fuss over how much or little he eats at each meal will lead to eating problems or weight problems later in life. Remember, just a tablespoon of food in his small stomach is equivalent to ½ cup in an adult. Your pediatrician will watch Baby's weight and suggest vitamins or food supplements if necessary.

Eat-Around

A grandma who spent her childhood on a farm shared this tip. Once a week, the family had "eat-around night." That meant each family member could take his plate and eat wherever he pleased—in a tree, on the lawn, in the barn. Baby could chose to eat in his room, the playhouse, or the living room floor with someone to supervise. It could be a fun family tradition and add variety to mealtime.

Small Portions

A first-time mother discovered that her less-than-eager eater was discouraged by the sight of a full plate of food. She began putting minute portions of each food on the plate, suggesting that her child could ask for seconds. It worked!

SLEEPING

Music Hath Charms

Some babies find it hard to go to sleep in a totally quiet room. Make a tape of soothing lullabies and tell Baby that if he lies quietly in his crib, you'll play his go-to-sleep music.

Sleep Habits

Sleeping habits vary with each child. If your child is an early riser, don't figure that you can change that by keeping him up later at night. Don't eliminate the afternoon nap in the hope that he'll go to bed earlier. Sleep can't be stored up. Also, you'll find that sleeping habits may vary during periods when Baby is learning a lot of new skills or is having a growth spurt.

Naps

Between twelve and sixteen months, most toddlers give up the morning nap. Baby will begin taking his morning nap later and later and sleeping longer. You end up with one long nap in the middle of the day instead of two short ones morning and afternoon.

DRESSING AND CHANGING

Shoe Time

Sit baby in his high chair with a toy to play with while you put on his shoes. He'll be more cooperative and your back will be more comfortable.

Velcro Closures

Shoes with velcro closures are great for three-year-olds and beyond but not for toddlers. You'll find that Baby will constantly remove his shoes. You'll spend a lot of time putting them back on or searching the house for one missing shoe.

HELPFUL HINTS

Ready

A working mom shared this idea with us. During times when her child refused to dress in the morning, she dressed him the night before in a clean sweatsuit after he'd had his bath. She would relax the next morning if he refused to dress or let her help him, knowing he was already dressed in clean clothes. Only another harried mom can appreciate the beauty of this idea.

Happy Traveler

Before you take Baby on a long car trip, check with your doctor about a motion sickness remedy. You'll want to have it on hand, just in case it's needed.

Plane Travel

Give Baby a bottle or a box of juice to suck on when the plane is taking off and landing. It will help equalize the air pressure in his ears.

Again and Again

Mom and Dad may think they cannot stand one more repetition of "The Three Bears" but Baby doesn't agree. He loves every single repeat performance. Keep reading the favorites until he decides he's bored.

Posey Fun

Baby loves to sort things. Those plastic bouquets you relegated to the attic for no good reason will fascinate him. He can sort out the roses and daises in containers you give him.

Singalong

The reason you hear teachers of toddlers singing while they work is that it makes the youngsters pay attention. Singing a simple song can encourage an independent-minded toddler to cooperate better than a direct request. Example: "Helper, helper, I need a helper to put away the toys. Janie is a helper, a helper, a helper. She puts her toys away." Make up your own tune. Words and music aren't as important as the invitation to join in.

Rings and Things

Mark each of Baby's fingernails with a different color and then show him how to slip on matching dime-store finger rings.

PARENTS, FRIENDS, AND ADMIRERS

Reminder

Now that Baby is saying a few words, be sure to include his "conversation" on the tapes you send to relatives and friends far away.

New Tools

Grandpa's tool bench will entrance Baby. Let him put screws in little boxes, pound with a small hammer (no nails necessary), and feel the sandpaper. As a special treat, he'd love to have a piece of very fine sandpaper for his very own.

Grandma's Cookies

Even if grandma isn't big on baking, Baby will never know if he and she share the fun of decorating cookies cut from a roll, then baking and eating them.

Simple Pleasures

Grandparents and friends who have no children may feel at a loss to entertain Baby when he visits. A smart grandmother we know emptied a small bottom drawer in the pantry (a small, two-section drawer would work, too) and filled it with little-used kitchen utensils, junk mail with colorful pictures, and other discarded items. This was her grandchild's own special drawer. He could rummage in it to his heart's content, and each time he came, there were new surprises.

Just for Mom

Give Mom a framed picture of Baby. She's so busy sending out pictures to others she may not take time to do it for herself. Photo refrigerator magnets and photo key chains are nice, too.

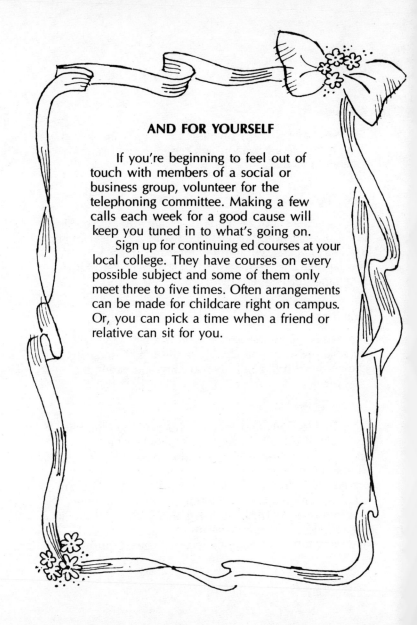

AND FOR YOURSELF

If you're beginning to feel out of touch with members of a social or business group, volunteer for the telephoning committee. Making a few calls each week for a good cause will keep you tuned in to what's going on.

Sign up for continuing ed courses at your local college. They have courses on every possible subject and some of them only meet three to five times. Often arrangements can be made for childcare right on campus. Or, you can pick a time when a friend or relative can sit for you.

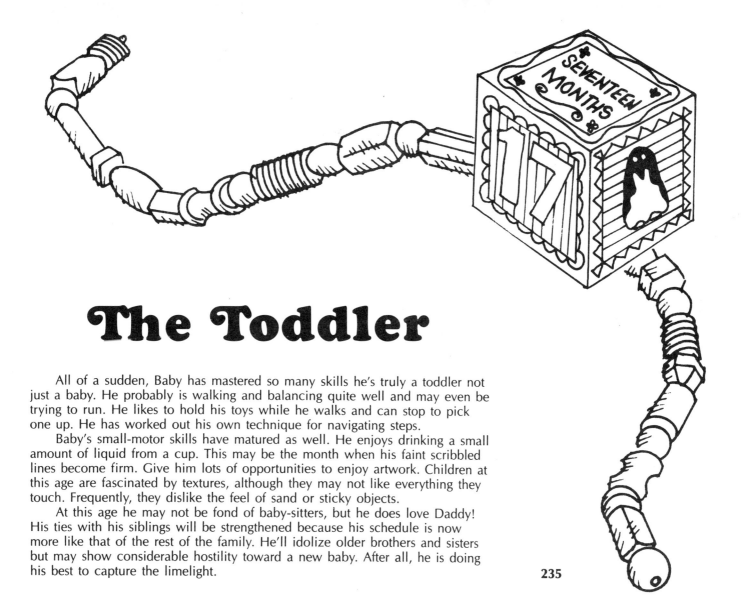

The Toddler

All of a sudden, Baby has mastered so many skills he's truly a toddler not just a baby. He probably is walking and balancing quite well and may even be trying to run. He likes to hold his toys while he walks and can stop to pick one up. He has worked out his own technique for navigating steps.

Baby's small-motor skills have matured as well. He enjoys drinking a small amount of liquid from a cup. This may be the month when his faint scribbled lines become firm. Give him lots of opportunities to enjoy artwork. Children at this age are fascinated by textures, although they may not like everything they touch. Frequently, they dislike the feel of sand or sticky objects.

At this age he may not be fond of baby-sitters, but he does love Daddy! His ties with his siblings will be strengthened because his schedule is now more like that of the rest of the family. He'll idolize older brothers and sisters but may show considerable hostility toward a new baby. After all, he is doing his best to capture the limelight.

235

This month you may find Baby enjoying a lot of imaginative play. He will like to dress up in other family members' clothes, carry a handbag like mother's, and talk on a play telephone. Dramatic play is a playback of what he has seen around him and helps him sort through his impressions of his world. Imaginative play can serve as a way for Baby to express his emotions. Try to provide him with plenty of interesting props.

ACTIVITIES, GAMES, AND SONGS

Maze Box

This month's very curious Baby will particularly enjoy this game. This toy is used in many schools. Make a maze box from a shoe box and cardboard tubes. You also need strong scissors, contact paper, and tape. Cover the box with colorful contact paper. Cut three holes in the lid, each about 3 in. × 1½ in. Cut out one hole—the same size as in the lid—in each of the three sides of the box. Insert a tube through a hole in the lid then out a hole on the side. Do the same with two more tubes. Tape the tubes in place and, if necessary, trim the ends so that the box lays flat. Now you can drop small bells or other objects into the top of the tube and they will fall out on the sides. Baby will try to guess which hole the toy will pop out of.

Balloon Swatter

Here's a toy for a rainy day. Bend a wire coat hanger into a diamond shape and cover it with an old nylon stocking. Cover the hook with tape for safety and show Baby how to use the wire to bat balloons around his room.

String Painting

Fold a piece of paper. Dip a piece of string in paint, put it in the fold of the paper. Close the paper and move the string around with your hands. Open the paper and find a string picture.

The Old Standards

Don't overlook the simple, traditional games—flying kites, rolling down a hill, catching fireflies, and hide-and-seek. This kind of roughhouse play is always special fun and shouldn't be reserved just for fathers and sons.

Dressing Up

Dress-up play is a great way for a child to use his imagination. Visit a thrift store and buy size eight or nine children's clothes for Baby to play in. The larger size will give him plenty of room without causing him to trip. Items such as jackets, skirts, hats, wigs, and bags will be thoroughly enjoyed.

Attractive Napkins

Baby will like to look at colored paper napkins that have seasonal motifs. Give him a few to feel and scrunch up. Put them in a discarded tissue box so Baby can pull them out and stuff them in.

Puzzled?

Store-bought puzzles can be very expensive. You can make dozens at home. Paste uncomplicated colored pictures on corrugated board. Cut into large puzzle pieces. Cut another piece of cardboard the same size. Attach velcro dots or pieces of magnetic tape (both are available at notions counters) to the puzzle pieces and to the second piece of cardboard. This will make the puzzle easier because a perfect fit is not required.

Periscope

Make a periscope with two 2 in. × 3 in. mirrors and an aluminum-foil box (without the cutter). Cut out two holes, one at each end of the box. Insert the mirrors at an angle, so that they will reflect images to each other, and secure them with tape. Baby peeks in one hole and sees things around him.

Song

This cute little song is sung to the tune of "Skip to My Lou": It is fun to add hand movements.

Eight long legs and two big eyes,
Salty tears whenever he cries,
Makes his home at the bottom of the sea,
Can you guess what this can be?
See him wiggle, see him slide.
Try to catch him, he will hide.
Throw him a fish so he won't fuss,
He's a baby octopus.

Baby will also enjoy seeing a picture of an Octopus and learning about him.

Which One Doesn't Belong?

Line up a series of pictures or objects that are similar and add one that is different. Example: three pictures of cats and one of a bird. Ask Baby to point out (or remove) the one that doesn't belong.

Roll a Picture

Cut a medium-sized rectangle from the bottom of a box. Draw pictures on a roll of adding machine tape and glue the end of the paper to an empty adding-machine-tape tube. Place the paper and rolls in the box, secured by pencils or dowels which are punched through the sides of the box. To see the pictures, you and Baby turn the pencils and watch the pictures through the rectangular hole.

Newspaper Tree

Roll a few sheets of newspaper into a tube and tape them together. At the top of the roll, make four 6 in. vertical cuts. Reach inside and carefully pull the inside up, letting cuts form branches that flop down to make a tree. These are fun and good props for imaginative play. Use bigger paper and more layers to make palm trees for Baby's playroom. Lay out sunglasses, a blanket and sand toys, and play Hawaiian music as you escape to the islands.

Pasta Strings

Get some large-sized pasta (rigatoni, wheels, elbow macaroni, etc.) and string them together. To make stringing easy, attach a large bobby pin or harden one end of the string with nail polish. You can easily store materials for his pasta creations in Baby's kitchen drawer or cabinet. Then they will be ready to amuse him when you must devote all your attention to cooking.

Tissue Paper Collage

Let Baby help arrange pieces of colored tissue paper on a large piece of white paper. Dip a thick

brush into thinned white glue or liquid starch and paint (or soak) the tissue paper. The pieces will dry and have a "stained-glass" effect.

Creative Clothespins

Once your child is able to handle clothespins, you have opportunities to create all kinds of games that utilize his new skill. You can color the pins with a marker and tape corresponding colors on the sides of loaf pans. Let Baby match the colors by placing the pins in their respective boxes.

A Crayon Variation

Peel the paper off a crayon. Cut a "V"-shaped notch extending the length of the crayon. When your child draws with the altered crayon, he'll get two parallel lines. You can cut a notch in the top of a fat crayon for the same result.

Egg-Carton People

Egg cartons can be used in a variety of quick, homemade games. One that Baby will like is "All the People." Invert an egg carton and poke a hole in each section. Let Baby help draw faces on twelve straight clothespins. He'll enjoy standing all the people up in their holes. This activity teaches Baby about objects in space. The same idea can be used as a letter, number, or color-matching game. Color code the pins with their respective egg-carton sections and let Baby match them.

ROUTINE TIMES

BATHING

Reluctant Bather

Try using a small inner tube while Baby plays before he is washed. This little bit of extra security may be all he needs to help him enjoy the "big tub" experience.

FEEDING

Yogurt Dip

To persuade a finicky eater to eat vegetables, try a dip made of yogurt. It's fun and tasty to dip cooked vegetables and fresh fruit. Cheese and peanut butter dips are good, too. Try unusual vegetables. Snow peas, crinkle-cut carrots, baby corn on the cob, water chestnuts, and zucchini sticks will fascinate Baby.

SLEEPING

Egg Timer

Set a kitchen timer or egg timer to signal when Baby's bedtime has arrived. This makes bedtime "official," and Mom and Dad don't have to take the blame for interrupting his play.

The Art of Sleeping

Have one of Baby's pictures put on an oversized T-shirt to use as his nightshirt. He'll coo to himself as he dozes off. You can have Baby's picture put on a plate as well. This might be an incentive for him to eat everything so he can see himself.

Pompons

Two soft, small, yarn pompons sewn securely on each of Baby's pajama sleeves will give him something to touch as he snuggles to sleep.

DRESSING AND CHANGING

Eight Balls in the Left-Hand Pocket

Toddlers love pockets big enough to store treasures. When shopping for clothes, remember that he'll appreciate lots of pockets.

Straighten Up

Have Baby help you "clean up" by giving him several objects to put away in their proper places. He can put dirty clothes in the hamper and shoes in the closet, for example.

More Coats

An outgrown jacket can become a vest. With a heavy sweater underneath, Baby will be almost as warm as he was in the original jacket. Don't get mad at an uncooperative dresser. Remember to play where's-your-hand, peek-a-boo, or there-it-is to help Baby push his hand through the sleeve. Use the same strategy for getting small feet into snowsuits.

Find the Bell

Put a bell in the pocket of Baby's overalls and have him find it while you're dressing him. Shake the overalls occasionally while you're putting on other items to keep him interested.

A Warm Bed

Blanket sleepers are the answer for the active toddler in winter. It will keep him cozy and give you peace of mind.

HELPFUL HINTS

Costumes

Keep Halloween costumes for year-round dress-up play.

Sun Times

Too much sun is dangerous for Baby. If you're going to the pool or beach take an umbrella or use a playpen turned upside down as shade for his sun-sensitive skin.

Comfort First

Baby seats can get very warm in summer. Cover the seat with a terrycloth towel to keep it cool and to absorb moisture.

Makeup With Cotton

Do you need to distract Baby while you apply your makeup? Keep small tongs near your cotton balls and let Baby fill a container while you do your face.

The Eyes Have It

Embroidered eyes on stuffed toys are much safer than button-type eyes that might be swallowed.

Important Records

Baby should have his own file folder, which contains his medical records and birth certificate.

Keep it with the family tax records for easy retrieval and updating.

Hot Clay

To rejuvenate modeling clay wrap it in a moistened paper towel and place it in a microwave oven for seven to ten seconds.

Toy Hampers

Canvas clothes hampers with wooden or metal frames make great toy chests. They come in bright colors and cost less than most toy chests. They have several advantages:

1. You never have to worry about a child hurting his fingers.
2. They can be used for other purposes when toy chests are no longer needed.
3. They are a breeze to clean.

Clean Toys

Wash Baby's toys in the washing machine. The same bag Mom washes pantyhose in is perfect.

Frame It

Make a frame for the refrigerator door to showcase Baby's artwork. A clear acrylic 8 in. × 10 in. frame with two large magnets attached with superglue is ideal.

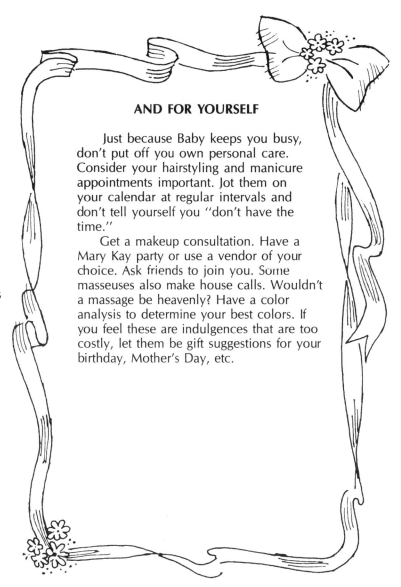

AND FOR YOURSELF

Just because Baby keeps you busy, don't put off you own personal care. Consider your hairstyling and manicure appointments important. Jot them on your calendar at regular intervals and don't tell yourself you "don't have the time."

Get a makeup consultation. Have a Mary Kay party or use a vendor of your choice. Ask friends to join you. Some masseuses also make house calls. Wouldn't a massage be heavenly? Have a color analysis to determine your best colors. If you feel these are indulgences that are too costly, let them be gift suggestions for your birthday, Mother's Day, etc.

PARENTS, FRIENDS, AND ADMIRERS

Artsy Gifts

Give an artistic gift from Baby to his admirers. You can have his favorite drawing transferred to a T-shirt. Give it to a friend or relative who simply must have one of Baby's creations. Baby's handprint is always appreciated. Use it to sign cards from him, frame one, put on backs of photographs as a personalized signature. Footprints and lip prints are also welcomed.

Make Some Dough

Cooked playdough? Yes, this recipe will yield a caring gift for a favorite small person—a batch of playdough.

1 cup flour
½ cup salt
1 cup water
1 tsp. cream of tartar
1 tbsp. vegetable oil
food coloring

Combine the ingredients, mix them well, and cook over medium heat until the mixture forms a ball. Cool and wrap in plastic.

But don't stop there. Include with your playdough some cookie cutters, a small rolling pin, a garlic press, or a plastic knife. Baby will appreciate some straws to poke with and a wooden spoon for mashing.

Stationery Art

Delight Baby's friends and admirers by using the back of his artwork for letters to his and your special friends, such as grandma and grandpa. Write on the papers what baby says about his picture syllable-by-syllable.

Snow Ice Cream

Snow ice cream will be enjoyed by kids of any age. Mix:

1 cup rich milk
1 beaten egg
½ cup sugar
1 tsp. vanilla
dash of salt
5 cups of clean, fresh snow

Wash it Now . . . Drive It Later

Nobody will enjoy helping to wash the family car more than Baby. Give him a sponge and he'll wash the tires and other areas close to the ground.

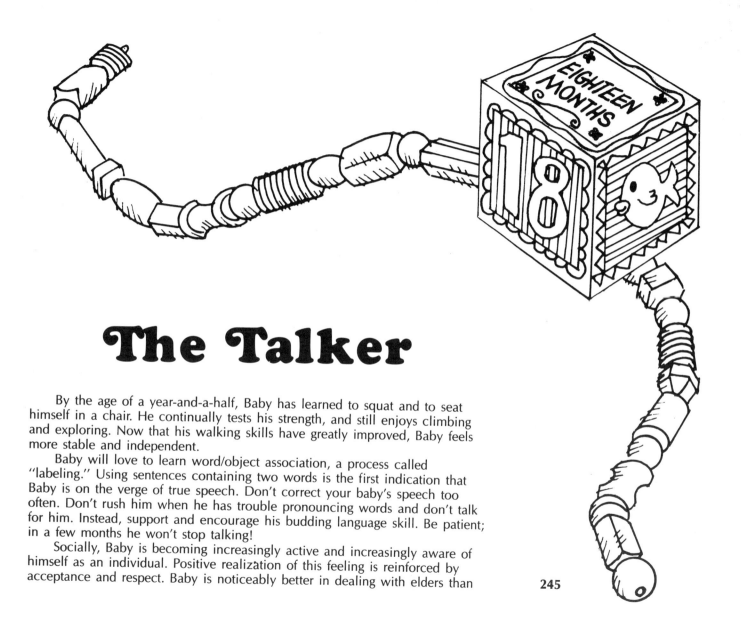

The Talker

By the age of a year-and-a-half, Baby has learned to squat and to seat himself in a chair. He continually tests his strength, and still enjoys climbing and exploring. Now that his walking skills have greatly improved, Baby feels more stable and independent.

Baby will love to learn word/object association, a process called "labeling." Using sentences containing two words is the first indication that Baby is on the verge of true speech. Don't correct your baby's speech too often. Don't rush him when he has trouble pronouncing words and don't talk for him. Instead, support and encourage his budding language skill. Be patient; in a few months he won't stop talking!

Socially, Baby is becoming increasingly active and increasingly aware of himself as an individual. Positive realization of this feeling is reinforced by acceptance and respect. Baby is noticeably better in dealing with elders than

245

with peers. The more time he spends with other children, the better developed his social skills will be.

A fear of the dark is common at this age, but with your help this and other fears can be controlled. Baby learns fear from his parents and others, from his own frightening experiences, and from what he hears. Try not to teach him fear. When Baby is frightened, deal with it seriously and calmly. To prevent needless fear, it is important that you never make Baby feel that he is a failure. Don't say things like, "You mustn't be a fraidy cat. You're a big boy now."

During the active months, don't expect perfection from Baby or yourself. No one is the perfect parent, and no one can guarantee that his child-rearing methods will produce Supreme Court judges or affluent owners of corporations. With patience, support, and a little luck, chances are that Baby will not, in his adulthood, pick up a copy of *The New Prison Times* for some easy Sunday reading before your weekly visit.

ACTIVITIES, GAMES, AND SONGS

Learning Emotions

To teach Baby about emotions, cut a piece of felt in the shape of a body and secure it to a sturdy piece of cardboard. Cut some felt circles and draw faces with a different emotions on each. Tell Baby a story like "Bobby broke his favorite toy and feels very sad. Can you find Bobby's sad face and put it on his body?" For a variation, make some felt hats, too. Tell Baby to put the hat on the happy face or the crying face.

Lunch Box I.D.

If your toddler totes a lunch pail to nursery school, he will always recognize it if you personalize it with his picture. To make it permanent, cover the picture with a square of clear contact paper.

Picture Block

Make a square block from a small milk carton. Glue a picture, color, etc. on each side. Cover the block with clear contact paper. Let your child roll it like a die and identify the picture that comes up on top.

Picture Calendar

Enhance learning skills by making a calendar with a picture of one activity you have planned for Baby each day. Use pictures from magazines of a grocery store, a car, or a wading pool. Establish a routine with the calendar by checking it every day. The calendar instills the concept of time for Baby and gives him something to anticipate and talk about each day.

Paint a Face

A face-painting kit can be a lot of fun for you and your inquisitive toddler. Let him watch in the mirror as you apply designs to his face. Increase his pleasure by letting him try the art on himself or on you.

Voices from Home

If you're planning a long trip, ask your child's nursery school teacher to make a tape of his group singing or playing a word game. What a surprise it will be when he hears his friends while he's riding in the car.

Art Kit

This is great gift for an aspiring artist. Pack a sturdy box that has a strong handle with a variety of art supplies. Include a glue stick, scissors (the new two-color, plastic ones that cut safely), markers, crayons, a short-handled flat paintbrush, a set of watercolors, several pads of paper, stickers, an envelope containing scraps of paper to paste, a plastic or cloth tarp (about 18 in. × 24 in.) for a work surface, and a smock or bib.

Make Stamp Prints

Baby can enjoy printing without expensive and hard-to-clean stamp prints. Use alphabet blocks that have raised letters or figures. Put some watercolor paint on a sponge and use it as a stamp pad. Watercolors are much easier to wash off than the ink on a stamp pad.

Sandpaper Pictures

Bright yarn and cotton balls will stick to sandpaper. You can make pictures without using glue. No mess! Hang the sandpaper paintings on the wall or the refrigerator to experience the true sticking effect.

Matching Squares

Cut sets of matching squares from wallpaper samples or wrapping paper. Glue four or five patterns on one piece of cardboard and let Baby play with the remaining squares by matching them to the glued-on patterns.

Sack Wings

Slit the sides of a sturdy brown grocery bag, leaving the bottom intact. Cut the sides into butterfly, angel, or bird wings. Place the bottom of the bag, between the two wings, on Baby's back. Make straps to hold the wings with ribbon, and staple the ribbon to the wings. When Baby slips his arms into the straps, he can flap his wings. The wings will be strong enough to withstand hard play because the bottom of the bag is reinforced.

Chalkboard Paint

If you haven't heard of chalkboard paint, visit your local art store. This nifty stuff will turn any surface you chose into a blackboard. Use the side or back of a garage for outdoor art or an inside garage wall or basement wall for an indoor gallery.

Vocabulary Building

When you read a story or say a familiar poem, pause and omit a key word, letting Baby say it. This will help him build his vocabulary and also learn to listen more carefully.

Backyard Icebergs

When the temperature soars, add new fun to Baby's wading pool with "icebergs." Fill balloons with water and freeze. Put them in the pool and let Baby splash with them.

Water Chute

Water slides are easy to make and work well when several age groups are using the water sprinkler together. Find a slight rise in the ground and place an old shower curtain or plastic table cloth on the side of the hill. Arrange the sprinkler so it wets the cloth. Baby can stand in the sprinkler while brother takes a running slide. Soon Baby will learn to slide, too, probably in a conservative, tummy-down position.

Poems

Toddlers love the suspense and action of these easy little rhymes. Act it out together often.

Down in a Box

Down in a box, still as can be.
Lift up the lid and what do you see?
Pop up!
Jumping jacks go up and down,
Up and down, up and down.
Jumping jacks go up and down.
Up—Down—Stop.
I'm a Spinning Top.
Round and round I goooo—
I spin and spin and spin and spin.
Spin until I DROP.
KER-PLOP.

Squish Bag

Put some vegetable oil, water, and food coloring in a zip-lock bag. Seal the bag and let Baby squish it to form colorful designs.

What Bobby Did Today

Make up a story about something your child did that day. "Bobby washed his ball today. He filled a pan with water and scrubbed his ball and scrubbed and scrubbed and scrubbed . . ."

Or make up a bedtime story about the whale family. Young children enjoy Mom's made-up stories even more than books.

ROUTINE TIMES

BATHING

Cleanup

Use baby oil or baby lotion to clean the paint and marker off Baby's skin. If this doesn't work, try a little hairspray to remove stubborn marker stains.

Safety

Form the habit of always turning the hot water off before putting Baby in the tub. That way, if the faucet drips you won't have to worry about burns.

Sure Footing

Invest in a nonslip bathmat for the tub. It is much safer than stick-on decals and provides a little cushioning in addition to surer footing. Baby insists on being upright in the tub so you should always be there and ready to catch him if he tumbles.

SLEEPING

Crib Climber

Climbing out of the crib is inevitable, so at least make it a safe maneuver. Here are some tips:

1. Put a chair next to the crib so he can reach the floor safely without a big leap.
2. Leave the crib gate down so it won't release while he's climbing over it.
3. Get Baby in the habit of reporting to you as soon as he's out of his bed. He'll do this if he thinks you're glad to see him. This way he won't go exploring without your knowledge.
4. Give Baby a noisemaker or a bell so he can let you know when he's awake.
5. Put a gate on the bedroom doorway so he can't get out of the room.

FEEDING

Balanced Diet

Your goal should be to train Baby to accept a wide variety of foods when he is older so that eating a balanced diet comes naturally. This may be impossible right now, but continue to work on it. Offer very small portions of new foods. If Baby rejects them, don't force the issue, just wait a few weeks or a month and try again.

Don't use food as a reward or a motivator. Having dessert shouldn't be the reason Baby eats his vegetables. Researchers believe that overeating and other nutritional problems may be the result of poor eating habits learned in childhood. Reward Baby with a hug, a word of praise, or a trip to the playground instead of food.

At this age, Baby may change his likes and dislikes for no reason. If he begins to reject a food, offer a substitute and reintroduce it later.

If Baby eats with older children, discourage them from loudly proclaiming that one food or another is "yucky." Baby will reject it too, even if he likes it.

Experiment with Textures

Children react strongly to texture as well as flavor. You may like your vegetables very crisp. Right now, Baby may like them softer. Color and size may also be issues for Baby. If he loves green peas he will grow to like green beans if you cut them about the same size. Ditto with baby lima beans.

Finger Food

Roll sandwich bread flat with a rolling pin. Put some meat or cheese on the bread and roll it to create a roll-up sandwich. Put in the toaster oven occasionally for a crisp texture.

Sandwich Surprise

Surprise Baby with a sandwich shaped like a letter or a face. With just a kitchen knife you can cut the slice into his initial or a big heart. Olive eyes, carrot curl hair, and a green pepper mouth will develop into a fun "facewich."

DRESSING AND CHANGING

Drawstrings

A very easy way to replace those long, limp drawstrings that Baby loves to pull out of his pants or jackets is to wet and freeze them. Then, it's a snap to push the string through the slot.

Space Saver

If closet space is a limited, consider hanging clothes on tiered skirt hangers. This method saves space and the hangers will always be useful.

Shoestring Trick

If you are tired of lacing Baby's shoes over and over again, try this little preschool trick. Tie knots in the ends of the laces in the shoes so they can be loosened, but not removed.

Money-saving Tip

When you switch Baby from diapers to training pants, he will wear a smaller size in shorts and overalls. You may discover that clothing items that didn't fit over bulky diapers can be worn now. Save good wearable clothes that you may be using at this time; he can use them later.

Easy Off

If you decide to begin toilet training, switch Baby from overalls to pull-on pants. Dress girls in skirts and tights. They are easier to pull off and on.

HELPFUL HINTS

Playground Safety

You can get the "Handbook for Playground Safety"—Volume 1" from the Consumer Products Safety Commission, Washington, DC 20207. Or you can call, toll-free, 1-800-638-2772.

Don't assume all play areas are safe. Asphalt surfaces and unprotected swings that a toddler can run into are dangerous.

Relax Together

Let some of the time you spend with Baby be mutually relaxing. Make it a looked-forward-to daily routine to sit and take a coffee/juice break. The two of you can relax and enjoy some quiet time together.

Telephone Trick

About this time, Baby may discover the telephone if he can reach it. Use a rubber band to hold down the piece that, when lifted, causes a dial tone or connection. If Baby removes the receiver from the hook, your phones will still function.

Coping with Emergencies

Here are a few things you can do to make sure you can handle any minor emergency.

1. Carry several safety pins attached to your key chain.
2. Carry a small sewing kit. Some are as small as a matchbox.
3. Carry an assortment of band-aids in your change purse.
4. Carry moist towelette in individual wrappers.
5. Carry a set of clothes in the trunk of the car.

Slick Idea

A nifty way to apply baby oil or other liquids without a big mess is to put the liquid in a clean roll-on deodorant bottle.

Play Table

Bed tables make ideal work tables for Baby when he's sitting on the floor. Put a plastic place mat on the table for easy cleanup.

Sticker Saver

Stick a piece of clear plastic contact paper on the inside of Baby's closet door or next to your washing machine. All of those stickers he leaves in his pockets can be placed there when you prepare to wash his clothes. They'll peel right off tomorrow and can be used again.

By the Sea

When planning a vacation to a resort area, invest in a portable high chair that safely clamps to any restaurant table. They cost less than fifteen dollars and are indispensable. All the parents waiting for a high chair or faced with the prospect of holding babies on their laps will envy you.

Gum

If you have the misfortune of having either candy or gum tangled in your child's hair don't go for the scissors! A generous amount of laundry prewash spray will usually work if you work it between your fingers. A good hair conditioner or cream rinse will also work in a pinch.

Toy Caddy

A carpenter's carrying case is handy for storing favorite toys. This way they are always together and take up minimal space. Having too many toys in one place only distracts Baby from creative play. Extras can be stored and then exchanged for new ones periodically.

Keep the Stroller

Always take your stroller on short or long excursions. Although Baby wants to trot along on his own, a toddler does not learn to follow a moving adult or stay with one until he's about three. Until then, he will ask you to "uppy" him the moment he sees you begin to move on. He knows he can't stay close to you once you start walking. The stroller will save your back and please him.

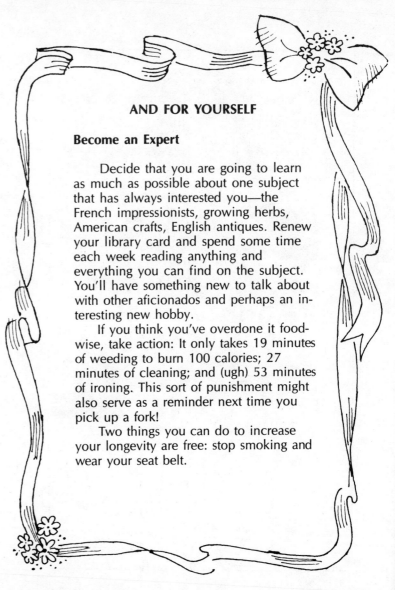

AND FOR YOURSELF

Become an Expert

Decide that you are going to learn as much as possible about one subject that has always interested you—the French impressionists, growing herbs, American crafts, English antiques. Renew your library card and spend some time each week reading anything and everything you can find on the subject. You'll have something new to talk about with other aficionados and perhaps an interesting new hobby.

If you think you've overdone it food-wise, take action: It only takes 19 minutes of weeding to burn 100 calories; 27 minutes of cleaning; and (ugh) 53 minutes of ironing. This sort of punishment might also serve as a reminder next time you pick up a fork!

Two things you can do to increase your longevity are free: stop smoking and wear your seat belt.

PARENTS, FRIENDS, AND ADMIRERS

Grandma's Ballgame

Make playing ball with Baby less strenuous for grandma and grandpa. Have grandma or grandpa hold one end of a large bath towel or tablecloth while Baby holds the other. Bounce the ball in the cloth. It's fun and does not require running.

Catering to Kneads

Baby will love to help grandma knead the dough and eat the delicious results. Here's a recipe that will satisfy Baby's "kneads." You need:

1 package dry yeast
1 cup warm water
1/3 cup sugar
1/3 cup oil
3 cups flour
dash of salt

Put the water in a bowel and sprinkle on the yeast. After it settles, mix in the rest of the ingredients and form a ball of dough. Knead the dough for 10 to 15 minutes (Baby loves this part) on a floured board. Cover the dough and let it rise for one hour (until it has doubled). Knead the dough again, cut it into small balls, place on a greased baking sheet, cover and let them rise until doubled. Bake 10 to 12 minutes at 450 degrees. These small rolls will be just the right size for Baby's sandwiches.

Ring Toss

Save a few games for the baby-sitter to play with Baby. Here's an easy one: Clip some clothespins to the edge of a box. Get a few mason jar rubber rings to toss onto the clothespins. You can paint the tops of the pins and have Baby identify the color where the ring has fallen.

Reminder

At this age, Baby's teeth should be brushed after each meal, using a soft baby's toothbrush. (Many children's dentists recommend you begin brushing as soon as the first tooth erupts.) It's not necessary to use toothpaste. Most babies dislike the strong flavor. It's a good idea to introduce Baby to a children's dentist at this age. Caries (decay) usually occur on the back of the teeth and may not be visible to casual examination. Also, the dentist will spot any abnormalities in the teeth or formation of the jaw. We said it before but it's worth repeating: Drinking at will from a bottle or taking a bottle filled with milk, juice, or other beverage to bed is the single most common cause of caries. As one dentist exclaimed, "We see absolutely devastating cases of caries in two-year-olds that are the result of taking a bottle to bed." If a bottle at bedtime is necessary, fill it with water.

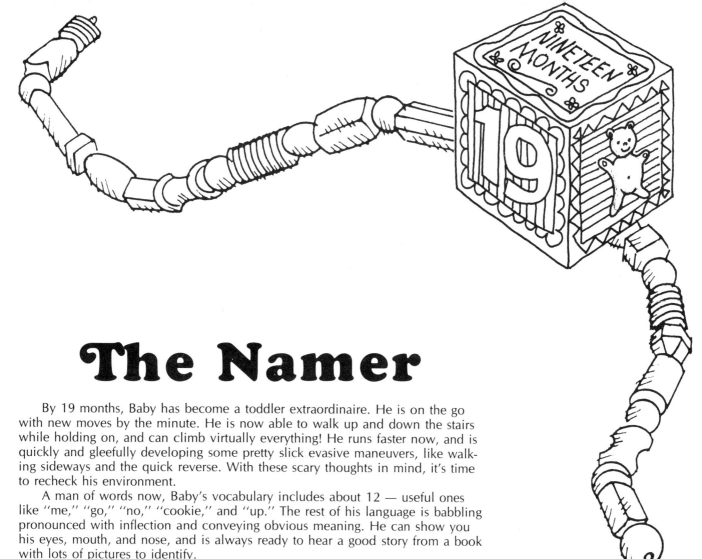

The Namer

By 19 months, Baby has become a toddler extraordinaire. He is on the go with new moves by the minute. He is now able to walk up and down the stairs while holding on, and can climb virtually everything! He runs faster now, and is quickly and gleefully developing some pretty slick evasive maneuvers, like walking sideways and the quick reverse. With these scary thoughts in mind, it's time to recheck his environment.

A man of words now, Baby's vocabulary includes about 12 — useful ones like "me," "go," "no," "cookie," and "up." The rest of his language is babbling pronounced with inflection and conveying obvious meaning. He can show you his eyes, mouth, and nose, and is always ready to hear a good story from a book with lots of pictures to identify.

Baby loves new adventures. The local park is great fun. He enjoys the swings and slides but will want you close by. Other children are exciting to be

257

around even though he doesn't play with them directly. He enjoys studying and imitating them. A huggable, energetic, busy little person, Baby is always working to become more independent. Parents, beware! We are approaching the land of tantrums and sheer stubbornness and are on the road through toddlerhood.

ACTIVITIES, GAMES, AND SONGS

Boulder Blocks

Stuff brown paper bags with leaves or newspapers and then tie or tape them shut so they are in the shape of large squarish boulders. These monster blocks will thrill baby with their size and light weight. This is a great game indoors or out.

Bubbles

Bubbles are always a captivator of young children. They are the thinnest things we can see with the naked eye. The shapes and sizes of bubbles are determined by the size and shape of wand you use. Try a straw, a juice can, a coffee can, a berry basket, or a shaped clothes hanger dipped in a shallow pan of solution for starters. Everything that touches the bubbles must be wet. Bubbles break when they touch a dry surface. Add food coloring for colored bubbles.

A variation on this is "bubble art": Divide your solution among several small glass bowls. In each bowl put several drops of food coloring. Using your wand, begin to blow but instead of having Baby pop these beauties, give him a sheet of white paper to catch them on. He will enjoy his colorful creation.

Our solution is:

1 qt. warm water
¼ cup liquid dishwashing detergent
1 T sugar
½ gallon plastic jug or jar with a lid

Magnet Game

Use a small metal cookie sheet, a horseshoe magnet (or other easy-to-hold magnet), and a small metal car. Draw a roadway on a piece of paper that will fit snugly in the pan. Place the car on the track and the magnet under the tray so that by moving the magnet Baby will propel his car. This mystery is guaranteed to hold the interest of any inquisitive toddler.

Lazy Boy Bean Bag Toss

Place a sturdy container on the floor about 5 feet from baby while he is sitting in his chair. Now tie a 6-foot length of string to a ball or beanbag. Tie the other end of the string around Baby's chair so that the ball can be tossed in the container and pulled out of the container without Baby getting up. It won't take many demonstrations before Baby will enjoy the beauty of this trick.

Kool Craft

On a too-hot-to-live day, pull out all the stops and design the perfect "kid cooler." Take a long shoelace or piece of string and place the string on a water-filled ice cube tray so that the string dips into each hole, leaving enough string at each end to tie together. You may want to add food coloring and flavoring to some of the holes just for fun. Freeze your creation. Now remove it from the tray and tie it in a loop that fits easily over Baby's head. What could be more refreshing than an ice-cube necklace?

"Who Says What"

One of Baby's most crowd-pleasing acts is his "Who Says What" game. He delights in telling anyone who will listen what the duck says and so on. Use his natural interest in animals as a way to expand his knowledge. Help him count the animals; tell Baby where they live; find the mothers and babies; and expand the number of animals he knows. Baby understands much more than he can tell and is absorbing much of what you say.

Bead Stringing

Don't overlook the obvious. A shoestring and large wooden beads has been a favorite of generations of babies. As a variation use a long colored pipe cleaner for a string and round breakfast cereal for beads. The taut string makes stringing much easier.

Neat Painters

A reasonably neat way to paint is done with bottles filled with water-based paints that have either roller ball or sponge applicator tops. These bottles can be purchased empty or full in craft stores, or you can collect and recycle them from such products as deodorant, glue, or spot remover. Tape a large piece of paper to the table or to the fence outside, stand back and let the artist create.

Creative Rods

Here are some uses for tension curtain rods that will please Baby. Stretched snug and secure in the door frame, they can provide the basis for all sorts of games.

With you there to supervise and cheer, try our suggestions and then make up a few of your own.

1. Place a rod at a height Baby has to squat to get under and he will have lots of fun. Add a little Limbo music for extra enjoyment.
2. Hang from a rod a set of old cafe curtains that part in the middle so Baby can part them and make his grand entrance.
3. Give the feel of the Orient by hanging paper streamers from a rod for Baby to hurry through.
4. Lower the rod so Baby must step over it to enter, or add a challenge with a second rod — one to squat under and one to step over in the same doorway.
5. Place your rod high above Baby's head and attach a slinky. Now attach a foam ball to the dangling end.

Batting this lively ball with his hand or a short cardboard tube will challenge and delight him.

Mouth Harp

A harmonica can be a wonderful toy for the young toddler. You will be amazed to listen to the range of notes he will play, quickly learning to both blow and draw the notes. Turn on the radio and give him some accompaniment for his music.

Mini Tramp

An exercise trampoline will not only be a good 20-dollar-or-less investment for you but great for Baby, too. With your help he will gleefully jump and bounce. You can add to the fun with music and by singing, counting, and chanting together as he jumps. Here is a jumping song we like.

"Tomatoes, lettuce, carrots, peas.
Mother says eat lots of these."

Reversed

A quick art project for your toddler can be in your kitchen drawer. Place a piece of contact paper—sticky side up—on the high chair tray or table. Turn the edges slightly under to secure to tray or table. Now give Baby an assortment of odds and ends of colored paper, yarn, cloth, and ribbon with which to make his picture. It's fun to watch his expression as this paper grips and holds his materials.

Mystery Painting

For this you'll need a coffee can or potato chip can with a lid, paint, and several small rubber balls. Place a sheet of paper inside the can covering the sides. Let Baby dip his balls in paint and toss them in the can. Place the lid on the can and let Baby shake it high and low. Open the can and remove the creation.

Life-Size Puzzles

Large floor puzzles can be costly but they are easy to make and great fun for toddlers. Take a picture of Baby or his pet and have it blown up into a poster or draw a life-size likeness. Now paste this to a large piece of corrugated cardboard. Cut the picture into four or five pieces. To ensure durability, have your puzzle laminated at the stationery store or cover the pieces with clear contact paper. As Baby grows, the large pieces can be cut into smaller ones, increasing the challenge.

Convertibles

Now that baby is getting older you may wonder what to do with all those stuffed animals he seems to have lost interest in. A great idea is to turn them into darling hand puppets. Open the bottom and remove most of the stuffing from the body. Now sew in a child's sock which will become the compartment for a hand. You can match a story to the puppet or make one up.

Juice Lid Matching Game

Lids from frozen juice cans with pull-tape openers can be used with stickers to make a durable matching game. Just wash, dry, and spray paint the lids. Once the paint has completely dried, attach stickers to make a set. Baby will have a lot of fun playing this game with you.

Smell Book

Don't toss away all those perfume samples from your magazines. Collect them and place each in a separate bag which can be zippered or closed with Velcro. String the bags together with yarn to form a book. You and Baby can open each "page" and enjoy the scents. This is a great activity to pull from your purse on the way to work or when waiting in lines.

Sticky Feet

Place a 6-in. × 4-ft. strip of self-stick paper on the floor with the adhesive side up. Tape the edges to the floor. Have Baby walk with bare feet across this beginner's balance beam.

Stocking Balls

Cut the legs off pantyhose and discard the tops. Tie a knot at the bottom and cut off fabric directly below the knot. Stuff the area directly above the knot with a handful or so of polyester stuffing which can be purchased in any fabric store. Tie another knot above the stuffing and cut the fabric above that knot. You now have a safe indoor ball that's just the right size for Baby's hands.

Matching

Baby is not too young to do simple matching. Cut out pictures of several objects that look like Baby's toys.

Mount them on cardboard and cover them with clear contact paper for durability. Lay three or four of the pictures on the floor in front of you and Baby. Name the pictures and point to them as you and Baby identify them. Now hand Baby the objects that match the pictures. Show him how to place the shoe on the picture of the shoe. Then, with the same object, let Baby do it himself. Soon he will have this game down perfectly. Lavish praise on Baby for his efforts. Good starting objects include a shoe, a cup, baby dolls, or a favorite kind of stuffed animal. The important thing is that the objects be very familiar to Baby.

Travel Tips

Now that Baby is wide awake and you can't count on him to sleep in the car, consider making his ride more enjoyable by trying these suggestions.

1. Decorate the back of the front seat with favorite pictures. Merely cut them out and apply with an easy-to-remove square of clear contact paper.
2. Attach several toys to his car seat with short strings so that he can easily throw and retrieve them.
3. Try boxes and cans that nest inside each other. Baby will entertain himself opening and shutting them, finally finding a favorite toy inside.
4. Take a musical tape recording you made together of his favorite songs for a "sing-along."
5. Make up a "traveling bag" for Baby that, besides diapers, includes a favorite hat, sunglasses, keys, toys, and a snack.

Telephone

A toy phone is a hit for children at this stage. Phones seem to hold a real fascination, and provide an opportunity for practicing verbal skills. You may learn some things about Baby's perception of what telephone conversations are all about if you watch him carefully. One handy dad we know mounted a discarded wall phone at Baby's height, just below the family's kitchen phone.

Gotcha

To help Baby extend his vocabulary and practice learning his body parts, play "Gotcha!" It goes like this:

> Gotcha, gotcha, gotcha!
> What can this be?
> It's a part of Baby.
> Please tell me.

This is a game for two. Baby will enjoy playing with you or a sibling. A great activity for the bath, and he will enjoy playing this game on your body, too.

Marker Art

Because he thinks he's a big kid, Baby will want to use markers. Markers are easier to use and get better results than crayons. They work well on any paper but slick surfaces are best. And remember, never throw away dried-up markers that are capless. They can often be reactivated with warm water, or the marker can be used as a kind of magic paintbrush. A piece or two of masking tape applied to each corner of the paper steadies it for Baby.

Noise Games

Don't miss the old classics like "Old MacDonald Had A Farm." Baby will relish putting to use his knowledge of what a cow and pig say. Some songs just seem to get better with time. This is a good example.

ROUTINE TIMES

Now that Baby is approaching two, more and more of the routine-time hints are focusing on ways for him to do things for himself. This can be a time-consuming project, but allowing for and encouraging his need for independence will certainly reduce the conflict and tantrums which may erupt in the coming months. Establishing and sticking to routines is especiall important now!

BATHTIME

Safety Check

If you haven't already done so, now's a good time to make sure that the temperature of your water heater is set no higher than 110°. This is essential to prevent accidental scalding. With Baby so nimble-fingered, there is every possibility that he may try to help you with the bathtime procedure and unintentionally turn on the faucet. Make sure the water isn't too hot to handle. Make it a habit to turn off the cold water last.

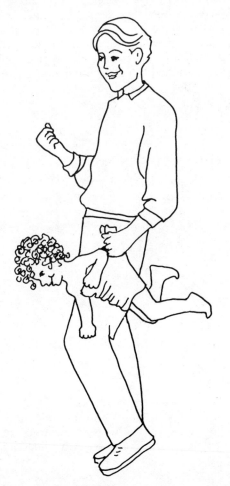

An Easy Out

An easy way to remove a toddler from the tub is to promise him a towel ride. Dry the child completely and then wrap the towel across the front of the child and under the arms and gather behind. Lift and you're off for a ride.

To help keep shampoo and soap out of Baby's eyes, have him wear swimming goggles. This way Baby can see while you are rinsing.

Toothbrushing

It's time to make toothbrushing a regular part of your toddler's routine. Have him select a colorful brush, and along with you, brush his teeth while you wash your face or apply makeup. When he thinks he's finished you can check his job. Mount a special mirror at his level so he can watch himself.

Tub Toys

To help make bathtime more interesting, try changing Baby's tub toys. A paint brush with foam soap, shaped sponges, spray or squirt bottles, colanders, strainers, and funnels are fun to experiment with. Can you think of a better place to work with water and bubbles?

SLEEPING

Bedtime Routine

If you haven't yet established a bedtime ritual— better late than never. Need we remind you that the "terrible twos" are fast approaching? This period is known for its difficulty in maintaining routines, to say nothing of establishing new ones! The best bedtime routines begin with consistency—same time, same format. Whatever your style, be it a story, a kiss and lights out, or a tickle, a hug and lights out, carry it out with *confidence* and *conviction*.

Nighttime Safety

Although we'd like to think that when we sleep, everyone sleeps, we know better. Placing glow-in-the-dark strips on the frame of Baby's bedroom door, around the knob, and on the edge of the door can help prevent nighttime collisions.

Naps

If the afternoon nap has become a hassle, try a new setting. One mom found that her toddler was thrilled at the prospect of resting in a large decorated cardboard playhouse. Another mom found that her child was able to settle down in a small pup tent outdoors while she gardened close by. On rainy days, one toddler curled up on pillows underneath a card table. These are nice changes of pace and place.

Night Light Alternative

Instead of a night light, use a dimmer switch on the overhead light. It doesn't cast the scary shadows that often occur with regular night lights.

Follow the Path

For a change of pace, lay some paper footprints on the floor that will lead Baby through the evening routine. Include the stop to kiss Daddy and a pre-bedtime bathroom stop.

EATING

Practice, Practice

When Baby wants to feed himself, your only course of action is to minimize the mess. Buy plastic bibs with long sleeves, which will keep Baby covered up to his elbows. A little petroleum jelly around Baby's mouth will allow food to be wiped off easily. Placing the high chair on a plastic tablecloth or old plastic shower curtain will save your floor or carpet.

Distractors

While your fussy, hungry baby waits for a meal, try these distractors on his high chair tray:

1. One or two ice cubes
2. Pieces of cooked spaghetti to twirl, or several lengths of clear or colored tape
3. A bright, wet sponge to pat, poke, or suck

Cakes and Muffins

Although you don't want to overdo sweet cakes in Baby's diet, you don't have to eliminate baked goodies completely. Deprivation is not the answer to a good diet. Nutritional balance and proper proportions are. The best idea is to control quantities and enhance the nutritional value by baking your own treats from wisely chosen ingredients. For example, try adding nut powder and fruit or whole wheat flour. Use the mini-muffin tins (petit four pans) for cupcakes. These bite-size morsels are truly baby portions. They can be baked and frozen—it takes only minutes to defrost one, less if a microwave is available.

Don't Forget the Tray

To bring the color back and sanitize baby's high chair tray, use a little bleach and water. Apply the bleach directly to the sponge and rub around. Let the tray soak for a few minutes.

Dining Out

For a treat, or on a day when cooking is not possible and you'll be sharing a meal with Baby in a restaurant, prepare yourself in the following ways:

1. Feed Baby ahead of time. Young children do not wait well. You can feed Baby dessert while you eat your meal.
2. In Baby's bag, have the following: a bib, a sweater (restaurants are usually cool), and a wash cloth or towelette. Also, carrying some familiar morsels is a good idea—anything from cheese to cereal.
3. Take Baby's shopping belt in case there's no way to keep him contained in the high chair. If you put a couple of sheets of newspaper underneath Baby you will almost guarantee good service from the restaurant.

4. Babies enjoy fingering and ripping various tabletop items, including straws, packages of crackers, and napkins.
5. You might take along his umbrella stroller—good for a restless baby.

Finally, remember to tip the waitress generously for her flexibility and thoughtfulness.

DRESSING AND CHANGING

Unisex and Simple

Now is the time to focus your style sense elsewhere. Sweatsuits and T-shirts and shorts are by far the easiest and best way to dress Baby. He can do much of the job himself. If you stick to basic colors all combinations work.

Ring-a-ling

For your little speedster, attach a small bell to the tip of his jacket hood so that even when you can't spot him you will hear where he is, at the playground or in your own backyard.

Socks

When it comes to socks, the tube type socks are the best bet. They're a cinch for youngsters to put on, have no fitting problems, and they all match. Some moms say they even last longer because they wear more evenly.

Fanny Fun

For the young toddler who loves to carry things with him, a handy fanny pack will become a favorite garment. This will let him carry all sorts of treasures. He will learn from experimenting with shapes and sizes as he struggles to make things fit.

Zipping

As your toddler becomes more independent, he will want to begin dressing himself. Zipping can be made easy for him if you make the pull a little bigger. Try adding an interesting key chain, a colorful shoelace, a ski-lift tag, a safety pin with stickers on it, or a luggage tag with a picture inside.

HELPFUL HINTS

Toys

A smart way to handle the problem of too many toys is to sort through them and put at least half away. You can then rotate the toys so that there are new ones which appear periodically. Too many toys overwhelm Baby and reduce his creative play. It also means endless cleanup for you.

Consignment Stores

If you have never had the experience of consignment store buying and/or selling, you're missing out on a great adventure. Across the country these stores (listed under "Used Clothes" in the Yellow Pages) are redefining the way mothers shop. Good ones are loaded with great buys on lightly used clothes, toys, equipment, and even juvenile furniture for less than 50 percent of the retail price. As a seller you will receive one half the selling price of your items.

Recycling

One of the great things the recycling movement has brought is the design of wonderful and reasonably priced storage containers. These attractive and colorful bins, cans, bags, and boxes which stack, fit together, or even roll around make excellent "baby-useable" storage for a toddler's toys or clothing. Baby will enjoy putting his belongings away—a habit that can never be established too soon.

Buttons

For the child learning to button, reinforce the buttons with fishing string. They will be stronger and you'll feel safer knowing they won't fall off and be eaten.

Fresh Paint

Keeping freshly painted walls and woodwork looking nice with Baby around is difficult. Save an old shoe polish bottle, the kind that has a built-in sponge applicator, for the next paint job. Fill the bottle with your wall paint. Keep this container handy to cover all those little marks from crayons and markers. With this tool, it's easy to spruce up the house and keep the repainting to a minimum.

Changing a Stained Favorite Back to New

If a favorite shirt has a spot or stain, use fabric paint or fake gemstones to decorate the shirt over the spot. These items can be purchased at any arts and crafts store for less than the cost of replacing the shirt.

Doorbells

If your toddler has learned how to open the doors, attach bells or chimes to the doors to let you know when they've been opened. Install latches high on the doors you don't want opened.

Fever

A fever is the natural response of the immune system. 95% of all fevers do not require medical treatment. You judge the importance of a fever by the child's actions, not the degrees. Listlessness, stiffness, pulling at the ears, vomiting, and diarrhea are all signs of illness. If your child is running a fever, encourage fluids and plenty of bed rest, and give non-aspirin if needed. If the fever persists more than 24 hours, contact your physician.

Baby Bottle Warmer

Remember that bottle warmer you carried faithfully when your toddler was younger? Don't put it in storage—it can be a great container for small toys. It's the perfect size for crayons or small cars, and your toddler will enjoy zipping and unzipping it.

Clean-up Time

Make cleanup part of your end-of-play or end-of-day routine. Have a special wagon or plastic storage container on wheels that your toddler can pull. He can walk around the house or room, pick up all his toys, and place them in the wagon—a big help for you and fun for him.

Dry Cleaning Plastic

To prevent your curious toddler from suffocating, don't forget to tie knots in your dry cleaning bags before placing them in the trash. This is very important!

Safety Re-check

It's time to re-check the house now that our toddler is getting older. Are all the outlets plugged and the cabinets latched? Is everything breakable put away? Make sure emergency phone numbers are placed on or near all the telephones. You never know which phone you will be using in an emergency.

Splinters

Don't rush; right after the insult may be the wrong time to confront splinters. Applying a vegetable oil-laced

Band-Aid until bathtime and allowing a long soak in the tub may even make your surgery unnecessary. However, if you must operate, first numb the spot with ice. This will make removal of the splinter less painful for everyone.

Playpen Re-use

If you have the type of playpen with one side that can pull down, here are some other uses: Open one side of the playpen and fill it with soft pillows. Now it can be used for a cozy, quiet reading area or a space for imaginative play. The addition of a blanket will turn it into a tent.

Child-Made Toy Box

Have your child make his own toy box by sponge painting an unfinished wooden box or plastic waste-paper basket. He will take pride in putting his toys in a container he helped create.

Bug Keeper

Baby is probably interested in bugs at this point, even if you're not! A humane home for his new ''pets'' can be made from an empty plastic bleach or milk bottle. Cut holes in the sides and slip an old stocking over it, securing the ends with rubber bands.

Cart Safety

For a trip through the aisles of the discount store, keep the youngest shopper secure by carrying his own special belt. A plastic, leather, or fabric adult belt with a wide midriff will hold Baby safe in any cart.

Medical Note

The best remedy for a bee sting, a bumped lip, or a pinched finger, is ice. Fold and freeze a wash cloth in a plastic bag to make a mini ice pack. Keep several in your freezer. A wet sponge frozen in a zipper-lock bag is also a good choice—and it's reusable.

Smart Drawers

No matter how hard you try, Baby is always into something—like someone's drawer. A quick trick to minimize the consequences is to arrange your dresser drawers in this order:

1. Put the items least likely to be damaged at the bottom, for example, underwear and socks.
2. Put sweaters or items that require special cleaning, handling, or pressing in higher drawers.
3. Put the most valuable items, such as jewelry or money, in the highest drawer possible.

Protect Your Pet

One of Baby's favorite play substances is water—he'll search the house to find some to play in. One source often overlooked by adults, but not by Baby, is Bowser's water dish. Even the most even-tempered pet can become a bit testy when his dish is being taken while he's drinking. Do give this steadfast friend his due—a place to eat and drink uninterrupted. Bowser has rights, too!

Toilets

Toilets can be a source of joy for toddlers, and not necessarily for toileting! Learning that toilet lids stay down and water play is done in the sink is essential. Encouraging sink play should help discourage potty play.

Screen Doors

On doors that are okay for Baby to use and ones you'd like him to learn to close and open with care, position a special door pull at his level. This will save screen doors from bowing, keep fingerprints to a minimum, and give Baby a real sense of competence.

Quick Check

Remember to check the batteries in the smoke alarms. Most of them have testers that beep when the battery is almost dead. About every four months is often enough for testing the home-use models. It's much harder to escape with a toddler in tow, so every extra second you can gain is precious.

A Reminder

Allowing a child to try something on his own is a kind of love, too. It's easy to be such concerned parents that we fail to let Baby have needed experiences, even if they are not always wonderful ones. If Baby is to develop his motor skills, he must fail as well as succeed. Keeping him too safe, too clean, too far away from dirt, germs and from others may be more harmful in the long run than small bumps or bruises or a few colds.

AND FOR YOURSELF

Because you no longer have a baby with all the bottles, pacifiers, and rattles to put in your purse, it's time to treat yourself to a new purse—something with style. You're doing great, Mom. You deserve it!

Couple Time

While you may have lost some spontaneity, you needn't miss out on the good times. Now you need to plan your time together as a couple. Consider unplanned moments a bonus, but don't allow them to be your only source of time together. The first step to success is developing a list of reliable, available sitters. You may wish to include flexible, ongoing arrangements to swap child care with other parents. Baby-sitters can be quite expensive.

Business Cards

If you are an ex-corporate woman who feels a little bit lost when your friends are exchanging business cards, surprise them with one of your own . . .

CAROL BRADBURY
MOTHER

12 LEIGH ST
BROWN, NJ
201-555-9098

PARENTS, FRIENDS AND ADMIRERS

Good Gift

Baby will be thrilled to receive a participation or pop-up book. All the classics, especially those around animal themes, will appeal to him. *Pat The Bunny* by Dorothy Kunhardt is still a number one favorite with babies this age. You will soon know every word by heart.

Prepare

If a baby is coming to visit with his family, prepare for this guest. Remove all small, precious objects and tipsy furniture. Borrow a gate that will fit in any door that leads to stairs, and consider entertaining in the backyard. Borrow an inflatable pool for water or sand play. No pool? Then buy a five-dollar bag of sand and get out your old shower curtain. Assemble some small combs, funnels, and containers from the kitchen, and the baby will have an instant sandbox that will keep him happily occupied. This will allow you and your friends to have an enjoyable time as well.

Great Gift

A super gift for both parents and children is a subscription to a parenting magazine or newsletter. Most not only deal with concerns of parents but also suggest activities to enhance daily routines. It can be a monthly morale builder. There are also magazines designed to give children a closer look at the animal world. Visit your library to preview copies or for information on subscribing.

Teacher's Trick

Did you ever wonder why teachers seem to warm up to kids easily while other adults can't? There's a technique for approaching children. First, make eye contact. Catch Baby's eye and smile. Talk to him. Next, get him to smile at you. A funny face will help. Say his name and use a familiar greeting. Then encourage him to come to you. If Baby seems reluctant, slowly move toward him, but don't try to touch him. Continue to smile and talk. Get down on his level by squatting or kneeling. Take it slowly, and speak to him for a few minutes while you're eye-to-eye, still encouraging him to move toward you. Try to interest him in something you have, such as a pin or a book.

Special Toy Box

Have a special box of toys and activities set aside for use only at times when special friends or playmates come over to visit. Even if the toys were old favorites at one time, everything will be new and the "host" won't mind sharing some of his "other" or "old" toys with the friends.

Another Great Gift

A great gift from Baby's grandparents is a small table and chairs. These can be twice-loved pieces from a garage sale that you've refurbished with a fresh coat of paint. Whether wooden or molded plastic, the important thing is that they be very sturdy. We guarantee they will be regularly used.

Special Bag

One clever grandma presented her grandchildren with a delightful homemade bag—a special catch-all and play surface in one. She cut out a 40-inch circle of solid color cotton. With cotton batting, bits of fabric, and iron-on crayon, she created a miniature design reminiscent of an aerial view. She ran a shiny blue river through the middle of her small world. She created a raised area to resemble mountains, made special places for animals to play, airplanes to land, and trucks to park, and finished by putting a roadway around the perimeter.

She then cut another 40-inch circle of cotton (perhaps a print) and sewed them, right sides together around the perimeter, leaving an opening to turn. Then she added two rows of stitching near the perimeter to form a casing and put in a drawstring, running two separate pieces of cord through. This allowed the bag to be drawn up at the end of playtime. Her grandchildren were thrilled and so was Mom, because all the little people, cars, airplanes, and animals could be neatly stowed away, ready for another day of fun.

Plants

Nearly all the families we know have at least five household plants, usually the hardy types that thrive on little water and benign neglect. One green-thumbed grandpa we know got his toddler grandson off to a good start by purchasing a special plant just for him. Most toddlers love to water, sprinkle, or spritz a plant. Besides, there's no telling what might happen when Baby starts talking to "his" plant. Good beginnings include wax begonias and most succulents. Check with your local nursery or garden supply store. Be sure to include facts about the location where the plant will be living. Give the plant the best possible start! Baby will droop momentarily if the plant does!

Family Event

If relatives are too far away to visit often, why not plan a get-together at a halfway point between your homes? Some inns, resorts, and hotels have special rates and facilities for families, plus entertainment for all ages, nightlife, outdoor activities for athletes, sight-seeing for camera buffs, and supervision for little ones. With this plan, no one need spend weeks planning, cooking, and cleaning; everyone can have a real vacation and catch up on all the news.

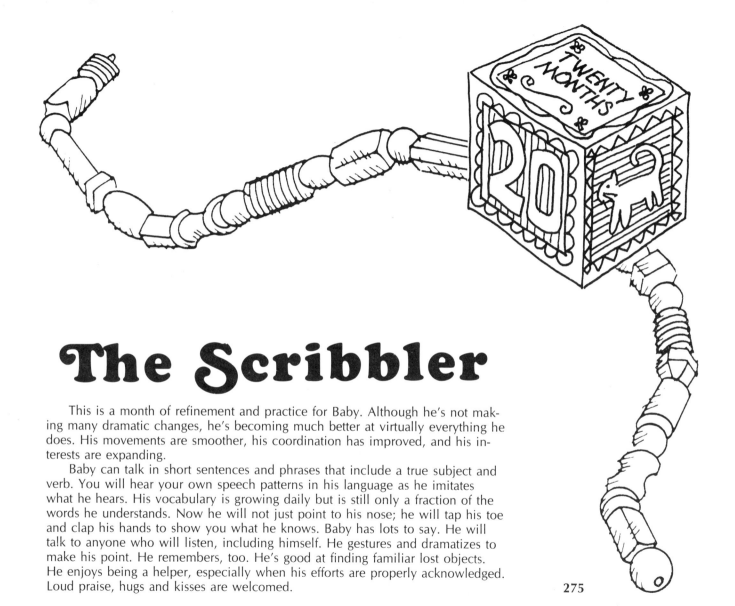

The Scribbler

This is a month of refinement and practice for Baby. Although he's not making many dramatic changes, he's becoming much better at virtually everything he does. His movements are smoother, his coordination has improved, and his interests are expanding.

Baby can talk in short sentences and phrases that include a true subject and verb. You will hear your own speech patterns in his language as he imitates what he hears. His vocabulary is growing daily but is still only a fraction of the words he understands. Now he will not just point to his nose; he will tap his toe and clap his hands to show you what he knows. Baby has lots to say. He will talk to anyone who will listen, including himself. He gestures and dramatizes to make his point. He remembers, too. He's good at finding familiar lost objects. He enjoys being a helper, especially when his efforts are properly acknowledged. Loud praise, hugs and kisses are welcomed.

275

Most babies are great undressers by now. Do encourage Baby to reverse this process and dress himself, too. An assortment of dress-up clothes will help Baby practice these skills and provide him with great fun. Hats, bags, and vests are of particular interest. And, of course, don't forget a mirror so his efforts can be admired.

Baby is becoming more independent every day. Be patient and tolerant, allowing him to try things on his own. We all learn through trial and error, and babies are no exceptions. Allowing a child to move on from babyhood can be quite difficult for parents. Being over-protective will just frustrate him and won't change a thing. He will still not be an infant any longer.

ACTIVITIES, GAMES, AND SONGS

Magnetic Fun

While you are cooking in the kitchen, it's convenient to have Baby right there so you can supervise his activities. A good way to accomplish this is to turn your refrigerator into a learning board. Keep a set of magnetic shapes in a box on top of the refrigerator to be used only during these times. When it's time to cook, bring these jewels down and let Baby sort and arrange them to his heart's content against the refrigerator. Check the magnets to make sure they are securely attached. He could choke on one that is not.

While he's doing this you can talk to him, identify the shapes, and praise his new arrangements. As he becomes more proficient, add a few numbers and letters. Make your cooking time a time you both look forward to and a rewarding experience for Baby.

The Kings

Balls have always been, and will always be, wonderful toys. Always challenging and yet almost indestructible, they must be the kings of toys. Don't overlook any sizes and types. Try lightweight, buoyant Ping-Pong balls, fluffy tennis balls, giant beach balls, kickable red rubber balls, and squishy foam balls. Encourage a variety of play-kicking, rolling, throwing, carrying, and chasing — all great skills to learn.

First Dishes

Instead of wrestling your silverware and cooking equipment back from Baby, buy Baby his own set. Baby will choose real plastic cups, saucers, salad plates, and pots over the miniature sets available in toy stores. Tea sets and toy dishes are often too fragile, contain far too many pieces, and are hard for little fingers to manage. Tough, durable plastic utensils and plates designed for grown-ups can be picked up for pennies at yard sales and second-hard stores. A big pot with some water and a wooden spoon placed on top of a towel on the kitchen floor holds Baby's interest.

Baby's Favorite

Baby has distinct preferences at this point. Note them here for future reference and for sharing with his special friends.

Games _____

_____

Songs _____

_____

Toys _____

_____

Favorite Outings _____

_____

"Nots"

Have fun together with the "not" song. Now it's okay for both of you to say no. Try starting this way:

This is my nose, this is my nose. (point to your nose)
This is not my nose. (point to your ear)
This is not my nose. (point to another body part)
This is my nose, this is my nose. (point to your nose)
And it's a part of me.

Pull Toys

The best pull toys are the ones you assemble yourself. With some twine, elastic cord, rubber bands, and tape or glue, you can combine many toys into original mobile masterpieces. Our formula is simple. Take a musical toy, combine it with any wheeled vehicle, add a string, and you've got a pull toy. The combinations are limitless and give Baby an inexpensive way to expand his toy collection.

More Hand Games

Baby enjoys exploring and playing with his hands. Here's a game you can play in the car, waiting for meals, or anytime at all:

Open, shut them. Open, shut them. Give a little clap.
Open, shut them. Open, shut them. Lay them in your lap.
Creep them, creep them. Slowly creep them right up to your chin.
Open wide your little mouth, but do not let them in!

Boxes

Boxes are among Baby's favorite toys. They have unlimited size and variety, and they're usually free. Be it a poke box for a finger, an arm and leg box to test and push through, or the ultimate, one large enough to put his whole self in, babies love boxes. Remember to check the box carefully for sharp staples and to make sure there's only cardboard. Then watch the fun.

A Sense of Wonder

Being in touch with nature builds self-esteem. Don't miss out on fleeting moments of amazement! Watch a first snowfall together, stop to watch a butterfly, lie in the backyard and watch some fluffy clouds. Allowing children to enjoy these simple, yet magical, moments contributes to a sense of vitality and unity with nature that is essential to us all.

New Old MacDonald

Do you love the song "Old MacDonald Had A Farm"? Then make a finger-puppet glove to go with it. All you need is a new garden glove, pom-poms, and felt. Glue a pom-pom to each glove finger. Make an Old MacDonald by using the felt to make a hat and glue it onto the pom-pom. A pig can be made with a pink pom-pom and felt ears and nose. A cat can be any color; a cow can be brown, white, or black, while a lamb is white. Make your child's favorite animals. A felt-tipped marker can be used to add additional details to the characters.

Zipper Bag Art

For a super no-mess activity, fill a plastic bag with jello or pudding of various colors and zip it securely shut. To insure closure, fold the top over about an inch and tape it. Your toddler will enjoy squeezing this pouch and watching the colors swirl together.

Bath Toy Alternative

Vinyl bath toy stick-ups are not limited to the tub. These soft "pat-on peel-off" forms stick to any wet sur- face. A quick swipe with a wet sponge makes any refrigerator door or cabinet ideal. We like using them on a stand-up easel or a cookie sheet. They come in a variety of shapes, letters, and numbers.

The Rocking Horse

Rocking horses have been around for ages and are still popular with children this age. A song to sing while on the rocking horse can be . . .

Giddy-up my pony, it looks like rain.
I'll be darn, my pants ain't sewn.
So, giddy-up, oh, giddy-up my pony-o.

Sponge Transfer

Place two dishpans or large bowls next to each other on the floor on an old shower curtain. Put about two inches of water in one pan. Let your toddler transfer the water from one bowl or pan to the other, using two sponges.

Recycling Spools

If you are not a "sewer" ask your sewing friends to save their empty spools of thread—the wooden ones are the best but hard to get. Your child will enjoy painting and stringing the spools into necklaces and bracelets.

Show Me How

Baby knows more than he can say, so let him show you rather than tell you. Ask, "How do you comb your hair, zip your coat, wash your face, brush your teeth, put on a shirt?" and let Baby show you just how.

Rocker

For the active baby, we suggest a rocker just for him in the family room, library, or wherever you read. It can occupy him and provide him with an opportunity to be close to the family. Make sure he has books to read and papers to scan while you catch up on your reading. Remember, children who value reading come from homes where they see adults and older chldren reading.

Pouring

What could be more fun than pouring? This is an important skill because it paves the way for a real understanding of measurements. To facilitate fun and learning for Baby, collect clear plastic measuring cups, spoons, funnels, and other items from your kitchen. Or save clear plastic containers—dish detergent bottles are good—and mark them at different levels with either a permanent marker or colored cloth tape. By marking the levels, you encourage precision pouring and learning to compare. You can also cut containers into different sizes. If the edges are sharp, cover them with adhesive-type tape. Then Baby can begin to add water.

Good places to practice pouring are the bathtub and splash pool. During the coldest months, try cornmeal or flour instead of water. As these are easy to clean up with a broom or a brush, you can place your little experimenter on the floor with his dishpan on an old shower curtain.

Inflatables

Better than a balloon and just as bouncy are inflatable toys—a real hit with Baby. What they may lack in toughness they gain in size, for they are big and

nearly weightless. Check your toy store for all sorts of wonderful animals and human shapes.

Building Blocks

All parents have heard that blocks teach important concepts. Most wonder how and when this process occurs. For a beginning builder, an excellent choice is a set of cardboard blocks. Without a lot of expense, noise, or special requirements, your toddler will enjoy all the positive attributes and learning potential of the more expensive hardwood blocks. Because they are lightweight,

Baby will be able to build larger structure with these than he could with large wooden blocks. These blocks can also be used for other play activities such as building a fortress. The one-inch cubes in the play refrigerator as ice cubes or to build a little house for a favorite stuffed animal.

The Suitcase

A suitcase can launch extended dramatic play with your toddler. An ideal weight for Baby would be a small duffle bag, a beach bag, a supply case, or a picnic basket. We've used an old makeup case with a mirror in the top—perfect for checking one's outfit and heavy enough to take some tough tugging. We fill the inside with glasses, hats, beads, jackets, shawls, and dresses.

Noisy

This is a fun poem for Baby to learn:

Noisy, noisy, noisy
I'm so noisy when I play.
Outside I stomp and bang and clap
And shout the livelong day.
But when outdoor play is over
And I am in to stay,
I take out all my quiet toys
And put noisy ones away.

Do Like Me

Now that Baby knows a variety of gestures and commands, he is ready for a game with a "do like me" format. Baby will enjoy mimicking gestures and getting you to perform them, too. Soon he will prefer being the leader himself, with you responding. This is a perfect way to build on his emerging verbal skills. Some examples are waving bye-bye, motioning to come forward, sitting down with a flip of your hand, stopping with a policeman's palm up, nodding yes and no. Siblings will enjoy joining you and your toddler.

Busy Boards

For the home carpenter, experienced or not, odds and ends become a source of great delight for Baby. Casters, hinges, boat locks, keys and locks, knobs, and pulleys attached to a flat board will give a toddler hours of fun. For the highly skilled carpenter, intricate boards can be made with a third dimension by cutting and hinging doors or fashioning boxes, making them even more challenging to the curious toddler.

Puzzle Power

Babies love wooden puzzles, as do toddlers. Begin with simple ones that have four to six separate non-interlocking spaces. Some of these are built with notches so they interlock off the puzzle board. One we recently saw features a bear that sits on a bicycle, with a hat that sits on his head. The multi-dimensional aspect of these puzzles will delight Baby. And don't throw away the remaining pieces to the puzzle when some have disappeared—they can be used with blocks, little cars, in toy houses, and so on. The value of any item to Baby's development can't be judged without considering how it's used and how you encourage its use.

ROUTINE TIMES

BATHING

Shape Sponges

To help make bathtime more fun and educational, cut shapes out of sponges and have the child help you identify and use them.

Surprises in the Soap

Make your own soap using soap flakes and a little water. Hide objects inside as you form the ball. As the soap dissolves when the child uses it, the small prize will appear.

Let's Make Brushing More Interesting

To make toothbrushing more interesting for your toddler, keep some sample-size toothpastes for your child's use only. Have him choose which tube he wants to use daily.

A Bath Spritz

A plant spritzer can be used to make bathtime with your toddler a little more fun. Fill it with hair shampoo and apply with spray. It can also be filled with water to rinse off the soapy body after the bath.

Baby Doll Bath

Bathtime is the ideal time to build a discussion with Baby about his body. This dialogue, which can start with you doing much of the talking, will help him during other routines. As Baby understands most of what you say to him, encourage his attempt to repeat words or to indicate by pointing, lifting, or touching his various body parts. It's also fun for Baby to bathe with his doll and show you his doll's arm and his own. A Baby wary about washing and shampooing may be reassured by watching you do these things to his doll. He may even get into the act and try to groom his doll. This kind of dramatic play is a typical and healthy way for children to become comfortable with different roles and situations.

SLEEPING

Sleeping Tips

Bedtime needn't be a battleground, even with a toddler bursting with energy. He may need some new structure in his sleeping routine, however. Here are some ideas:

1. Decide what time bedtime will be and resolve to honor it. This will allow you and your toddler to make your evening pleasurable. Sticking to this part of the schedule will create stability and establish good sleeping habits.

2. Let a clock remind your toddler that bedtime is fast approaching. Set the alarm to ring a few minutes before it's time for bed. There's no bad guy then—the clock is always right.

Moving On

For the baby who's moving to a full-size bed from his crib, a bed tent provides not only a lot of fun but also a safe transition. The tent has sides and is a cozy space.

Story Site

For most parents and toddlers, the bedtime story is an eagerly anticipated part of the day. Remember the fun of reading by a campfire or in a sleeping bag? Consider a different place than the rocker or your toddler's room to read together. How about in a different bed—maybe yours—or in a porch swing, on the steps inside or out? Pick a different place daily and have it coincide with one of the places in the story. For example, "Ferdinand" takes place under a cork tree, so you could sit under a tree to read this story.

A Special Book

If after snuggling, a story, and another sip of water, a toddler's eyes are still not shut, let him "read" a story to his doll or stuffed animal. A simple, familiar picture book with an easy story will do the trick, so long as the story is read quietly and lying down.

Fish Tanks

Another alternative to a night light is a lighted fish tank. The tank doesn't cast shadows and the fish make wonderful pets.

EATING

A Fussy Eater Remedy

If your toddler is one of many fussy eaters, try presenting the meal in a different way. Put food on a toothpick, serve food in its original container, like yogurt or fruit cup, rather than transferring it into a bowl, or use unusual serving or drink containers.

Reusable Containers

Instead of a juice box, keep reusable plastic drink containers filled with water in the refrigerator. When your toddler gets thirsty, all you need do is give him the container. It will be okay if it spills since it contains only water.

Yogurt

For a fussy baby who is unable to wait while you heat something up or on a day when you are low on energy and supplies, try yogurt. Babies love it plain, or mixed with pureed fruit or vegetables for added nutrition and interest. It's the quickest meal around!

Trick

Learning to eat solids is a messy task. It seems that most of the food becomes liquid and rolls down Baby's chin. So we use this idea that we borrowed from the beauty parlor to keep Baby comfortable and his clothes dry. Slip several tissues, soft paper napkins or toilet tissue around Baby's neck before you put on his bib. Cleanup will be much easier.

Needless Worry

Babies will not starve. If your baby is healthy and has his doctor's okay that his weight is fine, then you can relax and not worry if he doesn't seem to eat as much as you think he should. Force-feeding or tricking babies into eating is a mistake. Mealtime should be pleasant and relaxed. Baby will eat what he needs and only what he needs. Like you, he has preferences and feelings. There are times when he is hungrier than other times and things he likes better than others.

DRESSING AND CHANGING

Mitten Matching

Attach Velcro to a pair of mittens, one piece on each. This way, when not being worn, they can stick together and always remain a pair.

The Hood

Many babies hate hats. Hoods are often a sensible alternative. Before you let Baby wear the hood, carefully secure three wooden beads (too big to swallow) to each end of the cord. Not only is this cute, a handy toy, and a noisemaker, it also eliminates the frustration of losing the cord, which you need to tie the hood securely around Baby's head to keep his ears warm.

T-shirts

The T-shirt craze is still going strong. Toddlers we know are not only more comfortable in them, but they are perfect for the quick-change artist who gets dirty fast and also takes his shirt off. Keep the designs and decals in good condition. Before the first wear, soak them in a solution of cold water and plenty of salt—this keeps the colors bright and fast.

Clean and Neat

For the not-so-neat eater or drooler, spray any collar and dress or shirt front with non-aerosol fabric repellent. This keeps special-occasion clothes in good condition and makes clean-up a breeze.

Shoes and Socks

Having trouble getting shoes and socks on those wiggling little feet? Try putting them on while Baby is occupied in the high chair.

HELPFUL HINTS

Keeping Cool in a Crisis

The best way to handle any emergency is to keep your wits about you. These tips can help.

1. Keep an emergency information kit where it can be readily available. It should include: your insurance card; a list of any medications your child is currently taking or is allergic to; all immunization information; the name and telephone number of your child's physician; the name, phone number, and address of a close friend.

2. Keep a list of emergency numbers posted by the telephone. Don't forget to include your pediatrician's number, your local emergency service, your local poison control center, the numbers of two neighbors, both spouses' work numbers, your address and directions to your house from the nearest intersection.

3. Have a basic first-aid kit and keep it where you can get at it quickly. This kit should contain bandages of different sizes, gauze, cotton balls, rubbing alcohol, sterile tweezers, scissors, and wood for a splint.

Spot Cleaner

To make your own spot cleaner or pre-wash, mix together equal amounts of dish detergent and ammonia, not chlorine bleach. Put this mixture in a squeeze bottle and apply to spots before laundering. As with any pre-wash, test the clothing in an inconspicuous spot for colorfastness.

Fingerprints

Your little cruiser or walker is undoubtedly leaving his marks continually along baseboards and walls. To spruce up your home, try a squirt of commercial spray cleaner and a dab of toothpaste on a damp cloth. Rinse well and blot carefully. Most important, quick action is required.

Young Cleaners

Having trouble getting your housework done? We suggest you start now to take advantage of Baby's interest and delight in helping you with your routine household chores. Get him into the act. Give him a little apron. Buy him his own plastic caddies and add a dust rag or mitt, a non-aerosol spray with a touch of furniture polish, a sponge, a feather duster, or anything else you can think of that will please him. He's not too young to have his own tasks. Do check his work and praise him generously. This is an interest that will reap valuable rewards for you and the household in months to come.

Pets

If you're considering a pet for Baby, now is a good time to purchase a young cat or dog. Of course, there are positives and negatives to this approach. On the positive side, pets who grow up with young children tend to become quite gentle and child-centered. But when you buy a pet for a young child, you need to remember that you will be the one caring for this pet.

Also, make sure that the pet is suited to your lifestyle. Big dogs can be difficult to care for if you don't have the right outdoor accommodations.

Cats

One advantage of having a cat is that this pet is sturdy. A cat learns quickly to escape from your toddler when things get rough and requires little maintenance. A good-tempered cat will cope with your toddler by letting himself be petted when Baby is gentle but driving home his point when Baby is rough. Our experience with most toddlers is that there are very few scratches. It takes a relatively short time for cat and toddler to develop mutual respect.

Inexpensive Change

Wallpaper borders can change the look of a room in a flash; you'll be amazed at all the new designs available. Easy to install and relatively inexpensive, they are no longer used just around the ceiling. You can put them along walls at any angle. If you choose to put one around the middle of the room, add a piece of coordinating molding to the bottom of the border. This will give you something to hang things from and save your walls from tack holes.

Change-off

Now that Baby is walking, he will insist that this be his only mode of transportation. Don't give in to this—a good strategy is to let Baby push his stroller for the first half of the walk and be ready for him to ride on the way home.

Outgrown Clothing Box

Keep a box or basket in your toddler's closet for clothes as your child outgrows them. When the box or basket is full, just bring it to a resale shop.

Cleaning Tips

Colored marker spots can be removed from clothing and other surfaces with a little nail polish remover. Use sparingly and move quickly. Also, we have found that spots from permanent markers can be removed from clothing—if you act quickly—using cold water and fabric cleaners (the liquid types work best).

Glass Tip

The new order of the day for the bathroom is paper cups only. Baby will want to drink occasionally in the bathroom, so avoid the nightmare of accidents with glass or plastic. Paper is more hygienic, too.

Bathroom Tactics

Don't forget about the bathroom when you're accident-proofing your home. Now that Baby is a master locksmith, you'll want to make sure he can't lock himself in the bathroom. Those second-floor rescues are no fun. A good idea is a latch hook at the proper height for siblings and adults but too high for Baby. You'll find that one on each side is the best idea so that you can keep the bathroom off-limits to Baby while offering privacy to those using it.

Toy Bins

We think the best toy box is the open-bin type. This style allows Baby to put his things away easily and quickly. It's also the safest container. You'll find that teaching a two-year-old to put things on shelves is much more difficult. The box should be about 6 ft. long with slats about 6–10 in. apart. It can be hung flush with the wall at the height of your child's arms. Picture labels on the bins will make toy sorting almost like a game.

Rugs

Slip-proof small area rugs by sewing a rubber canning ring to each of the four corners. This is particularly helpful in hallways and in the kitchen in front of the sink.

Car Organizers

A shoe bag hung over the back seat of your car is sure to become a regular feature. When you have young riders, this bag is handy for extra clothes, art and craft supplies, toys, and even special snacks. This convenient caddy can be cut in half so that each side of the car has its fair share of storage space.

Shelves

If open shelving in your toddler's room seems to keep it from looking neat no matter how hard you clean, consider this nifty trick. Install a bamboo or fabric shade or mini-slat blind at the top of each shelf section. When the blinds are lowered, the clutter is neatly covered, yet when raised the shelves are accessible to you and your child.

Sounding the Alarm

A mom we know solved the problem of an exploring Baby creating havoc in her bedroom by installing a bell above the bedroom door. When the door was opened, the mother knew that Baby had entered her room and she could supervise or shoo the visitor out.

Mother's Crayon Saver

Baby wants his crayons to be whole but uses them so often and so exuberantly that the crayons tend to break. Try wrapping each crayon with a double or triple layer of masking tape. They will last far longer and give Baby something secure to hold onto. This also works with colored chalk. Remember, when selecting crayons for a toddler, the bigger the better.

Diary for Sitters

Rather than repeat instructions over and over or worry about missing an important detail (for example, Karoline is allergic to chocolate), write these important details down and keep them in a diary for sitters. With a looseleaf notebook, a set of dividers, paper, and a big marker, you're all set. This approach is convenient and makes additions easy. Add-ons will be necessary as your child grows. A big clamp on the inside can hold any new instructions, for example, medications or phone numbers. Divide as you like or use the following suggestions:

Section 1: Important Phone Numbers
    Pediatrician, ambulance service, and so on
    Contacts and their relationship to the child

Section 2: Napping and Sleeping
    Sequence of steps
    Rituals
    Special toys
Section 3: Food and Snacks: House Rules
    Example: no sugar, and so on
    Prejudices: likes and dislikes
    Recipes for good projects together
Section 4: Favorite Things
    A list of toys, music, and stories that are particular favorites with your child

Loving Tip

Sometimes your negative "Me-Do Almost Two" misses out on hugging and cuddling when the child actually needs it the most—when he is struggling to develop his own identity. Make a point to hug, kiss, and squeeze him even if he sometimes rejects you. Just as adults sometimes have trouble accepting affection, so does he, but, he really does like it. Learning to accept love is as important as learning to give it.

Clean Shoes

For cleaner shoes, keep a nylon net pot scrubber handy to clean off dirt and caked mud. A nylon bristle brush is the ideal cleaner for sneakers. To cover scuffs and make the polish adhere, rub the abraded surface of the shoe with a raw potato before you apply the polish.

Quiet

If slamming doors are driving you crazy, consider this trick. Take out your sewing kit and cut out two four-inch squares of fabric. Stitch these together on three sides, stuff with a small amount of padding, and tack the fourth side together. Now attach a loop of elastic to two sides of this pincushion. On the door, which has banged for the last time, place this little pillow on the edge of the door and loop the elastic over the knob on each side. Silence is golden.

Band-Aids Off

Once your young accident victim's bumps, scrapes, or bruises have begun to heal, remove Band-Aids without further tears by dabbing the edges with a cotton ball dipped in baby or salad oil.

PARENTS, FRIENDS, AND ADMIRERS

Make a Special Gift for a Lady

Fill a small bowl with Epsom salts, add a few drops of food coloring and a few squirts of perfume, and let your toddler stir it around. Fill some of those baby jars you've been saving and tie a ribbon around the top. Women love to relax in the bath with this special mixture Baby has made as a gift.

Sharing

If you're planning a "get together" with a friend who has a child, ask the friend to bring a few of the child's favorite playthings. This way both children have to share instead of just one.

Super Card

Instead of a card, a thoughtful aunt sent a growth chart to a toddler. When displayed in his room, this wall graphic showed the world how big her nephew had become. He was delighted because everyone seemed to tell him how little he was—and the chart proved otherwise.

Hot Tip

One savvy relative made it possible to have a hot meal in a hurry when his young nieces and nephews under four were in town. With the menus of his favorite restaurants posted close to the phone, he called his order ahead. As a result, the group was barely seated before dinner was served.

Tidbits

A single lady who wished to befriend her friends' young children shared an idea. Her plan, which required more effort than money, was simple. She saved up all the prizes, packages, decals, and small toys found in her purchases. Then she packed them in a fancy box. When little friends came to visit, she either chose or let them choose an item or two. What a treat for them, and a source of lots of lively discussion and fun together.

AND FOR YOURSELF

Take a dance class with your spouse. It's an intimate activity and will allow for time together. Even if you never plan to go out dancing after the class ends, these sessions can be great exercise.

Join an outside-the-home activity either on your own or with a significant other. Bowling and volleyball are great fun and the weekly meeting will give you something to look forward to.

An excellent alternative to low-impact aerobics is yoga. It actually promotes greater strength, flexibility, and relaxation and can be done at home while Baby is napping. Classes are offered at many park districts, YWCAs, and as adult continuing education through the local high school.

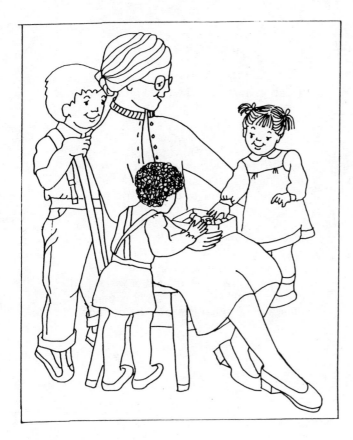

Super Toy

Start now looking for, commission, or create a classic toy for a special child who is approaching his second birthday. A durable cloth toy will be a constant companion. A doll, teddy bear, monkey, or other animal needs to be extra sturdy with all the pieces embroidered or appliqued to ensure long life and safety. One friend made a large yellow rabbit out of stretch terry with a jaunty pocketed vest and bow tie. She sent it to her toddler friend special delivery. The child and his mother went to the post office to pick it up. The mother reports that the child was almost as thrilled by the trip and the package as he was by the rabbit, which became a close personal friend.

Preservation Tip

One grandma claims she can make crayon drawings last much longer if she uses a recipe passed on to her by her grandmother. She dissolves several Milk of Magnesia tablets in two cups of club soda and lets this mixture rest overnight. The next day she soaks the drawing in the solution for about 60 minutes and pats it dry. She leaves the picture undisturbed until it's completely dry. This is a sure way to preserve a family heirloom.

Grandma's Apron

Grandmas tend to be an elite group, eager to share news, especially about their grandchildren. Many have photos, wear charm bracelets, and tell inspired stories, but one special lady we know is rarely seen without a certain gift from her daughter-in-law—a bright apron with cookie-cutter-style profiles of her grandchildren dancing around the hemline. Each little person is labeled by name and birthdate. Another grandma, an avid outdoor person, has a denim jacket festooned with patches, each bearing the name of a grandchild and a quick sketch of an object important to that child. Both garments are conversation starters, personal, and easy to wear. We also know of a grandfather who had a fancy fisherman's vest with patches just like the grandma's.

Silent Movie

One uncle caught the rapt attention of a two-year-old by presenting a silent movie at home. Through the flicker of a light cast by a huge candle, he made his hands dance and wiggle, creating a shadowy story across the living room wall. Another evening, the younger relatives participated in their own silent movie. By stapling simple cutouts to short sticks, simple puppets were created, and familiar tunes added to the evening's entertainment.

Gifts For The Family

Why not a gift that a whole family can share together? Here are some ideas:

1. Based on geographic location, present a membership to a nature center, arboretum, bird sanctuary, or state park. To add to the fun, include a map or guidebook of the area.
2. For a game-playing family, give a set of Checkers or the perennial favorite, Chinese Checkers.
3. For munching, give an electric popcorn popper. The newer ones make perfect popcorn without oil.

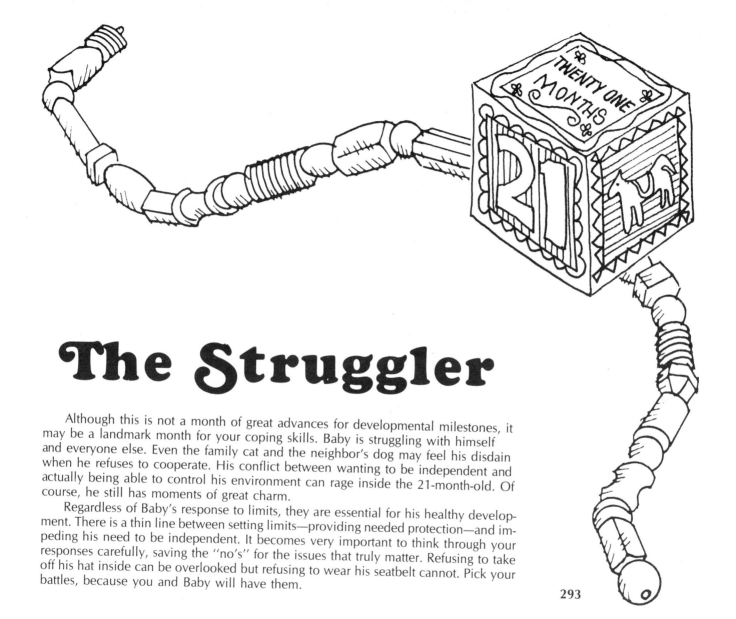

The Struggler

Although this is not a month of great advances for developmental milestones, it may be a landmark month for your coping skills. Baby is struggling with himself and everyone else. Even the family cat and the neighbor's dog may feel his disdain when he refuses to cooperate. His conflict between wanting to be independent and actually being able to control his environment can rage inside the 21-month-old. Of course, he still has moments of great charm.

Regardless of Baby's response to limits, they are essential for his healthy development. There is a thin line between setting limits—providing needed protection—and impeding his need to be independent. It becomes very important to think through your responses carefully, saving the "no's" for the issues that truly matter. Refusing to take off his hat inside can be overlooked but refusing to wear his seatbelt cannot. Pick your battles, because you and Baby will have them.

293

If you are thinking that your child doesn't seem to show any of these signs, keep reading. No one escapes this developmental stage; tantrum times will arrive before the age of four.

As you cope with these fits of anger, lead with your sense of humor and rely on your own maturity. Baby may be the offender but he deserves a baby-suited response. A stern look, a short chat, and lots of redirecting is appropriate. Hitting sends a confusing message. Hurting others is not tolerated, so how can hurting *him* be tolerated?

Baby's ball-playing skills are developing rapidly. He can throw a ball over his head and has learned to kick large balls. He can carry several things around with him and may even be able to pedal a small tricycle. Baby is talking more and constructing phrases with his vocabulary of about 25 words. He may be starting to ask questions, too. He'll ask, "What's that?" All children develop speech at different rates, so don't become anxious if he has a smaller vocabulary or speaks less than we have described.

Baby is very interested in smells and sounds. He loves to use colored markers. He's very interested in other children but doesn't enjoy sharing his toys or his Mom. He does empathize with someone who is sad and likes to refer to himself by name.

Baby can take off his clothes quite well and put on most of them. He loves to help around the house with dusting, picking things up, and doing the tasks he sees others do.

ACTIVITIES, GAMES, AND SONGS

Row Your Boat Variations

While singing "Row, Row, Row Your Boat" with your toddler, use different speeds and pitches. First sing it normally, then high-pitched and fast or low-pitched and slow.

Using Our Noses

Fill up net bags, easily made from material purchased at any fabric store, with common scents your toddler is familiar with, such as hot cocoa, orange peel, peppermint, cloves, cinnamon, and lemon. Make two bags of each scent. Have your toddler use his nose to match the scents that are alike.

Baby's Own Book

Using a small photo album, collect photographs of Baby during his daily routine. Print a short simple explanation under each picture (on the plastic covering) with a china marker. Your child will enjoy reading the story about himself and his activities. The writing can be easily removed from the plastic with a little petroleum jelly when you want to change the story. Plan on changing the story every other month.

What's Missing?

Your little detective may be ready for his first mystery game. How well does he pay attention and remember? Using a flat basket tray, assemble three objects such as a sock, spoon, cup, small toy, or book.

Name the items as you place them in the tray. Tell Baby you want him to cover his eyes while you hide something. Demonstrate while he's watching and ask him to respond. Say, "What's missing?" Repeat this procedure several times until you think he's got the right idea.

Now gently cover his eyes with your hand and play the game. This game is an early form of developing visual memory—an important readiness skill.

Baby's Vocabulary

Baby's word	Our translation of the word
_____	_____
_____	_____
_____	_____
_____	_____

Some of his first and best sentences

_____

_____

_____

_____

Song

Sung to the tune of "Frère Jacques," this action song can be fun for a busy Baby.

Up and down, up and down.
Turn around, turn around.
Rise up on your toes,
Rise up on your toes.
Now sit down, now sit down.

Inside Joke

Baby appreciates a little humor, too. He enjoys having an inside joke with you. Whatever your silly routine may be, whether it's a classic stomping motion signaling a chase, a certain funny face, or a silly sound that means a hug will follow, this game reflects Baby's growing memory and participation skills. These games will last through toddlerhood and be a source of delight to both of you.

Pockets

For your handyman who always needs to have his materials and tools with him, a smock with a variety of pockets will be a welcome garment. This will let him carry and sort his treasures. We like a variety of pocket sizes because this gives Baby an opportunity to learn to judge which sizes of things fit in which pockets—the beginning of math skills.

Hide and Wait

Baby loves to find things. Take any musical toy or attach bells to a pie plate. Ask Baby to wait in the next room. Rattle and ring as you move through the house and decide where to hide the musical object. This variation of hide-and-seek will appeal to a toddler who's excited by little mysteries, suspense, and action.

Basket Trick

Does Baby enjoy rolling a ball? And is your time to play with him limited? Set a bushel basket against the wall with the opening facing Baby. The basket will deflect the ball back to Baby regardless of his aim. Teach Baby to sit in front of the open basket and roll the ball, then watch it roll back. If Baby has trouble getting the ball up to the basket, move him closer or install a small cardboard ramp between him and the basket.

Lick and Stick

Tired of crayons? Markers a bit pale? A little sticker art may be just the thing for your young artist. Using either leftover stamps (wildlife, holiday) or special seasonal stickers, your toddler will love licking or sticking them onto paper. To add a bit more dash to this project, try different sorts of paper. Give him a sheet of foil, a plain paper cup and plate, a lace doily, a cut up brown paper bag, and/or a distinctive department store type of bag. You might try cutting background paper into seasonal shapes such as hearts, pumpkins, turkeys, eggs, or Christmas trees to match special stickers you have gathered.

Another Sniff Game

Another game that uses the toddler's sense of smell is the "Sniff Game." At this stage, your toddler is interested in smells of foods and spices that are part of his regular diet. Baby food jars are the perfect size to hold the following common scents: a slice of lemon, a spoonful of mustard, a sliver of onion, a cinnamon stick, some chocolate chips, and a little peanut butter. There is no reason to blindfold him at this point. Just let him sniff and talk about the smells and the foods he associates with them.

Transporter

Although Baby may not be as enthusiastic about gardening as you are, he can be a great help if you channel his efforts. A toddler's natural love and need to transport things can be a real asset. While he may not see the glories of a gladiolus, he can take your leaves to a wheelbarrow or basket, pick up and pull out extra pebbles from your flower bed, or collect and dump lawn clippings or leaves. Just keep the task simple, the route short, and the praise consistently extravagant.

Kitchen Furniture

Baby is now old enough to really enjoy dramatic role playing. Of course, his favorite role will be you in the kitchen. Children's kitchen furniture need not be costly; for one or two children the cardboard box type is sturdy, fun, and under $40. These heavy-duty painted boxes will last several years with reasonable care. There are also molded plastic sets and metal ones for under $100. The Cadillac type, made of wood, runs about $300 for the three-piece set of sink, stove, and refrigerator. If encouraged, Baby will convert these same basic pieces of furniture into restaurants, post offices, laundromats, or bakeries, providing endless hours of imaginative fun.

Messless

There is nothing quite like finger painting for fun or making a mess. A good way to keep the fun going and control the mess is to save a short cardboard beer box (the kind that holds 24 cans). Use it as a nifty paint tray. With its low sides, it requires no altering. Just tape Baby's paper to the bottom of the inside and let him go.

The Pan Guitar

Musical instruments are always fun to make and play, be they drums or pie plate cymbals. One instrument that is quick to make and great for the very young is the pan guitar. Pull out pans in various shapes, such as a loaf pan and square or circular cake pans. Stretch rubber bands around each pan so they go across the open side. All that's needed now is someone to strum. Each pan provides a different sound, depending on its shape. Several together make a band.

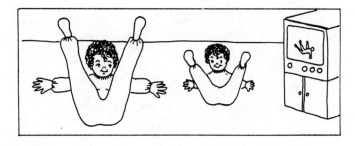

Fitness Partner

Wish you had your toddler's boundless energy and pep? Take a tip from a less-than-fit mom we know and turn your toddler into your best exercise partner. Whether you have a record or tape or tune into yoga, aerobics, or dance shows on television, your toddler will continue to imitate you by raising his toe, arm, or leg when he sees you lifting yours. Not only is this fun and good for you, it's excellent practice for Baby and will help him to coordinate and develop his large motor skills.

Roadway

Now that Baby enjoys real toys, he will greatly appreciate a roadway for his small vehicles. It can be a simple

cardboard highway, or a handy one Dad or Mom can make a more lasting wooden terrain. As Baby becomes more sophisticated, the simple roadway can be embellished by ramps and tunnels. What's important is that you encourage him to use it. Soon he will be able to play on his own for extended periods of time.

Thoughts on Toddler Art

Most toddlers love to use art materials—chalk, paint, clay, paste—and especially pencils, crayons, and Magic Markers. At this stage of his development, Baby is scribbling. Here are some things to keep in mind when assessing his work:

1. These marks are a source of considerable pride and satisfaction, among his first forms of artistic self-expression. He will soon recognize that this is his creation.

2. Praise him generously and often. Be as specific as you can about his efforts.

3. Help him extend his own work by identifying and labeling it. Example: "My, there are a lot of blue lines in this corner."

4. Observe and comment on the child's physical state as he works. Example: "You're moving your hand very fast when you're working with that red crayon." "Look at all those dots."

5. Most pictures at this stage are characterized by lots of lines and squiggles. There will be vertical squiggles if he is working on a vertical surface, like an easel. If he's working on a floor or a table, the squiggles will probably be going horizontally. Remember that the child is

using whole arm movement. The pumping motion occurs because the toddler only has control of his shoulders.

6. Later, he will learn to control his elbow, and this will signal the emergence of slight curves in his drawing.

Trips

Plan a walk outdoors with your toddler. Equip him with a sturdy bag, preferably plastic. Make sure he is given encouragement and the opportunity to collect things—sticks, leaves, paper, whatever catches his fancy—even a bug, if he's quick enough to catch it. On returning home do something with his new treasures. Since he's focused on learning about things, the materials gathered can provide an afternoon of fun. A muffin tin provides a good way to divide all of his finds and set each one off nicely. A clear plastic plate can be used to display his findings for the rest of the family to see. For the bug, see our bug keeper in Chapter 19.

Rip and Tear Art

Before tiny fingers can cut, they must learn the art of tearing and ripping. Assist Baby in mastering this process by providing odd bits of wrapping paper, foil, tissue, old magazines, and cellophane. Once the size and shape of materials have been changed by ripping and tearing, let your toddler reassemble them as he chooses. He might use glue or paste to arrange his design on a styrofoam tray. When the project is complete, he will have a simple wall plaque.

It's not too early, by the way, to introduce a pair of blunt scissors—but don't expect too much.

Sponge Paint

Save those tired sponges for a super-quick, easy-to-handle painting project well suited to a toddler's interests and abilities. Use scissors to cut large simple shapes from the sponges. Dip the shapes into water-based tempera paint plus a bit of detergent, thinned enough to barely cover the bottom of a styrofoam tray, and let your toddler at it. This is a good project to do in a high chair or a well-covered area of the kitchen floor. Sponge-painted newspaper done by toddlers makes excellent gift wrapping, too.

Cheap and Neat

Still a bargain at 25 cents, a box of colored chalk can provide an afternoon of fun for Baby. Just give him the chalk and he can create a wonderful mural on the sidewalk. Chalk is also a good item to take to a friend's—while Baby and his pal enjoy themselves in the park, you and his mom can have fun, too.

Special Clay

Make a quick batch of clay to use on a day when your toddler's energies are high and your ability to keep up with him is low. Direct his attention and give him something he can push, roll, squeeze, and pound. Use our recipe for oatmeal dough—one part flour, two parts oatmeal, one part water. Add water gradually and mix well. If you'd like additional texture, cornmeal or coffee grounds in small quantities add textural interest. Give your child a vinyl placemat or set him up on an oiled vinyl tablecloth to keep the mess to a minimum and to keep the dough from sticking. You might enjoy sitting down with him, too. Be sure to wrap up whatever dough remains in an airtight container after you put it in a plastic bag.

Pop Beads

Large pop beads are a great toddler toy. Building a necklace of these beads can amuse and provide Baby with experiences that will help busy little fingers practice connecting and disconnecting. Together you can practice pattern building—red-blue-red-blue—or use beads of all one color. When you're finished, you each have a necklace to wear. These are also fun to use in the car or to carry around in a purse or backpack. Because they are plastic, they are easy to keep clean. Put them in a lingerie bag and toss into the washer on the gentle cycle.

Downhill Roll

Although most toddlers adore going fast, they lack the necessary coordination to build up a lot of speed, and they still worry about falling. A particularly safe way to provide a toddler with the sensations that he enjoys so much is rolling down a hill. No hill or slope in your backyard? Consider a neighborhood park. You may need to demonstrate how to roll to get your toddler moving. This is a simple thrill that you can both share—especially fun in crunchy leaves, soft, clean snow, or fresh-cut grass.

ROUTINE TIMES

BATHING

Waterwheel

One of the best bath toys you can purchase is a waterwheel for Baby's tub. This plastic toy can be used in sand outdoors as well, but it is particularly fun to use in water. Babies of this age love rotating and spinning disks and dials, not to mention bicycle wheels. That's one of the reasons this waterwheel is so much fun for them.

Slipless

Prevent accidents In the tub. Make it a rule to go slow and keep checking that your adhesive strips, decals, or bath mats, which are essential for slippery bodies and fast feet, are still firmly attached. Accidents in the bathroom can be extremely serious.

Ode To The Belly Button

For the toddler who's finicky about undressing for the bath, finesse him with this little chant:

Belly button, belly button,
Small and deep and round,
I'll look right down and see you
And wiggle all around.

Let him take off his own shirt and see his own belly button.

Rinse Tip

If you let your toddler participate in the shampooing process, this part of bathing may be easier for you both. Most toddlers dislike water on their faces unless they are the ones directing the flow. Get a clear plastic bottle, punch lots of little holes in it using a hammer and nail, and let him rinse off the soap. You will probably need to finish the job but his participation may keep his opposition to your help to a minimum.

SLEEPING

New to the Routine

As part of the bedtime routine that you have developed, try a poem like this one, which will help reinforce the settling-down process:

I know a little baby who's ready to sleep.
I'm gonna hug and kiss him so he won't even peep.
I'm gonna lay him down and cover him tight,
I'm gonna pat his back and turn out the light.

Night Lights

There's something new in night lights, and it's more than just the shape. Today's night lights turn on and off automatically. They also include a safety feature that allows them to function in case of a power outage. With young children, we think they are indispensable in the bathroom, hallway, and Baby's room. Reasonably priced, they certainly beat fumbling for a flashlight and candles.

Pillowcase

A cheery pillowcase may be just the touch of novelty for the toddler. Whether it matches his sheets and blankets, or is hand-embroidered or silk-screened with a message like "Good night, Karoline," a toddler may find sleeping easier and cozier. A sibling will enjoy decorating one of these with his fabric crayons.

His Own Clock

If a toddler is not able to stay in bed once he's awake, try this idea from a parent who was exhausted from 5 a.m. go-arounds with her toddler. This mom bought a durable alarm clock with a luminous dial especially for the child. She let him wind it and set the alarm so he could hear it ring loudly. Then she told him he could have the clock in his room if he didn't get out of bed before the bell went off. Everyone slept better after that.

EATING

Snack Happy

Baby is feeding himself with increasing skill, and parents are looking for a range of things that will win Baby's vote. Since lunch and dinner are usually in the form of finger foods, Baby finds finger foods interesting not only to eat but to feel and look at. He may be so fascinated that he plays with his food. Encourage his interest and consumption by providing him with tasty tidbits like cubes of cheese, chunks of tuna, zucchini fingers, green beans, toast fingers, carrot rounds (cooked but still firm), chunks or wedges of melon, slivers of raw apple, and a waffle square.

Clean-up Chant

When it comes to speeding clean-up, use a quick rhyme. It goes like this:

One, two, three, get ready for me.
Put your hands in the air while I clean your chair.
Four, five, six, now none of your tricks.
Seven, eight, nine, now things look fine.

Peanut Butter

Peanut butter is an inexpensive, nutritious, and frequently overlooked source of protein. Check labels to determine salt and sugar content. Many brands have reduced the amount of both. Or make your own. For one cup of peanut butter, you need one pound of peanuts in the shell and 1–2 tbs. of cooking oil. Roast peanuts on a cookie sheet in a 350° oven for 15 minutes. Cool, then shell them and swirl about a cup of them at a time in the blender. Add oil and salt to taste. Try other nuts like walnuts, almonds, and cashews to discover your child's favorite. Baby may find he likes other nut butters as much as peanut butter.

New Foods

This is a good time to introduce new foods to your toddler. Expand his repertoire. Since all breads are not white or wheat, give Baby a variety. How about muffins, bagels, or breadsticks? Each is also a chance for little fingers to explore. Whether it's tofu and bean sprouts or the new yogurts made from milk, or spinach pasta, join your toddler in sampling. The two of you will enjoy comparing notes on each new taste treat.

Small Sandwiches

For a toddler whose desire to eat surpasses his ability to consume, make him a sandwich like "big kids" eat but use cocktail size bread—less mess, less waste, and definitely easier to eat.

DRESSING AND CHANGING

Your child won't wear mittens? Try long socks that go up over the jacket. The child can not pull these off as easily. Finger puppets also keep those little fingers warm and are fun to boot!

Shoe News

A teaspoon makes an ideal shoehorn for your toddler. It will take the struggle out of putting on shoes and encourage him to put them on himself.

Peek-a-boo Dressing

If your toddler is fussing while getting dressed, play peek-a-boo games. Wave or say "bye-bye" to a hand as it goes into the sleeve, and say "hello" when it reappears on the other side. This can also be done with a foot going into the pants and the head into a shirt.

Ode to the Clothes Hamper

For the sake of the wives and husbands of tomorrow, it's up to the mothers of today to teach their children how to use the clothes hamper. All clothes have but four homes—on Baby, on hangers, in drawers, or in the hamper.

HELPFUL HINTS

Remaining Calm

When Baby is frightened or injured, engage at least three of his senses to calm and reassure him. Make sure Baby can see you, and speak in a soft, loving tone. At the same time touch a part of his body that is not in pain. By occupying three of Baby's senses, you are reassuring him that he will be fine as well as diverting attention away from the anxiety and/or pain.

Safety Thought

One of Baby's favorite sports is opening any type of latch, fastener, knob, or handle. Don't underestimate his skills. The standard gate latch is certainly no challenge. Install an adult-height latch on top of the post if your gate is high enough or one on the back side of the gate that requires you to reach over the top of the gate to open it.

Your Child Is Changing

Realize that your child's developmental stages are changing all the time. Today he may not be able to reach the burners; suddenly tomorrow he can. Ask your physician what changes you can expect in the coming weeks and prepare your house to protect him from any mishaps.

Crayon Removal

To remove crayon from clothes, iron it between two paper towels. The crayon will melt onto the towels.

The Booster Seat

Instead of using a high chair for your child at a restaurant, try a booster seat. Your child will feel "grown-up" with this change of pace.

Work Surface

Children benefit from good work surfaces. An easy way to construct one is to place a flat, hollow door horizontally on milk crates. This will allow a toddler to lay out the various miniature environments that are now being produced for young children—the school, the farm, or the gas station. He will enjoy leaving these toys set up, and you will find that the pieces stay together much better than when you insist that the games be put away after each use. This surface works well for block play, art projects, and train or car track sets. When Baby is older, he'll have a desk with the addition of a few more crates.

Lickety-Split

If you really want to thrill your toddler, teach him the old preschool trick of putting on his coat. It's easy with practice. Lay the coat down so the collar is toward him and the front opening is on top. Open wide, showing the arm holes. The child bends down, puts a hand in each armhole, and picks up the coat, throwing it back over his head, and simultaneously thrusting his arms into its arms. It's on. He'll love it, but you'll love it even more when you think of all the time and energy you're saving.

Toothpaste Cleaning

If food coloring has gotten into Baby's clothing, try this tip. Rub the spot with some white toothpaste and allow the area to dry. Dip in cold water, wring out well, and launder as usual.

Clothing First Aid Kit

One playgroup mother claims that she can cope with any emergency clothing repair with the following items close at hand: masking tape, a small stapler, dental floss and needle, and safety pins. She keeps several of these kits with her at all times—in the kitchen, car, and in her purse. No hem ever falls and no button is ever lost for long.

Toy Display

Display special toys in the following ways. Sew an inexpensive curtain ring to the back of the toy or doll. Then hang these playthings from hooks positioned around the room. Baby enjoys them near the bed or changing table. They're fun to wake up to or look at while waiting for clean clothes.

Toy Nightmare

After almost two years of collecting, if you feel you could open a toy store without another purchase, it's time to organice, sort, trade, donate to a charity, or sell the extras.

ORGANIZE: Consider an indoor playhouse that will double as a toy chest now that the one you have is too small to hold the collection.

SORT: Consider a toy closet in which you will fill the walls with hooks. It's amazing how much you can hang. Think about pegboards, which can be hung in inconspicuous places such as behind stairways, on the garage wall, or in an unused part of the laundry room or attic.

TRADE: Help your toddler decide which items he wants to swap with his playgroup pals. Toy-swapping day will be something to look forward to, and kids will play with pre-owned toys as if they were brand new.

DONATE: Choose a favorite charity and donate toys.

SELL: A toy consignment shop in your area could be a bonanza. Don't take Baby with you when you drop off toys or you will leave with more than you came with.

Place Mats

Why not share some of Baby's great artwork with those who will appreciate it the most? Let Baby help you pick out some of his best efforts and seal them in a clear contact paper sandwich, or buy a set of the specially designed kits for making place mats found in local fabric shops. We guarantee these will be treasured by grandparents and other friends and admirers.

Tripping the Light Fantastic

Some families find taking trips with their children pleasant and easy. What are their secrets? If you like to travel and want to take your kids along, here are some ways to prepare:

1. A cooler filled with drinks and snacks is essential. Try for non-messy, non-sticky foods, like carrot sticks, cheese chunks, apple slices. The new single-serving-size drinks in paper cartons with straws attached will delight a child. Never travel without disposable wet-wipes.

2. Nothing beats a duffle bag to carry all of Baby's gear. It fits in any car and can be an extra pillow.
3. Containers with lids are indispensable for containing all those little bits and pieces of toys and art materials. Plastic cake pans with lids double as a desk for Baby.
4. Paper tablets and water-based, water-soluble markers are perfect for use in the car. Good-bye broken crayons.
5. Buy a new toy and give it to Baby as you're starting out. This will keep him occupied for quite a while.
6. A portable cassette tape deck and ear phones and a supply of the many children's tapes now available will provide some happy moments.
7. If you're considering a long trip for children, plan to leave near nap time or before bedtime.
8. For long day trips, parents cope with eating and snacking by scheduling a picnic along the way so that everyone can stretch as well as have a good nibble.

Tantrums

Growing up is hard on everyone. Your toddler is much more vulnerable than he may seem. His ego and confidence are fragile. All children have tantrums at some point; they are an important and healthy part of growth and development. A toddler needs to test his power and assert his independence. It doesn't mean that he's any less interested in your approval or loves you less. A sense of humor is indispensable to keep things in perspective. Certainly limits and rules are necessary, but the fewer the better. Try to save showdowns for things that truly matter. Many small issues and situations can and should be handled by redirecting and diverting.

Dogs

Unfortunately, not all dogs love children of this age. A toddler's short stature, quick moves, and noisy shrieks may lead dogs to momentarily confuse Baby with one of their own kind and act aggressively. Teaching Baby how to behave appropriately with a dog is time well spent. Before you approach any dog, you should say to the child, "You must ask someone if you can pet the dog first." Next teach Baby how to follow these rules: stick out his hand so the dog can sniff it, show the dog a flat hand with fingers together, pet the dog on or near his tail, not on the head. Most dogs are more willing to be petted on the back than on the head. Once the dog is friendly, you can help Baby pat the head. Don't leave Baby alone with a dog you don't know well.

Play Groups

At this point in his life, Baby may reap some benefits from regular socializing. For some moms, a play group is the answer, perhaps a group of four children, all about the same age and size, ideally living in the same locale so that all can walk to each home. Play groups usually meet one or two mornings a week, with the responsibility for planning and supervision rotating among the parents.

When you're the group leader, post your schedule and plan to supervise the children for about two hours of play. There are many resources available for games and activities, such as this book. For two hours of time, plan to have one quiet game, one noisy game, one action game, song, or dance, one group art project, and an age-appropriate story to share with the whole group. Begin and end your two-hour session with time for the children to explore individually the toys and environment you've provided as part of your program.

Out To Breakfast

There's no reason not to eat out with a toddler, but there's good reason to think through and plan these outings carefully. The most successful restaurant meal we have shared with our children has been breakfast. Some of the pluses are:

1. Breakfast food is the kind kids love most.
2. Everyone is in good form at this hour of the day.
3. Breakfast food is prepared quickly.
4. These breakfasts are usually enjoyed on the weekend when we have more leisure time and aren't feeling rushed.
5. These meals are usually relatively inexpensive.
6. Most important, the surrounding clientele are usually the same sort of people we are, that is, other families.

Thoughtfulness

Your thoughtfulness counts, especially when your toddler is not as charming and loving as he can be. Let his sitters or caregivers know how grateful you are for their affection and attention. Your actions show them that you know how trying Baby can be. Love has not caused you to lose your reason. We suggest giving caregivers baked cookies or a loaf of luscious fruit bread, a large jug of cider, a plant, or a magazine subscription to enjoy, maybe when Baby's asleep.

Pictures

It seems that once Baby gets to the running stage, we sometimes stop taking enough pictures. Make sure you always have an extra roll of film at home. Batteries, flashbulbs, and a mail-away developing envelope would be handy items to have on hand. You can never take too many pictures, and certainly there are still lots of wonderful moments to capture. Don't miss them.

Sleeping Bags

Even if yours is not a camping family, a sleeping bag can be a familiar and cozy way to cope with a traveling toddler. Whether it's used to visit relatives across the country or to stay with a sitter across the street, a zippered sleeping bag comes in handy. Besides the classic models with plaid or wild-west lining, the newest bags are upbeat and fanciful, light and easy to care for. One mother also uses a sleeping bag as an alternative on sick days, grouchy days, or when the routine of sleeping in one's own bed becomes boring. You can put a sleeping bag almost anywhere and Baby will be happy.

To Grandmother's House We Go

A trip to Grandma's house can be easier if you leave a set of Baby's gear at Grandma's—a duplicate blanket, toys, diapers, materials that he likes, and maybe one of his vehicles. Then you won't have to bring along a carful of equipment, nor load and unload it. This will make the trip more fun for everyone and allows for more spontaneous visits.

Car Trips

Children want to move around during long or short car trips. Make your trip safer and saner by establishing and constantly reinforcing a few simple rules and routines. All trips begin with seat belts buckled or

children secured in special car seats. Little hands and fingers need to be kept out of trouble. You might have a slogan like, "Give me a clap while I buckle your lap" while you fasten Baby in his chair. After the children are secured, make sure all doors are locked and that windows are locked at a safe level if open. Do this every time you start.

AND FOR YOURSELF
Keeping Current

Even when strangers stop and say, "What a cute baby!" don't be misled. Although you may eat, sleep, and breathe Baby's habits, your friends and relatives may prefer to discuss other things. Buy a major Sunday newspaper or leading news magazine and keep up with interests apart from Baby to stay current with the rest of the world.

Ticking, Ticking

Time doesn't need to be your enemy. Remember to enjoy where you are and what you're doing at the moment. Perspective is important. In ten years you won't have the opportunity to do the things you might be complaining about right now. Your positive attitude about time allows good things to happen.

Five Minutes of Peace and Beauty

Many cosmetics studios give free or reasonably priced make-overs and five-minute facials. Contact a local department store for details and promotions. Find a sitter for a portion of the afternoon, and create a new you!

PARENTS, FRIENDS, AND ADMIRERS

Gift Ideas

Fortunately, many grandparents take advantage of a quieter home life by pursuing creative interests. These generous folks often produce hand-wrought treasures for special grandchildren. This is a super time to begin thinking about Baby's soon-to-arrive second birthday. Grandma may be considering needlework, cross-stitching, poetry, samplers, appliques, wall hanging, or other items to be framed, while Grandpa may be painting, refurbishing, or designing a little toy boat or a simple piece of outdoor equipment.

Cooking

A trip into Grandmother's kitchen can be an adventure, especially when she shares a special recipe for a treat that can be eaten several ways. It's granola—healthy and crunchy. A big batch will satisfy even the most finicky eater and his nutrition-conscious parents. Once made, you can use the granola as a cereal, a cereal made into bars, a topping for fruit, or the prime ingredient in the greatest oatmeal cookies around. We like this recipe:

Ingredients:
3 cups oatmeal
2 cups unsweetened coconut
1 cup untoasted wheat germ
⅓ cup oil
1 Tbs. to ⅓ cup brown sugar, to taste, or
1 cup honey
Directions:
1. Mix first four ingredients in a bowl. Gradually add the honey or sugar.

2. Spread on a cookie sheet or baking pan.
3. Bake 30 minutes at 325°. Remove and let cool.

You can also add dried fruit such as cherries, apricots, dates, raisins, and any sort of seed. This makes about 4 cups of cereal or topping. If you want to make the bars, beat 2 eggs until fluffy and combine with 2 cups of granola. You can add a little cinnamon and vanilla and pour it into an 8-inch square. Bake at 350° for 15 minutes. When cool, cut into 8 bars. For a special treat spread with peanut butter or jam.

Stamps and Cars

Adults sometimes think they must always share a child's interests but forget to share their own with the child. Pass on your loves and passions. The "nearly-two" child can begin to love what you love—gardening, stamps, cars, cats, antiques. Your enthusiasm will be contagious. What could be better than learning about a subject from someone who likes it, knows it best, adores Baby, and wants to share with him?

A Spice Sack

Few of us can resist the aroma of a spice store. Take a toddler along on your next visit and let him pick out an assortment of aromatic spices and herbs for Grandma or a special someone. Whether the spices are used for cooking, as an inexpensive room freshener, or just for display, present them in sacks with bows to match the recipient's decor, or in lovely little baskets. Grandma will be pleased, and your toddler will be delighted because he's not too young to have a hand in making a gift for someone special.

The Museum

A special adventure for Baby can be a visit to the local museum. Museums are no longer somber archives full of ancient artifacts for intellectuals. Some of today's collections are developed with young visitors in mind. Exhibits are not always behind glass—children and adults can often touch, manipulate, and explore them. Check with your local Chamber of Commerce or tourist information bureau to learn about exhibits in your area.

Picture Cards

Rather than sending cards that must be read to your favorite pre-reader, send him one he can understand himself. If you're up to drawing stick men, you can produce a funny story line telling your special wish. Or consider photographs, as in this scenario for a card: On the front is a photo of Grandma preparing a cake, and inside, a photo of the cake with candles. Behind it are Grandma and Grandpa, holding open loving arms.

Good Gifts

For grandparents on a fixed income, the thought of buying toys for all their grandchildren can be daunting. One smart couple we know devised this system: Each child was given a purse and a small amount of money with an invitation to go shopping. The children were roused early and taken to the local swap-and-shop outdoor flea market. They had a wonderful time and came home with boxes of appealing toys. Other grandparents do the same with garage sales, followed by a luncheon stop at McDonald's.

Lunch With Grandpa

One grandpa shared lunch with all his visiting grandchildren and let them help with the preparations. They made mini-pizzas together. First he set out a plate of English muffins, a dish of tomato sauce, several bowls of different cheeses, mushrooms, peppers, and other toppings. Then each child made a mini-pizza and placed it on a cookie sheet. The pizzas went under the broiler for about five minutes, and while they were cooking, the table was set. In a jiffy, lunch was ready to eat and enjoy together. Baby is at no disadvantage at this kind of luncheon. He can participate fully.

Planning Ahead

More for grandparents: If your favorite grandchild is coming to visit, start your preparations with a visit to the local library. Tell the children's librarian a little bit about your special friend, especially his interests and his age. She can help you find the records, tapes, and stories that are sure to please. She may also be able to suggest activities to delight you both. Most libraries have story hours and some even have a bedtime story hour at 7 p.m.

Another Good Idea

Have Baby help with the signing of holiday or birthday cards. After you sign the card, give Baby a marker and have him make a mark. Or, use ink to make a hand or thumbprint at the bottom of the card.

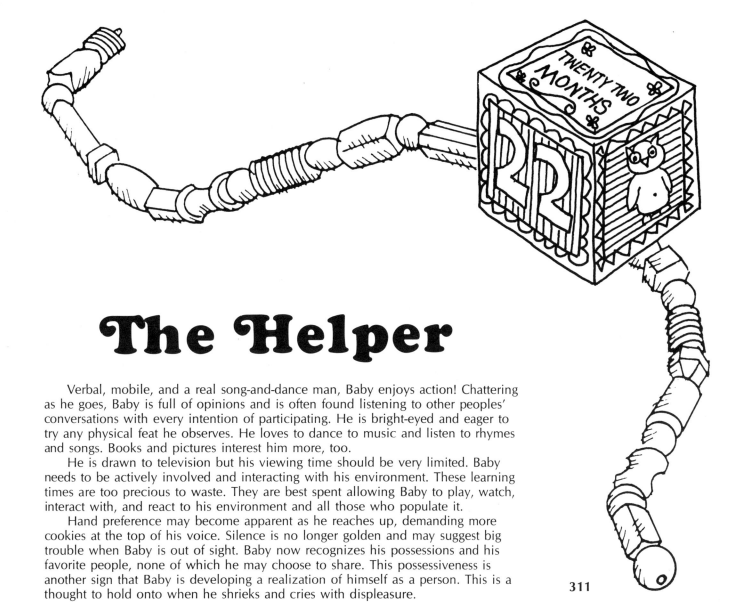

The Helper

Verbal, mobile, and a real song-and-dance man, Baby enjoys action! Chattering as he goes, Baby is full of opinions and is often found listening to other peoples' conversations with every intention of participating. He is bright-eyed and eager to try any physical feat he observes. He loves to dance to music and listen to rhymes and songs. Books and pictures interest him more, too.

He is drawn to television but his viewing time should be very limited. Baby needs to be actively involved and interacting with his environment. These learning times are too precious to waste. They are best spent allowing Baby to play, watch, interact with, and react to his environment and all those who populate it.

Hand preference may become apparent as he reaches up, demanding more cookies at the top of his voice. Silence is no longer golden and may suggest big trouble when Baby is out of sight. Baby now recognizes his possessions and his favorite people, none of which he may choose to share. This possessiveness is another sign that Baby is developing a realization of himself as a person. This is a thought to hold onto when he shrieks and cries with displeasure.

ACTIVITIES, GAMES, AND SONGS

Finger Song

"Put Your Finger In The Air" is a classic song by Woody Guthrie with tremendous toddler appeal. It's so simple, and the tune is so easy, that you and Baby will be singing it together in just a short time.

Put your finger in the air, in the air.
Put your finger in the air, in the air.
Put your finger in the air, leave it there about a year.
Put your finger in the air, in the air.

Pasta Sorting

Ask your supermarket clerk or a produce manager for some cardboard food-packing trays. The type used for apples and pears is sturdy enough. You and your toddler can use the depressions in these trays for sorting a variety of items. Start with pasta from your kitchen. Place a spiral, a shell, a rigatoni, or a wheel in one of the depressions and ask your toddler to match it with an identical shape from a box or a dish you've provided for him. This is a lot of fun and if a few go into his mouth, it doesn't matter.

String Painting

Consider a painting activity that requires no brush. Use yarn, string, or twine instead. Help your toddler fold a piece of paper length-wise. Then dip a foot-long piece of yarn or string into thick paint. Lay the twine on one side of the paper and fold the other side over the string. Then place the folded paper, with string enclosed, inside an old big catalogue. Let your child pull the string out.

Then open the catalogue and remove his paper and open it. For a toddler, the results are a great source of excitement and surprise. For best results, use no more than two colors and one string at a time.

More Water

The kitchen sink is a great site for water play, especially when you need to make a telephone call. Pull your toddler up to the sink and put an old raincoat on him backward. This will keep him fairly dry. Make sure he has plenty of real things to wash this time, like your plastic dishware or even your picnic set. In a pinch, you can always give him a baby doll or even his old socks and T-shirt to wash. Most toddlers think this is a lot of fun. After you have supervised this activity several times, you will find that water play is a good way to get through a troublesome period when Baby is fretting, angry, or just feeling contrary.

Pasta Magic

Hand your toddler a small piece of cardboard, thick paper, or a paper plate. Present him with some noodles which have been cooked but are not quite al dente. If still on the sticky side, the pasta will be perfect for him to twirl, twist, and fiddle with until he is satisfied with the design. Hand him only one piece at a time, giving the pasta some time to adhere to the paper, thus eliminating the need for glue or paste. What could be more suitable for a kitchen wall than this project, which can be spray painted for a festive touch?

Rainy Day Song

Sing to the tune "Frère Jacques"

I hear thunder, I hear thunder.
Say do you, say do you.
Trip trop raindrops, trip trop raindrops.
I'm wet through, you are too.

Social Butterfly

Here's a place to jot down Baby's first friends and playmates. Write a sentence or two about each.

Human _____

_____

_____

_____

Non-Human _____

_____

_____

Rainy Day Strategy

If you are stuck inside with a rowdy Baby, give into the rowdiness once in a while, but on your terms. Push back all the furniture and make sure all small things, such as knick-knacks and lamps, are out of the way. Then gather things to climb over—a stack of pillows, a large chair, a hassock, stools; things to crawl under—a coffee table, a piano bench; things to crawl around; and things to back in and out of, such as a laundry basket or even a large trash can. Make a tunnel out of a box by opening both ends, or line up a series of chairs and cover them with a sheet, making a scary, dark crawl space. The object is to move around without upsetting objects. The key to both fun and learning is to build something well constructed with clear limits set at the beginning of the game.

Jars And Lids

Before you throw out all those odd jars and unusual containers, put a dozen or so in a large box and sit down with your toddler. First, see if he can take the lids off—remember, little fingers can do magic. Second, can he match them up again? Consider spice jars, salad dressing bottles, and cans and jars that open in unique ways. After your toddler knows this game well, pass the set on to a play group, or take it to Grandma's.

Running

Can't get outside? Then make it okay for your toddler to run and play in a controlled running game. Pour yourself a cup of coffee, sit down, and let your toddler do the work. If you're really good at this game, you may even be able to leaf through a magazine, drink coffee, and help your toddler learn at the same time.

This game is called "Run and Touch." Say "Run and touch something you can sit on." He makes a decision, and when he gets your okay, he goes and then runs back to you. Then you send him off again with this instruction: "Run and touch something to look at." When he points to a picture, a mirror, or some other piece of artwork, or whatever you've decided, and you okay it, he runs off again. "Run and touch something that's growing." If he finds a plant and a fish in a fish tank, then he's succeeded in finding two things. Your child will enjoy this game, and it will help him learn and label important parts of his environment.

Shape Fun

Preparing an initial shape game needn't require special creativity. Use fabric this time; paper is too fragile. Start with a triangle, a circle, and a square. Cut three large examples of each shape in the same fabric. (Hint: If you use felt, the shapes can be used as a stick-on sorting game, perfect for a flannel or felt board.) Take one shape and hold it up. Say, "Find the shape that looks like this square." Allow your toddler time to hunt. Let him match it with yours. If your toddler doesn't know the name of the shapes, he can indicate whether they are the same or different, an important part of this concept-building game.

Magic Box

Maybe today is the day for a magic box. With a dark color, paint the inside, bottom, and sides of a shoe box or other small box. Any type of paint will do, but latex enamel is the best because it gives a hard, slick surface and a shiny finish. After the paint has dried, add a thin layer of salt to the bottom and show your toddler how he can make squiggles and designs by using his fingers. The salt will seem brilliant next to the painted walls of the box. When he's finished, demonstrate how a quick shake of the box erases what he's done—time to start over.

Clean-up Fun

Every parent's nightmare has to do with the end-of-day clean-up. Baby resists all calls that he help with the clean-up process. To the tune of "Twinkle, Twinkle," try this:

After my long day of play,
I take time to put away.
Put away, put away,
I take time to put away.
In my closet, drawers, and chest,
A clean room surely looks the best.

Face Game

Baby hasn't lost interest in the human face, or any other face for that matter. With his growing sense of humor, he adores the novel and the humorous. Remember potato faces? Buy the largest spud at the supermarket, grease it well with shortening, and cut a variety of facial features from vinyl—not the cloth-backed type. The shortening will allow these vinyl features to stick and to be moved around at will. To display this potato face, what could be more appropriate than leaning him against a potato masher?

Shark Puppets

Sharks can be made very easily from business-size envelopes, and they are perfect for your toddler's hand. Save a "junk mail" envelope and instead of opening it at the top, rip it open along the side and remove the contents. On the opposite end of the ripped opening, cut a "V" for the mouth. This piece can be glued or taped to the top as a fin. The envelope is now a shark and ready to be decorated by the toddler with crayons or markers. Your child will slip his hand into the puppet and make the shark swim.

Snake Mobile

On a day when Baby wants to color, stimulate him by giving him a paper plate and crayons or markers. Water colors are also a lot of fun for Baby at this age. Once he has finished decorating or painting the plate and the colors have dried, draw a spiral line from the edge of the plate ending in the center. Cut along the spiral line, punch a hole at the top, and add yarn. Hang the mobile at a window and watch it spin around and around.

Fun In The Snow

For a fun snow activity, fill an empty dish detergent bottle with water and food coloring. Make a few so that baby has a choice of colors. Let Baby squirt the snow and "paint" it different colors.

Make Your Own Placemat

Have your child make his own placemat. Print his name in large capital letters with a crayon and give it to him to paint with water colors. The wax from the crayon will resist the water in the paints and his name will peek through. Once dry, the picture can be covered in clear contact paper and used as his placemat. This is a great way to introduce Baby to his name!

Scavenger Hunt

Collect pictures of Baby's favorite toys or household objects that are familiar to him. Before his snack, show Baby a few pictures, one at a time. Have him find each object and bring it to you before presenting him with another picture. Celebrate a job well done by having him choose a special snack.

See And Say

Make a homemade "see and say" where Baby is the voice. On a paper plate, glue familiar pictures, and attach a cardboard arrow with a brass fastener. Baby can move the arrow to each picture and tell you the name of the picture.

Wipe-Off Board

Scribbling is fun on paper, but it is even more fun when you can erase your marks. You can easily make a wipe-off board by covering an old clipboard or cardboard with contact paper. Slide the covered board into a picture frame with the glass removed. We recommend dry erase markers because Baby can easily remove his creation with an ordinary chalkboard eraser. If you choose to use overhead projector markers, Baby can remove his marks with a damp sponge. Baby will enjoy many hours of fun with his new board.

Thumbprint Cookies

Cooking is always fun for Baby, especially if he is allowed to participate. Using ready-made cookie dough, cut the dough as instructed and place on cookie sheet. Have him make a depression in the uncooked cookie and fill the hole with raisins, chocolate chips, a Hershey Kiss, mini-marshmallows, or whatever you have available. Once cooked these tasty treats can be served for snacks or shared after dinner.

Pegboards

A super activity that helps Baby with eye-hand coordination is the use of pegboards. A colander can easily be converted into a pegboard when turned upside-down. Golf tees in a variety of colors will intrigue Baby and he will eagerly make designs on this odd shaped board.

Story Time

Instead of reading a story, why not act out one of Baby's favorite stories? Look around the house, use your imagination. By using three chairs of various sizes, three bowls, and a trip around to the bedrooms, you can act out *Goldilocks And The Three Bears.* It's a great way to share a story together and a change of pace from reading to him. Baby may be the next Tom Cruise.

Practicing Our Bending

A song that is full of actions and exciting to learn is "Head, Shoulders, Knees, and Toes." Baby touches each part of the body as it is sung. It goes like this:

Head, shoulders, knees, and toes, knees and toes.
Head, shoulders, knees, and toes, knees and toes.
And eyes, and ears, and mouth, and nose.
Head, shoulders, knees, and toes, knees and toes.

Baby's Brag Book

Make a picture book of Baby's favorite toys by placing pictures of things he is familiar with in a small photo album. Baby will learn to recognize family members, toys, and objects that can be found around the house. He will love sharing his knowledge with friends and admirers.

ROUTINE TIMES

BATHING

The Red Dot

Minimize your worries about accidents in the bathroom by putting a bright red stick-on dot on the hot water handles. Red means "red hot" and "hands-off." Make this a policy in the kitchen, too. Only grown-ups touch the handles.

Hand Washing

Now is a good time to teach a simple ritual for washing hands. An almost-two will revel in his ability to master this job. Let him help you gather soap, towels, nail brush, and if you want, some hand lotion. Although Montessori uses at least a ten-step process, we like this five-step strategy:

1. Roll up sleeves and step up to the sink on a stool or chair.
2. Fill sink about half way with warm water and wet hands.
3. Rub soap onto hands and return to soap dish.
4. Lather up. Use brush if necessary on nails or tough spots.
5. Rinse hands well, drain sink, and dry hands, working on one finger at a time.

Mix And Brush

For a not-so-cheerful toothbrusher, consider letting Baby make his own toothpaste. Mix one tablespoon baking soda, one teaspoon salt, and one teaspoon of your favorite flavoring, such as vanilla or peppermint. To keep this fresh, store in a jar.

Cautionary Note

Bath time is usually a happy, easy time for your toddler; here are some ways to keep it that way. Adding bubbles or suds to the water can create problems for young children. Avoid urinary tract or vaginal infections by leaving these fancy preparations for later. For a special effect, make a pink bath by adding a couple of drops of food coloring. Or add fun by floating several ice cubes in a warm bath.

Tub Toys

Save large, colored, two-liter plastic soda bottles for the tub. These boats fill slowly before they sink to the bottom.

SLEEPING

Light Play

If you can't beat them, join them. For the child who just can't fall asleep easily, consider a compromise. Maintain the bedtime routine and the time he must be in bed, but allow your bright-eyed child to take a flashlight with him when he goes to bed. The disposable type with no removable parts is best. He can quietly look around his room with the light until the sandman overtakes him.

Best Sleeping Song

The best sleeping song we know is the classic, "Hush, Little Baby, Don't Say A Word." Here is the first verse, but you may wish to learn the whole song.

> Hush, little baby. Don't say a word.
> Papa's gonna buy you a mockingbird.
> If that mockingbird don't sing,
> Papa's gonna buy you a diamond ring.

Wake-up Trick

Sometimes toddlers have to be awakened. One gentle, unobtrusive way is a little ear tickle. Caregivers we know tell us that children rouse each other effectively this way. Just gently tickle or lightly pull the lobe of the child's ear while saying his name.

Jammy Bags

For the toddler who is wearing pajamas, a ritual like putting his "jammies" into a special bag will be a routine that he will want to follow. Most of these pajama holders are cute animals, perfect to hang or add to the menagerie of animals on his bed. The best ones are homemade and can usually be found at craft stores or bazaars.

EATING

Finicky Eater

If lunchtime becomes a trial, presenting lunch in a different way will interest the finicky toddler. Using a tray, wicker basket, shoe box tied with ribbon, paper bag with each portion wrapped in foil, or the all-time favorite lunchbox will make the ordinary seem special.

Snack On A String

Fun for a play group or Baby alone is a snack on a string. Let him nibble off a string that you've strung with grapes, tiny marshmallows, small cubes of bread, olives, or even parboiled vegetables—carrots are a good choice. Use one kind of food or a combination. This different way to present snacks always interests toddlers. A sibling may enjoy stringing it for you.

Portable Meals

For the toddler who is always on the move, present a meal that can move with him. Prepare some tuna, egg, or ham salad and put it in an ice cream cone. He'll be able to eat the cone with the filling, and it's all easier to handle.

New Ways With Peanut Butter

Peanut butter is a top choice for sandwiches, but it's also ideal for a variety of other goodies. How about peanut butter balls with fruit or vegetable tidbits inside—raisins, grated carrots, apple chunks; peanut butter roll-ups in lettuce leaves; peanut butter boats made with a long strip of banana topped with peanut butter; or frosted pineapple bits made from chunks of pineapple topped with peanut butter? Delectable! Baby's admirers have been observed eating these treats with relish.

Breakfast With Dad

Sadly, the only time some parents have to visit with their little ones is before bed. In one household, the parents attacked this problem by rotating the time they rose in the morning so they could prepare a special breakfast for Baby. This gave one parent an extra hour of rest, while the toddler got total attention from the other. Soon the young breakfaster was grinding coffee beans, dropping muffins into the toaster, delivering the cat's food, and scooping granola into bowls. Can you imagine what he was doing by two and a half?

DRESSING AND CHANGING

Fish Bowl Storage

A clear plastic fish bowl can provide the perfect storage container for Baby's socks. He'll enjoy fishing and you'll enjoy keeping track of these elusive items.

Mitten Thoughts

If the mittens on a string running through the coat and armholes is not working for you or your toddler, and you've tried using mitten clips without success, consider sewing a button to the cuff of each glove. When the mittens are off, they can be buttoned to the coat.

Shoe Business

No doubt about it; toddlers outgrow their shoes at a rapid rate. In the meantime, keeping shoes on Baby's feet can be a challenge. Try these ideas:

1. Tie shoes and help them stay tied by dampening the laces first.
2. Never forget to double-knot.
3. Cut small slits in the sides of the tongue and pull the laces through them, then tie.

Softer Shoes

Soften and restore shoes that have "walked on water" by giving them a good rubbing with saddle soap before they dry. Not only will this old standby clean them up, but it will keep them from getting stiff. Dry shoes away from direct heat and finish with a coat of regular shoe polish and a good buffing.

Fancy Shirt

Buttons are fun for little fingers to explore, but a shirt covered in buttons could be an extra-special garment to wear. Empty your button box and start stitching buttons all over a T-shirt. Go glittery or plain, as you like. Make sure the buttons are on securely. One mom used a half dozen buttons positioned in a specific pattern as the basis of holiday shirts. She just buttoned on felt or fabric objects to denote the season—bunnies, hearts, or leaves. Another mother buttoned on a first initial and later the child's first name.

HELPFUL HINTS

Bumped Lips

Occasionally Baby will fall and hit his mouth, and ice may not be close at hand. One smart mom suggested an ice pop to her bruised toddler. He willingly sucked on the cold treat, reducing the swelling in no time.

No Spills

To give a child medicine without a spill, measure the proper dose and put it in a small cup. Then give the child a straw to drink the medicine. This works much better than a spoon, and the medicine goes down without a mess.

Fire Safety

Don't forget to put a TOT FINDER sign on your child's window in case there is a fire in your home. Most fire stations have them, and what a fun trip to see the fire trucks while picking up the sign!

The Fun Phone

Now is a good time to put the telephone high on a wall. It's so much more fun to use than the pretend phone in the playroom. Also, add a hook next to the phone to corral that enticing cord. It can be fun to play with but is so dangerous as a toy.

Room Decorations

When considering how to decorating Baby's room cost effectively, visit a teachers' supply center. Today's classroom graphics are delightful and far less expensive than wallpaper and designer coordinates. You can change them as Baby grows and use them as learning tools for Baby, too. You'll find everything from colorful alphabet lines to entire wall environments. They may be especially useful if you are renting your home and don't want to invest in decorating.

Recycling

Now that Baby is better able and more willing to help pick up his toys, it's time to provide him with the tools for success. Tiered recycling bins provide great toy storage that is just his height and color-coded, too. They are much easier to use than shelves which can frustrate Baby when things fall or roll off.

Hot Seat

Remember how hot your car seat can get in the summer? Well, Baby's seat gets just as hot. An easy cover is an old bassinet or crib sheet.

Car Safety

Now that your toddler has grown and gets very busy with all the things in the car, NEVER get out of the car with the keys in the ignition. It's so easy for the child to hit the door lock and be locked inside. Always take the keys out of the ignition before you open the door.

Working Moms

Don't play "Beat the Clock" in the morning. Figure out how long it takes you to get ready and then how long it takes Baby. Get up that much earlier. You will both be much happier and feel less pressure—a nice way to start your day, and Baby will love you for it. Harassed Moms are no fun.

Scoop Away

Dustpan those smaller toys away. Buy a dustpan for toys only and when your toddler's toys are everywhere, just scoop them up. Teach Baby this trick and before you know it, he may clean up without asking.

Getting To Know You

To help Baby feel more secure during an upcoming special family event or holiday, make a family picture tree. Show and tell him who each family member is and glue the picture on the tree. When your toddler sees the "not often seen" family members, he won't feel insecure because he "knows" these people. This also makes a nice keepsake.

Sore Throats

For a child who has a sore throat and won't or can't suck on a cough drop, place the cough drop in a bottle or cup with some juice. Let it dilute a little and then have the child drink it. This will usually help the throat and cough.

Sliding Straps

Do your toddler's shoulder straps spend most of their time around his waist? Sew a Velcro dot onto the shoulder of his shirt to grasp the strap. Or use a barrette to clip the straps together.

Footed Sleepwear

Do your toddler's feet sweat when in footed pajamas but get too cold without them? Use a hole punch to add ventilation for his little feet.

Laundry Day

Doing laundry? Give your toddler his own basket to play in. He can fill and dump clothes out of it or prepare doll clothes to be washed.

Sitting Still

When taking your toddler to church or another place where he is required to sit still and be quiet, always sit right in front so he can see what is going on. Bring an activity or treat. One book and a box of raisins will work. The raisins are a quiet food and easy to clean up.

Prevention

To protect your child's cheeks and face from becoming red and chapped on cold winter days, dab a little petroleum jelly on them.

Indoor Sandbox

Make an indoor sandbox from used coffee grounds. Dry the grounds quickly in the oven at 250°. Pour them onto a cookie sheet and have him drive cars through them.

Patching

For that inflatable toy that needs a quick patch, coat the hole with three or four layers of clear nail polish. Let it dry completely before re-inflating it.

Off Limits

Put a sock on the doorknob of the room you want to prevent Baby from entering. The elastic will hold the sock onto the knob, making the knob too slippery to use.

The Right Socks

To determine the right size sock to buy for your toddler, wrap a sock around the child's fist. If the toe meets the heel, you have the right size.

Winter Hat and Mitten Holder

Tired of looking for missing hats and mittens? Attach a strip of Velcro, rough side out, onto the inside of the door. Then when your toddler or any family member comes in, they can press the mittens and hats right onto the strip.

AND FOR YOURSELF

Doing What's Best For You

In the 1990's women have a wide range of choices. Having young children doesn't necessarily mean they are locked into a particular lifestyle. Some women work at home. Some women work outside for money. Some do a little of each. At the heart of this decision is self-acceptance. Decide what you want. Then take the action required to produce a happy lifestyle.

Research suggests that the best mothers are those who are the most personally content. Self-worth and positive image have nothing to do with whether or not you work outside the home. The happiest women have a variety of interests and skills and see different avenues for personal growth. Conversely, those who seem the least content feel they are suffering from lost identity and often experience boredom and isolation. Whether you choose to be at home and happy or working and loving it, moving ahead as a person is what counts.

Don't waste the time you have. There are so many things you can do if you've chosen to be at home. Community colleges often have baby-sitting services available. Use your time to:

—Learn art history
—Continue or launch a degree program
—Master a language

If you prefer an evening course, most husbands would encourage an hour or two away so you can learn to:

—Weave
—Sing
—Tune the family car

And don't waste time either:

—Study the piano or guitar, now that you can schedule practice time.
—Meet a friend for lunch.
—Volunteer in some community organization and acquire some new public relations skills

The Saving Way

If you've previous been an earner, it's often difficult to adjust to your new status. The new equation is: greater time = less money. You don't need to go without the niceties of life. Become a smarter shopper. Saving money is still the best game in town. Follow the sales, clip coupons, barter, trade tips and services with others.

PARENTS, FRIENDS, AND ADMIRERS

A Different Play Dough

For Grandma or a friend who is looking for an easy gift idea for Baby, consider a box of cookie cutters and a batch of this play dough which smells wonderful. Don't forget to include the recipe!

Kool-Aid Play Dough
Measure and mix together.
½ cup salt
1 Tbs. alum
2 pkgs. unsweetened Kool-Aid
3 Tbs. oil

Boil 2 cups of water. Add the oil, then the rest of the ingredients. Knead together until well mixed and let cool. Store in covered container in the refrigerator when not in use. The color and smell will vary according to the flavor you choose.

A Great Gift

Now that Baby can talk, a great gift he will love is a tape recorder with a microphone. He will enjoy listening to his own voice as well as playing tapes of songs both new and familiar. He will use it for years to come.

Picture Stationery

Another use for the scores of pictures your toddler is now creating is stationery. With the picture on the front, write the letter or message on the back, then roll it up and put it inside a paper towel roll so the picture remains intact. This will brighten the day of any grandpa and grandma.

That Terrific Toddler

Now that our favorite toddler is so busy, it's not easy for Mom or Dad to start or finish a task. Offering to take Baby for a walk or even for an occasional afternoon out will allow the often frustrated parent a chance to complete the task.

A Special Gift

A special gift for Mom or Grandma on Mother's Day is a rose bush. Start it the first Mother's Day a child is able to help plant, and continue every year. Rose bushes are inexpensive and precious to a Mom or Grandma. Other kinds of perennials can be used in the same way.

Wrapping Alternative

When giving a gift that has several parts or pieces, like Duplo or Bristle Blocks, instead of wrapping the original container in wrapping paper, present the gift in a storage container. You can use a clear plastic shoebox with a bow, a brightly colored drawstring bag, or a basket. Baby will associate the container with the present and it gives Mom a place to keep all the pieces together. This is one present both Mom and Baby will enjoy.

Special To Grandma

Not all stories come from books. Many of the best are fables and legends that have existed in your family for years. And who can tell them better than a grandparent, aunt, or uncle? Make a tape for the toddler. And while you're at it, after telling your favorite story, give

Baby a brief catch-up talk about the news in *your* home. Sing him a song, recite a poem, share a little chant. If you aren't up to telling a story, you might want to read a book; send it along with him so that Mom can hold the book while you tell the story to Baby.

Circle Glider

One grandfather's favorite trick was a wonderful paper glider. It was made of paper circles, a straw, and two paper clips. It never looked as if it could fly and yet it did. Here's the trick: Cut two strips of paper, nine inches by one inch, and six inches by one inch, from medium-weight construction paper. Make loops from these strips and clip them to both ends of the straw. Sail it forward, small loop in front. If it doesn't fly beautifully, check the proportions and weight.

Candied Nuts

It is parents who transmit enthusiasm and place a value on family gatherings. Start teaching Baby the importance of family, community, and belonging. Every year before the family holiday gathering, the children in a family we know made traditional candied nuts. All year long they saved containers and gathered their fixings. Finally, on the appointed night, the nuts were baked and cooled, then placed in jars decorated with a circle of red gingham and a green yarn bow. Upon arrival at the family party, the children would go from relative to relative delivering the nuts. It was an event they always looked forward to and will be one of their fondest memories—a tradition they will share with their own children.

Ladybug Races

A ladybug race is fun for a bunch of active children or for a mixed group of grown-ups and kids. Give all the racers a paper plate or two and let them decorate the plate as a ladybug, or any bug they like, adding additional pieces of paper for wings, legs, and head. The next steps: Punch a hole for a string near the top of the plate. Thread a ten-foot-long piece of string through the hole and secure one end to a chair leg or the lower rung of another piece of furniture. When the signal to begin the race is given, jiggle the string with the ladybug attached. The object is to move the ladybug from one end of the string to the other. Practice and time will improve the technique. It's also fun to decorate the plates with faces to represent the players, or to turn the paper plate into a car with wheels attached sideways. This is a game that can be played anywhere!

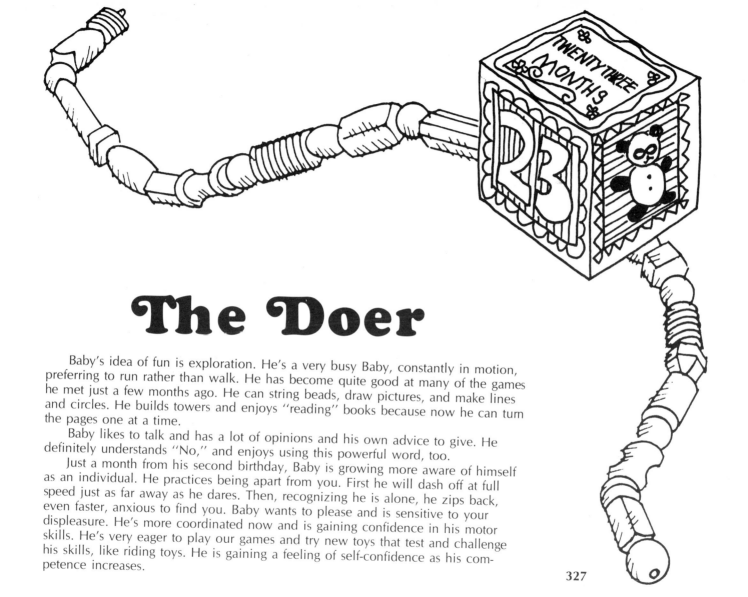

The Doer

Baby's idea of fun is exploration. He's a very busy Baby, constantly in motion, preferring to run rather than walk. He has become quite good at many of the games he met just a few months ago. He can string beads, draw pictures, and make lines and circles. He builds towers and enjoys "reading" books because now he can turn the pages one at a time.

Baby likes to talk and has a lot of opinions and his own advice to give. He definitely understands "No," and enjoys using this powerful word, too.

Just a month from his second birthday, Baby is growing more aware of himself as an individual. He practices being apart from you. First he will dash off at full speed just as far away as he dares. Then, recognizing he is alone, he zips back, even faster, anxious to find you. Baby wants to please and is sensitive to your displeasure. He's more coordinated now and is gaining confidence in his motor skills. He's very eager to play our games and try new toys that test and challenge his skills, like riding toys. He is gaining a feeling of self-confidence as his competence increases.

327

This is a time when Baby may seem to develop a fear of noises or large animals. This is certainly not unusual and is part of his growing awareness of himself. You may also find that although he plays well with adults he can be possessive and aggressive with peers.

Baby anticipates routines and events. He loves to dress up and insists on picking out his own clothes. The outdoors is favored because it's a place he can test his motor skills and is full of interesting things, including bugs, mud, puddles, flowers, stones, and animals.

ACTIVITIES, GAMES, AND SONGS

Free Form Puzzles

A good investment for a toddler is a set of painted, one-inch wooden cubes. Besides the obvious uses for these—sorting, color identification, matching, counting, stacking, filling containers, and so on—try a "do like me" game to build visual and imitative skills. In this game, show Baby a pattern you've created with his cubes and ask if he can copy it.

Begin with a two-color pattern. With time and practice, your design can become quite elaborate. This activity allows your toddler to make something beautiful without the fine motor skills needed to complete a design with crayons or markers.

Unlike commercial puzzles, the range of designs with these cubes is limitless. Baby will not be bored when the games are repeated.

The cubes are also a good way to learn color values. Try this. Create a background of yellow cubes and insert a red one. Baby will remember the red cube because it's different. These are the most free-form puzzles in any medium we know.

Magnet Magic

A magnet experiment provides a kind of magic and a good guessing game to share with siblings or a play group. Buy the largest magnet you can find. A horseshoe magnet is distinctive and is often colorfully painted. Gather some common objects—a pencil, large paper clips, wood, combs, sponges, tin cans, fabric scraps, large nails, nuts, pennies, rubber bands, cotton balls, large safety pins, and so on.

Let your toddler check the items and hold the magnet. After a few minutes ask, "Can you pick something up with the magnet?" Let him experiment until he finds things. Listen to what he says and encourage him. It will be enough the first time to discover that magnets pick up some things but not others.

Next time, separate the items that can be picked up from the ones that can't and let Baby test your choices.

Buttoning and Unbuttoning

Your toddler loves to button and unbutton things. To help develop this skill, turn a cloth ball into a toddler's dream. Sew buttons onto the cloth ball. Then cut shapes of different sizes and color out of felt. Cut a slit in the middle, and the shape can be buttoned to the ball. Baby will love to practice buttoning by moving the shapes around or changing them as he desires. This is also a great traveling activity since it is compact and holds Baby's attention.

I Spy

Do your own variation of "I Spy" to work on Baby's language and vocabulary acquisition. Choose various objects around the room. Say, "I spy a book. Can you find it? Can you say it?" One intuitive mom played this game in the car with her active son to keep him occupied while she drove.

Another Tactile Game

Create a "feely box." Ask Baby to match the "feel" of the item in the box with that of the item glued on top. First, glue a variety of materials with different textures to the lid of a shoe box—sandpaper, cotton, satin, corduroy, and plastic are some suggestions. Place the same materials inside the box. Make a hole in the side of the box just big enough for Baby's hand to fit. Ask him to feel one of the textures on the top and find one that feels the same inside the box. When he thinks he has found it, remove the lid to see which texture he has chosen.

Zoom Pictures

Using a file folder as a frame, cut a square to reveal only part of a picture. Place pictures of people or items that Baby is familiar with—Grandma, dogs, toys, tree, bird, Grandpa, trucks, cars, bottle, cookie, shoe, hat, etc., in the folder so that Baby sees only a portion. Can he guess what the picture is from the part he can see? Reward Baby for his accomplishments.

Color Sort Game

Crafts sticks (like small tongue depressors) are fun for Baby to handle and are available at craft stores. Color the tops of the craft sticks, and Baby can use them to sort. Start by making three sticks of each of three colors. Then gradually add to the selection as Baby becomes familiar with the game. He can sort the sticks into coffee or juice cans that have been covered or marked with the appropriate color paper, or put them in piles on the floor.

Magnets on the Go

Magnets don't have to stay on the refrigerator—you can make them mobile by placing them in a coffee can or on a cookie sheet. The coffee can is ideal for storing them and also provides a different kind of surface to attract them. The cookie sheet resembles the smooth, straight refrigerator surface but is horizontal and can move between rooms with your toddler or to the car.

Summer Water Fun

If you're "painting" a fence with water and a brush on a hot day, try a small paint roller instead. It's fun, and cool for Baby, too.

Lacing

Now that Baby is older, an enjoyable stringing activity is to make Mom or Grandma a beautiful straw necklace. Cut up straws into easy-to-handle lengths about an inch long. Give Baby some yarn with the ends taped to make the job easier and keep it from unraveling. Paper flowers with holes cut in the middle or round o's cereal can be added for an interesting effect.

Stair Practice

Bedside steps which can be purchased unpainted at a furniture store are ideal for your toddler to practice stair-climbing. Place a set of steps next to his bed or put two back to back so he can go up and down. Reasonably priced, these mini-steps are a useful introduction to the real thing.

Napkin Ring Stacker

Stacking and sorting activities are always a big hit. Make your own stacker by filling paper towel tubes with newspaper and inserting them halfway into an upright box. Cover the box and tubes with contact paper. Your toddler can sort and place napkin rings and/or curtain rings on this new "stacker."

Sorting Hook Board

Now that your toddler is becoming more familiar with shapes, he will be able to sort and hang them on his own. Make him an easy-to-use, colorful board to work on. Poster board in many wonderful colors can be purchased at any store that sells art supplies. Using construction paper, cut out the shapes that Baby is familiar with, add new ones, and glue them onto the poster board. Attach a plastic self-stick mug hook just above each shape. Now cut four or five of each shape out of different colored papers, and punch a hole in the top so Baby can hang each shape in the appropriate spot.

Finger Painting Made Easy

Finger painting is easy, but finger painting on a cookie sheet can be even more fun! The smooth non-porous surface gives an unusual texture to the finger paint and leaves perfect track marks. Baby can easily create the design of his choice. No finger paint in the house? Here's an easy recipe we found, using ingredients you might have around your kitchen:

FINGERPAINT
½ cup cornstarch
1 cup cold water
1 envelope unflavored gelatin
food coloring

1. Combine cornstarch and ¾ cup of the cold water in a saucepan. Mix well.
2. In a separate dish, soak the gelatin in the remaining ¼ cup of cold water.
3. Add the boiling water to the cornstarch mixture, stirring as you pour. Cook over medium heat, stirring constantly until boiling. When mixture is thick and clear, remove from heat and add dissolved gelatin, stirring constantly. When mixture is cool, divide into separate containers and add food coloring.

Crayon Cookies

No matter how much tape you use or how careful your toddler is with his crayons, they break. Broken crayons can be made into multicolored "crayon cookies" by placing two or three broken pieces in each section of a muffin tin and baking them at 325° for about four minutes or until melted. Remove them from the tins when cool, and you'll have new crayons for drawing. These round crayons will be a welcome change from the long ones Baby is used to.

Spinners

Almost any game is more fun if it has a spinner. Happily, spinners are easy to make. They require a simple brass paper fastener and a sheet of construction paper. Cut out an arrow, then make a grid and attach the arrow to it. Mark the grid like the face of a clock. For the non-reader, pictures or symbols are best. If you need more information on constructing or using spinners, there are books on them and on games you can play with them. Spinners can be used to select chores on a "home-chore chart" or to practice saying colors, words, or sounds. They can be used for giving directions if you're playing a motor game—for example, spinning to see how many steps to take. Uses for spinners are limited only by your imagination.

Values

One of the best ways to teach values is through stories. The brothers Grimm had the right idea. Listening to a story about a character with similar problems can be an enormous help to a child who's struggling with an issue. For the almost-two, this could be a story on biting,

running away, or being nice to the cat. Simply begin with "once upon a time" and drive your point home.

Dominoes

This game provides a creative way to learn numbers. Because it is essentially a matching game, it's perfect for toddlers. You can use the standard Domino tiles or make your own. Dominoes can also double as building blocks. You can expand the matching lesson beyond numbers by using sets of pictures that go together. Examples are shoes and laces, brush and comb, bowl and spoon. Hardwood picture sets, as well as number sets, are usually inexpensive.

Rubber Stamps

Rubber stamps can provide the basis for colorful print art. Since stamps can be expensive, buy only the ones with numbers and letters, then sort through the toy box and refrigerator for other objects and shapes that will print. Cookie cutters make wonderful printers. Small metal cars and other small toys can also be used. For a handy stamp pad, use a sponge soaked in water-based dye—water that has been richly colored with food coloring. You can create a rainbow of special colors this way. Stamps and printers can be used to personalize paper for all occasions, to make a special book cover for Grandma, and to make bright holiday cards.

Holiday Stamps

You can make additional rubber stamps from rubber erasers. Get the hard green or pink ones, which are about 1 in. × 2 in. × 4 in. Draw your design on a piece of paper and then, using a piece of carbon paper, transfer it to the eraser. Now, using an X-acto knife, cut the design so that the raised part will print. Although you will have to do the actual cutting of the design, Baby will love these activities because he sees his art transformed into a stamp he can use forever. Stamps are great tools for encouraging number and letter recognition, as in "Print me three apples."

Jumping Game

Using colored chalk, draw a variety of shapes in the driveway, one or two jumps apart. Let your toddler help in this process. Now explain the jumping game. You give the directions and he jumps the pattern you give. If you feel shapes are too hard, use object pictures, but do give your jumping jack his day.

If you want some exercise, too, reverse roles and let Baby give directions while you do the jumping. This is a good play group activity for several children at a time. Here's the model:

Jump in the square.
Jump two times.
Jump to the circle.
Wriggle to and fro.
Land in the heart.
Shake your head.

Pretend Places

If you think back, some of your happiest childhood hours were spent in "pretend places." Although the days of clotheslines are fading, string one up for your toddler. Hanging a blanket tent or a tepee can be great fun. Hold the edges down with bricks and stretch the cloth as tightly as you can. Another good source for a pretend structure is a playpen. If you have a wooden one you no longer need, take off one side and turn it upside down. It makes a wonderful hideout.

Large cardboard boxes from refrigerators or other appliances are also good playhouses. In nursery school playgrounds we have seen the hull of an old row boat and the body of a discarded Volkswagen. Almost any enclosure is fun if you get inside it with friends.

Macaroni Art

A standard item on most kitchen shelves is pasta. In the past your toddler sorted pasta. Now he can dip it, string it, or glue it. To create lovely bright colors, let him dip the pasta in a strong solution of food coloring, with a splash of white vinegar and a bit of water added. The longer the pasta sits, the darker and more intense the color. Overnight is best, but who can wait? Drain on wax paper.

Small pieces of pasta work well—bows, wheels, macaroni, and ziti. If Baby would prefer to paint, watercolors work fine with pasta. Use a small brush. Once colored, painted, or tinted, the pasta can be glued onto light cardboard for an unusual collage.

Another good idea is to string these colorful beauties. Yarn, with ends dipped in clear nail polish or wrapped with tape to prevent fraying, or a shoelace make ideal necklace strings. The shoelace is guaranteed to have a perfect point every time.

Folding Art

A lovely project for Baby or a group is a folding activity with white paper napkins or towels, or even coffee filters. By dipping corners into a strong food coloring and water mix (10 drops of food coloring for ¼ cup of water) your toddler can create abstract designs. First, help him fold the paper into rectangles or squares, letting him press the edges together. Next dip the corners of the paper in the mix. When the paper is opened, you get a wonderful splotch of color. To make circular designs, use a coffee filter.

Painting

If Baby enjoys painting often, plan ahead. Save junior sized baby food jars with lids. Invert a shoe box and trace around the jar bottom. Cut out the cardboard and set the baby food jars in the box for a tipless paint dispenser. Or use a sponge. Cut a circle out of the center of the sponge to fit around paint containers. The sponge will catch paint drips and keep the jar upright.

Don't fill the jars too full because shaking is still the best way to mix paint. For a young watercolor artist, an ashtray is an ideal water pan because it has a built-in holder for the paint brush. Add a double suction cup to the bottom to keep a water dish or ashtray steady.

Mr. Flexy

For someone so silly that he just flops around, introduce the "Mr. Flexy" game and do as the song suggests.

Mr. Flexy is so flexible he spends his time just so.
He bends, he twists, he turns his head, but is he finished? No.
He will move and he will squat and he will stretch so low.
How can Mr. Flexy do such things? We will never know.

ROUTINE TIMES

BATHING

Liquid Soap

The new way to cleanliness may be soaps dispensed with a squirt. Make your own by saving small snippets of soap and adding them to a blender with about a half cup water and a bit of glycerine for added smoothness. Children love these soaps. Squeeze bottles make great dispensers, too, as do old hand lotion or syrup bottles with pumps.

Helper

Let Baby help clean the tub. Since he is right there and undoubtedly willing, make it a cooperative venture. Hand him a sponge when you pick up yours. Let him scour while you rinse, or the reverse. He may prefer to clean the soap dish or try polishing the fixtures. As always, keep the job description simple and the instructions specific.

Faces In The Tub

Throw in some Ping-Pong balls you've decorated with faces. Permanent fine-point markers will do the job nicely.

The Cape

Avoid the post-bath tussle with a special towel that is really a cape. Cut large enough, this cozy alternative to a robe can be used at the beach as well as after bathtime. Young friends of ours like to dress up as superheroes, who of course dry off faster with the aid of this garment. A brightly colored bath-size towel is suitable for most toddlers. Add a strip of pre-shrunk grosgrain ribbon for ties, or any other fabric and a Velcro tab, so he can fasten the ends of this towel cape himself.

SLEEPING

Crib to Bed

To help your toddler make the transition into the big bed from his crib, roll blankets and put them under the fitted sheet on either side of him. This will make hills that should keep him from rolling out of bed. Also, store the crib mattress under his new bed and slide it out at night. If your toddler does manage to roll over the hills, he'll have a soft landing.

A Busy Basket

If your early riser can be encouraged to amuse himself, develop this tendency by presenting him with his own special basket. Then each evening, before you go to bed, leave something familiar, something novel, and something easy to eat (wrapped well!) to keep him occupied for as long as 15 minutes in the morning after he wakes up.

Bedroom Slippers

When purchasing bedroom slippers for your live wire, we suggest the pull-on sock types. Kids slip and trip less often in these models. They're washable and they'll truly stay on.

Reminder

Check your toddler's room, hallways, and bathroom to allow enough light for your child to move about safely. Growing fearless at night, your toddler may now feel confident enough to try and go to you if he feels ill or out of sorts, or is upset by a dream. Let him select a night-light for additional safety.

Bedtime Story

Need a bit of inspiration at bedtime? If you've read every story too many times and you're not up to telling your own, try tuning into a radio storytime. It might be the sort of diversion to win over a wriggler. Even if you pre-recorded the program to be replayed at bedtime, this could be the beginning of a shared family tradition. Most of us remember (or have witnessed the revival of) the Green Hornet, the Lone Ranger, and other exciting stories. Educational radio stations around the country regularly run such series. Consult local newspapers for specifics.

EATING

Tins

A microwave muffin pan is a convenient way to heat up various little dabs of food all at once and give Baby the fun of eating from a different sort of dish. Who knows, this may have been the forerunner of today's TV dinner! Make sure the tin cools enough to be safe for Baby.

Some Thoughts on Food

Especially during growth spurts or periods of illness, it's not at all uncommon for toddlers to eat less. Some toddlers eat a large breakfast, no lunch, and some dinner. There are endless variations on this pattern. The only sanity-saving strategy for parents is to accept the premise that if nutritious food is offered on a regular basis, children will eat what they need to stay healthy. All kinds of research confirms that this does indeed happen.

Quick Snack

Take some of the mess out of eating by placing food on a stick. Bananas work best, but Baby will enjoy orange wedges, melon cubes, peach and pear pieces, grapefruit sections, bits of apple, and even pineapple wedges, stacked. Dip these tidbits in wheat germ or toasted coconut for extra flavor. Remember that the food should be in chunks no smaller than one inch. Any smaller and they'll crumble when a stick is inserted. These are fun as desserts as well as snacks.

Dripless

One play group mom we know has a cute trick for sharing ice cream cones with a group of toddlers. If they're pointed ice cream cones, she puts a piece of marshmallow in the bottom of each cone. For the flat bottomed model, a small, round, vanilla flavored cookie keeps the mess to a minimum and fun to the maximum. These goodies absorb the drips and keep the cone from collapsing when it gets too moist.

Circle Time

Try this cup trick to decrease the number of spills. Place a circle of tape or a colored-dot sticker on the table or high-chair tray to signal where the cup should sit. This works well for the dish, too. You'd be amazed at how orderly almost-twos will be if given encouragement.

DRESSING AND CHANGING

Socks Up

There's nothing more annoying for Baby than having his sock disappear down inside his shoe. To prevent further sock nibbling, position a strip of adhesive tape across the inside back of the shoe's heel and the socks will stay up.

Dressing Made Easy

There's no reason for dressing to be a complicated, time-consuming, nerve and temper-shattering routine, if it's well-planned. To begin, clothes should be simple and coordinated. The best-dressed toddlers we know are ones who have already begun selecting clothing and dressing themselves by combining outfits from drawers where everything—pants and shirts, socks and underwear—is in one or two colors. This makes combinations a snap. Often toddlers will try to dress themselves if the neck openings give and there are few buttons or snaps. Pants can be a real trial if they're too tight. Buying clothes a bit on the loose side encourages Baby's efforts. The favorite toddler attire remains the jogging suit.

Boot Trick

Keep boots leak-proof and in good repair. If a slash, rip, or hole occurs, an inner tube kit from a hardware store will repair boots and return them to service. Additional idea: an oversized, colorful clothespin holds boots together, making a "boot hunt" unnecessary.

Haircut

If it's time for a haircut, a summer visor is especially handy. A clear or tinted visor, also indispensable when cutting bangs, allows kids to look around without interrupting the haircut. Best of all, it keeps hair out of eyes and off the face.

Snowsuits

To us, snowsuits are an expensive and questionable purchase. We think it's better to spend money on a warm parka and several pairs of lined pants. The one-piece outfits virtually immobilize an almost-two. Because children grow so quickly, and because a snowsuit is limited to the coldest months and climates, think carefully about this purchase.

HELPFUL HINTS

Birthday Bash for a Two

If the approach of your toddler's birthday party has thrown you into a dither, ask for help. Advance planning can make the day wonderful for you and your two-year-old. Teachers of toddlers will happily provide ideas for games and songs. The library is also an excellent source and so are other parents. Avoid expensive favors and decorations. Remember that the first priority is to let the kids have a good time.

Second thoughts on organization: get help at the party. Check bulletin boards in grocery stores or think about hiring a college student, particularly an early childhood education major, perhaps one who can play an instrument and sing children's songs. The days of Mom doing everything are over. Have Dad pitch in, too. Not only do you need this help, but you don't want him to miss the fun. If the weather is good, have the party outdoors—everyone has a happier time.

Toilet Training

One of the first signs of your toddler's readiness for toilet training is his awareness—and disgust—that he's wet. At about the age of two these signs become extremely common. Encouraging and developing his awareness of toilet functions and giving him a chance to learn about and try the potty will help him ease into bigger steps. There's no hurry.

For most children it isn't until the mid-twos to early threes that they have the necessary physical control to be successful at toilet training. At that point because they are capable and ready, children will need only praise and some help to cope successfully with this transition. Starting this process too soon frustrates all involved.

The Big Bash

If you'd like to have a big party for friends and family but are overwhelmed by the thought of cleaning house and cooking, consider reserving a site at your favorite state park or neighborhood recreation area. You can provide the main dish, and others can bring side dishes, dessert, and beverages. This is a good way for families with small children to get together happily with all the open space and park facilities.

Toy Boxes

There are never enough of these—toys seem to reproduce as you sleep. A good strategy is to consider buying containers that can be used later for other purposes. We like a wicker trunk that later became a coffee table in a den. Or if you like antiques, how about a dough box, a wardrobe with shelves, a pie safe, or a dry sink? Use your imagination.

Car Trick

One mom we know can spot trouble in the back seat without turning around. She attached a clip-on mirror to the visor and another one to the dashboard. These allow for silent surveillance and help her keep things calm in the back without ever raising her voice.

Kit for the Car

A smart dad who often takes jaunts with his young son shared this tip with us. Keep the following items in a small sack or bag: a book, a small box of raisins, a rubber toy, a large bib just in case there is a stop for a snack or ice cream, a hooded jacket, a complete change of clothes, and a juice box. This dad said there is almost no emergency that he's not prepared to handle, knowing that the kit is in the car.

Tummy Trouble

When your toddler complains of a stomachache but cannot tell you where it hurts, offer a bandage. Ask him to show you where it hurts by placing the bandage on the spot. This will help you focus on the pain site without playing frustrating guessing games.

Special Dinner Napkins

During special dinners when cloth napkins are being used by everyone, give your toddler a pretty washcloth as a napkin. He will enjoy having a cloth napkin like the grown-ups, and a washcloth makes cleaning the face much easier.

Pajama Feet

A mom we know keeps those annoying all-in-one pajama feet in place on her toddler with the use of terry-cloth elastic wristbands or sweatbands. She slides them over the pajama feet around her toddler's ankles. The bands hold the pajama feet in place and keep him from tripping over them as he walks.

Clean-up Helper

To help your toddler make clean-up a game, make silhouettes of his toys out of contact paper and apply them to the places where the toy should be kept. This system turns a clean-up into a matching game for both of you rather than a chore.

Straps That Stay Put

If the straps on your toddler's jumpers or overalls are always coming down, try snapping on a child's barrette. The barrettes come in many different colors and designs and will hold even the most fidgety toddler's straps in place.

Car Box

Keep a wooden box, like a wine bottle gift box, filled with appealing items under the seat of the car. It's durable and can hold paper, crayons, small cars, and books. The top can be used as a desk, depending on your car seat.

Purse Alternative

Now that junior is so active, consider placing that traditional handbag in storage and using a fanny pack or backpack when shopping. This will free your hands to maneuver your child and a cart or stroller.

Another Phone Activity

Useful items to keep near the phone are a water-only or paint-with-water coloring book and some cotton swabs. Give your toddler a small amount of water with the book. These can keep him occupied while you hold your conversation relatively uninterrupted.

Shoe Tricks

Do your toddler's shoes keep slipping off? Try adding tongue or heel pads, sold at shoe stores. Also, to tie your toddler's shoes tighter, lace the last hole of his shoes through the top, not the bottom.

Your Own Blocks

Recycle your own juice boxes and have your toddler turn them into blocks. After cleaning them thoroughly, either cover them in contact paper or have your toddler paint them. These blocks are just the right size and weight for his hands and easy for him to handle.

Cereal Necklaces

Remember those round cereal necklaces your toddler made with yarn or pipe cleaners? These make a great traveling snack to keep in the car in case he gets hungry unexpectedly. The next time he makes one of these delicious necklaces, save it in a self-closing plastic bag to carry along for a special treat.

Whisper

When you're ready to scream, try using "whisper power." Preschool teachers use it routinely. Children will quiet quickly and listen to you if you whisper, because they fear they might miss something. Once conversation returns to a normal tone, you can start moving in a positive direction. Whisper power doesn't work well in a quiet place like a church or temple, since it is apt to produce a loud "What?" in response.

Juice-up

Fruit juice spills are a common event at this age of quick moves and little attentiveness. You can eliminate sticky surfaces by using a little vinegar in your clean-up water. Keep in mind that without dangerous chemicals, your toddler can do this clean-up job, too. Provide a spray bottle and a sponge. Having to clean up does discourage accidents.

Hair Clips

Most of us eventually give in to the temptation to buy hair clips for little girls. Impractical for Baby's fine hair, they look wonderful for the few minutes they stay put. You can now buy Velcro barrettes that require only a few strands of hair, but if you have the clips, here are two ways to help them hold elusive strands: Glue a small piece of foam rubber on the inside surface of the clip, or glue a small piece of rubber band on the inside of the clip. Both methods will keep clips in the hair at least long enough to get a picture.

Thorny Spots

Every mom has a thorny hour, be it 7:30 a.m. or 6:30 p.m. It's that time when everyone needs you and your energy is at its lowest ebb—along with your good humor. Recognizing your own trouble spots can allow you to make adjustments and get support and assistance. Having a 5 o'clock snack might make the 6 o'clock onslaught easier. Arranging to be first in the shower, even if Dad does have to go to work, would give you more time to speed the troops on. Instead of practicing endurance exercises, try problem-solving.

Band-Aids

For a toddler who thinks he is wounded, nothing soothes his feelings like a little TLC, words of reassurance, and a Band-Aid. Just as taking vitamins make some people feel stronger, Band-Aids are a source of relief, too. These little strips signify that he must be getting better.

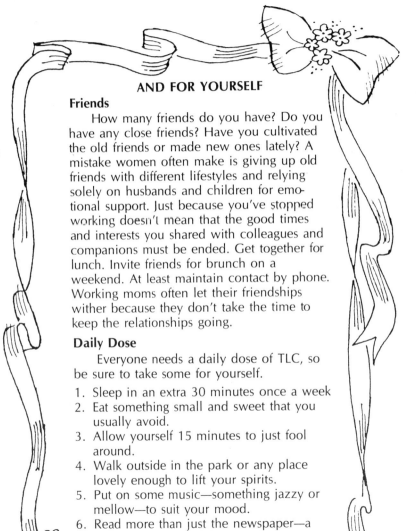

AND FOR YOURSELF

Friends

How many friends do you have? Do you have any close friends? Have you cultivated the old friends or made new ones lately? A mistake women often make is giving up old friends with different lifestyles and relying solely on husbands and children for emotional support. Just because you've stopped working doesn't mean that the good times and interests you shared with colleagues and companions must be ended. Get together for lunch. Invite friends for brunch on a weekend. At least maintain contact by phone. Working moms often let their friendships wither because they don't take the time to keep the relationships going.

Daily Dose

Everyone needs a daily dose of TLC, so be sure to take some for yourself.

1. Sleep in an extra 30 minutes once a week
2. Eat something small and sweet that you usually avoid.
3. Allow yourself 15 minutes to just fool around.
4. Walk outside in the park or any place lovely enough to lift your spirits.
5. Put on some music—something jazzy or mellow—to suit your mood.
6. Read more than just the newspaper—a spicy mystery or a juicy novel.

Goodies

The ultimate self-indulgence, in our estimation, is a visit to a health spa. Whethe your budget allows for the Golden Door or the wooden one, if there's any way you can spring a week away, take it. A jaunt to a spa is guaranted to rejuvenate anyone. Still wonderful, if not as luxurious, are:

1. An all-day makeover special at a great beauty salon;
2. A professional full body one-hour-of-ecstacy massage;
3. A full-hour salon facial;
4. A salon pedicure with wild-colored polish;
5. A professional makeup lesson;
6. An individual color analysis.

There's bound to be something on this list for everyone. It's our firm belief that moms who take care of themselves are the best at taking care of others, especially their families.

PARENTS, FRIENDS, AND ADMIRERS

Keepsake

A keepsake to treasure for any relative is a classic gift that improves with age—a handprint. Mix up a batch of special dough for this purpose. Here's our recipe:

1 cup cornstarch
1 cup baking soda
1¼ cups water

Add food coloring or not as you prefer. Mix thoroughly in a saucepan and cook over medium heat for four minutes, stirring constantly. The consistency will resemble moist mashed potatoes. Cover with a damp cloth and cool. Knead as with dough.

Form a small portion of the dough into a circle large enough to accommodate Baby's hand. Help him print his hand in the dough. Poke a small hole in the top with a straw so this treasure can be hung. When the dough has hardened, it can be painted and then sprayed with clear plastic or coated with a half-and-half mixture of white glue and water.

Birthday in a Box

For a friend or relative who must miss the birthday party of a special small friend, consider sending your own birthday party in a box. A child can never have too many parties, and a chance to replay the big event will be fun for your favorite family. Send a hat, birthday bib, juice, goodies, party games, paper goods, streamers, and balloons. We hope the family has a camera ready to capture the excitement when the box arrives and is opened by a favorite little person.

Shaping Wood

A good project for an uncle or friend and a two-year-old is shaping wood. Sandpaper, with its rough texture, is intriguing, and the way it changes the wood from rough to smooth seems almost magical. Use soft wood and a sanding block for best results. Any shape will do, and it's extra fun if you can end with a finished project. For example, by drilling two holes and rubbing your project with furniture polish at the end, you have the basis of a neckerchief slide or necklace. All you'll need to add is a scarf or small chain—something wonderful for a proud two-year-old to wear.

Gift Idea

A large set of durable rubber animals is fun for toddlers. These animals are guaranteed to have a long and busy life. They'll be carried around and incorporated into block building, sand play, car and transportation play, and all sorts of exciting events for years to come.

Pictures

Why not make the family portrait that you plan to give Grandma and Grandpa extra special this year? Have everyone in the family autograph it. Even your nearly-two can "sign" his name with his own mark to let Grandma know that he sends her his love.

Special Calendar

Now that your toddler is getting older and more creative, you are accumulating a lot of good pictures. One parent we know collected inexpensive calendars from office supply stores and local merchants and pasted her toddler's pictures over the monthly illustrations. These unique calendars were shared with grandparents and close friends.

Sand Combs

Inspired by a day at the beach, an uncle made sand combs for his favorite niece and nephew. The combs create unusual patterns in the sand when dragged through it. The uncle cut his combs out of thin plywood, about a ¼ in. thick, with a coping saw, but you could use thick cardboard instead. The texture of the combed sand enhances children's building projects as they discover interesting ways to use cars, blocks, toys, and wood in the trails they make.

Mom's Beads

It started with a book of wallpaper samples. After collages and fancy picture frames were made, and the dollhouse redecorated, the leftover pieces were rolled up for beads. Even the youngest member of the family participated in making a necklace for Mom. Here's how:

1. Cut triangle shaped wedges, 12 in. long × 1½ in. wide.
2. Carefully roll the paper end over end around a large pencil or nail.
3. With a dab of white glue, paste the pointed end down and slide the bead off the pencil.
4. After making 10 to 12 beads, spray them with an adhesive glue or paint them with a mixture of glue and water. Allow the beads to dry and string them on a thin grosgrain ribbon, combining patterns and colors.

The Needlewoman

A great gift for Grandma or a doting aunt is a representation of your child's early art. Colorful abstracts can be easily transformed into needlepoint canvas or embroidered linen. When properly framed and dated, this is a lasting family heirloom.

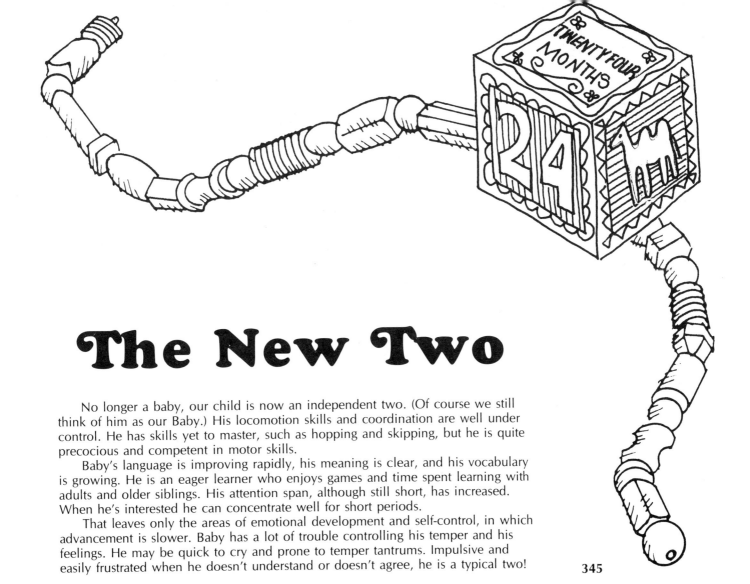

The New Two

No longer a baby, our child is now an independent two. (Of course we still think of him as our Baby.) His locomotion skills and coordination are well under control. He has skills yet to master, such as hopping and skipping, but he is quite precocious and competent in motor skills.

Baby's language is improving rapidly, his meaning is clear, and his vocabulary is growing. He is an eager learner who enjoys games and time spent learning with adults and older siblings. His attention span, although still short, has increased. When he's interested he can concentrate well for short periods.

That leaves only the areas of emotional development and self-control, in which advancement is slower. Baby has a lot of trouble controlling his temper and his feelings. He may be quick to cry and prone to temper tantrums. Impulsive and easily frustrated when he doesn't understand or doesn't agree, he is a typical two!

345

Remember that all children develop at different rates. For some parents these are terrible times, while for others they are remembered as the golden years before the terrible times. The message is that no parents escape tough times during the child-rearing period. If we truly knew what to expect, there would be few parents. However, the joys and daily rewards—if you relax, laugh and let yourself enjoy them—are more than worth the duress.

Our toddler now has an emerging personal style and individuality that will be characteristic of his life. He is creative in his dealings with others, and you will notice he can now use adults as resources when the going gets rough with his siblings. He is trusting and enjoys pleasing. You may even see a decrease in his negativism this month. Like all of us he does not like to be scolded, and his feelings are easily hurt. Although he has come far in many ways, he still needs more time to practice and refine his skills.

He may show some fleeting interest in the potty, probably to please you. It is not yet time for toilet training. The vast majority of children are trained between two-and-a-half and three-and-a-half. With those taught before this period, the question often is whether the children or the parents are trained.

You will notice that Baby is now playing with his toys in a more sophisticated way and even briefly with other children. This month is the prelude to another year of pleasure with your child. Happy Birthday!

ACTIVITIES, GAMES, AND SONGS

Playdough

Of all the playdough recipes we've used, we like this one the best as an all-purpose blend. It lasts about six weeks in the refrigerator if it's kept in a plastic bag. For the most vivid colors, use the paste or powder type of food coloring found in a pastry store.

1 cup flour
1 cup colored water (tinted with food coloring)
½ cup salt
2 teaspoons cream of tartar
1 tablespoon oil

Mix together and cook the ingredients until the mixture clumps on the spoon. Then knead lightly.

Body Painting

Get out your camera before you start this summer-time activity, a priceless photo opportunity. Put the children in swimsuits. Give them brushes and paint made from no-tears shampoo, water, and food coloring. Provide a mirror and a hose. Now stand back and watch the fun as they paint themselves and each other. The best part is that when the hose reduces the art to bubbles, you are left with happy, clean kids.

Clothesline Story

A good way to teach about sentencing and left-to-right progression, both important reading-readiness skills, is to develop clothesline stories. String a short clothesline in a handy place. We suggest using picture-frame wire and picture hooks, hung beneath a windowsill. Attach about ten large paper clips to your wire. From these you can hang almost anything. Start with a very easy sequence. For example, use these three pictures: a bare foot, a foot with a sock, and a foot with a sock and shoe. Tell the story, laying them on the floor as you talk.

Now mix them up. Let Baby hang the story. Simple processes are the easiest, but made-up stories can be developed from any picture or object. Numbers and letters can also be arranged, as can coming events. If you don't have the time or inclination to cut out pictures to make cards, use representative objects. For instance, a mitten, a leaf, and a spoon might represent this story: "Remember when we put on our mittens and went out and gathered leaves, and then we came in and we ate pudding with a spoon?" Soon Baby will delight you with his collections and his stories.

Special Occasion Story

Just for a change or for a special occasion, try adding a little atmosphere to storytime. Use a novel source of light—try the flicker of a big spicy or scented candle, a large flashlight or glow-stick, or the glow of a hurricane lamp. All add a soothing glow and a touch of magic. In some households, this technique has even helped children begin to manage darkness with greater ease. For safety's sake, always snuff out the candle before you give your goodnight kiss.

Artistic Answer

Have paper ready to go for any sort of drawing, painting, or writing project by mounting it on the wall. Mount a three-inch dowel, a metal pipe, or a closet pole in a convenient spot. We suggest using a roll of paper 12–16 in. wide (the butcher type is good). A wall dispenser allows the artist to draw or paint vertically or snip off sheets for use on the floor or table.

Footprint Game

This is a good activity with a play group or a few toddlers in an outdoor place such as a beach or park. It's especially fun in wet sand or snow. Make footprints that are either far apart of close together, and invite Baby and his friends to walk in them. Then let them make footprints for you to walk in. This will be greeted with lots of giggles. Using a stick, create a pattern that resembles a hopping rabbit or a four-legged animal, or a snake-like line where they have to shuffle their feet, or a straight line on which they pretend to be jets. Whatever design you make with the stick will provide a model for the way the children will move—wiggly lines, straight lines, jagged lines, long lines, and so on.

Flannel Board

If you have a flannel board and haven't used it in a while, try some of these suggestions:

1. Use the flannel board for storytime instead of a book, especially when a story has been repeated it is so often practically memorized. By tracing, photocopying, or cutting up an old version of the book, you and your toddler can tell the story together.

2. Gather two sets of matching objects and let him match yours, using two flannel boards or dividing your big one in half. This is fun for matching faces and facial parts—eyes, nose, mouth. Or try vehicles—adding decals, windows, and steering wheels to trucks and cars. After Baby understands the game, let him take the lead.

3. Baby will also enjoy practicing with letters and initials. Sets of these for flannel boards are commercially available. Make a model on which he can lay his letters over his name, which you have written.

Categories

Get three large coffee cans or three shoe boxes, all about the same size. Cut an opening in the plastic lid or box top so your toddler can stick his hand through. Then gather some pictures and divide them into categories—animals, vehicles, things to eat, clothing, birds, and so on. Can labels and box fronts are good sources for things to eat. Paste these onto 3 × 5 in. index cards, making a series for each of the categories. On each can or box attach a card representing one of the categories. Now help baby deposit the remaining cards in the appropriate slots.

Cards from this game can be used for other games, especially vocabulary games. They're natural conversation starters. A toddler is practicing his words at every opportunity. You may find him demonstrating his knowledge with new adults or even practicing in front of the mirror.

Puddle Art

On a warm, rainy day, nothing is better than a walk right after the last raindrop falls, to see what the rain has done. Driveways, parking lots, fields, and gutters seem to be paved with mirrors. Beautiful rainbows shine on well-glazed surfaces. As you look at reflections of the sky, it will seem as if you are standing on the clouds above you. What fun it is to splash and look at the

wonderful colors. The puddled world is certainly a work of art.

You'll have no trouble generating enthusiasm for this activity because toddlers love splashing in puddles. Make sure Baby has a suitable pair of boots.

Color Cubes

For a cooking project, make some super-gelatin. When ready to eat, these thick, shimmering cubes won't melt, do not require refrigeration, and can be carried to school by a sibling to share with friends at snacktime. Eaten right out of the hand, they are a real treat. Here's our recipe:

    3 Tbs. plain gelatin
    1 cup cold water
    2 pkg. commercial flavored gelatin
    1 cup boiling water
    10 ice cubes

1. Place the plain gelatin in a small bowl. Add the cold water. Let soften five minutes and stir well.
2. Empty the flavored gelatin into a large bowl. Add the boiling water and the ice cubes. Let Baby add them one at a time and help you stir until the gelatin is dissolved.
3. Add the plain gelatin to this mixture and stir thoroughly.
4. Pour into an 8 × 8-in. pan and refrigerate until set. This will take about 15 minutes.
5. Cut into one-inch cubes. You'll get 64 one-inch cubes.

Family Photos

A good project for the family is making a set of photo figures. Have a head-to-toe picture of each family member enlarged so that it measures about 10–12 in. Mount them on heavy 1/8-in. cardboard with rubber cement, and cut around the figures with a jigsaw. A piece of half-round molding, one inch in diameter, with a slit cut in it will make a good stand. Let the children invent their own stories, using the figures as puppets—they are effective vehicles for expressing feelings. They are also good props for the block corner.

Fun in the Snow

The magic of fresh-fallen snow is a treat to be savored by kids of all ages, especially if they are dressed for outdoor fun. Remember to layer and to cover mittens with sandwich bags or rubber gloves. Add a shoelace bow on each wrist to keep hands dry. Rub a bit of petroleum jelly on cheeks to prevent chapping.

A toddler can use a plastic dustpan for pushing snow around. An old bassinet or dishpan makes the perfect sled when you add a rope. Older kids will make snow forts, which Baby will love to play in.

One mom who prefers to be indoors doesn't deprive her children of fun with snow. She supplies a baby bathtub full of snow and lets the kids experiment, play, and poke around in it on the kitchen floor or in the bathtub.

Pretzel Project

A project perfect for a rainy day is to make a batch of pretzels. They can be shaped as decorations or enjoyed as a snack. This recipe takes about 90 minutes from start to finish and makes a dozen.

3 cups unsifted flour
2 Tbs. sugar
½ tsp. salt
1 pkg. active dry yeast
1 cup water
1 Tbs. margarine
1 egg yolk, beaten
1 Tbs. water

1. Mix one cup of flour, sugar, salt, and yeast.
2. Heat one cup water and margarine to 120–130°. Gradually add that mixture to the dry ingredients and beat for 2 minutes on medium speed with a mixer.
3. Add half a cup of flour and beat at high speed for 2 minutes. Stir in enough additional flour to make the dough soft. Now call for help.
4. On a floured board, knead for 5 minutes. Set in a greased bowl (turn to grease top). Cover and let rise in a warm, draft-free place for 40 minutes.
5. Divide the dough into 12 equal pieces and roll into a 12-in. rope.
6. Now shape the pretzels into any form you like. Baby will develop wonderful new shapes. Place on greased cookie sheets, cover, and let rise for 5 minutes.
7. Mix the egg yolk and tablespoon of water. Brush on pretzels. Sprinkle with coarse salt or omit.
8. Bake at 375° for 15 minutes or until done. Cool on racks.

Home Painter

What toddler can resist the lure of paint and painter's equipment? Give Baby his own kit—brushes, rollers, pans, some pint-size and gallon-size empty paint cans, stirring sticks, drop cloth and rags. Show him some paint chips so he can tell you which colors he wishes to use (pretend, of course). Get him his uniform, that is, speckled jeans and shirt and a painter's cap, usually free at the paint store. Since Baby will want to know his job, be prepared with the specifics of his project or assignment. Even if your toddler only "paints" your Formica-top surface, your table, cabinets, and counter, or spends his time outside on the fence or lower portion of the building, he will have a wonderful time. Mix him up a special batch of magic paint—plain water with a squirt of liquid detergent. That "paint" is guaranteed to make the desired surfaces darker—because they're wet.

Riding Toys

All types of vehicles will be a hit with a two-year-old. Not content just to sit on a tricycle or push with his feet, Baby is ready for the real thing—pedals. We like the low-slung, heavy plastic type for new riders. They seem to be the easiest to ride and the best balanced. But you can't beat the heavy metal tricycles for durability. If there is more than one child in the family, the metal type is probably the best buy. The medium-sized one will last the longest, since it can be ridden by someone a little too small or too big.

Clarify the rules of the road on the first day: where, when, and how Baby rides. You also need rules for visitors and older children.

Riding Song

(To the tune of "I'm A Little Teapot")

Riding on the sidewalk is such fun.
Zooming up, zooming back, here I come.
If I leave the sidewalk, my ride is done.
So I stay on the sidewalk and have great fun.

Bingo

Remember how much fun you had with Bingo? The concept of that game can provide the basis for vocabulary-building games. First, purchase some packages of stickers that feature items that are familiar to your toddler or soon will be. Or cut geometric shapes or shapes in a certain category (kinds of fruit, for example) from construction paper.

Make four 6-in.-square cards out of heavy cardboard. With a marker and ruler, divide each card into six equal sections, and make picture cards to match.

The game is simple. Put the picture cards in a pile. Each player takes a grid and takes turns picking and naming cards and matching the pictures to the ones on his grid. The first one to fill his card wins the game. Control the level of difficulty with the pictures you choose. Control the game's length by the number of non-matching items included in the pile. This game challenges a toddler's memory and provides him with some early experiences in social games and sharing.

Cheese ABCs

Learning is most enjoyable when it's presented in an unexpected way. A mom we know makes delightful learning lunches. Her child may open his lunchbox to find sliced cheese As, carrots cut into small 6s, or a secret message in a picture code tied to his apple. Even his teachers look forward to each lunchtime and the new learning experience it will bring.

Grass Letters

Another form of letter fun is seed writing. All you need are some hardy grass seeds and a sponge. Sprinkle the seeds onto the sponge in the shape that you want to grow—the first letter of a name perhaps—and then water. Place the sponge in the sun and wait for your seeds to sprout. Grass grows so quickly that children don't lose interest. If you encourage them to mist their growing letters and to use a magnifying glass to search for the new seedlings, they will be enthralled.

Dolls

Doll play gives children a chance to work through emotions and experiences. Nothing is more familiar to them than a doll. Regardless of sex, playing with dolls helps children verify their rolls. Little boys can learn to be gentle and to role-play a concerned and caring parent. As a child cares for his doll, he shows you his interpretations of having been loved and mothered or fathered.

The best dolls for Baby can, without much harm, be carried, dropped, bathed, combed, spanked, dressed, and forgotten outside. For good doll play, a baby bed, a bottle, and a change of clothes are all that's necessary. Big dolls and bears that can wear three- to six-month baby clothes can be purchased at thrift shops.

Children are so inventive they can create intriguing scenarios with simple props. Start an afternoon of play by saying, "Why not give your baby a bath today?" Through dramatic play children explore the world and learn to model behavior.

Cutting

For the first pair of scissors, choose a pair that really works. Since you will be cutting with your child, the scissors should be sharp. The new super-scissors have several desirable qualities. They can be used by right- or left-handed children. They're sharp without points, and they have cushioned finger pieces.

The best way to start is to give your child projects that guarantee success. For example, draw a line on a paper that takes only one snip to cut. Cutting is even more rewarding if the pieces can be used for something afterward. Cut up paper into confetti and use it to make a collage. Make a snake out of playdough, or use cookie dough. Start with a snake about $1/8$-in. thick. Cut the dough snake into half-inch lengths and attach these snippets to a round cookie, using bits of dough for hair. Add beads for eyes and a bit of red licorice whip for a mouth. Baby can make a gallery of tasty faces.

Puppets

The simplest and quickest puppets are those drawn on your thumb, fingers, or hand. Draw them with colored markers and use them for dancing, singing, or talking activities. Sing "Thumbulina" or try this one about the two smiling gentlemen. Decorate your thumbs with hats, eyes, nose, and mustache, and say:

Two smiling gentlemen met in Wayne,
Bowed most politely, bowed once again.
Said how do you do, how do you do,
How do you do again.

Use your other fingers in the same manner. The little fingers could be babies. The third finger could be a tall policeman. Do whatever your imagination and your child suggest. Remove decorations with a little soap and water.

Update on Talking

Two-year-olds are like sponges, soaking up information as we do, piecemeal, so keep right on talking and explaining while doing anything—using real terms and appropriate language. One day you'll be pleasantly surprised at how capably your child shares what he's heard and remembered.

If you used the tape recorder months ago to make a tape of your child's babbles, add to it, now that your child is a more proficient talker. He will enjoy listening to his voice and comparing it to his younger voice and will also enjoy the tapes 10 years from now.

Giant Letters

Introduce a child to the first letter of his name in a big way. Cut a giant letter out of fabric or wrapping paper and display it in a prominent place. Every time the toddler finds or sees an object or picture that starts with his letter, he has a place to hang it. For "B," for example, he may find a balloon, a berry, or a picture of a baby in a magazine. Keep masking tape, safety pins, string, and glue handy to attach his findings to his letter sign.

Balance Beam

Baby will find a low balance beam challenging. It's easy to assemble and fine for use indoors and out. To make it, cut a piece of wood 1 in. thick by 4 in. wide by 10 ft. long. If you lack the tools the lumberyard will cut it. Place a cinder block or brick under each end of the board.

Paper Dolls

Make a string of paper dolls. The trick is all in the folding. Fold and pleat the paper back and forth, like an accordian. To string the dolls together, make sure there's a portion of every fold that has not been cut through. Open carefully and there you have it, all the little dolls—boys or girls—holding hands together.

Every parent should know how to make snowflakes. The best ones are made from circles. Once you have the perfect circle, fold it in half, in half a second time, and in half a third time. Cut down along the top and sides of the folded circle. Then open it carefully to delight Baby with the most beautiful snowflake, no two of which are ever alike.

ROUTINE TIMES

BATHING

After Bath

If you have a toddler who won't get in or out of the bathtub, resort to bribery and let the world be fragrant. One mom saves perfume and after-shave samples in an after-bath box. The toddler who successfully completes a bath in a reasonable time can partake of sweet smells.

Brontosaurus in a Bath

A two-year-old we know was enamored of dinosaurs and owned an impressive collection. His mother surprised him with some that were perfect for use in the tub. She cut out several dinosaur pictures, mounted them individually on heavy cardboard, then cut out the shapes. Next, she punched a hole in each and tied a long piece of string through the hole. She melted bits of old wax crayons and added them to paraffin left over from a canning project. She kept dipping each cardboard animal into this mixture until she built up a complete layer of wax around each one. These wax wonders floated in her son's bathtub and were a real joy to him.

Knowing When to Quit

A dad we know who's in charge of bathtime eliminated protests about leaving the tub by setting his digital alarm-clock watch, which plays a tune. When "The Yellow Rose Of Texas" begins to play, that's the signal to pull the plug and grab a towel.

Soap Crayons

These items are easy to make, useful in the bathtub or for an outdoor activity, and they make a great rainy-day project. To make soap crayons, combine powdered food coloring, available at shops for bakers, soap flakes, and water. Make a thick paste and compress it into an ice cube tray. Set it aside for a day or two until the cubes are thoroughly dry. You'll have chubby cubes of color for drawing on the skin or on wet or dry paper. After a child has finished a picture on paper, you can use the drawings as a finger-painting experience simply by wetting Baby's hands. The result will be bubbles of fun. Finish off this project with a dunk in the bathtub.

Soap Mitts

Add some scrubbing magic to the bath. Design a soap mitt for Baby. Using either terry cloth or washcloths, cut a silly shape or cut and stitch a basic hand puppet to which you add features. A car or a teddy bear is fun. Use leftover socks in which a small bar of soap is concealed. Both aid scrubbing in the bath.

SLEEPING

Love of Books

Keep in mind as you're reading a story by popular request for the zillionth time that story reading develops a love of books. We have known two-year-olds who have slept with books under their pillows and have memorized book after book. These children are usually early readers, and good ones. It's impossible to read to a child too much.

Norma's Technique

One teacher of toddlers seems to have solved the naptime resistance problem. Her technique is to set the right "tone" to help young children ease into sleep. She uses very little light and a slow, soft, lulling classical music album. The only problem she encountered was resisting the desire to join the children!

New Bed

Baby can become very attached to his bed. When your toddler begins to climb out of his crib, start thinking about the first bed. There is no reason to rush the transition, however, if Baby seems hesitant. When you do buy the first bed, do it right. A good bed is worth the investment—it may last until your child is ready for college! The new Captain's beds, which have storage drawers under the frame, are great space savers.

If you're expecting another child, move your toddler into his bed several months before the baby arrives. This will help reduce the feeling that the new baby is replacing him.

Take your child with you to pick out some sheets for his new bed. This insures that the bed will be easier to make and pleasing to Baby.

Talk Time

The moments just before you say goodnight and turn off the lights is important family time. Regardless of how disastrous the day has been, you can make sure Baby goes to bed feeling warm, loving, and loved. This is a time to talk, dream, and share memories or the prospect of pleasant plans. It's a time for serious talk, reassurance, thankfulness, and remembrance of others. It's a special close time that only parents and their children share.

Bed Diversions

For a toddler who must stay in bed, a set of table blocks is a manageable game that will provide a quiet diversion. We like to use a metal, rimmed cookie sheet for a bed table. Table blocks are small colored wooden blocks that vary in size and shape. They provide for creative play. A few small people or vehicles can add to the fun. Another appropriate bed toy is a magnetic puzzle.

EATING

Mealtime Strategies

Parents who are successfully managing mealtimes with toddlers recommend the following:

1. Make the largest portion of the meal finger food.
2. Keep the amounts small.
3. Serve one or two items at a time in a single plate with dividers.
4. Always save the best for last.
5. Be sure that Baby's menu resembles the adults' menu. Baby wants to eat the same foods you eat.

Tea Party

Teaching manners can be done subtly and with flair. Many niceties have been picked up at a tea party. First, have Baby help you set a fancy table—a flower or two in a vase, a tablecloth, even if it's vinyl, and napkins. Bring out tea cups or fancy glasses for lemonade and plates for tiny sandwiches and cookies.

Provide the other guests—teddy bear, dolls, and so on—with chairs, cups, and napkins. This game of "let's pretend" is an opportunity for Baby to practice good table manners, the best way to sit, and how to ask for more. Perhaps most important is learning how to participate in a conversation, with other people or with Bobby Bear.

Grandmas are especially good at this game. Teas can make social and dining events less traumatic for both you and Baby, who will want to be included in holiday parties and family events.

Special Meals

As an antidote to gloom or when Baby has decided not to eat, try presenting the meal in a new location. If spirits are sagging for the housebound, how about a picnic on a beach towel on the back porch, or cooking a hot dog—under full supervision—in the fireplace. One mom we know often serves dinner Japanese-style with everyone sitting on cushions around a low table with chopsticks, tea, and rice.

Bread Lovers

Bread is the favorite food of many two-year-olds. Here are a few ways to liven up the fare:

1. Hide an egg in a hamburger bun. Make a depression large enough to hold an egg, slip the raw egg into the hole, and cover with a slice of cheese. Bake in a 350° oven 10 minutes, or until the egg is cooked and the cheese melted.
2. Wrap a breadstick with ham, adding some mustard to make the ham stick to the breadstick.

3. Bagatelles are always fun to dress up and eat—anything mini is special.

4. When making soft pretzels, tuck a healthy surprise inside; try nuts, raisins, or dried fruit.

Yeah, Yogurt

Yogurt is to kids what tomato sauce is to adults—everything tastes better with it. Low in fat and sugar, nutritious, and easy to digest, yogurt is also flexible. Add it to sauces; use it for dessert. Camouflage the least-desired items, like liver, with it. Make creamy yogurt popsicles or use it as a vehicle for small good things like raisins, nuts, pieces of fruits and vegetables.

DRESSING AND CHANGING

Boots

Stop! Don't fight with boots and galoshes. Use the old plastic sandwich-bag trick. Put one on each foot and slip the boot on easily. Or spray the inside of the boots with a little fabric softener, which will add a nice odor as well.

Hats

If you really mean to have Baby wear a hat, and he's resisting, there must be some compromise. The only way we know is to let him pick out the hat. One mom we know in Nebraska took this advice to heart. She sewed earmuffs onto her son's choice, a man's felt dress-up hat. He drew occasional stares when they went shopping, but his mom never had an argument about wearing a hat for the entire winter.

Mitten Madness

Buy two or three pairs of mittens that are identical so there will be spares. Lost mittens are inevitable, but with this plan, you can make a match. Give yourself extra points if the mittens are reversible and will fit either hand.

Training Pants

We vote no on training pants. Extra-thick training pants are bulky, take more time to dry, and really aren't as comfortable as standard pants. Few parents we know use them for long, and they are an unnecessary expense. For children who have frequent accidents, pull-on disposable diapers that resemble training pants are available and much more convenient and comfortable.

Higher Authority

A mom we know, in a fit of frustration, took her problem, a child who would not get dressed, to a higher authority—the dressing fairy. Each morning a note appeared that would suggest she wear her yellow pants and blue top today, or that she be the first member of the family to appear dressed at breakfast. One morning there was a checklist to help her be sure she had on all her garments. A little silly, but it really worked.

HELPFUL HINTS

Dental Visit

Now is the time to schedule the first dental appointment for your toddler. A visit to the family dentist or periodontist may require some play-acting and casual talk beforehand. A baby's first teeth last until the sixth year or so, and they can get cavities. These must be filled to avoid large dental bills in the future and to keep your child's teeth looking and feeling good! The proper formation of a toddler's teeth and gums require regular dental examinations to ensure that growth is occurring normally.

There are several children's books to read in preparation for this visit. We recommend:

A Visit to the Dentist by Mary Packard (New York: Simon & Schuster, 1981)
At the Dentist by Sandra Ziegler (Elgin, IL: Child's World, 1976)
My Dentist by Harlow Rockwell (New York: William Morrow/Greenwillow Books, 1975)

Fears

Children's fears often catch parents off-guard because they appear without warning. Treat all fears seriously and acknowledge that we all have fears. Try to deal directly with fears and develop a solution. Even mystical monsters can be banished: use monster spray, or capture them and flush them down the toilet. You can even explain them away logically. Remember—there is no fear greater than fear itself.

Fill In

Well, you've completed the second year. Baby now walks, talks, and definitely has a mind and style of his own. Take a few moments to reflect on this last year—its trials and tribulations and wonderful moments.

_____

_____

_____

_____

_____

_____

Thinking Chair

When your child disobeys, help him learn to sit on a thinking chair—a device used by many pre-school teachers. This gives you time to repair the damage and collect yourself and it gives him time to realize that his last move was not his best, even if he doesn't understand why. Twos are not capable of real remorse, but that will develop later. For now, having to stop playing will suffice. After the two- or three-minute thinking period, release him and redirect him into a more appropriate activity.

Trips to the Store

A shopping trip with your "two" along, especially to the grocery store, need not be a hassle if you have a plan. Involve him, talk to him, and give him a pictorial list so he can remind you of things you need to buy. In a store there is a wealth of information to keep him busy—colors, sizes, comparisons, items and brands to identify. Most two-year-olds get into trouble when they are bored. Baby can certainly pick out which apples to buy, alert you when you've reached the bread aisle, and remind you to buy chicken legs for dinner. Assigning ahead of time what he needs to buy can short-circuit the "Buy me, buy me" syndrome. In our house, the rule is to buy only what's on the list.

Temper, Temper

Nothing hurts one's self-esteem more than a bout of temper. Black moments are rarely the best time to make policy or to discipline. Backing off means neither retreat nor defeat but rather an opportunity for thoughtful consideration. When an imperious two has pushed too hard too many times, it's difficult if not impossible to maintain control. Remember then to step back.

Decision-Making

Giving a two the opportunity to make choices is the way he develops self-direction and responsibility. Choices are more significant when two or three options of equal weight are offered. Through this process, the child develops confidence, especially when these choices affect his work or play situation. He will soon be able to generate alternatives and talk through the consequences after you provide the model.

For example, say, "We're going to the store. We'll need to leave at 2 o'clock. You'll need to eat your lunch and get dressed. Which are you going to do first?"

Giving

If your child attends a child-care center or play setting, be one of the parents who asks if there's anything you can do to help make it the best possible experience. This is a big part of your child's life and deserves your interest, too. Research has shown that the best environments for children are those where parents are willing to participate in some small way, even if it's only to send in cookies, or a good story book on a rainy day. Your child's teacher will appreciate your efforts.

When you think your day is tough, keep these professionals in mind and think about spending a day with a group of two-year-olds.

Be Aware

Baby's need to explore, his driving curiosity, his desire to try, taste, and open, make it absolutely vital that your safety measures be flawless. Putting poisons up high isn't enough. You need a locked cabinet and child-proof latches. Protect now and teach later. This is no area to test his sense of responsibility, cooperativeness, or behavior skills.

Accidents

Accidents happen even to the careful. The point is to let Baby know what happened and why. Treating these inevitabilities with words instead of angry silence or dark looks makes a positive impression on a child. When there is a slip-up, explain how the accident occurred and how to keep it from occurring again. Don't react as if only twos have accidents. Sharing your goofs with Baby will let him know that no one is perfect and will allow him the opportunity to support you through the clean-up process.

Parts Replacement

With the high cost of today's games and toys, it's maddening when key pieces are lost. Most manufacturers will gladly sell you the missing parts at a reasonable cost if you write them. What a happy discovery, when you consider the investment you have in most toys!

Maximizing Space

Children love nooks and special spaces. If you think that nooks and lofts and landings in children's rooms can only be made by the rich or talented, you're wrong. Many imaginative designs are quite easy to construct, and there are "how-to" books galore in libraries and bookstores with cost-saving ideas.

Carpet Squares

Carpet squares, handy to sit on, can be acquired free or cheaply from a carpet store. Join four or five squares together to form a cozy, colorful corner for games or block building. They also protect your carpets from messy projects. Cleaning up the pieces of an interlocking toy is a snap when carpet squares are used—just pick up the square and dump the contents into the toy box.

Color Favorite

Buy several rolls of plastic tape in your child's favorite color and apply a strip to all his school possessions. This will allow him to find his own boots, lunchbox, and so on, when he goes to nursery school. The teachers will love you, too.

Eye to Eye

When things get serious, eyeball-to-eyeball is the only way to talk. Stooping down to Baby's level may be in order, but you can also bring him up to your level—perching him on a countertop, for example—as a way to drive home your feelings about the importance of the matter under discussion.

Warning to Working Moms

Now that your child is older, don't be lulled into failing to have a backup child-care arrangement. Remember that every child will sooner or later require more than a few days at home. If you have an arrangement with a neighbor, be sure you've done your share already. Ask any working parent: there's a connection between kids getting sick and a busy period at work.

TV Alert

TV is a controversial topic with most parents. It's an appealing and powerful medium, and children find it entertaining and addictive—like adults. Turning on the tube is a quick way to absorb Baby when you're tired and need a respite, but evaluate this decision carefully.

Research confirms that children who seem to have the greatest success in school, who are the best readers and creative self-starters, are given only limited access to TV programs. There are good ones, but on the whole TV programs are designed to entertain, not to educate.

Mattress Covers

Protecting your child's mattress is important during the toilet-training process. You can buy zippered plastic covers that completely encase and protect the mattress. If you use a cotton mattress pad over the plastic one, the mattress will be fully protected, with a comfortable, cozy surface that won't be too hot for your child. Protect the pillows, too, with attractive pillow jackets.

Avoiding Problems

Conflicts with toddlers are inevitable, but if you use four simple rules, you can reduce their intensity and frequency.

1. Think through your response. Don't respond impulsively.
2. Be clear about your expectations.
3. Clarify feelings that are involved.
4. Follow through with your decision.

Room Decor

If you haven't already begun, now is the time to spruce up your toddler's room. Try decorations that encourage the learning of colors, numbers, and letters. Number dresser drawers from top to bottom to make dressing fun, or make your own number chart.

Put up a big first initial on the wall or hang it from the ceiling. One mother hung a big "K" for her daughter, Karoline, and went on to hang all the other letters of the alphabet.

Towel Jumble

Assign each member of the family a separate color towel to avoid "towel jumble" in the bathroom and instill Baby's pride in personal neatness. This system will also keep Dad from complaining that he can never find a clean, dry towel. Install a special hook for your toddler's towel and washcloth.

Toothbrushing Alert

If your child doesn't like the taste or foaming qualities of toothpaste, let him clean his teeth without it. Fluoride in toothpaste helps protect the teeth from decay, but it's not the most important part of cleaning. Good old-fashioned elbow grease with the toothbrush is what gets them clean.

The Broom Bunch

Having a kids' party? Instead of tying balloons to a tree to mark the spot, greet guests with a bunch of endearingly silly broomstick people. Make features from pine cones, felt cutouts, and large buttons. Dress them with scarfs, hats, leaves, string mops, or vines. Tip: A glue gun is the surest, quickest way to keep your zany add-ons from blowin' in the wind.

Trash Bag Smock

For messy art projects at home, a simple smock can be made from a plastic garbage bag. Using sharp scissors, cut a hole in the bottom large enough for Baby's head. Then cut an arm slit on either side of the bag. Cut about two inches off the open end for a sash.

Zipping

A man's toiletry case makes a perfect traveling storage container for many of your toddler's little toys. He will love being like Dad, zipping and unzipping the container to get the toys in and out.

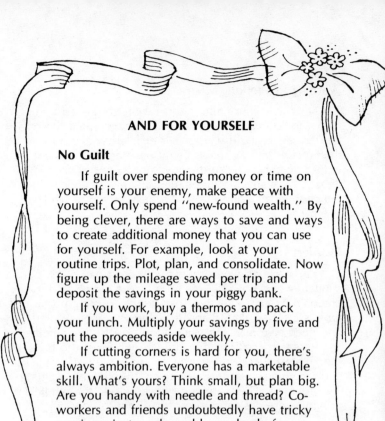

AND FOR YOURSELF

No Guilt

If guilt over spending money or time on yourself is your enemy, make peace with yourself. Only spend "new-found wealth." By being clever, there are ways to save and ways to create additional money that you can use for yourself. For example, look at your routine trips. Plot, plan, and consolidate. Now figure up the mileage saved per trip and deposit the savings in your piggy bank.

If you work, buy a thermos and pack your lunch. Multiply your savings by five and put the proceeds aside weekly.

If cutting corners is hard for you, there's always ambition. Everyone has a marketable skill. What's yours? Think small, but plan big. Are you handy with needle and thread? Co-workers and friends undoubtedly have tricky repair projects and would pay dearly for skilled work. Can you type, cook, clean, or write? Make it a game. Attitude is everything. Whole businesses are developed and succeed with simple ideas.

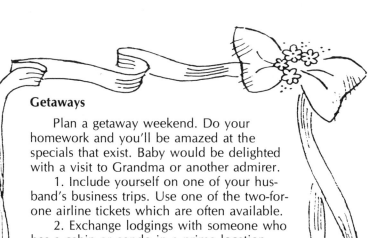

Getaways

Plan a getaway weekend. Do your homework and you'll be amazed at the specials that exist. Baby would be delighted with a visit to Grandma or another admirer.

1. Include yourself on one of your husband's business trips. Use one of the two-for-one airline tickets which are often available.

2. Exchange lodgings with someone who has a cabin or condo in a prime location.

3. House-sit for a weekend. You'll have seclusion and earnings at the same time.

4. Check into a hometown hotel with a "couples only" bargain. Many have specials featuring champagne, Continental breakfast, pool, and other treats.

5. Even if supersavers are too rich for your blood, why not arrange to spend an evening in a friend's downtown apartment when she is out of town?

Undercover

Pretty lingerie makes every woman feel good. Today you can get beauty and control together. Take the money you're saving with coupons, invest in yourself, and get rave reviews.

PARENTS, FRIENDS, AND ADMIRERS

Tinker Box

Any suitcase or old hat box at a friend's house can be turned into a container that Baby can enjoy. It can hold hats, scarfs, old shoes, and maybe some bangle bracelets. When the toddler pays a visit, there can be new and different things in the Tinker box, which he will always associate with the friend.

Good Gift

A hobbyhorse, a great gift for a rambunctious two, is easily made from patterns found in a fabric store or may often be purchased at church bazaars and craft fairs for a reasonable price.

Participation Books

Children love to hear stories, especially if they have the opportunity to become involved. Keep books like *Bartholomew And The Oobleck* by Dr. Seuss with all the necessary supplies handy so that you and Baby can enjoy the book together. After you've read the book, to make the magic Oobleck, just add cornstarch and water. What you end up with is an interesting solid/liquid formation that is solid until you touch it and then takes on the property of a liquid. A little food coloring can be added to this mixture.

Windowpane Cookies

Cooking in Grandma's or Auntie's kitchen is always a treat. Why not practice color recognition with Baby while you cook? Windowpane cookies are special fun and very easy. We like the ones that are free shapes but can be made with cookie cutters. All you need is a basic cookie recipe, or use this one.

⅓ cup shortening
⅓ cup sugar
1 egg
3 cups flour
½ tsp. baking soda
1 tsp. salt
⅔ cup honey

1. Mix ingredients and chill until firm. Roll the dough into snake strips about ¼ in. thick and shape into connected squares. Make your squares on foil over a cookie sheet.
2. Crack pieces of lollipop or Lifesavers and sprinkle them into the openings in your squares.
3. Bake at 375° for 8–10 minutes.
4. Cool and peel squares from the foil when the dough is firm.

Good Neighbors

The two-year-old will be the one who really knows the neighbors. You can help him learn how to be a good friend and neighbor by encouraging him to give his time and energy freely. Encourage him to put the newspaper of an elderly couple next door on their porch each day. Having this responsibility will make him feel important, besides pleasing his friends and saving them steps. Helpful children are a delight and should be shared with all.

Silhouettes

A quick gift for a friend is a silhouette of the whole family. Use a slide projector or a powerful lamp without its shade as a light source. Mount a large piece of white paper on the wall, and while one family member sits, another can trace his outline. The result is an attractive composition that can be cut out and mounted on a dark background. Or you can take it to a print shop and have it reduced in size. Silhouettes may also be cut from dark paper and mounted on colorful paper or on small-print denim fabrics.

Multi-use Pool

One dad made an attractive small sandbox for his daughter by using a fiberglass or molded plastic fountain-pool form and sinking it in the ground. It was an item of interest in the garden because of its unusual shape. Depending on the season, the sandbox could be converted to a miniature ice pond or a wading pool. The pool was about 36 × 30 × 6 inches.

Friend's Gift

An adult friend of a two-year-old is guaranteed to hit the spot with a picture poster of his small friend made from a photo. What a way to please with a bigger-than-life-copy of the best poster for a toddler's room! A poster usually costs less than $20. The same process can be used to make a photo puzzle, a photo T-shirt, or a tote bag—great gifts for Baby, who is very interested in seeing himself.

Biking

Since your toddler is mastering his tricycle now, take it along when you're ambling, snapping photos, or just enjoying the outdoors. Good places to roam, especially on weekends, are schoolyards and areas in front of municipal buildings. Art museums usually have wide walkways and interesting things to look at. If you take your child on a bike hike, make sure you both wear your helmets to ensure a safe and worry-free ride. In some states, it's the law.

APPENDIX A

HANDLING THE FUSSY BABY

Babies cry because it is their only way to summon help to meet their needs. You do not need to worry about spoiling a young infant. In fact, research suggests that the best way to decrease Baby's crying is your consistent responsiveness to his cries.

There are degrees of crying. Imagine Baby's cries as running along a continuum; he starts with a fussy, halfhearted cry that eventually develops into a panicky, desperate cry of rage. Your response is most effective if it comes before this final, desperate stage.

As Baby becomes secure in your ability to meet his needs, his crying diminishes and becomes more of a select signal. As you learn Baby's ways, you will be able to distinguish between a cry of hunger and one of pain. As Baby grows and develops, his routines will become more regular. Since you will be increasingly able to anticipate his needs, you can cut down on his crying by eliminating problems before they happen.

The first thing to do when Baby cries is to run through a checklist of possible problems. We suggest the following:
1. Is Baby hungry or thirsty?
2. Does Baby have a gas pain or a need to burp?
3. Does Baby need a diaper change or some fresh ointment on his bottom?
4. Is Baby tired?
5. Is Baby too hot or cold? (Use the temperature of his back or tummy as an indicator.)
6. Is Baby lonely or is there too much stimulation?
7. Does Baby need to suck?
8. Is Baby sick? Is he running a temperature? Are there any other symptoms?

Babies cry for a reason. Unfortunately, we are not always able to determine just what the reason is. If you can answer *no* to all of the above questions and your child continues to cry, consult your pediatrician. If Baby is simply fussy every now and then, we suggest the following techniques to help calm him.

Physical Positions

1. Pick Baby up, hold him tightly over your shoulder, and pat his back.
2. Use Position 1 as you pace.
3. Lay Baby gently across your knees and bounce him rhythmically. Pat him gently on the back.
4. Hold Baby over your arm while he rests on your hip.
5. Put Baby, tummy down, on your lap and push his knees up to his chest.
6. Hold Baby closely and firmly and sit in your rocker and rock, or sit on the edge of a chair and pretend to rock.
7. Hold Baby with his back against your stomach, encircle his waist with your arm, and exert a bit of pressure.

Other Suggestions

1. Swaddle Baby by wrapping him snugly in a light blanket.
2. Give Baby something to suck—a finger, fist, or pacifier. Hold him close and pat his back.
3. Add a ticking clock to the scene; the rhythmic noise can be very soothing.
4. Make the crib smaller by adding a few pillows and stuffed friends. A smaller space is often comforting to Baby.
5. Turn Baby over on his tummy, pull up his cover, and turn on the radio to soft tunes. Pat his back or gently rock his crib.
6. Take Baby for a ride in the car.
7. Put Baby in a front carrier or an umbrella stroller and take a walk around the block.
8. Put Baby in a wind-up swing.
9. Sing to Baby.
10. Whisper in Baby's ear.
11. Take Baby to the mirror so he can see himself; talk to him.
12. Dance with Baby.
13. If Baby finds water soothing, give him a bath, or shower together.

If nothing works, call for reinforcements and let them try.

APPENDIX B

HAVE BABY, WILL TRAVEL

Many happy moments can be spent traveling with Baby. Day trips to visit friends, museums, or shopping centers are a must for a caregiver with an infant. Keep a travel bag ready to go for these short trips. On longer trips, use the same bag as an airplane, train, or car bag; pack the rest of Baby's things with the family luggage.

Your travel bag should be durable and sturdy. It should have both a handle and shoulder straps. If it is not made of waterproof material, it should at least have several waterproof inside pockets. It should be large enough to easily hold all of Baby's necessities and a small handbag of your own. The following list of essential items for traveling with Baby should be included in your bag. Take only the amount of each that you will really need.

1. Disposable diapers
2. Disposable wipes
3. Diaper cream and powder (buy the sample sizes)
4. A small comb and brush if Baby has enough hair to warrant their use
5. Tissues
6. Plastic zip-lock bags, the larger size
7. Two complete changes of clothes
8. A complete change of outer clothes
9. A small blanket
10. A bib
11. A few small toys
12. Enough food and bottles for the trip

Long-Distance Traveling

Planning for Your Arrival

Be sure to discuss with your host or hostess in advance the kinds of physical arrangements that are to be made for Baby. This will make plans easier for them to complete, and will help you know what to bring.

If the people you are visiting do not have small children, ask them to investigate pediatricians and baby-sitters in advance. Babies always seem to get sick at 3 A.M. in a strange city when you've made no arrangements.

By Airplane

Remember to call the airlines a few days before your departure to tell them that you are traveling with an infant. If they know this, they will usually let you board a little early so that you can get settled without being crowded. Specify any special arrangements you wish to make about food; the flight attendants will generally be happy to warm bottles or baby food for you.

Be sure to get to the airport early. Rushing around at the last minute will leave both you and Baby frazzled and unprepared for the flight. An early arrival will also let you choose your seat. Ask for a seat in the nonsmoking section—healthier and more pleasant for everyone.

By Car

Long car trips with a baby can be difficult for everyone. Try to plan an easy driving schedule that begins early and ends early enough in the afternoon so that everyone can have a rest. Stop frequently.

Even the youngest baby should be securely strapped into a car seat in the back seat. There is a great temptation, particularly on long trips, to let Baby sit in front on someone's lap. This is unsafe and should never be permitted, no matter how fussy Baby gets.

It is wise to pack a cooler in the morning before you leave. Stock it with small containers of prepared food for very young babies, or with peanut butter and jelly sandwiches, cheese and crackers, and fruit for older ones. Remember to bring small containers of juice and milk, and Baby's cup, bottle, and utensils. A large thermos of cool water is a must. Warmed formula can also be kept in a large thermos and poured into bottles when needed.

No Matter How You're Going

—If you plan to be gone any length of time, take a portfolio of Baby's pictures with you. Photos of Baby's house, pets, toys, and friends and admirers are take-alongs that keep him connected with his loved ones.

—A roll of masking tape can provide creative diversions for Baby. This sticky stuff is fun to play with; it is also ideal for retaping disposable diapers.

—A cool washcloth can refresh a wilting baby traveling in hot weather. Simply wrap a dry cloth around an ice cube and place in a zip-lock plastic bag. It will be ready when you are.

—Carrying your young infant in a sling is an easy way to keep your hands free. An umbrella stroller is a good traveling aid for the older baby.

APPENDIX C

FIGHTING THE MEAN MOTHER GUILTS

According to government statistics, only 17 percent of all American families include a father who is the sole breadwinner, a wife who is a full-time homemaker, and one or more children still at home. Nonetheless, this is the stereotype with which most of us have been brought up; many women feel tremendous guilt about working because of it. Here are some things you might want to know that will help you fight the "mean mother guilts" and develop a perspective.

Although current research concerning working mothers and their young children is limited, there have not been any noticeable negative differences between children who spend their day at home and those who spend it in day care. In fact, positive differences have been noted in some testing situations. Children from high-quality care programs were consistently more socially independent, outgoing, task-oriented, and curious. Another important finding contributing to your peace of mind is that the mother-child relationship is not weakened when a child is in day care.

Whether you must work or choose to work, it is important that you feel confident about the care situation you select for your child. There are many kinds of day-care arrangements. No matter which you choose, work hard to develop a relationship of trust and mutual respect with your child's caregivers. Make a real effort to keep the lines of communication open both ways. After all, your child's daily welfare is at stake. The following chart provides a brief comparison of the four basic types of child care and a few thoughts about their advantages and disadvantages.

Type	Advantages	Disadvantages
Baby-sitter in your home	Most convenient Greatest flexibility in terms of hours Will care for a sick child Most individualized care	Hard to locate Not always licensed Most expensive No backup in event of illness No consistent program No social contact(s) for parents
Baby-sitter away from home	Convenient Reasonably flexible hours Will care for a sick child Some individualized care	Hard to locate Not always licensed Expensive No backup in event of illness No consistent program No social contact(s) for parents Sitter may have other household duties
Family group	Convenient Moderately flexible hours Limited number of children lowers cost Some socialization with other babies May have consistent program Some interaction with other parents May be licensed	Usually will *not* accept a sick child No backup in event of illness Other children may not be appropriate playmates

Type	Advantages	Disadvantages
Day-care center	Convenient Maximum dependability regarding services Licensed, trained personnel whose job it is to interact with children Competitively priced Consistent program with planned activities Maximum social interaction with other parents	Least flexibility in hours Center will not accept sick child Larger group size Possible concern over changes in staff

Working outside the home and raising a family, and doing both happily, is very demanding indeed. Here are some tips from working parents we know.

1. Be sure to arrange a special time with your child(ren) each weekend. This should be a time when you are not distracted by anything else. An outing is especially relaxing for both of you—try a walk in the park, a trip to the zoo, a ride around the block in a wagon. In addition, you should arrange a private time—even if it is for only five minutes—to say good-night with a song or a book and a talk with each child each evening.
2. Parents need to have some time alone together, make this one of your priorities.
3. Everyone needs a little time alone, even if it is just to read a magazine for half an hour or to take a nice, hot bath.
4. Subscribing to a working woman's magazine can help fight that feeling of being isolated and burdened.
5. Streamline your housework and learn to live with slightly less than perfectionist standards. Read a book about hints and shortcuts to help reduce your workload.

APPENDIX D

DOWN MEMORY LANE

Name _____

Place of birth _____

Date of birth _____ Day _____ Time _____

Who was present _____

Arrived home for first time _____

Motor Development Milestones

	DATE	COMMENTS
Lifts head	_____	_____
Rolls from back to stomach	_____	_____
Rolls from stomach to back	_____	_____
Rolls completely over	_____	_____
Crawls	_____	_____
Sits alone	_____	_____
Crawls up stairs	_____	_____
Pulls to standing position	_____	_____
Stands alone	_____	_____
Walks alone	_____	_____

Watch Me Grow!

	WEIGHT	LENGTH
1 Month	_____	_____
3 Months	_____	_____
6 Months	_____	_____
12 Months	_____	_____
18 Months	_____	_____

Feeding Firsts

	DATE	COMMENTS
Begins solids	_____	_____
Drinks from cup	_____	_____
Tries a spoon	_____	_____
Feeds self	_____	_____
Weaned	_____	_____

Cognitive Cuties

	DATE	COMMENTS
Follows objects with eyes	_____	_____
Imitates actions	_____	_____
Points to body parts	_____	_____
Looks for hidden object	_____	_____

Listen to Me!

	DATE	COMMENTS
Vocalizes to get attention	_____	_____
Responds when talked to	_____	_____
Understands name	_____	_____
Understands *no!*	_____	_____
First word	_____	_____

Social Steps

	DATE	COMMENTS
Smiles	_____	_____
Plays peek-a-boo	_____	_____
Teases family	_____	_____
Disturbed by strangers	_____	_____
Gives a kiss or hug	_____	_____

Routine Relief

	DATE	COMMENTS
Sleeps through the night	_____	_____
Splashes, plays, and enjoys bath	_____	_____
Tries to undress self	_____	_____